2011 Case Supplement

Recent Developments in Constitutional Law

2011 Case Supplement

Recent Developments in Constitutional Law

Randy E. Barnett
Carmack Waterhouse Professor of Legal Theory
Georgetown University Law Center

Wolters Kluwer
Law & Business

Published by Wolters Kluwer Law & Business in New York.

Wolters Kluwer Law & Business serves customers worldwide with CCH, Aspen Publishers, and Kluwer Law International products. (www.wolterskluwerlb.com)

To contact Customer Service, e-mail customer.service@wolterskluwer.com,
call 1-800-234-1660, fax 1-800-901-9075, or mail correspondence to:

Wolters Kluwer Law & Business
Attn: Order Department
PO Box 990
Frederick, MD 21705

Printed in the United States of America.

1 2 3 4 5 6 7 8 9 0

ISBN 978-0-7355-0726-5

Library of Congress Cataloging-in-Publication Data

Barnett, Randy E.
Constitutional law : cases in context / Randy E. Barnett.
p. cm.
Includes index.
ISBN 978-0-7355-6344-5 (text)
ISBN 978-0-7355-0726-5 (supplement)
1. Constitutional law—United States—Cases. I. Title.

KF4550.B373 2008
342.73—dc22

2007052607

About Wolters Kluwer Law & Business

Wolters Kluwer Law & Business is a leading global provider of intelligent information and digital solutions for legal and business professionals in key specialty areas, and respected educational resources for professors and law students. Wolters Kluwer Law & Business connects legal and business professionals as well as those in the education market with timely, specialized authoritative content and information-enabled solutions to support success through productivity, accuracy and mobility.

Serving customers worldwide, Wolters Kluwer Law & Business products include those under the Aspen Publishers, CCH, Kluwer Law International, Loislaw, Best Case, ftwilliam.com and MediRegs family of products.

CCH products have been a trusted resource since 1913, and are highly regarded resources for legal, securities, antitrust and trade regulation, government contracting, banking, pension, payroll, employment and labor, and healthcare reimbursement and compliance professionals.

Aspen Publishers products provide essential information to attorneys, business professionals and law students. Written by preeminent authorities, the product line offers analytical and practical information in a range of specialty practice areas from securities law and intellectual property to mergers and acquisitions and pension/benefits. Aspen's trusted legal education resources provide professors and students with high-quality, up-to-date and effective resources for successful instruction and study in all areas of the law.

Kluwer Law International products provide the global business community with reliable international legal information in English. Legal practitioners, corporate counsel and business executives around the world rely on Kluwer Law journals, looseleafs, books, and electronic products for comprehensive information in many areas of international legal practice.

Loislaw is a comprehensive online legal research product providing legal content to law firm practitioners of various specializations. Loislaw provides attorneys with the ability to quickly and efficiently find the necessary legal information they need, when and where they need it, by facilitating access to primary law as well as state-specific law, records, forms and treatises.

Best Case Solutions is the leading bankruptcy software product to the bankruptcy industry. It provides software and workflow tools to flawlessly streamline petition preparation and the electronic filing process, while timely incorporating ever-changing court requirements.

ftwilliam.com offers employee benefits professionals the highest quality plan documents (retirement, welfare and non-qualified) and government forms (5500/PBGC, 1099 and IRS) software at highly competitive prices.

MediRegs products provide integrated health care compliance content and software solutions for professionals in healthcare, higher education and life sciences, including professionals in accounting, law and consulting.

Wolters Kluwer Law & Business, a division of Wolters Kluwer, is headquartered in New York. Wolters Kluwer is a market-leading global information services company focused on professionals.

Contents

2011 Case Supplement

Recent Developments in Constitutional Law

Chapter 9

Article I — The Legislative Power

ASSIGNMENT S-1

STUDY GUIDE: Is the following case a revolutionary expansion of the powers of Congress under the Necessary and Proper Clause? Or merely a narrow ratification of the penal power of Congress when exercising its enumerated powers? How does Justice Kennedy's concurrence in the judgment seek to qualify the holding of the majority? Notice also Justice Kennedy's invocation of an "external" federalism constraint akin to that which he advocated in his concurring opinion in Lopez, *and his distinction between Due Process and Commerce Clause scrutiny. How might his discussion of the "rational basis" test in the context of the Commerce Clause (and Justice Alito's discussion of the Necessary and Proper Clause) be significant in future cases? Might it indicate any second thoughts about Justice Stevens' opinion in* Raich, *with which Justice Kennedy joined without an opinion? (Note that, because Justice Breyer's opinion was joined by Chief Justice Roberts, and Justices Stevens, Ginsburg, and Sotomayor, Justices Kennedy or Alito's votes were not essential to the outcome of the case.) Exactly what connection to an enumerated power does Justice Thomas think is absent in this statute? Does he adopt the "two-step" test attributed to him by Justice Breyer? In light of his joining the majority in* Raich, *does Justice Scalia's joining Justice Thomas's dissent (and the citations therein to his opinions in* Raich *and* Printz*) suggest that* Raich *may not have augured the death of federalism as some believe?*

UNITED STATES v. COMSTOCK

560 U.S. _____ (2010)

JUSTICE BREYER delivered the opinion of the Court.

A federal civil-commitment statute authorizes the Department of Justice to detain a mentally ill, sexually dangerous federal prisoner beyond the date the prisoner would otherwise be released. We have previously examined similar statutes enacted under state law to determine whether they violate the Due Process Clause. But this case presents a different question. Here we ask whether the Federal Government has the authority under Article I of the Constitution to enact this federal civil-commitment program or whether its doing so falls beyond the reach of a government "of enumerated powers." McCulloch v. Maryland (1819). We conclude that the Constitution grants Congress the authority to enact §4248 as "necessary and proper for carrying into Execution" the powers "vested by" the "Constitution in the Government of the United States." Art. I, §8, cl. 18.

I

The federal statute before us allows a district court to order the civil commitment of an individual who is currently "in the custody of the [Federal] Bureau of Prisons," if that individual (1) has previously "engaged or attempted to engage in sexually violent conduct or child molestation," (2) currently "suffers from a serious mental illness, abnormality, or disorder," and (3) "as a result of" that mental illness, abnormality, or disorder is "sexually dangerous to others," in that "he would have serious difficulty in refraining from sexually violent conduct or child molestation if released." . . .

Confinement in the federal facility will last until either (1) the person's mental condition improves to the point where he is no longer dangerous (with or without appropriate ongoing treatment), in which case he will be released; or (2) a State assumes responsibility for his custody, care, and treatment, in which case he will be transferred to the custody of that State. The statute establishes a system for ongoing psychiatric and judicial review of the individual's case, including judicial hearings at the request of the confined person at six-month intervals. . . .

II

The question presented is whether the Necessary and Proper Clause, Art. I, §8, cl. 18, grants Congress authority sufficient to enact the statute before us. In resolving that question, we assume, but we do not decide, that other provisions of the Constitution — such as the Due Process Clause — do not prohibit civil commitment in these circumstances. In other words, we assume for argument's sake that the Federal Constitution would permit a State to enact this statute, and we ask solely whether the Federal Government, exercising its enumerated powers, may enact such a statute as well. On that assumption, we conclude that the Constitution grants Congress legislative power sufficient to enact §4248. We base this conclusion on five considerations, taken together.

First, the Necessary and Proper Clause grants Congress broad authority to enact federal legislation. Nearly 200 years ago, this Court stated that the Federal "[G]overnment is acknowledged by all to be one of enumerated powers," *McCulloch*, which means that "[e]very law enacted by Congress must be based on one or more of" those powers, United States v. Morrison (2000). But, at the same time, "a government, entrusted with such" powers "must also be entrusted with ample means for their execution." *McCulloch*. Accordingly, the Necessary and Proper Clause makes clear that the Constitution's grants of specific federal legislative authority are accompanied by broad power to enact laws that are "convenient, or useful" or "conducive" to the authority's "beneficial exercise." Chief Justice Marshall emphasized that the word "necessary" does not mean "absolutely necessary." In language that has come to define the scope of the Necessary and Proper Clause, he wrote:

> "Let the end be legitimate, let it be within the scope of the constitution, and all means which are appropriate, which are plainly adapted to that end, which are not prohibited, but consist with the letter and spirit of the constitution, are constitutional."

We have since made clear that, in determining whether the Necessary and Proper Clause grants Congress the legislative authority to enact a particular federal statute, we look to see whether the statute constitutes a means that is rationally related to the implementation of a constitutionally enumerated power. Sabri v. United States (2004) (using term "means-ends rationality" to describe the necessary relationship); see Gonzales v. Raich (2005) (holding that because "Congress had a rational basis" for concluding that a statute implements Commerce Clause power, the statute falls within the scope of congressional "authority to 'make all Laws which shall be necessary and proper' to 'regulate Commerce . . . among the several States'"; see also United States v. Lopez (1995).

Of course, as Chief Justice Marshall stated, a federal statute, in addition to being authorized by Art. I, §8, must also "not [be] prohibited" by the Constitution. *McCulloch.* But as we have already stated, the present statute's validity under provisions of the Constitution other than the Necessary and Proper Clause is an issue that is not before us. Under the question presented, the relevant inquiry is simply "whether the means chosen are 'reasonably adapted' to the attainment of a legitimate end under the commerce power" or under other powers that the Constitution grants Congress the authority to implement. *Gonzales* (SCALIA, J., concurring in judgment) (quoting United States v. Darby (1941)).

We have also recognized that the Constitution "addresse[s]" the "choice of means"

> "primarily . . . to the judgment of Congress. If it can be seen that the means adopted are really calculated to attain the end, the degree of their necessity, the extent to which they conduce to the end, the closeness of the relationship between the means adopted and the end to be attained, are matters for congressional determination alone." Burroughs v. United States (1934).

See also *Lottery Case* (1903) ("[T]he Constitution . . . leaves to Congress a large discretion as to the means that may be employed in executing a given power"); *Morrison* (applying a "presumption of constitutionality" when examining the scope of Congressional power); *McCulloch.*

Thus, the Constitution, which nowhere speaks explicitly about the creation of federal crimes beyond those related to "counterfeiting," "treason," or "Piracies and Felonies committed on the high Seas" or "against the Law of Nations," nonetheless grants Congress broad authority to create such crimes. See *McCulloch* ("All admit that the government may, legitimately, punish any violation of its laws; and yet, this is not among the enumerated powers of

Congress"). And Congress routinely exercises its authority to enact criminal laws in furtherance of, for example, its enumerated powers to regulate interstate and foreign commerce, to enforce civil rights, to spend funds for the general welfare, to establish federal courts, to establish post offices, to regulate bankruptcy, to regulate naturalization, and so forth.

Similarly, Congress, in order to help ensure the enforcement of federal criminal laws enacted in furtherance of its enumerated powers, "can cause a prison to be erected at any place within the jurisdiction of the United States, and direct that all persons sentenced to imprisonment under the laws of the United States shall be confined there." Ex parte Karstendick (1876). Moreover, Congress, having established a prison system, can enact laws that seek to ensure that system's safe and responsible administration by, for example, requiring prisoners to receive medical care and educational training, and can also ensure the safety of the prisoners, prison workers and visitors, and those in surrounding communities by, for example, creating further criminal laws governing entry, exit, and smuggling, and by employing prison guards to ensure discipline and security.

Neither Congress' power to criminalize conduct, nor its power to imprison individuals who engage in that conduct, nor its power to enact laws governing prisons and prisoners, is explicitly mentioned in the Constitution. But Congress nonetheless possesses broad authority to do each of those things in the course of "carrying into Execution" the enumerated powers "vested by" the "Constitution in the Government of the United States," Art. I, §8, cl. 18—authority granted by the Necessary and Proper Clause.

Second, the civil-commitment statute before us constitutes a modest addition to a set of federal prison-related mental-health statutes that have existed for many decades. We recognize that even a longstanding history of related federal action does not demonstrate a statute's constitutionality. A history of involvement, however, can nonetheless be "helpful in reviewing the substance of a congressional statutory scheme," *Gonzales*, and, in particular, the reasonableness of the relation between the new statute and pre-existing federal interests.

Here, Congress has long been involved in the delivery of mental health care to federal prisoners, and has long provided for their civil commitment. . . . [O]ver the span of three decades, Congress created a national, federal civil-commitment program under which any person who was either charged with or convicted of any federal offense in any federal court could be confined in a federal mental institution. These statutes did not raise the question presented here, for they all provided that commitment in a federal hospital would end upon the completion of the relevant "terms" of federal "imprisonment" as set forth in the underlying criminal sentence or statute. But in the mid-1940's that proviso was eliminated. . . .

Between 1948 and 1949, . . . Congress modified the law. It provided for the civil commitment of individuals who are, or who become, mentally incompetent at any time after their arrest and before the expiration of their federal sentence. . . . In 1984, Congress modified these basic statutes . . . so as to authorize (explicitly) civil commitment if, in addition to the other conditions, the prisoner's "release would create a substantial risk of bodily injury to another person or serious damage to the property of another." . . .

With these modifications, the statutes continue to authorize the civil commitment of individuals who are both mentally ill and dangerous, once they have been charged with, or convicted of, a federal crime. They continue to provide for the *continued* civil commitment of those individuals when they are "due for release" from federal custody because their "sentence is about to expire." And, . . . they establish various procedural and other requirements.

In 2006, Congress enacted the particular statute before us. It differs from earlier statutes in that it focuses directly upon persons who, due to a mental illness, are sexually dangerous. Notably, many of these individuals were likely already subject to civil commitment under which, since 1949, has authorized the postsentence detention of federal prisoners who suffer from a mental illness and who are thereby dangerous (whether sexually or otherwise). Aside from its specific focus on sexually dangerous persons, §4248 is similar to the provisions first enacted in 1949. In that respect, it is a modest addition to a longstanding federal statutory framework, which has been in place since 1855.

Third, Congress reasonably extended its longstanding civil-commitment system to cover mentally ill and sexually dangerous persons who are already in federal custody, even if doing so detains them beyond the termination of their criminal sentence. For one thing, the Federal Government is the custodian of its prisoners. As federal custodian, it has the constitutional power to act in order to protect nearby (and other) communities from the danger federal prisoners may pose. . . . If a federal prisoner is infected with a communicable disease that threatens others, surely it would be "necessary and proper" for the Federal Government to take action, pursuant to its role as federal custodian, to refuse (at least until the threat diminishes) to release that individual among the general public, where he might infect others (even if not threatening an interstate epidemic). And if confinement of such an individual is a "necessary and proper" thing to do, then how could it not be similarly "necessary and proper" to confine an individual whose mental illness threatens others to the same degree?

Moreover, §4248 is "reasonably adapted," *Darby*, to Congress' power to act as a responsible federal custodian (a power that rests, in turn, upon federal criminal statutes that legitimately seek to implement constitutionally enumerated authority). Congress could have reasonably concluded that federal inmates who suffer from a mental illness that causes them to "have serious difficulty in refraining from sexually violent conduct," §4247(a)(6), would pose an especially high danger to the public if released. And Congress could also have reasonably concluded (as detailed in the Judicial Conference's report) that a reasonable number of such individuals would likely *not* be detained by the States if released from federal custody, in part because the Federal Government itself severed their claim to "legal residence in any State" by incarcerating them in remote federal prisons. Here Congress' desire to address the specific challenges identified in the Reports cited above, taken together with its responsibilities as a federal custodian, supports the conclusion that §4248 satisfies "review for means-end rationality," i.e., that it satisfies the Constitution's insistence that a federal statute represent a rational means for implementing a constitutional grant of legislative authority.

Fourth, the statute properly accounts for state interests. Respondents and the dissent contend that §4248 violates the Tenth Amendment because it "invades the province of state sovereignty" in an area typically left to state control. New York v. United States (1992). But the Tenth Amendment's text is clear: "The powers *not delegated to the United States* by the Constitution, nor prohibited by it to the States, are reserved to the States respectively, or to the people." (Emphasis added.) The powers "delegated to the United States by the Constitution" include those specifically enumerated powers listed in Article I along with the implementation authority granted by the Necessary and Proper Clause. Virtually by definition, these powers are not powers that the Constitution "reserved to the States." See *New York* ("[I]f a power is delegated to Congress in the Constitution, the Tenth Amendment expressly disclaims any reservation of that power to the States . . . ." "In the end . . . it makes no difference whether one views the question at issue in these cases as one of ascertaining the limits of the power delegated to the Federal Government under the affirmative provisions of the Constitution or one of discerning the core of sovereignty retained by the States under the Tenth Amendment").

Nor does this statute invade state sovereignty or otherwise improperly limit the scope of "powers that remain with the States." (THOMAS, J., dissenting). To the contrary, it requires *accommodation* of state interests: The Attorney General must inform the State in which the federal prisoner "is domiciled or was tried" that he is detaining someone with respect to whom those States may wish to assert their authority, and he must encourage those States to assume custody of the individual. §4248(d). He must also immediately "release" that person "to the appropriate official of" either State "if such State will assume [such] responsibility." And either State has the right, at any time, to assert its authority over the individual, which will prompt the individual's immediate transfer to State custody. §4248(d)(1). . . .

Fifth, the links between §4248 and an enumerated Article I power are not too attenuated. Neither is the statutory provision too sweeping in its scope. Invoking the cautionary instruction that we may not "pile inference upon inference" in order to sustain congressional action under Article I, *Lopez*, respondents argue that, when legislating pursuant to the Necessary and Proper Clause, Congress' authority can be no more than one step removed from a specifically enumerated power. But this argument is irreconcilable with our precedents. . . . In [Greenwood v. United States (1956)] we upheld the (likely indefinite) civil commitment of a mentally incompetent federal defendant who was accused of robbing a United States Post Office. The underlying enumerated Article I power was the power to "Establish Post Offices and Post Roads." But, as Chief Justice Marshall recognized in *McCulloch*,

> "the power 'to establish post offices and post roads' . . . is executed by the single act of *making* the establishment . . . . [F]rom this has been inferred the power and duty of *carrying* the mail along the post road, from one post office to another. And, from

this *implied* power, has again been inferred the right to *punish* those who steal letters from the post office, or rob the mail." (emphasis added).

And, as we have explained, from the implied power to punish we have *further* inferred both the power to imprison, and, in *Greenwood*, the federal civil-commitment power. . . .

Indeed even the dissent acknowledges that Congress has the implied power to criminalize any conduct that might interfere with the exercise of an enumerated power, and also the additional power to imprison people who violate those (inferentially authorized) laws, and the additional power to provide for the safe and reasonable management of those prisons, and the additional power to regulate the prisoners' behavior even after their release. Of course, each of those powers . . . is ultimately "derived from" an enumerated power. And, as the dissent agrees, that enumerated power is "the enumerated power that justifies the defendant's statute of conviction." Neither we nor the dissent can point to a single specific enumerated power "that justifies a criminal defendant's arrest or conviction," in *all* cases because Congress relies on different enumerated powers (often, but not exclusively, its Commerce Clause power) to enact its various federal criminal statutes. But every such statute must itself be legitimately predicated on an enumerated power. And the same enumerated power that justifies the creation of a federal criminal statute, and that justifies the additional implied federal powers that the dissent considers legitimate, justifies civil commitment under §4248 as well. Thus, we must reject respondents' argument that the Necessary and Proper Clause permits no more than a single step between an enumerated power and an Act of Congress.

Nor need we fear that our holding today confers on Congress a general "police power, which the Founders denied the National Government and reposed in the States." *Morrison*. As the Solicitor General repeatedly confirmed at oral argument, §4248 is narrow in scope. It has been applied to only a small fraction of federal prisoners. And its reach is limited to individuals already "in the custody of the" Federal Government. §4248. Indeed, the Solicitor General argues that "the Federal Government would not have . . . the power to commit a person who . . . has been released from prison and whose period of supervised release is also completed." Thus, far from a "general police power," §4248 is a reasonably adapted and narrowly tailored means of pursuing the Government's legitimate interest as a federal custodian in the responsible administration of its prison system. . . .

* * *

We take these five considerations together. They include: (1) the breadth of the Necessary and Proper Clause, (2) the long history of federal involvement in this arena, (3) the sound reasons for the statute's enactment in light of the Government's custodial interest in safeguarding the public from dangers posed by those in federal custody, (4) the statute's accommodation of state interests, and (5) the statute's narrow scope. Taken together, these considerations lead us to conclude that the statute is a "necessary and proper" means of exercising the federal authority that permits Congress to create federal criminal laws, to punish their violation, to imprison violators, to provide appropriately for those imprisoned, and to maintain the security of those who are not imprisoned but who may be affected by the federal imprisonment of others. The Constitution consequently authorizes Congress to enact the statute. . . .

The judgment of the Court of Appeals for the Fourth Circuit with respect to Congress' power to enact this statute is reversed, and the case is remanded for further proceedings consistent with this opinion.

It is so ordered.

JUSTICE KENNEDY, concurring in the judgment.

The Court is correct, in my view, to hold that the challenged portions of 18 U.S.C. §4248 are necessary and proper exercises of congressional authority.

Respondents argue that congressional authority under the Necessary and Proper Clause can be no more than one step removed from an enumerated power. This is incorrect. When the inquiry is whether a federal law has sufficient links to an enumerated power to be within the scope of federal authority, the analysis depends not on the number of links in the congressional-power chain but on the strength of the chain.

Concluding that a relation can be put into a verbal formulation that fits somewhere along a causal chain of federal powers is merely the beginning, not the end, of the constitutional inquiry. See United States v. Lopez (1995). The inferences must be controlled by some limitations lest, as Thomas Jefferson warned, congressional powers become completely unbounded by linking one power to another *ad infinitum* in a veritable game of "'this is the house that Jack built.'" Letter from Thomas Jefferson to Edward Livingston (Apr. 30, 1800).

This separate writing serves two purposes. The first is to withhold assent from certain statements and propositions of the Court's opinion. The second is to caution that the Constitution does require the invalidation of congressional attempts to extend federal powers in some instances.

The Court concludes that, when determining whether Congress has the authority to enact a specific law under the Necessary and Proper Clause, we look "to see whether the statute constitutes a means that is rationally related to the implementation of a constitutionally enumerated power."

The terms "rationally related" and "rational basis" must be employed with care, particularly if either is to be used as a stand-alone test. The phrase "rational basis" most often is employed to describe the standard for determining whether legislation that does not proscribe fundamental liberties nonetheless violates the Due Process Clause. Referring to this due process inquiry, and in what must be one of the most deferential formulations of the standard for reviewing legislation in all the Court's precedents, the Court has said: "But the law need not be in every respect logically consistent with its aims to be constitutional. It is enough that there is an evil at hand for correction, and that it might be thought that the particular legislative measure was a rational way to correct it." Williamson v. Lee Optical of Okla., Inc. (1955). This formulation was in a case presenting a due process challenge and a challenge to a State's exercise of its own powers,

powers not confined by the principles that control the limited nature of our National Government. The phrase, then, should not be extended uncritically to the issue before us.

The operative constitutional provision in this case is the Necessary and Proper Clause. This Court has not held that the *Lee Optical* test, asking if "it might be thought that the particular legislative measure was a rational way to correct" an evil, is the proper test in this context. Rather, under the Necessary and Proper Clause, application of a "rational basis" test should be at least as exacting as it has been in the Commerce Clause cases, if not more so. Indeed, the cases the Court cites in the portion of its opinion referring to "rational basis" are predominantly Commerce Clause cases, and none are due process cases.

There is an important difference between the two questions, but the Court does not make this distinction clear. *Raich*, *Lopez*, and *Hodel* were all Commerce Clause cases. Those precedents require a tangible link to commerce, not a mere conceivable rational relation, as in *Lee Optical*. "[S]imply because Congress may conclude that a particular activity substantially affects interstate commerce does not necessarily make it so." *Lopez*. The rational basis referred to in the Commerce Clause context is a demonstrated link in fact, based on empirical demonstration. While undoubtedly deferential, this may well be different from the rational-basis test as *Lee Optical* described it.

The Court relies on *Sabri* for its conclusion that a "means-ends rationality" is all that is required for a power to come within the Necessary and Proper Clause's reach. *Sabri* only refers to "means-ends rationality" in a parenthetical describing the holding in McCulloch v. Maryland (1819); it certainly did not import the *Lee Optical* rational-basis test into this arena through such a parenthetical. See *Sabri* (THOMAS, J., concurring in judgment) ("A statute can have a 'rational' connection to an enumerated power without being obviously or clearly tied to that enumerated power"). It should be remembered, moreover, that the spending power is not designated as such in the Constitution but rather is implied from the power to lay and collect taxes and other specified exactions in order, among other purposes, "to pay the Debts and provide for the common Defence and general Welfare of the United States." Art. I, §8, cl. 1; see South Dakota v. Dole (1987). The limits upon the spending power have not been much discussed, but if the relevant standard is parallel to the Commerce Clause cases, then the limits and the analytic approach in those precedents should be respected.

A separate concern stems from the Court's explanation of the Tenth Amendment. I had thought it a basic principle that the powers reserved to the States consist of the whole, undefined residuum of power remaining after taking account of powers granted to the National Government. The Constitution delegates limited powers to the National Government and then reserves the remainder for the States (or the people), not the other way around, as the Court's analysis suggests. And the powers reserved to the States are so broad that they remain undefined. Residual power, sometimes referred to (perhaps imperfectly) as the police power, belongs to the States and the States alone.

It is correct in one sense to say that if the National Government has the power to act under the Necessary and Proper Clause then that power is not one reserved to the States. But the precepts of federalism embodied in the Constitution inform which powers are properly exercised by the National Government in the first place. See *Lopez* (KENNEDY, J., concurring); see also *McCulloch* (powers "consist[ent] with the letter and spirit of the constitution, are constitutional"). It is of fundamental importance to consider whether essential attributes of state sovereignty are compromised by the assertion of federal power under the Necessary and Proper Clause; if so, that is a factor suggesting that the power is not one properly within the reach of federal power.

The opinion of the Court should not be interpreted to hold that the only, or even the principal, constraints on the exercise of congressional power are the Constitution's express prohibitions. The Court's discussion of the Tenth Amendment invites the inference that restrictions flowing from the federal system are of no import when defining the limits of the National Government's power, as it proceeds by first asking whether the power is within the National Government's reach, and if so it discards federalism concerns entirely.

These remarks explain why the Court ignores important limitations stemming from federalism principles. Those principles are essential to an understanding of the function and province of the States in our constitutional structure. . . .

This is not a case in which the National Government demands that a State use its own governmental system to implement federal commands. See Printz v. United States (1997). It is not a case in which the National Government relieves the States of their own primary responsibility to enact laws and policies for the safety and well being of their citizens. See United States v. Morrison (2000). Nor is it a case in which the exercise of national power intrudes upon functions and duties traditionally committed to the State. See *Lopez* (KENNEDY, J., concurring).

Rather, this is a discrete and narrow exercise of authority over a small class of persons already subject to the federal power. Importantly, §4248(d) requires the Attorney General to release any civil detainee "to the appropriate official of the State in which the person is domiciled or was tried if such State will assume responsibility for his custody, care, and treatment," providing a strong assurance that the proffered reason for the legislation's necessity is not a mere artifice.

With these observations, I concur in the judgment of the Court.

JUSTICE ALITO, concurring in the judgment.

I am concerned about the breadth of the Court's language, (KENNEDY, J., concurring in judgment), and the ambiguity of the standard that the Court applies, (THOMAS, J., dissenting), but I am persuaded, on narrow grounds, that it was "necessary and proper" for Congress to enact the statute at issue in this case in order to "carr[y] into Execution" powers specifically conferred on Congress by the Constitution, see Art. I, §8, cl. 18.

Section 4248 was enacted to protect the public from federal prisoners who suffer from "a serious mental illness, abnormality, or disorder" and who, if released, would have "serious difficulty in refraining from sexually violent conduct or child molestation." Under this law, if neither the State of a prisoner's domicile nor the State in which the prisoner was tried will assume the responsibility for the prisoner's "custody, care, and treatment," the Federal Government is authorized to undertake that responsibility. The statute recognizes that, in many cases, no State will assume the heavy financial burden of civilly committing a dangerous federal prisoner who, as a result of lengthy federal incarceration, no longer has any substantial ties to any State.

I entirely agree with the dissent that "[t]he Necessary and Proper Clause empowers Congress to enact only those laws that 'carr[y] into Execution' one or more of the federal powers enumerated in the Constitution," but §4248 satisfies that requirement because it is a necessary and proper means of carrying into execution the enumerated powers that support the federal criminal statutes under which the affected prisoners were convicted. The Necessary and Proper Clause provides the constitutional authority for most federal criminal statutes. In other words, most federal criminal statutes rest upon a congressional judgment that, in order to execute one or more of the powers conferred on Congress, it is necessary and proper to criminalize certain conduct, and in order to do that it is obviously necessary and proper to provide for the operation of a federal criminal justice system and a federal prison system.

All of this has been recognized since the beginning of our country. The First Congress enacted federal criminal laws, created federal law enforcement and prosecutorial positions, established a federal court system, provided for the imprisonment of persons convicted of federal crimes, and gave United States marshals the responsibility of securing federal prisoners.

The only additional question presented here is whether, in order to carry into execution the enumerated powers on which the federal criminal laws rest, it is also necessary and proper for Congress to protect the public from dangers created by the federal criminal justice and prison systems. In my view, the answer to that question is "yes." Just as it is necessary and proper for Congress to provide for the apprehension of escaped federal prisoners, it is necessary and proper for Congress to provide for the civil commitment of dangerous federal prisoners who would otherwise escape civil commitment as a result of federal imprisonment. . . .

The Necessary and Proper Clause does not give Congress *carte blanche.* Although the term "necessary" does not mean "absolutely necessary" or indispensable, the term requires an "appropriate" link between a power conferred by the Constitution and the law enacted by Congress. See McCulloch v. Maryland (1819). And it is an obligation of this Court to enforce compliance with that limitation.

The law in question here satisfies that requirement. This is not a case in which it is merely possible for a court to think of a rational basis on which Congress might have perceived an attenuated link between the powers underlying the federal criminal statutes and the challenged civil commitment provision. Here, there is a substantial link to Congress' constitutional powers.

For this reason, I concur in the judgment that Congress had the constitutional authority to enact 18 U. S. C. §4248.

JUSTICE THOMAS, with whom JUSTICE SCALIA joins in all but Part III–A–1–b, dissenting.

The Court holds today that Congress has power under the Necessary and Proper Clause to enact a law authorizing the Federal Government to civilly commit "sexually dangerous person[s]" beyond the date it lawfully could hold them on a charge or conviction for a federal crime. I disagree. The Necessary and Proper Clause empowers Congress to enact only those laws that "carr[y] into Execution" one or more of the federal powers enumerated in the Constitution. Art. I, §8, cl. 18. Because §4248 "Execut[es]" no enumerated power, I must respectfully dissent.

I

"As every schoolchild learns, our Constitution establishes a system of dual sovereignty between the States and the Federal Government." Gregory v. Ashcroft (1991). In our system, the Federal Government's powers are enumerated, and hence limited. See, *e.g.*, McCulloch v. Maryland (1819) ("This government is acknowledged by all to be one of enumerated powers"). Thus, Congress has no power to act unless the Constitution authorizes it to do so. United States v. Morrison (2000) ("Every law enacted by Congress must be based on one or more of its powers enumerated in the Constitution"). The States, in turn, are free to exercise all powers that the Constitution does not withhold from them. Amdt. 10 ("The powers not delegated to the United States by the Constitution, nor prohibited by it to the States, are reserved to the States respectively, or to the people").[1] This constitutional structure establishes different default rules for Congress and the States: Congress' powers are "few and defined," while those that belong to the States "remain . . . numerous and indefinite." The Federalist No. 45 (J. Madison).

The Constitution plainly sets forth the "few and defined" powers that Congress may exercise. Article I "vest[s]" in Congress "[a]ll legislative Powers herein granted," §1, and carefully enumerates those powers in §8. The final clause of §8, the Necessary and Proper Clause, authorizes Congress "[t]o make all Laws which shall be necessary and proper for carrying into Execution the foregoing Powers, and all other Powers vested by this Constitution in the Government of the United States, or in any Department or Officer thereof." As the Clause's placement at the end of §8 indicates, the "foregoing Powers" are those granted to Congress in the preceding clauses of that section. The "other Powers" to which the Clause refers are those "vested" in Congress and the other branches by other specific provisions of the Constitution.

Chief Justice Marshall famously summarized Congress' authority under the Necessary and Proper Clause in *McCulloch*, which has stood for nearly 200 years as this Court's definitive interpretation of that text:

1. "With this careful last phrase, the [Tenth] Amendment avoids taking any position on the division of power between the state governments and the people of the States: It is up to the people of each State to determine which 'reserved' powers their state government may exercise." U.S. Term Limits, Inc. v. Thornton (1995) (THOMAS, J., dissenting).

"Let the end be legitimate, let it be within the scope of the constitution, and all means which are appropriate, which are plainly adapted to that end, which are not prohibited, but consist with the letter and spirit of the constitution, are constitutional."

McCulloch's summation is descriptive of the Clause itself, providing that federal legislation is a valid exercise of Congress' authority under the Clause if it satisfies a two-part test: First, the law must be directed toward a "legitimate" end, which *McCulloch* defines as one "within the scope of the [C]onstitution" — that is, the powers expressly delegated to the Federal Government by some provision in the Constitution. Second, there must be a necessary and proper fit between the "means" (the federal law) and the "end" (the enumerated power or powers) it is designed to serve. *McCulloch* accords Congress a certain amount of discretion in assessing means-end fit under this second inquiry. The means Congress selects will be deemed "necessary" if they are "appropriate" and "plainly adapted" to the exercise of an enumerated power, and "proper" if they are not otherwise "prohibited" by the Constitution and not "[in]consistent" with its "letter and spirit."

Critically, however, *McCulloch* underscores the linear relationship the Clause establishes between the two inquiries: Unless the end itself is "legitimate," the fit between means and end is irrelevant. In other words, no matter how "necessary" or "proper" an Act of Congress may be to its objective, Congress lacks authority to legislate if the objective is anything other than "carrying into Execution" one or more of the Federal Government's enumerated powers.

This limitation was of utmost importance to the Framers. During the State ratification debates, Anti-Federalists expressed concern that the Necessary and Proper Clause would give Congress virtually unlimited power. See, *e.g.*, Essays of Brutus. Federalist supporters of the Constitution swiftly refuted that charge, explaining that the Clause did not grant Congress any freestanding authority, but instead made explicit what was already implicit in the grant of each enumerated power. Referring to the "powers declared in the Constitution," Alexander Hamilton noted that "it is *expressly* to execute these powers that the sweeping clause . . . authorizes the national legislature to pass all *necessary* and *proper* laws." The Federalist No. 33. James Madison echoed this view [in the Virginia ratification convention], stating that "the sweeping clause . . . only extend[s] to the enumerated powers." Statements by delegates to the state ratification conventions indicate that this understanding was widely held by the founding generation. *E.g.* (statement of George Nicholas) ("Suppose [the Necessary and Proper Clause] had been inserted, at the end of every power, that they should have power to make laws to carry that power into execution; would that have increased their powers? If, therefore, it could not have increased their powers, if placed at the end of each power, it cannot increase them at the end of all").[2]

2. See also (statement of William Maclaine) ("This clause specifies that [Congress] shall make laws to carry into execution *all the powers vested* by this Constitution, consequently they can make no laws to execute any other power"); (statement of James Wilson) ("[W]hen it is said that Congress

Roughly 30 years after the Constitution's ratification, *McCulloch* firmly established this understanding in our constitutional jurisprudence. Since then, our precedents uniformly have maintained that the Necessary and Proper Clause is not an independent fount of congressional authority, but rather "a caveat that Congress possesses all the means necessary to carry out the specifically granted 'foregoing' powers of §8 'and all other Powers vested by this Constitution.'" Kinsella v. United States ex rel. Singleton (1960); see Alden v. Maine (1999); Martin v. Hunter's Lessee (1816); see also Gonzales v. Raich (2005) (SCALIA, J., concurring in judgment) (stating that, although the Clause "empowers Congress to enact laws . . . that are not within its authority to enact in isolation," those laws must be "in effectuation of [Congress'] enumerated powers" (citing *McCulloch*)).

II

. . . No enumerated power in Article I, §8, expressly delegates to Congress the power to enact a civil-commitment regime for sexually dangerous persons, nor does any other provision in the Constitution vest Congress or the other branches of the Federal Government with such a power. Accordingly, §4248 can be a valid exercise of congressional authority only if it is "necessary and proper for carrying into Execution" one or more of those federal powers actually enumerated in the Constitution.

Section 4248 does not fall within any of those powers. The Government identifies no specific enumerated power or powers as a constitutional predicate for §4248, and none are readily discernable. Indeed, not even the Commerce Clause—the enumerated power this Court has interpreted most expansively, see, *e.g.*, NLRB v. Jones & Laughlin Steel Corp. (1937) can justify federal civil detention of sex offenders. Under the Court's precedents, Congress may not regulate noneconomic activity (such as sexual violence) based solely on the effect such activity may have, in individual cases or in the aggregate, on interstate commerce. *Morrison*; United States v. Lopez (1995). That limitation forecloses any claim that §4248 carries into execution Congress' Commerce Clause power, and the Government has never argued otherwise.[3] . . .

Section 4248 closely resembles the involuntary civil-commitment laws that States have enacted under their *parens patriae* and general police powers. Indeed, it is clear, on the face of the Act and in the Government's arguments

---

shall have power to make all laws which shall be necessary and proper, those words are limited and defined by the following, 'for carrying into execution the foregoing powers.' [The Clause] is saying no more than that the powers we have already particularly given, shall be effectually carried into execution"); Barnett, The Original Meaning of the Necessary and Proper Clause, 6 U. Pa. J. Const. L. 183, 185-186 (2003); Lawson & Granger, The "Proper" Scope of Federal Power: A Jurisdictional Interpretation of the Sweeping Clause, 43 Duke L. J. 267, 274-275, and n. 24 (1993).

3. For the reasons explained in Part III-A-2, the enumerated power that justifies a particular defendant's criminal arrest or conviction cannot justify his subsequent civil detention under §4248.

urging its constitutionality, that §4248 is aimed at protecting society from acts of sexual violence, not toward "carrying into Execution" any enumerated power or powers of the Federal Government. See Adam Walsh Child Protection and Safety Act of 2006, (entitled "[a]n Act [t]o protect children from sexual exploitation and violent crime"), §102 (statement of purpose declaring that the Act was promulgated "to protect the public from sex offenders"); Brief for United States (asserting the Federal Government's power to "*protect the public from harm* that might result upon these prisoners' release, even when that harm might arise from conduct that is *otherwise beyond the general regulatory powers of the federal government*" (emphasis added)). . . .

In my view, this should decide the question. Section 4248 runs afoul of our settled understanding of Congress' power under the Necessary and Proper Clause. Congress may act under that Clause only when its legislation "carr[ies] into Execution" one of the Federal Government's enumerated powers. Art. I, §8, cl. 18. Section 4248 does not execute *any* enumerated power. Section 4248 is therefore unconstitutional.

III

The Court perfunctorily genuflects to *McCulloch*'s framework for assessing Congress' Necessary and Proper Clause authority, and to the principle of dual sovereignty it helps to maintain, then promptly abandons both in favor of a novel five-factor test supporting its conclusion that §4248 is a "'necessary and proper'" adjunct to a jumble of *unenumerated* "authorit[ies]." The Court's newly minted test cannot be reconciled with the Clause's plain text or with two centuries of our precedents interpreting it. It also raises more questions than it answers. Must each of the five considerations exist before the Court sustains future federal legislation as proper exercises of Congress' Necessary and Proper Clause authority? What if the facts of a given case support a finding of only four considerations? Or three? And if three or four will suffice, which three or four are imperative? At a minimum, this shift from the two-step *McCulloch* framework to this five-consideration approach warrants an explanation as to why *McCulloch* is no longer good enough and which of the five considerations will bear the most weight in future cases, assuming some number less than five suffices. (Or, if not, why all five are required.) The Court provides no answers to these questions.

A

I begin with the first and last "considerations" in the Court's inquiry. The Court concludes that §4248 is a valid exercise of Congress' Necessary and Proper Clause authority because that authority is "broad," and because "the links between §4248 and an enumerated Article I power are not too attenuated." In so doing, the Court first inverts, then misapplies, *McCulloch*'s straightforward two-part test.

1

a

First, the Court describes Congress' lawmaking power under the Necessary and Proper Clause as "broad," relying on precedents that have upheld federal laws under the Clause after finding a "'rationa[l]'" fit between the law and an enumerated power (quoting Sabri v. United States (2004)). It is true that this Court's precedents allow Congress a certain degree of latitude in selecting the means for "carrying into Execution" an end that is "legitimate."[4] But in citing these cases, the Court puts the cart before the horse: The fit between means and ends matters only if the end is in fact legitimate—*i.e.*, only if it is one of the Federal Government's enumerated powers.

By starting its inquiry with the degree of deference owed to Congress in selecting means to further a legitimate end, the Court bypasses *McCulloch*'s first step and fails carefully to examine whether the end served by §4248 is actually one of those powers. See Part III-A-2, *infra.*

b[5]

Second, instead of asking the simple question of what enumerated power §4248 "carr[ies] into Execution" at *McCulloch*'s first step, the Court surveys other laws Congress has enacted and concludes that, because §4248 is related to those laws, the "links" between §4248 and an enumerated power are not "too attenuated"; hence, §4248 is a valid exercise of Congress' Necessary and Proper Clause authority. This unnecessarily confuses the analysis and, if followed to its logical extreme, would result in an unwarranted expansion of federal power.

The Court observes that Congress has the undisputed authority to "criminalize conduct" that interferes with enumerated powers; to "imprison individuals who engage in that conduct"; to "enact laws governing [those] prisons"; and to serve as a "custodian of its prisoners." From this, the Court assumes that §4248 must also be a valid exercise of congressional power because it is "'reasonably adapted'" to *those* exercises of Congress' incidental—and thus unenumerated—authorities. But that is not the question. The Necessary and Proper Clause does not provide Congress with authority to enact any law simply because it furthers *other laws* Congress has enacted in the exercise of its incidental authority; the Clause plainly requires a

4. Justice Kennedy concludes that the Necessary and Proper Clause requires something beyond rational-basis scrutiny when assessing the fit between an enumerated power and the means Congress selects to execute it. Other arguments regarding the degree of fit between means and end have been lodged elsewhere. See, e.g., Gonzales v. Raich (2005) (Thomas, J., dissenting) (arguing that, for a law to be within the Necessary and Proper Clause, it must bear an "obvious, simple, and direct relation" to an exercise of Congress' enumerated powers and must not subvert basic principles of federalism and dual sovereignty). But I find that debate beside the point here, because it concerns the analysis employed at *McCulloch*'s second step, while the Court's decision today errs by skipping the first.

5. [Justice Scalia did not join this section of Justice Thomas's dissent—Ed.]

showing that every federal statute "carr[ies] into Execution" one or more of the Federal Government's *enumerated* powers.[6]

Federal laws that criminalize conduct that interferes with enumerated powers, establish prisons for those who engage in that conduct, and set rules for the care and treatment of prisoners awaiting trial or serving a criminal sentence satisfy this test because each helps to "carr[y] into Execution" the enumerated powers that justify a criminal defendant's arrest or conviction. For example, Congress' enumerated power "[t]o establish Post Offices and post Roads," would lack force or practical effect if Congress lacked the authority to enact criminal laws "to punish those who steal letters from the post office, or rob the mail." *McCulloch*. Similarly, that enumerated power would be compromised if there were no prisons to hold persons who violate those laws, or if those prisons were so poorly managed that prisoners could escape or demand their release on the grounds that the conditions of their confinement violate their constitutional rights, at least as we have defined them. Civil detention under §4248, on the other hand, lacks any such connection to an enumerated power.

2

After focusing on the relationship between §4248 and several of Congress' implied powers, the Court finally concludes that the civil detention of a "sexually dangerous person" under §4248 carries into execution the enumerated power that justified that person's arrest or conviction in the first place. In other words, the Court analogizes §4248 to federal laws that authorize prison officials to care for federal inmates while they serve sentences or await trial. But while those laws help to "carr[y] into Execution" the enumerated power that justifies the imposition of criminal sanctions on the inmate, §4248 does not bear that essential characteristic for three reasons.

First, the statute's definition of a "sexually dangerous person" contains no element relating to the subject's crime. It thus does not require a federal court to find any connection between the reasons supporting civil commitment and the

6. *McCulloch* makes this point clear. As the Court notes, *McCulloch* states, in discussing a hypothetical, that from Congress' enumerated power to establish post offices and post roads "has been inferred the power and duty of carrying the mail," and, "from this implied power, has again been inferred the right to punish those who steal letters from the post office, or rob the mail." Contrary to the Court's interpretation, this dictum does not suggest that the relationship between Congress' implied power to punish postal crimes and its implied power to carry the mail is alone sufficient to satisfy review under the Necessary and Proper Clause. Instead, *McCulloch* directly links the constitutionality of the former to Congress' enumerated power "to establish post offices and post roads." (explaining that "the right to . . . punish those who rob [the mail] is not indispensably necessary to the establishment of a post office and post road," but is "essential to the beneficial exercise of th[at] power"). More importantly, *McCulloch*'s holding, as well as the holdings of this Court's subsequent decisions, make plain that congressional action is valid under the Necessary and Proper Clause only if it carries into execution one or more enumerated powers. (upholding Congress' incorporation of a bank because it was a "means . . . to be employed only for the purpose of carrying into execution *the given powers*" (emphasis added)) . . . .

enumerated power with which that person's criminal conduct interfered. As a consequence, §4248 allows a court to civilly commit an individual without finding that he was ever charged with or convicted of a federal crime involving sexual violence. That possibility is not merely hypothetical: The Government concedes that nearly 20% of individuals against whom §4248 proceedings have been brought fit this description.

Second, §4248 permits the term of federal civil commitment to continue beyond the date on which a convicted prisoner's sentence expires or the date on which the statute of limitations on an untried defendant's crime has run. The statute therefore authorizes federal custody over a person at a time when the Government would lack jurisdiction to detain him for violating a criminal law that executes an enumerated power.

The statute this Court upheld in Greenwood v. United States (1956), provides a useful contrast. That statute authorized the Federal Government to exercise civil custody over a federal defendant declared mentally unfit to stand trial only "until the accused shall be mentally competent to stand trial or until the pending charges against him are disposed of according to law." Thus, that statute's "end" reasonably could be interpreted as preserving the Government's power to enforce a criminal law against the accused. Section 4248, however, authorizes federal detention of a person even *after* the Government loses the authority to prosecute him for a federal crime.

Third, the definition of a "sexually dangerous person" relevant to §4248 does not require the court to find that the person is likely to violate a law executing an enumerated power in the future. Although the Federal Government has no express power to regulate sexual violence generally, Congress has passed a number of laws proscribing such conduct in special circumstances. All of these statutes contain jurisdictional elements that require a connection to one of Congress' enumerated powers—such as interstate commerce—or that limit the statute's coverage to jurisdictions in which Congress has plenary authority. Section 4248, by contrast, authorizes civil commitment upon a showing that the person is "sexually dangerous," and presents a risk "to others." It requires no evidence that this sexually dangerous condition will manifest itself in a way that interferes with a federal law that executes an enumerated power or in a geographic location over which Congress has plenary authority.

In sum, the enumerated powers that justify a criminal defendant's arrest or conviction cannot justify his subsequent civil detention under §4248.

B

The remaining "considerations" in the Court's five-part inquiry do not alter this conclusion. . . .

I cannot agree with JUSTICE ALITO that §4248 is a necessary and proper incident of Congress' power "to protect the public from dangers created by the federal criminal justice and prison systems." A federal criminal defendant's "sexually dangerous" propensities are not "created by" the fact of his incarceration or his relationship with the federal prison system. The fact that the Federal Government has the authority to imprison a person for the purpose of punishing him for a federal crime — sex-related or otherwise — does not provide the Government with the additional power to exercise indefinite civil control over that person.[7] . . .

[Furthermore,] the Court overstates the relevant history. . . . The historical record . . . supports the Federal Government's authority to detain a mentally ill person against whom it has the authority to enforce a criminal law. But it provides no justification whatsoever for reading the Necessary and Proper Clause to grant Congress the power to authorize the detention of persons without a basis for federal criminal jurisdiction. . . .

Absent congressional action that is in accordance with, or necessary and proper to, an enumerated power, the duty to protect citizens from violent crime, including acts of sexual violence, belongs solely to the States. *Morrison* ("[W]e can think of no better example of the police power, which the Founders denied the National Government and reposed in the States, than the suppression of violent crime"); see Cohens v. Virginia (1821) (Marshall, C. J.) (stating that Congress has "no general right to punish murder committed within any of the States").

* * *

Not long ago, this Court described the Necessary and Proper Clause as "the last, best hope of those who defend ultra vires congressional action." *Printz*. Regrettably, today's opinion breathes new life into that Clause, and — the Court's protestations to the contrary notwithstanding — comes perilously close to transforming the Necessary and Proper Clause into a basis for the federal police power that "we *always* have rejected," *Lopez* (THOMAS, J., concurring). In so doing, the Court endorses the precise abuse of power Article I is designed to prevent — the use of a limited grant of authority as a "pretext . . . for the accomplishment of objects not intrusted to the government." *McCulloch*.

I respectfully dissent.

ASSIGNMENT S-2

STUDY GUIDE: *The next case is important background to assessing the constitutionality of the Patent Protection and Affordable Care Act of 2010. Does the Court reject the original meaning of "commerce" in favor of an updated meaning to accommodate changing times? Does its analysis of the meaning of "commerce" comport with the evidence considered in Chapter 2? How did the previous decisions of the Court comport with that evidence? How did the Court in Paul v. Virginia reach its contrary conclusion about the meaning of*

7. The fact that Congress has the authority to "provide for the apprehension of escaped federal prisoners," (ALITO, J., concurring in judgment), does not change this conclusion. That authority derives from Congress' power to vindicate the enumerated power with which the escaped defendant's crime of conviction interfered, not a freestanding police power.

"commerce?" How does the Court distinguish these previous cases? Does the Court consider itself bound by stare decisis or "precedent"? Was there any reliance on the previous line of cases? Does the Court demonstrate the error of this previous line of cases?

UNITED STATES v. SOUTH-EASTERN UNDERWRITERS

322 U. S. 533 (1944)

MR. JUSTICE BLACK delivered the opinion of the Court.

For seventy-five years, this Court has held, whenever the question has been presented, that the Commerce Clause of the Constitution does not deprive the individual states of power to regulate and tax specific activities of foreign insurance companies which sell policies within their territories. Each state has been held to have this power, even though negotiation and execution of the companies' policy contracts involved communications of information and movements of persons, moneys, and papers across state lines. Not one of all these cases, however, has involved an Act of Congress which required the Court to decide the issue of whether the Commerce Clause grants to Congress the power to regulate insurance transactions stretching across state lines. Today, for the first time in the history of the Court, that issue is squarely presented, and must be decided.

Appellees—the South-Eastern Underwriters Association (SEUA), and its membership of nearly 200 private stock fire insurance companies, and 27 individuals—were indicted in the District Court for alleged violations of the Sherman Anti-Trust Act.... [D]o fire insurance transactions which stretch across state lines constitute "Commerce among the several States" so as to make them subject to regulation by Congress under the Commerce Clause?...

Ordinarily courts do not construe words used in the Constitution so as to give them a meaning more narrow than one which they had in the common parlance of the times in which the Constitution was written. To hold that the word "commerce," as used in the Commerce Clause, does not include a business such as insurance would do just that. Whatever other meanings "commerce" may have included in 1787, the dictionaries, encyclopedias, and other books of the period show that it included trade: business in which persons bought and sold, bargained and contracted.[1] And this meaning has persisted to modern times. Surely, therefore, a heavy burden is on him who asserts that the plenary power which the Commerce Clause grants to Congress to regulate "Commerce among the several States" does not include the power to regulate trading in insurance to the same extent that it includes power to regulate other trades or businesses conducted across state lines.[2]

1. See Gibbons v. Ogden, 9 Wheat. 1; also, Hamilton and Adair, The Power to Govern (N.Y.1937), pp. 53-63.

2. Alexander Hamilton, in 1791, stating his opinion on the constitutionality of the Bank of the United States, declared that it would "admit of little if any question" that the federal power to

The modern insurance business holds a commanding position in the trade and commerce of our Nation. Built upon the sale of contracts of indemnity, it has become one of the largest and most important branches of commerce. . . . Perhaps no modern commercial enterprise directly affects so many persons in all walks of life as does the insurance business. Insurance touches the home, the family, and the occupation or the business of almost every person in the United States.

This business is not separated into 48 distinct territorial compartments which function in isolation from each other. Interrelationship, interdependence, and integration of activities in all the states in which they operate are practical aspects of the insurance companies' methods of doing business. A large share of the insurance business is concentrated in a comparatively few companies located, for the most part, in the financial centers of the East. Premiums collected from policyholders in every part of the United States flow into these companies for investment. As policies become payable, checks and drafts flow back to the many states where the policyholders reside. The result is a continuous and indivisible stream of intercourse among the states composed of collections of premiums, payments of policy obligations, and the countless documents and communications which are essential to the negotiation and execution of policy contracts. Individual policyholders living in many different states who own policies in a single company have their separate interests blended in one assembled fund of assets upon which all are equally dependent for payment of their policies. The decisions which that company makes at its home office—the risks it insures, the premiums it charges, the investments it makes, the losses it pays—concern not just the people of the state where the home office happens to be located. They concern people living far beyond the boundaries of that state. . . .

Despite all of this, despite the fact that most persons, speaking from common knowledge, would instantly say that, of course, such a business is engaged in trade and commerce, the District Court felt compelled by decisions of this Court to conclude that the insurance business can never be trade or commerce within the meaning of the Commerce Clause. We must therefore consider these decisions.

In 1869, this Court held, in sustaining a statute of Virginia which regulated foreign insurance companies, that the statute did not offend the Commerce Clause because "issuing a policy of insurance is not a transaction of commerce." [Paul v. Virginia (1868).][3] Since then, in similar cases, this statement has been

---

regulate foreign commerce included "the regulation of policies of insurance." 3 Works of Alexander Hamilton (Fed.Ed., N.Y.1904) pp. 445, 469-470. Speaking of the need of a federal power to regulate "commerce," Hamilton had earlier said,

> It is, indeed, evident on the most superficial view that there is no object, either as it respects the interests of trade or finance, that more strongly demands a federal superintendence.

Federalist No. XXII, The Federalist (Rev. Ed., N.Y. 1901) 110.

3. "The defect of the argument lies in the character of their business. Issuing a policy of insurance is not a transaction of commerce. The policies are simple contracts of indemnity against

repeated, and has been broadened. In Hooper v. California, decided in 1895, the *Paul* statement was reaffirmed, and the Court added that, "The business of insurance is not commerce." In 1913, the New York Life Insurance Company, protesting against a Montana tax, challenged these broad statements, strongly urging that its business, at least, was so conducted as to be engaged in interstate commerce. But the Court again approved the *Paul* statement and held against the company, saying that "contracts of insurance are not commerce at all, neither state nor interstate." New York Life Ins. Co. v. Deer Lodge County [1913].

In all cases in which the Court has relied upon the proposition that "the business of insurance is not commerce," its attention was focused on the validity of state statutes—the extent to which the Commerce Clause automatically deprived states of the power to regulate the insurance business. Since Congress had at no time attempted to control the insurance business, invalidation of the state statutes would practically have been equivalent to granting insurance companies engaged in interstate activities a blanket license to operate without legal restraint. As early as 1866, the insurance trade, though still in its infancy, was subject to widespread abuses. To meet the imperative need for correction of these abuses, the various state legislatures, including that of Virginia, passed regulatory legislation. Paul v. Virginia upheld one of Virginia's statutes. To uphold insurance laws of other states, including tax laws, Paul v. Virginia's generalization and reasoning have been consistently adhered to.

Today, however, we are asked to apply this reasoning not to uphold another state law, but to strike down an Act of Congress which was intended to regulate certain aspects of the methods by which interstate insurance companies do business, and, in so doing, to narrow the scope of the federal power to regulate the activities of a great business carried on back and forth across state lines. But past decisions of this Court emphasize that legal formulae devised to uphold state power cannot uncritically be accepted as trustworthy guides to determine Congressional power under the Commerce Clause.[4] Furthermore, the reasons given in support of the generalization that "the business of insurance is not commerce" and can never be conducted so as to constitute "Commerce among the States" are inconsistent with many decisions of this Court which have upheld federal statutes regulating interstate commerce under the Commerce Clause.

One reason advanced for the rule in the *Paul* case has been that insurance policies "are not commodities to be shipped or forwarded from one State to another." But both before and since Paul v. Virginia, this Court has held that

---

loss by fire, entered into between the corporations and the assured, for a consideration paid by the latter. These contracts are not articles of commerce in any proper meaning of the word. They are not subjects of trade and barter offered in the market as something having an existence and value independent of the parties to them. They are not commodities to be shipped or forwarded from one State to another, and then put up for sale. They are like other personal contracts between parties which are completed by their signature and the transfer of the consideration. Such contracts are not interstate transactions, though the parties may be domiciled in different States. The policies do not take effect—are not executed contracts—until delivered by the agent in Virginia. They are, then, local transactions, and are governed by the local law." 75 U.S. 8 Wall. 168, 75 U.S. 183.

4. See, e.g., Wickard v. Filburn. . . .

Congress can regulate traffic though it consist of intangibles.[5] Another reason much stressed has been that insurance policies are mere personal contracts subject to the laws of the state where executed. But this reason rests upon a distinction between what has been called "local" and what "interstate," a type of mechanical criterion which this Court has not deemed controlling in the measurement of federal power. Cf. Wickard v. Filburn. . . . We may grant that a contract of insurance, considered as a thing apart from negotiation and execution, does not itself constitute interstate commerce. But it does not follow from this that the Court is powerless to examine the entire transaction, of which that contract is but a part, in order to determine whether there may be a chain of events which becomes interstate commerce. Only by treating the Congressional power over commerce among the states as a "technical legal conception," rather than as a "practical one, drawn from the course of business" could such a conclusion be reached. Swift & Co. v. United States [1905]. In short, a nationwide business is not deprived of its interstate character merely because it is built upon sales contracts which are local in nature. Were the rule otherwise, few businesses could be said to be engaged in interstate commerce. . . .

The real answer to the question before us is to be found in the Commerce Clause itself, and in some of the great cases which interpret it. Many decisions make vivid the broad and true meaning of that clause. It is interstate commerce subject to regulation by Congress to carry lottery tickets from state to state. So also is it interstate commerce to transport a woman from Louisiana to Texas in a common carrier; to carry across a state line in a private automobile five quarts of whiskey intended for personal consumption; to drive a stolen automobile from Iowa to South Dakota. Diseased cattle ranging between Georgia and Florida are in commerce, and the transmission of an electrical impulse over a telegraph line between Alabama and Florida is intercourse, and subject to paramount federal regulation. Not only, then, may transactions be commerce though noncommercial; they may be commerce though illegal and sporadic, and though they do not utilize common carriers or concern the flow of anything more tangible than electrons and information. These activities having already been held to constitute interstate commerce, and persons engaged in them therefore having been held subject to federal regulation, it would indeed be difficult now to hold that no activities of any insurance company can ever constitute interstate commerce so as to make it subject to such regulation;—activities which, as part of the conduct of a legitimate and useful commercial enterprise, may embrace integrated operations in many states and involve the transmission of great quantities of money, documents, and communications across dozens of state lines.

The precise boundary between national and state power over commerce has never yet been, and doubtless never can be, delineated by a single abstract definition. The most widely accepted general description of that part of commerce which is subject to the federal power is that given in 1824 by Chief Justice Marshall: "Commerce, undoubtedly, is traffic, but it is something more: it is

5. See, for illustration, . . . Lottery Case. . . .

intercourse. It describes the commercial intercourse between nations, and parts of nations, in all its branches. . . ." [Gibbons v. Ogden] Commerce is interstate, he said, when it "concerns more States than one." No decision of this Court has ever questioned this as too comprehensive a description of the subject matter of the Commerce Clause. To accept a description less comprehensive, the Court has recognized, would deprive the Congress of that full power necessary to enable it to discharge its Constitutional duty to govern commerce among the states.[6]

The power confined to Congress by the Commerce Clause is declared in *The Federalist* to be for the purpose of securing the "maintenance of harmony and proper intercourse among the States." But its purpose is not confined to empowering Congress with the negative authority to legislate against state regulations of commerce deemed inimical to the national interest. The power granted Congress is a positive power . It is the power to legislate concerning transactions which, reaching across State boundaries, affect the people of more states than one;—to govern affairs which the individual states, with their limited territorial jurisdictions, are not fully capable of governing. This federal power to determine the rules of intercourse across state lines was essential to weld a loose confederacy into a single, indivisible Nation; its continued existence is equally essential to the welfare of that Nation.

Our basic responsibility in interpreting the Commerce Clause is to make certain that the power to govern intercourse among the states remains where the Constitution placed it. That power, as held by this Court from the beginning, is vested in the Congress, available to be exercised for the national welfare as Congress shall deem necessary. No commercial enterprise of any kind which conducts its activities across state lines has been held to be wholly beyond the regulatory power of Congress under the Commerce Clause. We cannot make an exception of the business of insurance. . . . Having power to enact the Sherman Act, Congress did so; if exceptions are to be written into the Act, they must come from the Congress, not this Court. . . .

REVERSED.

MR. JUSTICE ROBERTS and MR. JUSTICE REED took no part in the consideration or decision of this case.

MR. CHIEF JUSTICE STONE, dissenting. . . .

The numerous and unvarying decisions of this Court that "insurance is not commerce" have never denied that acts of interstate commerce may be incidental to the business of writing and performing contracts of insurance, or that those incidental acts are subject to the commerce power. Our decisions on this subject have uniformly rested on the ground that the formation of an insurance

6. . . . . "A government ought to contain, in itself, every power requisite to the full accomplishment of the objects committed to its care, and to the complete execution of the trusts for which it is responsible, free from every other control, but a regard to the public good and to the sense of the people." Federalist No. XXX.

contract, even though it insures against risk of loss to property located in other states or moving in interstate commerce, is not interstate commerce, and that, although the incidents of interstate communication and transportation which often attend the formation and performance of an insurance contract are interstate commerce, they do not serve to render the business of insurance itself interstate commerce. . . .

If an insurance company in New York executes and delivers, either in that state or another, a policy insuring the owner of a building in New Jersey against loss by fire, no act of interstate commerce has occurred. True, if the owner comes to New York to procure the insurance or, after delivery in New York, carries the policy to New Jersey, or the company sends it there by mail or messenger, such would be acts of interstate commerce. Similarly, if the owner pays the premiums by mail to the company in New York, or the company's New Jersey agent sends the premiums to New York, or the company in New York sends money to New Jersey on the occurrence of the loss insured against, acts of interstate commerce would occur. But the power of the Congress to regulate them is derived not from its authority to regulate the business of insurance, but from its power to regulate interstate communication and transportation. And such incidental use of the facilities of interstate commerce does not render the insurance business itself interstate commerce. Nor is the nature of a single insurance transaction or a few such transactions not involving interstate commerce altered in that regard merely because their number is multiplied. The power of Congress to regulate interstate communication and transportation incidental to the insurance business is not any more or any less because the number of insurance transactions is great or small. . . . The contract of insurance makes no stipulation for the sale or delivery of commodities in interstate commerce or for any other interstate transaction. It provides only for the payment of a sum of money in the event of the loss insured against. . . .

The conclusion seems inescapable that the formation of insurance contracts, like many others, and the business of so doing, is not, without more, commerce within the protection of the commerce clause of the Constitution and thereby, in large measure, excluded from state control and regulation. This conclusion seems, upon analysis, not only correct on principle and in complete harmony with the uniform rulings by which this Court has held that the formation of all types of contract which do not stipulate for the performance of acts of interstate commerce, are likewise not interstate commerce, but it has the support of an unbroken line of decisions of this Court beginning with Paul v. Virginia, seventy-five years ago, and extending down to the present time. . . . Such has ever since been the practical construction by the other branches of the Government of the application to insurance of the commerce clause and the Sherman Act. Long continued practical construction of the Constitution or a statute is of persuasive force in determining its meaning and proper application. . . .

From what has been said, it seems plain that our decisions that the business of insurance is not commerce are not unsound in principle, and involve no inconsistency or lack of harmony with accepted doctrine. They place no field of activity beyond the control of both the national and state governments, as did

Hammer v. Dagenhart, overruled three years ago by a unanimous Court in United States v. Darby. On the contrary the ruling that insurance is not commerce, and is therefore unaffected by the restrictions which the commerce clause imposes on state legislation, removed the most serious obstacle to regulation of that business by the states. Through their plenary power over domestic and foreign corporations which are not engaged in interstate commerce, the states have developed extensive and effective systems of regulation of the insurance business, often solving regulatory problems of a local character with which it would be impractical or difficult for Congress to deal through the exercise of the commerce power. And in view of the broad powers of the federal government to regulate matters which, though not themselves commerce, nevertheless affect interstate commerce, Wickard v. Filburn, there can be no doubt of the power of Congress, if it so desires, to regulate many aspects of the insurance business mentioned in this indictment.

But the immediate and only practical effect of the decision now rendered is to withdraw from the states, in large measure, the regulation of insurance, and to confer it on the national government, which has adopted no legislative policy and evolved no scheme of regulation with respect to the business of insurance. . . .

The judgment should be AFFIRMED.

In response to this case, in 1945, Congress enacted the McCarran–Ferguson Act, 15 U.S.C. §§1011-1015, exempting the business of insurance from most federal regulation, including federal anti-trust laws to a limited extent. It did so by providing that Acts of Congress that do not expressly purport to regulate the "business of insurance" will not preempt state laws or regulations that regulate the "business of insurance." As a result of this Act, until 2010, the business insurance was largely regulated by state insurance commissions.

In March of 2010, Congress passed the Patient Protection and Affordable Care Act (ACA). The day after its passage, it was challenged in the Northern District of California as unconstitutional by a group of state attorneys general and the National Federation of Independent Business. In their lawsuit, the attorneys general challenged the constitutionality of the provision of the ACA that requires all Americans to purchase qualifying health insurance policies or pay a monetary penalty, which is commonly referred to as the "individual mandate." They also challenged the expansion of Medicaid contained in the ACA. The number of attorneys general in the lawsuit has since grown to 26. In addition, at least four other challenges were made in other courts. Three district court judges (in Michigan, Virginia, and the District of Columbia) upheld the constitutionality of the individual mandate; two district court judges (in Virginia and Florida) held that the mandate was unconstitutional. The judge in Florida denied the states' challenges to the new Medicaid requirements. Each of these cases was then appealed to their respective court of appeals.

As this supplement goes to press, only the Court of Appeals for the Sixth Circuit has reached a decision on the appeal before it, though by the time you are reading this, decisions will have been issued by the courts of appeals for the Fourth and Eleventh Circuits. (The Circuit Court of Appeals for the District of Columbia will hear oral argument at the end of September 2011.) Given the timing of these decisions, petitions for certiorari will be filed in the Supreme Court by the fall of 2011, and there is a good chance the Supreme Court will hear argument in the winter of 2012, and reach a decision on the constitutionality of the ACA by June of 2012.

The three opinions by the divided panel in the Sixth Circuit in the next case provide a nice cross-section of analyses of the constitutionality of the individual mandate.

***Study Guide:** Notice how Judge Martin identifies the "class of activities" being regulated by the statute. Why does he think that Congress may reach this activity under the Supreme Court's Commerce Clause cases? How does Judge Graham contest that characterization? Is this disagreement central to the outcome? All three judges seem to reject the proposition that Congress may not regulate "inactivity"? Given that, by what reasoning does Judge Graham conclude that the mandate is beyond the powers of Congress. Does it turn on the meaning of "economic activity," rather than "activity"? Try to identify each step in his logic. In a footnote, Judge Martin questions the availability of "as applied" Commerce Clause challenges after* Raich, *while Judge Sutton contends that "facial challenges" are extraordinarily difficult to sustain. Where does that leave the judicial enforcement of any limits on the enumerated powers of Congress?*

THOMAS MORE LAW CENTER v. BARACK HUSSEIN OBAMA

U.S. Court of Appeals for the Sixth Circuit, No. 10-2388 (2011)

Boyce F. Martin, Jr., Circuit Judge. This is an appeal from the district court's determination that the minimum coverage provision of the Patient Protection and Affordable Care Act is constitutionally sound. Among the Act's many changes to the national markets in health care delivery and health insurance, the minimum coverage provision requires all applicable individuals to maintain minimum essential health insurance coverage or to pay a penalty. . . .

Plaintiffs sought a declaration that Congress lacked authority under the Commerce Clause to pass the minimum coverage provision. . . . We find that the minimum coverage provision is a valid exercise of legislative power by Congress under the Commerce Clause and therefore AFFIRM the decision of the district court.

I. BACKGROUND

Congress found that the minimum coverage provision is an essential cog in the Affordable Care Act's comprehensive scheme to reform the national markets in health care delivery and health insurance. The Act contains five essential components designed to improve access to the health care and health insurance markets, reduce the escalating costs of health care, and minimize cost-shifting. First, the Act builds upon the existing nationwide system of employer-based health insurance. It establishes tax incentives for small businesses to purchase health insurance for their employees, and requires certain large employers to offer health insurance to their employees. Second, the Act provides for the creation of state-operated "health benefit exchanges." These exchanges allow individuals and small businesses to leverage their collective buying power to obtain price-competitive health insurance. Third, the Act expands federal programs to assist the poor with obtaining health insurance. For eligible individuals who purchase insurance through an exchange, the Act offers federal tax credits for payment of health insurance premiums, and authorizes federal payments to help cover out-of-pocket expenses. The Act also expands eligibility for Medicaid. Fourth, the Act bars certain practices in the insurance industry that have prevented individuals from obtaining and maintaining health insurance. The guaranteed issue requirement bars insurance companies from denying coverage to individuals with preexisting conditions, and the community rating requirement prohibits insurance companies from charging higher rates to individuals based on their medical history.

Finally, the Act's "Requirement to Maintain Minimum Essential Coverage," 26 U.S.C. §5000A, takes effect in 2014 and requires every "applicable individual" to obtain "minimum essential coverage" for each month. The Act directs the Secretary of Health and Human Services in coordination with the Secretary of the Treasury to define the required essential health benefits, which must include at least ten general categories of services.

Applicable individuals who fail to obtain minimum essential coverage must include with their annual federal tax payment a "shared responsibility payment," which is a "penalty" calculated based on household income. The Act exempts from its penalty provision certain individuals, including those deemed to suffer a hardship with respect to their capability to obtain coverage.

A number of Congressional findings accompany the minimum coverage requirement. Congress determined that "the Federal Government has a significant role in regulating health insurance," and "[t]he requirement is an essential part of this larger regulation of economic activity." Congress found that without the minimum coverage provision, other provisions in the Act, in particular the guaranteed issue and community rating requirements, would increase the incentives for individuals to "wait to purchase health insurance until they needed care." This would exacerbate the current problems in the markets for health care delivery and health insurance. Conversely, Congress found that "[b]y significantly reducing the number of the uninsured, the [minimum coverage] requirement, together with the other provisions of this Act, will lower health insurance premiums." Congress concluded that the minimum coverage provision "is essential to creating effective health insurance markets in which improved health insurance products that are guaranteed issue and do not exclude coverage of pre-existing conditions can be sold." . . .

III. IS THE MINIMUM COVERAGE PROVISION A CONSTITUTIONAL EXERCISE OF CONGRESS'S COMMERCE POWER?

The question squarely presented here is whether the minimum coverage provision is consistent with the Commerce Clause of the Constitution. We review de novo plaintiffs' constitutional challenge to the provision. At the outset, it is important to note that our elected officials and the public hotly debated the merits and weaknesses of the Act before Congress voted, and will undoubtedly continue to in the future. However, it is not this Court's role to pass on the wisdom of Congress's choice. See, e.g., Gibbons v. Ogden (1824) ("The wisdom and the discretion of Congress, their identity with the people, and the influence which their constituents possess at elections[] are . . . the sole restraints on which they have relied, to secure them from its abuse."). We consider only whether the Constitution grants Congress the power to enact this legislation.

The minimum coverage provision, like all congressional enactments, is entitled to a "presumption of constitutionality," and will be invalidated only upon a "plain showing that Congress has exceeded its constitutional bounds." United States v. Morrison (2000). The presumption that the minimum coverage provision is valid is "not a mere polite gesture. It is a deference due to deliberate judgment by constitutional majorities of the two Houses of Congress that an Act is within their delegated power. . . ." United States v. Five Gambling Devices (1953).

A. The Supreme Court's Commerce Clause Jurisprudence

In our dual system of government, the federal government is limited to its enumerated powers, while all other powers are reserved to the states or to the people. U.S. Const. amend. X. States have authority under their general police powers to enact minimum coverage provisions similar to the one in the Affordable Care Act. See Mass. Gen. Laws Ann. ch. 111M, §2 (West 2011). However, the federal government has no police power and may enact such a law only if it is authorized by one of its enumerated powers. See, e.g., United States v. Lopez (1995). Our task is to review the district court's conclusion that Congress properly relied on its authority under the Commerce Clause to enact the minimum coverage provision.

Recognizing that uniform federal regulation is necessary in some instances, the Commerce Clause of the Constitution grants Congress the power "[t]o regulate commerce with foreign Nations, and among the several States, and with the Indian Tribes." U.S. Const. Art. I, §8, cl. 3. The Supreme Court has held that Congress has broad authority to regulate under the Commerce Clause. From

1937 to 1994 it did not invalidate a single law as unconstitutional for exceeding the scope of Congress's Commerce Power. The Court has explained that Congress's Commerce Clause power encompasses three broad spheres: (1) "the use of the channels of interstate commerce"; (2) "the instrumentalities of interstate commerce, or persons or things in interstate commerce"; and (3) "those activities having a substantial relation to interstate commerce, . . . *i.e.*, those activities that substantially affect interstate commerce." *Lopez.*

Because the United States does not contend that the minimum coverage provision falls within either of the first two categories, we proceed to consider whether the provision falls within Congress's power to regulate activities that substantially affect interstate commerce. Current Supreme Court jurisprudence reveals that Congress may use this category of its Commerce Power to regulate two related classes of activity. First, it has long been established that Congress may regulate economic activity, even if wholly intrastate, if it substantially affects interstate commerce. See Gonzales v. Raich (2005); *Morrison*; *Lopez.*

Second, Congress may also regulate even non-economic intrastate activity if doing so is essential to a larger scheme that regulates economic activity. For example, in Wickard v. Filburn, the Court upheld regulations limiting the amount of wheat that farmers could grow, even for non-commercial purposes. Even though producing and consuming home-grown wheat is non-economic intrastate activity, Congress rationally concluded that the failure to regulate this class of activities would undercut its broader regulation of the interstate wheat market. This is because individuals would be fulfilling their own demand for wheat rather than resorting to the market, which would thwart Congress's efforts to stabilize prices. Similarly, in Gonzales v. Raich, the Court held that the federal Controlled Substances Act could be applied to prohibit the local cultivation and possession of marijuana authorized under California law. Leaving home-grown and homeconsumed marijuana outside federal control would undercut Congress's broader regulation of interstate economic activity. Thus, *Wickard* and *Raich* establish that "Congress can regulate purely intrastate activity that is not itself 'commercial,' in that it is not produced for sale, if it concludes that failure to regulate that class of activity would undercut the regulation of the interstate market in that commodity." *Id.*

Despite the Supreme Court's broad interpretation of the Commerce Power, it has emphasized in two recent cases that this power is subject to real limits. In United States v. Lopez and United States v. Morrison, the Court struck down single-subject criminal statutes as beyond Congress's power under the Commerce Clause. The Supreme Court held that the statutes at issue in these cases, the Gun Free School Zones Act and the Violence Against Women Act, exceeded Congress's Commerce Clause power based on four main factors: (1) the statutes regulated non-economic, criminal activity and were not part of a larger regulation of economic activity; (2) the statutes contained no jurisdictional hook limiting their application to interstate commerce; (3) any Congressional findings regarding the effects of the regulated activity on interstate commerce were not sufficient to sustain constitutionality of the legislation; and (4) the link between the regulated activity and interstate commerce was too attenuated. The Court found that accepting Congress's proffered reasons for the statutes would have paved the way for Congress to regulate those quintessentially local actions that the Constitution left within the purview of the states.

B. Whether the Minimum Coverage Provision is a Valid Exercise of the Commerce Power under *Lopez*, *Morrison*, and *Raich*

In applying this jurisprudence, our first duty is to determine the class of activities that the minimum coverage provision regulates. See, e.g., Perez v. United States (1971) (directing courts to determine first whether the class of activities regulated by a statute is within the reach of Congress's power). There is debate over whether the provision regulates activity in the market of health insurance or in the market of health care. In the most literal, narrow sense, the provision might be said to regulate conduct in the health insurance market by requiring individuals to maintain a minimum level of coverage. However, Congress's intent and the broader statutory scheme may help to illuminate the class of activities that a provision regulates. See, e.g., Swift & Co. v. United States (1905) ("[C]ommerce among the states is not a technical legal conception, but a practical one, drawn from the course of business."); United States v. Ambert (11th Cir. 2009) ("Congress did not focus on individual local registration as an end in itself, but rather as part of its goal to create a system to track and regulate the movement of sex offenders from one jurisdiction to another."). The Act considered as a whole makes clear that Congress was concerned that individuals maintain minimum coverage not as an end in itself, but because of the economic implications on the broader health care market. Virtually everyone participates in the market for health care delivery, and they finance these services by either purchasing an insurance policy or by self-insuring. Through the practice of self-insuring, individuals make an assessment of their own risk and to what extent they must set aside funds or arrange their affairs to compensate for probable future health care needs.[7] Thus, set against the Act's broader statutory scheme, the minimum coverage provision reveals itself as a regulation on the activity of participating in the national market for health care delivery, and specifically the activity of self-insuring for the cost of these services.

Plaintiffs challenge the minimum coverage provision on its face as an unconstitutional exercise of congressional authority. They accept the class of activities that the provision purports to reach: participating in the national market for health care services without maintaining insurance that meets the minimum coverage requirement. Unlike the plaintiffs in *Raich*, they do not attempt to carve out a subset class of activities and to deny that their conduct has substantial effects on interstate commerce. Rather, like the plaintiffs in *Lopez* and *Morrison*, they claim that the entire class of activities that the provision attempts to reach is

7. We use the term self-insurance for ease of discussion. We note, however, that it is actually a misnomer because no insurance is involved, and might be better described as risk retention.

beyond Congress's power to regulate.[8] In this Circuit, "[f]acial invalidation of a statute . . . is reserved only for when there are no set of circumstances in which the statute's application would be constitutional." United States v. Faasse (6th Cir. 2001) (en banc); see also United States v. Salerno (1987).

By regulating the practice of self-insuring for the cost of health care delivery, the minimum coverage provision is facially constitutional under the Commerce Clause for two independent reasons. First, the provision regulates economic activity that Congress had a rational basis to believe has substantial effects on interstate commerce. In addition, Congress had a rational basis to believe that the provision was essential to its larger economic scheme reforming the interstate markets in health care and health insurance.

1. The minimum coverage provision regulates economic activity with a substantial effect on interstate commerce

Congress may regulate economic activity, even if wholly intrastate, that substantially affects interstate commerce. See Raich; *Morrison*; *Lopez*. Additionally, "[w]e need not determine whether [the] activities, taken in the aggregate, substantially affect interstate commerce in fact, but only whether a 'rational basis' exists for so concluding." *Raich* (citing *Lopez*). Thus, our task is to determine whether self-insuring for the cost of health care services is an economic activity, and whether Congress had a rational basis to conclude that, in the aggregate, this activity substantially affects interstate commerce.

The minimum coverage provision regulates activity that is decidedly economic. In *Raich*, the Supreme Court explained that "'[e]conomics' refers to 'the production, distribution, and consumption of commodities.'" *Id.* (quoting Webster's Third New International Dictionary 720 (1966)). Consumption of health care falls squarely within *Raich*'s definition of economics, and virtually every individual in this country consumes these services. Individuals must finance the cost of health care by purchasing an insurance policy or by self-insuring, cognizant of the backstop of free services required by law. By requiring individuals to maintain a certain level of coverage, the minimum coverage provision regulates the financing of health care services, and specifically the practice of self-insuring for the cost of care. The activity of foregoing health

8. If a group of plaintiffs brought an as-applied challenge, in contrast, they would claim that their conduct does not have substantial effects on interstate commerce, either because they never access the health care market or because they are fully capable of paying for any health care services that they consume. We have no occasion to address these situations in detail but note only that if the minimum coverage provision is facially constitutional, then it is difficult to imagine a circumstance under which an as-applied Commerce Clause challenge to the provision would succeed. See, e.g., United States v. Maxwell (11th Cir. 2006) ("[*Raich*] leaves some doubt as to whether, in the Commerce Clause context, an as-applied challenge may ever be sustained so long as Congress may constitutionally regulate the broader class of activities of which the intrastate activity is a part. . . .").

insurance and attempting to cover the cost of health care needs by self-insuring is no less economic than the activity of purchasing an insurance plan. Thus, the financing of health care services, and specifically the practice of self-insuring, is economic activity.

Furthermore, Congress had a rational basis to believe that the practice of self insuring for the cost of health care, in the aggregate, substantially affects interstate commerce. An estimated 18.8% of the non-elderly United States population (about 50 million people) had no form of health insurance for 2009. U.S. Census Bureau, Income, Poverty, and Health Insurance Coverage in the United States (2010). Virtually everyone requires health care services at some point, and unlike nearly all other industries, the health care market is governed by federal and state laws requiring institutions to provide services regardless of a patient's ability to pay. The uninsured cannot avoid the need for health care, and they consume over $100 billion in health care services annually. Families USA, Hidden Health Tax: Americans Pay a Premium, at 2 (2009). The high cost of health care means that those who self-insure, as a class, are unable to pay for the health care services that they receive. Congress found that the aggregate cost of providing uncompensated care to the uninsured in 2008 was $43 billion. Congress also determined that the cost of uncompensated care is passed on from providers "to private insurers, which pass on the cost to families." This cost-shifting inflates the premiums that families must pay for their health insurance "by on average over $1,000 a year." Rising premiums push even more individuals out of the health insurance market, further increasing the cost of health insurance and perpetuating the cycle. See *47 Million and Counting: Why the Health Care Marketplace Is Broken: Hearing Before the S. Comm. on Finance*, 110th Cong. 49 (2008) (Statement of Mark A. Hall). Thus, the practice of self-insuring substantially affects interstate commerce by driving up the cost of health care as well as by shifting costs to third parties.

Self-insuring for the cost of health care directly affects the interstate market for health care delivery and health insurance. These effects are not at all attenuated as were the links between the regulated activities and interstate commerce in *Lopez* and *Morrison*. Similar to the causal relationship in *Wickard*, self-insuring individuals are attempting to fulfill their own demand for a commodity rather than resort to the market and are thereby thwarting Congress's efforts to stabilize prices. Therefore, the minimum coverage provision is a valid exercise of the Commerce Power because Congress had a rational basis for concluding that, in the aggregate, the practice of self-insuring for the cost of health care substantially affects interstate commerce.

2. The minimum coverage provision is an essential part of a broader economic regulatory scheme

Alternatively, even if self-insuring for the cost of health care were not economic activity with a substantial effect on interstate commerce, Congress could still properly regulate the practice because the failure to do so would undercut its regulation of the larger interstate markets in health care delivery and health insurance. In *Raich*, the Supreme Court explained that Congress can regulate non-commercial intrastate activity if it concludes that it is necessary in order to regulate a larger interstate market. The Court found relevant that unlike the single-subject criminal statutes at issue in *Morrison* and *Lopez*, the classification of marijuana at issue in *Raich* was "merely one of many 'essential part[s] of a larger regulation of economic activity, in which the regulatory scheme could be undercut unless the intrastate activity were regulated.'" *Id.* (alteration in original) (quoting *Lopez*). The *Raich* Court highlighted two aspects of Congress's broad power under the Commerce Clause. First, Congress may aggregate the effects of non-commercial activity and assess the overall effect on the interstate market. Second, the rational basis test applies to Congress's judgment that regulating intrastate non-economic activity is essential to its broader regulatory scheme. Thus, where Congress comprehensively regulates interstate economic activity, it may regulate non-economic intrastate activity if it rationally believes that, in the aggregate, the failure to do so would undermine the effectiveness of the overlying regulatory scheme.[9]

We have applied this doctrine to uphold laws prohibiting intrastate possession of child pornography and intrastate transfer of firearms that are part of broader economic regulatory schemes. See, e.g., *Bowers* ("*Raich* indicates that Congress has the ability to regulate wholly intrastate manufacture and possession of child pornography, regardless of whether it was made or possessed for commercial purposes, that it rationally believes, if left unregulated in the aggregate, could work to undermine Congress's ability to regulate the larger interstate commercial activity."); United States v. Rose (6th Cir. 2008) ("Congress had a rational basis for concluding that the intrastate transfer of firearms would undercut its regulation of the interstate firearms market. . . . "). . . . Similarly, Congress had a rational basis to conclude that failing to regulate those who self-insure would undermine its regulation of the interstate markets in health care delivery and health insurance.

As plaintiffs concede, Congress has the power under the Commerce Clause to regulate the interstate markets in health care delivery and health insurance. It has long been settled that "Congress plainly has power to regulate the price of [products] distributed through the medium of interstate commerce . . . [and] it possesses every power needed to make that regulation effective." United States v. Wrightwood Dairy Co. (1942); see United States v. South-Eastern Underwriters Ass'n (1944). In doing so, Congress may decide "to give protection to sellers or purchasers or both." Currin v. Wallace, 306 U.S. 1, 11 (1939). The Act uses this power to regulate prices and protect purchasers by banning certain practices in the insurance industry that have prevented

9. The Supreme Court has applied this larger regulatory scheme doctrine only in *Raich*, which addressed an as-applied challenge, while this case involves a facial challenge. However, because the larger regulatory scheme doctrine was articulated in *Lopez*, which addressed a facial challenge, it applies to facial challenges as well.

individuals from obtaining and maintaining insurance coverage. Under the process of "medical underwriting," insurance companies review each applicant's medical history and health status to determine eligibility and premium levels. As a result of this practice, approximately thirty-six percent of applicants in the market for individual health insurance are denied coverage, charged a substantially higher premium, or offered only limited coverage that excludes pre-existing conditions. Department of Health and Human Services, Coverage Denied: How the Current Health Insurance System Leaves Millions Behind, at 1 (2009). The Act bans this practice through a guaranteed issue requirement, which bars insurance companies from denying coverage to individuals with pre-existing conditions; and a community rating requirement, which prohibits insurance companies from charging higher rates to individuals based on their medical history. No one denies that Congress properly enacted these reforms as part of its power to regulate the interstate markets in health care delivery and health insurance.

Furthermore, Congress had a rational basis for concluding that leaving those individuals who self-insure for the cost of health care outside federal control would undercut its overlying economic regulatory scheme. Congress found that without the minimum coverage provision, the guaranteed issue and community rating provisions would increase existing incentives for individuals to delay purchasing health insurance until they need care. The legislative record demonstrated that the seven states that had enacted guaranteed issue reforms without minimum coverage provisions suffered detrimental effects to their insurance markets, such as escalating costs and insurance companies exiting the market. In contrast, Congress found that "[i]n Massachusetts, a [minimum coverage] requirement has strengthened private employer-based coverage: despite the economic downturn, the number of workers offered employer-based coverage has actually increased." It was reasonable for Congress to conclude that failing to regulate those who self-insure would "leave a gaping hole" in the Act. *Cf. Raich* (holding that Congress had a rational basis to conclude that failing to regulate intrastate manufacture and possession of marijuana would "leave a gaping hole" in the Controlled Substances Act). Congress rationally found that the minimum coverage provision "is essential to creating effective health insurance markets in which improved health insurance products that are guaranteed issue and do not exclude coverage of pre-existing conditions can be sold." Congress had a rational basis for concluding that the minimum coverage requirement is essential to its broader reforms to the national markets in health care delivery and health insurance. Therefore, the minimum coverage provision is a valid exercise of the Commerce Clause power.

C. Whether the Minimum Coverage Provision Impermissibly Regulates Inactivity

Thomas More argues that the minimum coverage provision exceeds Congress's power under the Commerce Clause because it regulates inactivity. However, the text of the Commerce Clause does not acknowledge a constitutional distinction between activity and inactivity, and neither does the Supreme Court. Furthermore, far from regulating inactivity, the provision regulates active participation in the health care market.

As long as Congress does not exceed the established limits of its Commerce Power, there is no constitutional impediment to enacting legislation that could be characterized as regulating inactivity. The Supreme Court has never directly addressed whether Congress may use its Commerce Clause power to regulate inactivity, and it has not defined activity or inactivity in this context. However, it has eschewed defining the scope of the Commerce Power by reference to flexible labels, and it consistently stresses that Congress's authority to legislate under this grant of power is informed by "broad principles of economic practicality." *Lopez* (Kennedy, J., concurring); see Wickard (explaining that Congress's power cannot be determined "by reference to any formula which would give controlling force to nomenclature such as 'production' and 'indirect' and foreclose consideration of the actual effects of the activity in question upon interstate commerce").

Similarly, this Court has also refused to focus on imprecise labels when determining whether a statute falls within Congress's Commerce Power. For example, we rejected the argument that the Child Support Recovery Act is unconstitutional because it regulates an individual's failure to place an item in commerce. Instead, we held that Congress had a rational basis for concluding that a non-custodial spouse's failure to send court-ordered child support payments across state lines substantially affects interstate commerce. *Faasse.* Focusing on the broader economic landscape of the legislation revealed the unworkability of relying on inexact labels because there was "no principled distinction between the parent who fails to send any child support through commerce and the parent who sends only a fraction of the amount owed." *Faasse.* Here, too, the constitutionality of the minimum coverage provision cannot be resolved with a myopic focus on a malleable label. Congress had a rational basis for concluding that the practice of self-insuring for the cost of health care has a substantial effect on interstate commerce, and that the minimum coverage provision is an essential part of a broader economic regulatory scheme. Thus, the provision is constitutional notwithstanding the fact that it could be labeled as regulating inactivity.

Furthermore, far from regulating inactivity, the minimum coverage provision regulates individuals who are, in the aggregate, active in the health care market. The Supreme Court has stated that "when it is necessary in order to prevent an evil to make the law embrace more than the precise thing to be prevented [Congress] may do so." Westfall v. United States (1927). The vast majority of individuals are active in the market for health care delivery because of two unique characteristics of this market: (1) virtually everyone requires health care services at some unpredictable point; and (2) individuals receive health care services regardless of ability to pay.

Virtually everyone will need health care services at some point, including, in the aggregate, those without health insurance. Even dramatic attempts to protect one's health and minimize the need for health care will not always be successful, and the health care market is characterized by unpredictable and unavoidable needs for care. The ubiquity and unpredictability of the need for medical care is born out by the statistics. More than eighty percent of adults nationwide visited a doctor or other health care professional one or more times in 2009. Centers for Disease Control and Prevention National Center for Health Statistics, Summary Health Statistics for U.S. Adults: National Health Interview Survey, 2009, table 35 (2010). Additionally, individuals receive health care services regardless of whether they can afford the treatment. The obligation to provide treatment regardless of ability to pay is imposed by the Emergency Medical Treatment and Active Labor Act, state laws, and many institutions' charitable missions. The unavoidable need for health care coupled with the obligation to provide treatment make it virtually certain that all individuals will require and receive health care at some point. Thus, although there is no firm, constitutional bar that prohibits Congress from placing regulations on what could be described as inactivity, even if there were it would not impact this case due to the unique aspects of health care that make all individuals active in this market. . . .

D. Conclusion

Congress had a rational basis for concluding that, in the aggregate, the practice of self-insuring for the cost of health care substantially affects interstate commerce. Furthermore, Congress had a rational basis for concluding that the minimum coverage provision is essential to the Affordable Care Act's larger reforms to the national markets in health care delivery and health insurance. Finally, the provision regulates active participation in the health care market, and in any case, the Constitution imposes no categorical bar on regulating inactivity. Thus, the minimum coverage provision is a valid exercise of Congress's authority under the Commerce Clause, and the decision of the district court is AFFIRMED.

SUTTON, Circuit Judge [concurring]. The National Government is "one of enumerated" and limited "powers," a feature of the United States Constitution "universally admitted" in 1819, McCulloch v. Maryland, 17 U.S. (4 Wheat.) 316, 405, and still largely accepted today. "But the question respecting the extent of the powers actually granted, is perpetually arising, and will probably continue to arise, as long as our system shall exist." *Id.* . . .

[The Supreme Court] has never considered the validity of this type of mandate before, at least under the commerce power. True enough, Heart of Atlanta Motel, Inc. v. United States (1964), sustained Congress's power to compel affirmative acts — to require the owner of any "inn, hotel, motel or other establishment which provides lodging to transient guests" to offer lodging to all on non-discriminatory grounds. But the Civil Rights Act of 1964 applies only to service providers *already in* the relevant interstate market. If covered entities offer lodging in interstate commerce, Congress tells them how to do so and requires action in the process. Congress did not try to solve this policy problem by compelling individuals to open inns in the first instance.

The same is true of the *Wickard* and *Raich* plaintiffs. The laws regulated individuals who chose to grow wheat and marijuana on their own—by punishing individuals who grew too much of one product (wheat) and any of the other (marijuana). In *Wickard* and *Raich*, it is true, the Court permitted Congress to regulate individuals who did not offer to buy or sell anything, who merely raised their crops and plants at home, who consumed them at home and who in one instance (*Raich*) were prohibited from buying and selling the product in any market. Yet that reality confirms only the breadth of the substantial-effects doctrine. It does not show that Congress may compel individuals to buy products they do not want.

Not only has the Court never crossed this line, neither has Congress, as the reports of two federal agencies confirm:

> (1) "The government has never required people to buy any good or service as a condition of lawful residence in the United States." CBO Memorandum, *The Budgetary Treatment of an Individual Mandate to Buy Health Insurance*, at 1 (Aug. 1994);
>
> (2) "[W]hether the individual responsibility requirement would be constitutional under the [Commerce Clause] is a challenging question, as it is a novel issue whether Congress may use the clause to require an individual to purchase a good or a service." Congressional Research Service, *Requiring Individuals to Obtain Health Insurance: A Constitutional Analysis*, at 8-9 (Oct. 15, 2010).

The efforts of the government and its *amici* to counter this point serve only to confirm it. That Congress may conscript individuals to serve in the military, or to pay taxes, proves only that Congress may require individuals to undertake tasks under other enumerated powers, not under the commerce power. That the Second Congress not only required certain individuals to serve in the military but to arm themselves as well (by purchasing a gun and ammunition), Second Militia Act of 1792, comes to the same end: It amounts to a necessary, proper and utterly sensible means of implementing Congress's authority to raise an army. To argue that Congress's power to enlist individuals to defend the country's borders proves that it may enlist individuals to improve the availability of medical care gives analogy a bad name. There is a difference between drafting a citizen to join the military and forcing him to respond to a price quote from Aetna. . . .

Legislative novelty typically is not a constitutional virtue. More than once, and quite often in separation-of-powers cases, the Court has said that a "[l]ack of historical precedent can indicate a constitutional infirmity" in a congressional act. Va. Office for Prot. & Advocacy v. Stewart (2011); see also Free Enter. Fund v. Pub. Co. Accounting Oversight Bd. (2010) ("Perhaps the most telling indication of the severe constitutional problem with the PCAOB is the lack of historical precedent for this entity."); Printz v. United States (1997) ("[I]f . . . earlier Congresses avoided use of this highly attractive power, we would have reason to believe that the power was thought not to exist.").

The plaintiffs . . . present (1) a theory of constitutional invalidity that the Court has never considered before, (2) a legislative line that Congress has never crossed before, and (3) a theory of commerce power that has the potential to succeed where others have failed: by placing a categorical cap on congressional power. Why not accept the invitation?

The first point proves only that the Supreme Court has considerable discretion in resolving this dispute. It does not free lower court judges from the duty to respect the language and direction of the Court's precedents, particularly in view of the reality that this law has the purpose and effect of regulating commerce and in view of the save-before-destroy imperatives of reviewing facial challenges. The Supreme Court can decide that the legend of *Wickard* has outstripped the facts of *Wickard* — that a farmer's production only of *more than* 200 bushels of wheat a year substantially affected interstate commerce. A court of appeals cannot. The Supreme Court can decide that *Raich* was a case only about the fungibility of marijuana, not a decision that makes broader and more extravagant assertions of legislative power more impervious to challenge. A court of appeals cannot. . . .

[There is a] lingering intuition — shared by most Americans, I suspect — that Congress should not be able to compel citizens to buy products they do not want. If Congress can require Americans to buy medical insurance today, what of tomorrow? Could it compel individuals to buy health care itself in the form of an annual check-up or for that matter a health-club membership? Could it require computer companies to sell medical-insurance policies in the open market in order to widen the asset pool available to pay insurance claims? And if Congress can do this in the healthcare field, what of other fields of commerce and other products?

These are good questions, but there are some answers. In most respects, a mandate to purchase health insurance does not parallel these other settings or markets. Regulating how citizens pay for what they already receive (health care), never quite know when they will need, and in the case of severe illnesses or emergencies generally will not be able to afford, has few (if any) parallels in modern life. Not every intrusive law is an unconstitutionally intrusive law. And even the most powerful intuition about the meaning of the Constitution must be matched with a textual and enforceable theory of constitutional limits, and the activity/inactivity dichotomy does not work with respect to health insurance in many settings, if any of them.

The very force of the intuition also helps to undo it, as one is left to wonder why the Commerce Clause does the work of establishing this limitation. Few doubt that Congress could pass an equally coercive law under its taxing power by imposing a healthcare tax on everyone and freeing them from the tax if they purchased health insurance. If Congress may engage in the same type of compelling/conscripting/commandeering of individuals to buy products under the taxing power, is it not strange that only the broadest of congressional powers carves out a limit on this same type of regulation?

Why construe the Constitution, moreover, to place this limitation — that citizens cannot be forced to buy insurance, vegetables, cars and so on — solely in a grant of power to Congress, as opposed to due process limitations on power with respect to all American legislative bodies? Few doubt that the States may require individuals to buy medical insurance, and indeed at least two of them have. See Mass. Gen. Laws 111M §2; N.J. Stat. Ann. §26:15-2. The same goes for a related and familiar mandate of the States—that most adults must purchase car insurance. Yet no court has invalidated these kinds of mandates under the Due Process Clause or any other liberty-based guarantee of the Constitution. That means one of two things: either compelled purchases of medical insurance *are* different from compelled purchases of other goods and services, or the States, even under plaintiffs' theory of the case, may compel purchases of insurance, vegetables, cars and so on. Sometimes an intuition is just an intuition.

For now, whatever else may be said about plaintiffs' activity/inactivity theory of commerce power, they have not shown that the individual mandate exceeds that power in all of its applications. Congress may apply the mandate in at least four settings: (1) to individuals who already have purchased insurance voluntarily and who want to maintain coverage, but who will be required to obtain more insurance in order to comply with the minimum-essential-coverage requirement; (2) to individuals who voluntarily obtained coverage but do not wish to be forced (at some indeterminate point in the future) to maintain it; (3) to individuals who live in States that already require them to obtain insurance and who may have to obtain more coverage to comply with the mandate or abide by other requirements of the Affordable Care Act; and (4) to individuals under 30, no matter where they live and no matter whether they have purchased health care before, who may satisfy the law by obtaining only catastrophic-care coverage. The valid application of the law to these groups of people suffices to uphold the law against this facial challenge.

While future challenges to the law have hills to climb, nothing about this view of the case precludes individuals from bringing as-applied challenges to the mandate as the relevant agencies implement it, and as the "lessons taught by the particular," [Sabri v. United States (2004)], prove (or disprove) that Congress crossed a constitutional line in imposing this unprecedented requirement. Just as courts should refrain from needlessly pre-judging the *invalidity* of a law's many applications, they should refrain from doing the same with respect to their *validity*.

Any remaining doubt about rejecting this facial challenge is alleviated by the most enduring lesson of *McCulloch*, which remains an historical, not a doctrinal, one. No debate in the forty years after the country's birth stirred the people more than the conflict between the federalists and anti-federalists over the role of the National Government in relation to the States. And no issue was more bound up in that debate than the wisdom of creating a national bank. In upholding the constitutionality of a second national bank, not a foregone conclusion, the Supreme Court erred on the side of allowing the political branches to resolve the conflict. Right or wrong, that decision presented the challengers with a short-term loss (by upholding the bank) and set the platform for a potential long-term victory (by allowing them to argue that Congress should not make the same mistake again). There was no third national bank. *But see* Federal Reserve Act, ch. 6, 38 Stat. 251 (1913).

Today's debate about the individual mandate is just as stirring, no less essential to the appropriate role of the National Government and no less capable of political resolution. Time assuredly will bring to light the policy strengths and weaknesses of using the individual mandate as part of this national legislation, allowing the peoples' political representatives, rather than their judges, to have the primary say over its utility.

GRAHAM, Senior District Judge [dissenting]. . . . This case presents the issue whether Congress acted within its powers under the Commerce Clause when it passed legislation requiring nearly all citizens to maintain health insurance coverage beginning in 2014. Individuals who fail to satisfy the "individual responsibility requirement" must pay a monetary penalty.

I

The mandate is a novel exercise of Commerce Clause power. No prior exercise of that power has required individuals to purchase a good or service. This fact alone does not answer the constitutional question, but it does highlight the need for judicial scrutiny. Federal courts have the duty to construe and enforce the "outer limits" of congressional power. *Lopez* (finding the Gun-Free School Zones Act unconstitutional).

The Commerce Clause authorizes Congress "[t]o regulate Commerce . . . among the several States." U.S. Const., Art. I, §8, cl. 3. The Supreme Court has interpreted the power as reaching three areas: (1) the channels of interstate commerce, (2) the instrumentalities of interstate commerce, and (3) "activities that substantially affect interstate commerce." *Lopez.*

Because the mandate regulates decisions not to purchase health insurance–conduct falling outside the ordinary sense of the word "commerce" (the trade or exchange of a good, see Gibbons v. Ogden (1824))–Congress expressly invoked the third category of Commerce Clause power as its authority for enacting the mandate. See ACA §1501(a)(1). And in various suits across the nation challenging the constitutionality of the mandate, the government has consistently defended the mandate under Congress's power to regulate activities that substantially affect interstate commerce.

II

In evaluating the mandate's validity, one must identify what market or conduct it regulates. Plaintiffs argue that the health insurance market is the immediate subject of the mandate, while the government contends that the mandate represents but one component of the ACA's broader regulation of the market for health care services.

The challenged statute is a requirement to obtain health insurance. The text of §1501 reflects Congress's view that it was regulating the insurance market when it enacted the statute. In the legislative findings, Congress found that the insurance requirement is what "substantially affects interstate commerce," ACA §1501(a)(1), and it specifically noted that "*insurance* is interstate commerce subject to Federal regulation." §1501(a)(3) (emphasis added) (citing United States v. South-Eastern Underwriters Ass'n (1944)). The findings further state that the federal government "has a significant role in regulating health insurance," §1501(a)(2)(F), and the mandate will serve to "broaden the health insurance risk pool to include healthy individuals, which will lower health insurance premiums." §1501(a)(2)(G). Moreover, the findings provide that "[t]he requirement is essential to creating effective health insurance markets that do not require underwriting and eliminate its associated administrative costs." §1501(a)(2)(H).

The government now attempts to recast the exercise of power as regulating the market for health care services. The ACA's numerous provisions seek to widen access to health care services and improve the quality of those services. The mandate itself rests among provisions aimed at reforming the health insurance market. Other parts of the Act make changes to public programs like Medicaid, and enact reforms intended to improve the quality and efficiency of health care, strengthen the health care workforce, and encourage innovative medical therapies. The government argues that the mandate is best viewed as regulating one aspect–financing–of the overall health care market.

The government's argument for viewing the mandate as regulating health care in general suffers from many flaws. First, it gives "Congress a perverse incentive to legislate broadly pursuant to the Commerce Clause–nestling questionable assertions of its authority into comprehensive regulatory schemes–rather than with precision." Gonzales v. Raich (2005) (O'Connor, J., dissenting). Within the ACA as a whole, the mandate represents a separate exercise of congressional power. To say that the mandate simply concerns the financing end of health care proves the point–it is insurance that the mandate requires of all citizens.

Second, the government's argument ignores what Congress itself said about the mandate. Congress found that the insurance requirement in particular is what substantially affects interstate commerce, and it referenced a Supreme Court ruling that the insurance industry is subject to Congress's Commerce Clause powers. As noted above, other findings in §1501 demonstrate that Congress had its sights on the health insurance market. When Congress has spoken so clearly on the basis for its attempted exercise of power, the exercise should be judged on those terms, even if its ultimate conclusion need not be accepted at face value. See Hodel v. Virginia Surface Mining & Reclamation Ass'n, Inc. (1981) (Rehnquist, J., concurring in judgment) ("Moreover, simply because Congress may conclude that a particular activity substantially affects interstate commerce does not necessarily make it so.").

Third, the government's argument turns the mandate into something it is not. The requirement that all citizens obtain health insurance does not depend on them receiving health care services in the first place. Individuals must carry insurance each and every month regardless of whether they have actually entered the market for health services. Simply put, the mandate does not regulate the commercial activity of obtaining health care. It regulates the status of being uninsured.

III

Congress's legislative finding that the "individual responsibility requirement... substantially affects interstate commerce" turns the analysis on its head. ACA §1501(a)(1). Without question, forcing all individuals to purchase a product that not everyone would otherwise purchase will have an effect on commerce. But Congress cannot be tolerated to justify its exercise of power by creating its own substantial effects. In determining whether the substantial effects test is satisfied, the focus must be on the existing economic activity Congress seeks to regulate, not on the impact the regulation would have. See Wickard v. Filburn (1942) (examining whether "appellee's activity," together with the activities of those similarly situated, "exerts a substantial economic effect on interstate commerce"); *Lopez*, 514 U.S. at 558-59 (holding that Congress may regulate an activity that substantially affects interstate commerce).

The inquiry then is whether plaintiffs' "activity," as it were, substantially affects interstate commerce. Much has been made in this litigation of the distinction between activity and inactivity. The Supreme Court has often employed the word "activity" to describe the regulatory subjects of Congress's power over interstate commerce. See *Wickard*; *Lopez*; *Morrison*; *Raich*. Yet I do not interpret those cases as drawing a constitutional line between activity and inactivity. That distinction would suffer from the same failings as the "direct" and "indirect" effects test of prior Commerce Clause jurisprudence. See NLRB v. Jones & Laughlin Steel Corp. (1937) (rejecting the direct/indirect distinction and stating that the question of Congress's authority is "necessarily one of degree"); *Lopez* (Kennedy, J., concurring) (noting that questions of constitutional law are often "not susceptible to the mechanical application of bright and clear lines"). Imposing an activity/inactivity line could hinder Congress in future cases from removing burdens on commerce that certain classes of individuals have passively enabled. See United States v. Faasse (6th Cir. 2001) (upholding the constitutionality of the Child Support Recovery Act and rejecting the argument that the willful failure to make a court-ordered, out-of-state child support payment from California to Michigan was insufficient for Commerce Clause purposes).

The inquiry should start by considering the "economic nature of the regulated activity." *Morrison*; see also *Lopez* (finding that possession of a gun in a school zone was not an economic activity); *Raich* (finding that growing and consuming a crop was "quintessentially economic"). Congress here attempts to regulate a class of individuals who have refrained from purchasing health insurance. The conduct being regulated is the decision not to enter the market for insurance. Plaintiffs have not bought or sold a good or service, nor have they manufactured, distributed, or consumed a commodity. See *Raich* (defining "economics" as the "production, distribution, and consumption of commodities"). Rather, they are strangers to the health insurance market. This readily differentiates the present case from others cited by the government. See *Wickard* (Filburn cultivated wheat); *Raich* (Raich cultivated marijuana); Heart of Atlanta Motel, Inc. v. United States (1964) (appellant operated a motel). Certainly there is an interstate market for health insurance, but, unlike the plaintiffs in *Wickard* and *Raich*, plaintiffs here have not entered the market. In no other instance has Congress before attempted to force a non-participant into a market.

The government contends that virtually every American has or will participate in the market for health care services. The timing of the need for health care can be unpredictable and the costs substantial. By not purchasing insurance, individuals like the plaintiffs have made a decision to accept risk. In the government's view, plaintiffs' financial planning choices and position on risk are quintessentially economic in nature because they inevitably lead to cost-shifting when the uninsured obtain care they cannot afford. The mandate concerns a failure to pay for services obtained, argues the government, not a failure to engage in economic activity.

This argument deftly switches the focus from the private, non-commercial nature of plaintiffs' conduct (the decision to be uninsured) to the perceived economic effects of their absence from the insurance market. Certainly, plaintiffs' conduct may be considered in the aggregate with the conduct of similarly-situated individuals, *see Raich*; however, the Commerce Clause cannot be satisfied when economic activity is lacking in the first instance.[10] "Where economic activity substantially affects interstate commerce, legislation regulating that activity will be sustained." *Lopez*, 514 U.S. at 560; see also *Morrison*, 529 U.S. at 611 ("[I]n those cases where we have sustained federal regulation of intrastate activity based upon the activity's substantial effects on interstate commerce, the activity in question has been some sort of economic endeavor."); *Raich*, 545 U.S. at 17 (Congress may regulate "purely local activities that are part of an economic 'class of activities' that have a substantial effect on interstate commerce").

It is true that decisions not to purchase insurance are in some sense economic ones. They are choices about risk and finances. When viewed in the aggregate, these decisions have economic consequences. Congress, for instance, has found that:

> The cost of providing uncompensated care to the uninsured was $43,000,000,000 in 2008. To pay for this cost, health care providers pass on the cost to private insurers,

10. Justice Scalia has stated that under the Necessary and Proper Clause, "Congress may regulate even noneconomic local activity if that regulation is a necessary part of a more general regulation of interstate commerce." *Raich* (Scalia, J., concurring). I do not believe that this view of the Necessary and Proper Clause would save the mandate. As Judge Vinson correctly explained, an attempted exercise of power–the mandate–cannot be justified because it is "necessary" to cure the economic disruption caused another part of the legislation–the "guaranteed issue" provision, ACA §1001. See Florida v. United States Dep't of Health and Human Services (N.D. Fla. Jan. 31, 2011).

> which pass on the cost to families. This cost-shifting increases family premiums by on average over $1,000 a year. By significantly reducing the number of the uninsured, the requirement, together with the other provisions of this Act, will lower health insurance premiums.

42 U.S.C. §18091(F). In an *amicus* brief, certain economic scholars point to other costshifting effects caused by decisions to be uninsured. The first relates to adverse selection, or the positive correlation between demand for insurance and the risk of loss. When healthy individuals opt not to buy insurance, the pool of insured persons is smaller and less healthy as a whole, thus raising premiums. Second, when previously uninsured individuals do obtain insurance, they tend to do so when they have a significant medical need and thereby consume more and costlier services.

Lopez and *Morrison* rejected a view of causation whereby the cost-shifting to society caused by violent conduct can satisfy the substantial effects test. *See Lopez* (rejecting the government's "costs of crime" and loss of "national productivity" reasoning); *Morrison* (same). The government fails to show why a view of cost-shifting caused by risky conduct should fare any better. The problem with the government's line of reasoning here is that it has no logical end point, and it illustrates precisely Justice Thomas's concerns with the substantial effects test. See *Morrison* (Thomas, J., concurring) (calling the test "rootless and malleable"). That test, when paired with the aggregation principle, invites manipulation and "draw[ing] the circle broadly enough to cover an activity that, when taken in isolation, would not have substantial effects on commerce." *Lopez* (Thomas, J., concurring).

The government insists that a decision not to buy insurance is more clearly financial in nature than the acts of crime at issue in *Lopez* and *Morrison.* But the statutes struck down in *Lopez* and *Morrison* at least waited to impose their criminal penalties until the commission of the acts that allegedly caused the cost-shifting. Here, several layers of inferences must materialize for the government's cost-shifting reasoning to work, but the mandate waits for none of them. *See Lopez* (rejecting as too attenuated a substantial effects theory that "pile[s] inference upon inference"). The mandate and its penalty are not conditioned on the failure to pay for health care services, or, for that matter, conditioned on the consumption of health care. Congress instead chose a more coercive and intrusive regulation. The proper object of Congress's power is interstate commerce, not private decisions to refrain from commerce.

The ACA represents Congress's attempt to solve national problems in the health insurance market. That problems are felt nationwide does not mean that Congress can try to solve them in any fashion it pleases. Congress must choose from the limited powers granted to it by the Constitution, and federal courts have a duty to uphold the Constitution when Congress has exceeded its authority. Marbury v. Madison (1803) ("This is of the very essence of judicial duty."). *Lopez* and *Morrison* firmly establish that the Commerce Clause power is "not without effective bounds." *Morrison* (citing *Lopez*); see also *Lopez* (Kennedy, J., concurring) ("[T]he Court as an institution and the legal system as a whole have an immense stake in the stability of our Commerce Clause jurisprudence as it has evolved to this point.").

The "hard work for courts" is identifying "objective markers for confining the analysis in Commerce Clause cases." *Raich* (O'Connor, J., dissenting). When dealing with the outer limits of Congress's powers, "first principles" must be heeded. See *Lopez*. The federal government is one of enumerated powers. Congress's authority must have limits, lest the Tenth Amendment's reservation of powers to the States and the people be without meaning. Principles of federalism thus should guide a court's examination of novel exercises of Commerce Clause power. See *id.* (Kennedy, J., concurring) ("[W]e must inquire whether the exercise of national power seeks to intrude upon an area of traditional state concern."); *Raich* (O'Connor, J., dissenting) (noting that "fundamental structural concerns about dual sovereignty animate our Commerce Clause cases").

Here, Congress's exercise of power intrudes on both the States and the people. It brings an end to state experimentation and overrides the expressed legislative will of several states that have guaranteed to their citizens the freedom to choose not to purchase health insurance. See Idaho Code Ann. §39-9003; Utah Code Ann. §63M-1-2505.5; Va. Code Ann. §38.2-3430.1:1. The mandate forces law-abiding individuals to purchase a product—an expensive product, no less–and thereby invades the realm of an individual's financial planning decisions. Cf. Maryland v. Wirtz (1968) ("Neither here nor in *Wickard* had the Court declared that Congress may use a relatively trivial impact on commerce as an excuse for broad general regulation of state or private activities."). In the absence of the mandate, individuals have the right to decide how to finance medical expenses. The mandate extinguishes that right.

Congress may of course provide incentives (in the Tax and Bankruptcy Codes, for instance) to steer behavior, and it may impose certain requirements or prohibitions once an individual decides to engage in a commercial activity. See, e.g., *Wickard* (Congress had power to impose a harvesting limit on farmer who grew wheat); *Heart of Atlanta Motel* (Congress had power to impose anti-discrimination requirement on individual who operated a motel). It is a different matter entirely to force an individual to engage in commercial activity that he would not otherwise undertake of his own volition.

The government recites the common refrain that the health insurance market is unique and attributes this to some blend of free-riding, adverse selection, universal participation, and unpredictability as to when and how much care might be needed. This should comfort the court, the government says, because Congress will not need to resort to such measures as the mandate again, or at least not very often.

This assurance is troubling on many levels and should hardly be heard to come from a body with limited powers. The uniqueness that justifies one exercise of power becomes precedent for the next contemplated exercise. And permitting the mandate would clear the path for Congress to cause or contribute to certain "unique" factors, such as free-riding and adverse selection,[11] and then impose a solution that is ill-fitted to the others.[12]

To the fatalistic view that Congress will always prevail and courts should step back and let the people, if offended, speak through their political representatives, I say that "courts were designed to be an intermediate body between the people and the legislature, in order, among other things, to keep the latter within the limits assigned to their authority." *The Federalist* No. 78 (A. Hamilton). In this arena, the "public force" is entrusted to the courts. Oliver Wendell Holmes, *The Path of the Law*, 10 Harv. L. Rev. 457, 457 (1897). "[W]here the will of the legislature, declared in its statutes, stands in opposition to that of the people, declared in the Constitution, the judges ought to be governed by the latter rather than the former." *The Federalist* No. 78.

This is the "hard work" Justice O'Connor referred to in her dissent in *Raich*. It is hard work in part because it can place a federal court in the position of choosing between powerful competing political ideologies with the risk that the court's judgment may be branded as "political." We must not lose sight of the fact however that the Constitution we interpret and apply itself embodies a resolution of powerful competing political ideologies, including the extent of the power of the federal government–a resolution that the States and the people accepted in the ratification process. See *The Federalist* No. 45 (J. Madison) ("The powers delegated by the proposed Constitution to the federal government are few and defined. Those which are to remain in the State governments are numerous and indefinite.").

In *Lopez* the Supreme Court recognized that the direction of its existing Commerce Clause jurisprudence threatened the principle of a federal government of defined and limited powers, and it began the process of developing a new jurisprudence more compatible with the Constitution. That process was interrupted by *Raich*, where a majority of the Court was unwilling to expressly overrule a landmark Commere Clause case in *Wickard*, which had been the law of the land for over sixty years.

Notwithstanding *Raich*, I believe the Court remains committed to the path laid down by Chief Justice Rehnquist and Justices O'Connor, Scalia, Kennedy, and Thomas to establish a framework of meaningful limitations on congressional power under the Commerce Clause. The current case is an opportunity to prove it so.

If the exercise of power is allowed and the mandate upheld, it is difficult to see what the limits on Congress's Commerce Clause authority would be. What

11. The free-riding problem is substantially one of Congress's own creation, *see* Emergency Medical Treatment and Active Labor Act (requiring hospitals with emergency departments to provide the care necessary to stabilize patients with emergency medical conditions, without regard to a patient's ability to pay for the care received), and the adverse selection problem will be exacerbated by the guaranteed issue provision, in that supply will be guaranteed to high-risk individuals. Though these policies might be reasonable, Congress's compassion does not allow it to exceed the limits of its constitutional powers.

12. Again, the mandate does not wait until an individual participates in the market for health care.

aspect of human activity would escape federal power? The ultimate issue in this case is this: Does the notion of federalism still have vitality? To approve the exercise of power would arm Congress with the authority to force individuals to do whatever it sees fit (within boundaries like the First Amendment and Due Process Clause), as long as the regulation concerns an activity or decision that, when aggregated, can be said to have some loose, but-for type of economic connection, which nearly all human activity does. *See Lopez*, ("[D]epending on the level of generality, any activity can be looked upon as commercial."). Such a power feels very much like the general police power that the Tenth Amendment reserves to the States and the people. A structural shift of that magnitude can be accomplished legitimately only through constitutional amendment.

Study Guide: *Does this decision tell us anything at all about the viability of the sorts of Commerce Clause challenges that were seen in* Lopez, Morrison, Raich, *and the pending challenges to the Affordable Care Act? When combined with his concurring opinion in Comstock, does the following opinion by Justice Kennedy—who concurred in* Lopez *and joining the majority in* Raich*—tell us anything new about his thinking with respect to enumerated powers? Does the fact this decision was unanimous—and that even the government supported its result—add to or detract from its significance?*

BOND V. UNITED STATES

564 U.S. _____ (2011)

Justice Kennedy delivered the opinion of the Court.

This case presents the question whether a person indicted for violating a federal statute has standing to challenge its validity on grounds that, by enacting it, Congress exceeded its powers under the Constitution, thus intruding upon the sovereignty and authority of the States.

The indicted defendant, petitioner here, sought to argue the invalidity of the statute. She relied on the Tenth Amendment, and, by extension, on the premise that Congress exceeded its powers by enacting it in contravention of basic federalism principles. The statute was enacted to comply with a treaty; but petitioner contends that, at least in the present instance, the treaty cannot be the source of congressional power to regulate or prohibit her conduct.

The Court of Appeals held that because a State was not a party to the federal criminal proceeding, petitioner had no standing to challenge the statute as an infringement upon the powers reserved to the States. Having concluded that petitioner does have standing to challenge the federal statute on these grounds, this Court now reverses that determination. The merits of petitioner's challenge to the statute's validity are to be considered, in the first instance, by the Court of Appeals on remand and are not addressed in this opinion

I

This case arises from a bitter personal dispute, leading to the criminal acts charged here. Petitioner Carol Anne Bond lived outside Philadelphia, Pennsylvania. After discovering that her close friend was pregnant and that the father was Bond's husband, Bond sought revenge. Bond subjected the woman to a campaign of harassing telephone calls and letters, acts that resulted in a criminal conviction on a minor state charge. Bond persisted in her hostile acts, placing caustic substances on objects the woman was likely to touch, including her mailbox, car door handle, and front doorknob. Bond's victim suffered a minor burn on her hand and contacted federal investigators, who identified Bond as the perpetrator.

Bond was indicted . . . for, among other offenses, two counts of violating §229. Section 229 forbids knowing possession or use of any chemical that "can cause death, temporary incapacitation or permanent harm to humans or animals" where not intended for a "peaceful purpose." The statute was enacted as part of the Chemical Weapons Convention Implementation Act of 1998. The Act implements provisions of the Convention on the Prohibition of the Development, Production, Stockpiling and Use of Chemical Weapons and on their Destruction, a treaty the United States ratified in 1997.

In the District Court, Bond moved to dismiss the §229 charges, contending the statute was beyond Congress' constitutional authority to enact. The District Court denied the motion. Bond entered a conditional plea of guilty, reserving the right to appeal the ruling on the validity of the statute. She was sentenced to six years in prison.

In the Court of Appeals for the Third Circuit, Bond renewed her challenge to the statute, citing, among other authorities, the Tenth Amendment to the Constitution. The Court of Appeals asked for supplemental briefs on the question whether Bond had standing to raise the Tenth Amendment as a ground for invalidating a federal statute in the absence of a State's participation in the proceedings.

In its supplemental brief in the Court of Appeals, the Government took the position that Bond did not have standing. The Court of Appeals agreed.

When Bond sought certiorari, the Government advised this Court that it had changed its position and that, in its view, Bond does have standing to challenge the constitutionality of §229 on Tenth Amendment grounds. The Court granted certiorari and appointed an *amicus curiae* to defend the judgment of the Court of Appeals. Stephen McAllister, a member of the bar of this Court, filed an *amicus* brief and presented an oral argument that have been of considerable assistance to the Court. . . .

III

. . . In *amicus*' view, to argue that the National Government has interfered with state sovereignty in violation of the Tenth Amendment is to assert the legal rights and interests of States and States alone. That, however, is not so. As explained below, Bond seeks to vindicate her own constitutional interests. The individual, in a proper case, can assert injury from governmental action taken in excess of the authority that federalism defines. Her rights in this regard do not belong to a State.

A

The federal system rests on what might at first seem a counterintuitive insight, that "freedom is enhanced by the creation of two governments, not one." Alden v. Maine (1999). The Framers concluded that allocation of powers between the National Government and the States enhances freedom, first by protecting the integrity of the governments themselves, and second by protecting the people, from whom all governmental powers are derived.

Federalism has more than one dynamic. It is true that the federal structure serves to grant and delimit the prerogatives and responsibilities of the States and the National Government vis-à-vis one another. The allocation of powers in our federal system preserves the integrity, dignity, and residual sovereignty of the States. The federal balance is, in part, an end in itself, to ensure that States function as political entities in their own right.

But that is not its exclusive sphere of operation. Federalism is more than an exercise in setting the boundary between different institutions of government for their own integrity. "State sovereignty is not just an end in itself: 'Rather, federalism secures to citizens the liberties that derive from the diffusion of sovereign power.'" New York v. United States (1992).

Some of these liberties are of a political character. The federal structure allows local policies "more sensitive to the diverse needs of a heterogeneous society," permits "innovation and experimentation," enables greater citizen "involvement in democratic processes," and makes government "more responsive by putting the States in competition for a mobile citizenry." Gregory v. Ashcroft (1991). Federalism secures the freedom of the individual. It allows States to respond, through the enactment of positive law, to the initiative of those who seek a voice in shaping the destiny of their own times without having to rely solely upon the political processes that control a remote central power. True, of course, these objects can not be vindicated by the Judiciary in the absence of a proper case or controversy; but the individual liberty secured by federalism is not simply derivative of the rights of the States.

Federalism also protects the liberty of all persons within a State by ensuring that laws enacted in excess of delegated governmental power cannot direct or control their actions. See *ibid.* By denying any one government complete jurisdiction over all the concerns of public life, federalism protects the liberty of the individual from arbitrary power. When government acts in excess of its lawful powers, that liberty is at stake.

The limitations that federalism entails are not therefore a matter of rights belonging only to the States. States are not the sole intended beneficiaries of federalism. See *New York.* An individual has a direct interest in objecting to laws that upset the constitutional balance between the National Government and the States when the enforcement of those laws causes injury that is concrete, particular, and redressable. Fidelity to principles of federalism is not for the States alone to vindicate.

The recognition of an injured person's standing to object to a violation of a constitutional principle that allocates power within government is illustrated, in an analogous context, by cases in which individuals sustain discrete, justiciable injury from actions that transgress separation-of-powers limitations. Separation-of-powers principles are intended, in part, to protect each branch of government from incursion by the others. Yet the dynamic between and among the branches is not the only object of the Constitution's concern. The structural principles secured by the separation of powers protect the individual as well.

In the precedents of this Court, the claims of individuals—not of Government departments—have been the principal source of judicial decisions concerning separation of powers and checks and balances. For example, the requirement that a bill enacted by Congress be presented to the President for signature before it can become law gives the President a check over Congress' exercise of legislative power. See U. S. Const., Art. I, §7. Yet individuals, too, are protected by the operations of separation of powers and checks and balances; and they are not disabled from relying on those principles in otherwise justiciable cases and controversies. In INS v. Chadha (1983), it was an individual who successfully challenged the so-called legislative veto—a procedure that Congress used in an attempt to invalidate an executive determination without presenting the measure to the President. The procedure diminished the role of the Executive, but the challenger sought to protect not the prerogatives of the Presidency as such but rather his own right to avoid deportation under an invalid order. Chadha's challenge was sustained. A cardinal principle of separation of powers was vindicated at the insistence of an individual, indeed one who was not a citizen of the United States but who still was a person whose liberty was at risk.

Chadha is not unique in this respect. Compare . . . Clinton v. City of New York (1998) (injured parties have standing to challenge Presidential line-item veto) with Raines v. Byrd (1997) (Congress Members do not); see also, *e.g.*, Free Enterprise Fund v. Public Company Accounting Oversight Bd. (2010). . . Youngstown Sheet & Tube Co. v. Sawyer (1952); A. L. A. Schechter Poultry Corp. v. United States, 295 U. S. 495 (1935). If the constitutional structure of our Government that protects individual liberty is compromised, individuals who suffer otherwise justiciable injury may object.

Just as it is appropriate for an individual, in a proper case, to invoke separation-of-powers or checks-and balances constraints, so too may a litigant, in a proper case, challenge a law as enacted in contravention of constitutional principles of federalism. That claim need not depend on the vicarious assertion of a State's constitutional interests, even if a State's constitutional interests are also implicated.

B

In this regard it is necessary to address a misconception in the position the Government now urges this Court to adopt. . . . The Government contends petitioner asserts only that Congress could not enact the challenged statute under its enumerated powers. Were she to argue, the Government insists, that the statute "interferes with a specific aspect of state sovereignty," either instead of or in addition to her enumerated powers contention, the Court should deny her standing. . . .

There is no basis to support the Government's proposed distinction between different federalism arguments for purposes of prudential standing rules. The principles of limited national powers and state sovereignty are intertwined. While neither originates in the Tenth Amendment, both are expressed by it. Impermissible interference with state sovereignty is not within the enumerated powers of the National Government, see *New York*, and action that exceeds the National Government's enumerated powers undermines the sovereign interests of States. See United States v. Lopez (1995). The unconstitutional action can cause concomitant injury to persons in individual cases.

An individual who challenges federal action on these grounds is, of course, subject to the Article III requirements, as well as prudential rules, applicable to all litigants and claims. Individuals have "no standing to complain simply that their Government is violating the law." Allen v. Wright (1984). It is not enough that a litigant "suffers in some indefinite way in common with people generally." Frothingham v. Mellon (1923). If, in connection with the claim being asserted, a litigant who commences suit fails to show actual or imminent harm that is concrete and particular, fairly traceable to the conduct complained of, and likely to be redressed by a favorable decision, the Federal Judiciary cannot hear the claim. These requirements must be satisfied before an individual may assert a constitutional claim; and in some instances, the result may be that a State is the only entity capable of demonstrating the requisite injury.

In this case, however, where the litigant is a party to an otherwise justiciable case or controversy, she is not forbidden to object that her injury results from disregard of the federal structure of our Government. Whether the Tenth Amendment is regarded as simply a "'truism,'" *New York* (quoting United States v. Darby (1941)), or whether it has independent force of its own, the result here is the same.

* * *

There is no basis in precedent or principle to deny petitioner's standing to raise her claims. The ultimate issue of the statute's validity turns in part on whether the law can be deemed "necessary and proper for carrying into Execution" the President's Article II, §2 Treaty Power. This Court expresses no view on the merits of that argument. It can be addressed by the Court of Appeals on remand.

The judgment of the Court of Appeals is reversed, and the case is remanded for further proceedings consistent with this opinion.

It is so ordered.

Chapter 12

The Executive Power

ASSIGNMENT S-3

STUDY GUIDE: *In this case, we revisit the debate over "formalist" and "functionalist" approaches to separation of powers issues. Does the "formalist" approach of the majority have pragmatic advantages? Does the "functionalist" approach create any pragmatic costs? Notice Justice Breyer's reliance on the Necessary and Proper Clause and McCulloch v. Maryland, which typically signals a rational basis level of scrutiny. Does rational basis scrutiny + a functionalist analysis = a recipe for upholding any scheme of Congress against a separation of powers challenge? If so, is that a good thing or a bad thing? Is this decision informed by, and illustrate the need for, "first principles" that underlie, but are not expressed does the text? If so, how are these first principles to be identified, and is their application consistent with interpreting the text according to its original meaning?*

FREE ENTERPRISE FUND v. PUBLIC COMPANY ACCOUNTING OVERSIGHT BOARD

561 U.S. _____ (2010)

CHIEF JUSTICE ROBERTS delivered the opinion of the Court.

Our Constitution divided the "powers of the new Federal Government into three defined categories, Legislative, Executive, and Judicial." INS v. Chadha (1983). Article II vests "[t]he executive Power . . . in a President of the United States of America," who must "take Care that the Laws be faithfully executed." Art. II, §1, cl. 1; *id.*, §3. In light of "[t]he impossibility that one man should be able to perform all the great business of the State," the Constitution provides for executive officers to "assist the supreme Magistrate in discharging the duties of his trust." Writings of George Washington (J. Fitzpatrick ed. 1939).

Since 1789, the Constitution has been understood to empower the President to keep these officers accountable — by removing them from office, if necessary. See generally Myers v. United States (1926). This Court has determined, however, that this authority is not without limit. In Humphrey's Executor v. United States (1935), we held that Congress can, under certain circumstances, create independent agencies run by principal officers appointed by the President, whom the President may not remove at will but only for good cause. Likewise, in

United States v. Perkins (1886), and Morrison v. Olson (1988), the Court sustained similar restrictions on the power of principal executive officers—themselves responsible to the President—to remove their own inferiors. The parties do not ask us to reexamine any of these precedents, and we do not do so.

We are asked, however, to consider a new situation not yet encountered by the Court. The question is whether these separate layers of protection may be combined. May the President be restricted in his ability to remove a principal officer, who is in turn restricted in his ability to remove an inferior officer, even though that inferior officer determines the policy and enforces the laws of the United States?

We hold that such multilevel protection from removal is contrary to Article II's vesting of the executive power in the President. The President cannot "take Care that the Laws be faithfully executed" if he cannot oversee the faithfulness of the officers who execute them. Here the President cannot remove an officer who enjoys more than one level of good-cause protection, even if the President determines that the officer is neglecting his duties or discharging them improperly. That judgment is instead committed to another officer, who may or may not agree with the President's determination, and whom the President cannot remove simply because that officer disagrees with him. This contravenes the President's "constitutional obligation to ensure the faithful execution of the laws."

I

After a series of celebrated accounting debacles, Congress enacted the Sarbanes-Oxley Act of 2002 (or Act). Among other measures, the Act introduced tighter regulation of the accounting industry under a new Public Company Accounting Oversight Board. The Board is composed of five members, appointed to staggered 5-year terms by the Securities and Exchange Commission. It was modeled on private self-regulatory organizations in the securities industry—such as the New York Stock Exchange—that investigate and discipline their own members subject to Commission oversight. Congress created the Board as a private "nonprofit corporation," and Board members and employees are not considered Government "officer[s] or employee[s]" for statutory purposes. The Board can thus recruit its members and employees from the private sector by paying salaries far above the standard Government pay scale.

Unlike the self-regulatory organizations, however, the Board is a Government-created, Government-appointed entity, with expansive powers to govern an entire industry. Every accounting firm—both foreign and domestic—that participates in auditing public companies under the securities laws must register with the Board, pay it an annual fee, and comply with its rules and oversight. The Board is charged with enforcing the Sarbanes-Oxley Act, the securities laws, the Commission's rules, its own rules, and professional accounting standards. To this end, the Board may regulate every detail of an accounting firm's practice, including hiring and professional development, promotion, supervision of audit work, the acceptance of new business and the continuation of old, internal inspection procedures, professional ethics rules, and "such other requirements as the Board may prescribe." . . .

The Act places the Board under the SEC's oversight, particularly with respect to the issuance of rules or the imposition of sanctions (both of which are subject to Commission approval and alteration). But the individual members of the Board — like the officers and directors of the self-regulatory organizations — are substantially insulated from the Commission's control. The Commission cannot remove Board members at will, but only "for good cause shown," "in accordance with" certain procedures.

Those procedures require a Commission finding, "on the record" and "after notice and opportunity for a hearing," that the Board member

> "(A) has willfully violated any provision of th[e] Act, the rules of the Board, or the securities laws;
> "(B) has willfully abused the authority of that member; or
> "(C) without reasonable justification or excuse, has failed to enforce compliance with any such provision or rule, or any professional standard by any registered public accounting firm or any associated person thereof."

Removal of a Board member requires a formal Commission order and is subject to judicial review. Similar procedures govern the Commission's removal of officers and directors of the private self-regulatory organizations. The parties agree that the Commissioners cannot themselves be removed by the President except under the *Humphrey's Executor* standard of "inefficiency, neglect of duty, or malfeasance in office," and we decide the case with that understanding.

Beckstead and Watts, LLP, is a Nevada accounting firm registered with the Board. The Board inspected the firm, released a report critical of its auditing procedures, and began a formal investigation. Beckstead and Watts and the Free Enterprise Fund, a nonprofit organization of which the firm is a member, then sued the Board and its members, seeking (among other things) a declaratory judgment that the Board is unconstitutional and an injunction preventing the Board from exercising its powers. . . .

III

We hold that the dual for-cause limitations on the removal of Board members contravene the Constitution's separation of powers.

A

The Constitution provides that "[t]he executive Power shall be vested in a President of the United States of America." Art. II, §1, cl. 1. As Madison stated on the floor of the First Congress, "if any power whatsoever is in its nature Executive, it is the power of appointing, overseeing, and controlling those who execute the laws." (1789).

The removal of executive officers was discussed extensively in Congress when the first executive departments were created. The view that "prevailed, as most consonant to the text of the Constitution" and "to the requisite responsibility and harmony in the Executive Department," was that the executive power included a power to oversee executive officers through removal; because that traditional executive power was not "expressly taken away, it remained with the President." Letter from James Madison to Thomas Jefferson (June 30, 1789). "This Decision of 1789 provides contemporaneous and weighty evidence of the Constitution's meaning since many of the Members of the First Congress had taken part in framing that instrument." Bowsher v. Synar (1986). And it soon became the "settled and well understood construction of the Constitution." Ex parte Hennen (1839).

The landmark case of Myers v. United States reaffirmed the principle that Article II confers on the President "the general administrative control of those executing the laws." It is *his* responsibility to take care that the laws be faithfully executed. The buck stops with the President, in Harry Truman's famous phrase. As we explained in *Myers*, the President therefore must have some "power of removing those for whom he can not continue to be responsible."

Nearly a decade later in *Humphrey's Executor*, this Court held that *Myers* did not prevent Congress from conferring good-cause tenure on the principal officers of certain independent agencies. That case concerned the members of the Federal Trade Commission, who held 7-year terms and could not be removed by the President except for "'inefficiency, neglect of duty, or malfeasance in office.'" The Court distinguished *Myers* on the ground that *Myers* concerned "an officer [who] is merely one of the units in the executive department and, hence, inherently subject to the exclusive and illimitable power of removal by the Chief Executive, whose subordinate and aid he is." By contrast, the Court characterized the FTC as "quasi-legislative and quasi-judicial" rather than "purely executive," and held that Congress could require it "to act independently of executive control." Because "one who holds his office only during the pleasure of another, cannot be depended upon to maintain an attitude of independence against the latter's will," the Court held that Congress had power to "fix the period during which [the Commissioners] shall continue in office, and to forbid their removal except for cause in the meantime."

Humphrey's Executor did not address the removal of inferior officers, whose appointment Congress may vest in heads of departments. If Congress does so, it is ordinarily the department head, rather than the President, who enjoys the power of removal. This Court has upheld for-cause limitations on that power as well. . . . *Morrison* . . . concerned the Ethics in Government Act, which provided for an independent counsel to investigate allegations of crime by high executive officers. The counsel was appointed by a special court, wielded the full powers of a prosecutor, and was removable by the Attorney General only "'for good cause.'" We recognized that the independent counsel was undoubtedly an executive officer, rather than "'quasi-legislative'" or "'quasi-judicial,'" but we stated as "our present considered view" that Congress had power to impose good-cause restrictions on her removal. The Court noted that the statute "g[a]ve the Attorney General," an officer directly responsible to the President and "through [whom]" the President could act, "several means of supervising or controlling" the independent counsel — "[m]ost importantly . . . the power to remove the counsel for good cause." Under those circumstances, the Court sustained the statute. *Morrison* did not, however, address the consequences of more than one level of good-cause tenure — leaving the issue, as both the court and dissent below recognized, "a question of first impression" in this Court.

B

As explained, we have previously upheld limited restrictions on the President's removal power. In those cases, however, only one level of protected tenure separated the President from an officer exercising executive power. It was the President — or a subordinate he could remove at will — who decided whether the officer's conduct merited removal under the good-cause standard.

The Act before us does something quite different. It not only protects Board members from removal except for good cause, but withdraws from the President any decision on whether that good cause exists. That decision is vested instead in other tenured officers — the Commissioners — none of whom is subject to the President's direct control. The result is a Board that is not accountable to the President, and a President who is not responsible for the Board.

The added layer of tenure protection makes a difference. Without a layer of insulation between the Commission and the Board, the Commission could remove a Board member at any time, and therefore would be fully responsible for what the Board does. The President could then hold the Commission to account for its supervision of the Board, to the same extent that he may hold the Commission to account for everything else it does.

A second level of tenure protection changes the nature of the President's review. Now the Commission cannot remove a Board member at will. The President therefore cannot hold the Commission fully accountable for the Board's conduct, to the same extent that he may hold the Commission accountable for everything else that it does. The Commissioners are not responsible for the Board's actions. They are only responsible for their own determination of whether the Act's rigorous good-cause standard is met. And even if the President disagrees with their determination, he is powerless to intervene — unless that determination is so unreasonable as to constitute "inefficiency, neglect of duty, or malfeasance in office." *Humphrey's Executor.*

This novel structure does not merely add to the Board's independence, but transforms it. Neither the President, nor anyone directly responsible to him, nor even an officer whose conduct he may review only for good cause, has full control over the Board. The President is stripped of the power our precedents have preserved, and his ability to execute the laws — by holding his subordinates accountable for their conduct — is impaired.

That arrangement is contrary to Article II's vesting of the executive power in the President. Without the ability to oversee the Board, or to attribute the

Board's failings to those whom he *can* oversee, the President is no longer the judge of the Board's conduct. He is not the one who decides whether Board members are abusing their offices or neglecting their duties. He can neither ensure that the laws are faithfully executed, nor be held responsible for a Board member's breach of faith. This violates the basic principle that the President "cannot delegate ultimate responsibility or the active obligation to supervise that goes with it," because Article II "makes a single President responsible for the actions of the Executive Branch." Clinton v. Jones (1997) (BREYER, J., concurring in judgment).[1]

Indeed, if allowed to stand, this dispersion of responsibility could be multiplied. If Congress can shelter the bureaucracy behind two layers of good-cause tenure, why not a third? At oral argument, the Government was unwilling to concede that even *five* layers between the President and the Board would be too many. The officers of such an agency—safely encased within a Matryoshka doll of tenure protections—would be immune from Presidential oversight, even as they exercised power in the people's name.

Perhaps an individual President might find advantages in tying his own hands. But the separation of powers does not depend on the views of individual Presidents, nor on whether "the encroached-upon branch approves the encroachment," New York v. United States (1992). The President can always choose to restrain himself in his dealings with subordinates. He cannot, however, choose to bind his successors by diminishing their powers, nor can he escape responsibility for his choices by pretending that they are not his own.

The diffusion of power carries with it a diffusion of accountability. The people do not vote for the "Officers of the United States." Art. II, §2, cl. 2. They instead look to the President to guide the "assistants or deputies subject to his superintendence." The Federalist No. 72 (A. Hamilton). Without a clear and effective chain of command, the public cannot "determine on whom the blame or the punishment of a pernicious measure, or series of pernicious measures ought really to fall." *Id.* That is why the Framers sought to ensure that "those who are employed in the execution of the law will be in their proper situation, and the chain of dependence be preserved; the lowest officers, the middle grade, and the highest, will depend, as they ought, on the President, and the President on the community." 1 Annals of Cong. (J. Madison).

By granting the Board executive power without the Executive's oversight, this Act subverts the President's ability to ensure that the laws are faithfully

1. Contrary to the dissent's suggestion, the second layer of tenure protection does compromise the President's ability to remove a Board member the Commission wants to retain. Without a second layer of protection, the Commission has no excuse for retaining an officer who is not faithfully executing the law. With the second layer in place, the Commission can shield its decision from Presidential review by finding that good cause is absent—a finding that, given the Commission's own protected tenure, the President cannot easily overturn. The dissent describes this conflict merely as one of four possible "scenarios," but it is the central issue in this case: The second layer matters precisely when the President finds it necessary to have a subordinate officer removed, and a statute prevents him from doing so.

executed—as well as the public's ability to pass judgment on his efforts. The Act's restrictions are incompatible with the Constitution's separation of powers.

C

Respondents and the dissent resist this conclusion, portraying the Board as "the kind of practical accommodation between the Legislature and the Executive that should be permitted in a 'workable government.'" Metropolitan Washington Airports Authority v. Citizens for Abatement of Aircraft Noise, Inc. (1991) (quoting Youngstown Sheet & Tube Co. v. Sawyer (1952) (Jackson, J., concurring)). According to the dissent, Congress may impose multiple levels of for-cause tenure between the President and his subordinates when it "rests agency independence upon the need for technical expertise." The Board's mission is said to demand both "technical competence" and "apolitical expertise," and its powers may only be exercised by "technical professional experts." In this respect the statute creating the Board is, we are told, simply one example of the "vast numbers of statutes governing vast numbers of subjects, concerned with vast numbers of different problems, [that] provide for, or foresee, their execution or administration through the work of administrators organized within many different kinds of administrative structures, exercising different kinds of administrative authority, to achieve their legislatively mandated objectives."

No one doubts Congress's power to create a vast and varied federal bureaucracy. But where, in all this, is the role for oversight by an elected President? The Constitution requires that a President chosen by the entire Nation oversee the execution of the laws. And the "'fact that a given law or procedure is efficient, convenient, and useful in facilitating functions of government, standing alone, will not save it if it is contrary to the Constitution,'" for "'[c]onvenience and efficiency are not the primary objectives—or the hallmarks—of democratic government.'" *Bowsher* (quoting *Chadha*).

One can have a government that functions without being ruled by functionaries, and a government that benefits from expertise without being ruled by experts. Our Constitution was adopted to enable the people to govern themselves, through their elected leaders. The growth of the Executive Branch, which now wields vast power and touches almost every aspect of daily life, heightens the concern that it may slip from the Executive's control, and thus from that of the people. This concern is largely absent from the dissent's paean to the administrative state.

For example, the dissent dismisses the importance of removal as a tool of supervision, concluding that the President's "power to get something done" more often depends on "who controls the agency's budget requests and funding, the relationships between one agency or department and another purely political factors (including Congress' ability to assert influence)," and indeed whether particular *unelected* officials support or "resist" the President's policies. The Framers did not rest our liberties on such bureaucratic minutiae. As we said in *Bowsher*, "[t]he separated powers of our Government cannot be permitted to turn on judicial assessment of whether an officer exercising executive power is on good terms with Congress." . . .

In a system of checks and balances, "[p]ower abhors a vacuum," and one branch's handicap is another's strength. . . . Congress has plenary control over the salary, duties, and even existence of executive offices. Only Presidential oversight can counter its influence. That is why the Constitution vests certain powers in the President that "the Legislature has no right to diminish or modify." 1 Annals of Cong. (J. Madison).

The Framers created a structure in which "[a] dependence on the people" would be the "primary controul on the government." The Federalist No. 51 (J. Madison). That dependence is maintained, not just by "parchment barriers," but by letting "[a]mbition . . . counteract ambition," giving each branch "the necessary constitutional means, and personal motives, to resist encroachments of the others." A key "constitutional means" vested in the President—perhaps *the* key means—was "the power of appointing, overseeing, and controlling those who execute the laws." 1 Annals of Cong. [J. Madison]. And while a government of "opposite and rival interests" may sometimes inhibit the smooth functioning of administration, The Federalist No. 51, "[t]he Framers recognized that, in the long term, structural protections against abuse of power were critical to preserving liberty." *Bowsher.*

Calls to abandon those protections in light of "the era's perceived necessity," *New York*, are not unusual. Nor is the argument from bureaucratic expertise limited only to the field of accounting. The failures of accounting regulation may be a "pressing national problem," but "a judiciary that licensed extraconstitutional government with each issue of comparable gravity would, in the long run, be far worse." Neither respondents nor the dissent explains why the Board's task, unlike so many others, requires *more* than one layer of insulation from the President—or, for that matter, why only two. The point is not to take issue with for-cause limitations in general; we do not do that. The question here is far more modest. We deal with the unusual situation, never before addressed by the Court, of two layers of for-cause tenure. And though it may be criticized as "elementary arithmetical logic," two layers are not the same as one.

The President has been given the power to oversee executive officers; he is not limited, as in Harry Truman's lament, to "persuad[ing]" his unelected subordinates "to do what they ought to do without persuasion." In its pursuit of a "workable government," Congress cannot reduce the Chief Magistrate to a cajoler-in-chief. . . .

We do not decide the status of other Government employees, nor do we decide whether "lesser functionaries subordinate to officers of the United States" must be subject to the same sort of control as those who exercise "significant authority pursuant to the laws." [Buckley v. Valeo (1976).]

Nor do the employees referenced by the dissent enjoy the same significant and unusual protections from Presidential oversight as members of the Board. Senior or policymaking positions in government may be excepted from the competitive service to ensure Presidential control, and members of the Senior Executive

Service may be reassigned or reviewed by agency heads (and entire agencies may be excluded from that Service by the President). While the full extent of that authority is not before us, any such authority is of course wholly absent with respect to the Board. Nothing in our opinion, therefore, should be read to cast doubt on the use of what is colloquially known as the civil service system within independent agencies.[2]

Finally, the dissent wanders far afield when it suggests that today's opinion might increase the President's authority to remove military officers. Without expressing any view whatever on the scope of that authority, it is enough to note that we see little analogy between our Nation's armed services and the Public Company Accounting Oversight Board. Military officers are broadly subject to Presidential control through the chain of command and through the President's powers as Commander in Chief. Art. II, §2, cl. 1. The President and his subordinates may also convene boards of inquiry or courts-martial to hear claims of misconduct or poor performance by those officers. Here, by contrast, the President has no authority to initiate a Board member's removal for cause.

There is no reason for us to address whether these positions identified by the dissent, or any others not at issue in this case, are so structured as to infringe the President's constitutional authority. Nor is there any substance to the dissent's concern that the "work of all these various officials" will "be put on hold." As the judgment in this case demonstrates, restricting certain officers to a single level of insulation from the President affects the conditions under which those officers might some day be removed, and would have no effect, absent a congressional determination to the contrary, on the validity of any officer's continuance in office. The only issue in this case is whether Congress may deprive the President of adequate control over the Board, which is the regulator of first resort and the primary law enforcement authority for a vital sector of our economy. We hold that it cannot. . . . The Sarbanes-Oxley Act remains "'fully operative as a law'" with these tenure restrictions excised. *New York*. . . .

* * *

The Constitution that makes the President accountable to the people for executing the laws also gives him the power to do so. That power includes, as a general matter, the authority to remove those who assist him in carrying out his duties. Without such power, the President could not be held fully accountable for discharging his own responsibilities; the buck would stop somewhere else. Such diffusion of authority "would greatly diminish the intended and necessary responsibility of the chief magistrate himself." The Federalist No. 70.

2. For similar reasons, our holding also does not address that subset of independent agency employees who serve as administrative law judges. Whether administrative law judges are necessarily "Officers of the United States" is disputed. And unlike members of the Board, many administrative law judges of course perform adjudicative rather than enforcement or policymaking functions, or possess purely recommendatory powers. . . .

While we have sustained in certain cases limits on the President's removal power, the Act before us imposes a new type of restriction—two levels of protection from removal for those who nonetheless exercise significant executive power. Congress cannot limit the President's authority in this way.

The judgment of the United States Court of Appeals for the District of Columbia Circuit is affirmed in part and reversed in part, and the case is remanded for further proceedings consistent with this opinion.

It is so ordered.

JUSTICE BREYER, with Whom JUSTICE STEVENS, JUSTICE GINSBURG, and JUSTICE SOTOMAYOR join, dissenting.

The Court holds unconstitutional a statute providing that the Securities and Exchange Commission can remove members of the Public Company Accounting Oversight Board from office only for cause. It argues that granting the "inferior officer[s]" on the Accounting Board "more than one level of good-cause protection . . . contravenes the President's 'constitutional obligation to ensure the faithful execution of the laws.'" I agree that the Accounting Board members are inferior officers. But in my view the statute does not significantly interfere with the President's "executive Power." Art. II, §1. It violates no separation-of-powers principle. And the Court's contrary holding threatens to disrupt severely the fair and efficient administration of the laws. I consequently dissent. . . .

I

. . . In answering the question presented, we cannot look to more specific constitutional text, such as the text of the Appointments Clause or the Presentment Clause, upon which the Court has relied in other separation-of-powers cases. That is because, with the exception of the general "vesting" and "take care" language, the Constitution is completely "silent with respect to the power of removal from office." Ex parte Hennen (1839); see also [Morrison v. Olson (1988)] (SCALIA, J., dissenting) ("There is, of course, no provision in the Constitution stating who may remove executive officers . . . ") . . . .

When previously deciding this kind of nontextual question, the Court has emphasized the importance of examining how a particular provision, taken in context, is likely to function. Thus, in Crowell v. Benson (1932), a foundational separation-of-powers case, the Court said that "regard must be had, as in other cases where constitutional limits are invoked, not to mere matters of form, but to the substance of what is required." . . . See . . . *Morrison* ("The analysis contained in our removal cases is designed *not to define rigid categories* of those officials who may or may not be removed at will by the President," but rather asks whether, given the "functions of the officials in question," a removal provision "interfere[s] with the President's exercise of the 'executive power'" (emphasis added)). The Court has thereby written into law Justice Jackson's wise perception that "the Constitution . . . contemplates that practice will integrate the dispersed powers into *a workable government.*" Youngstown

Sheet & Tube Co. v. Sawyer (1952) (opinion concurring in judgment) (emphasis added).

It is not surprising that the Court in these circumstances has looked to function and context, and not to bright-line rules. For one thing, that approach embodies the intent of the Framers. As Chief Justice Marshall long ago observed, our Constitution is fashioned so as to allow the three coordinate branches, including this Court, to exercise practical judgment in response to changing conditions and "exigencies," which at the time of the founding could be seen only "dimly," and perhaps not at all. [McCulloch v. Maryland (1819).]

For another, a functional approach permits Congress and the President the flexibility needed to adapt statutory law to changing circumstances. That is why the "powers conferred upon the Federal Government by the Constitution were phrased in language broad enough to allow for the expansion of the Federal Government's role" over time. New York v. United States (1992). Indeed, the Federal Government at the time of the founding consisted of about 2,000 employees and served a population of about 4 million. Today, however, the Federal Government employs about *4.4 million workers* who serve a Nation of more than 310 million people living in a society characterized by rapid technological, economic, and social change.

Federal statutes now require or permit Government officials to provide, regulate, or otherwise administer, not only foreign affairs and defense, but also a wide variety of such subjects as taxes, welfare, social security, medicine, pharmaceutical drugs, education, highways, railroads, electricity, natural gas, nuclear power, financial instruments, banking, medical care, public health and safety, the environment, fair employment practices, consumer protection and much else besides. Those statutes create a host of different organizational structures. Sometimes they delegate administrative authority to the President directly; sometimes they place authority in a long-established Cabinet department; sometimes they delegate authority to an independent commission or board; sometimes they place authority directly in the hands of a single senior administrator; sometimes they place it in a sub-cabinet bureau, office, division or other agency; sometimes they vest it in multimember or multiagency task groups); sometimes they vest it in commissions or advisory committees made up of members of more than one branch; sometimes they divide it among groups of departments, commissions, bureaus, divisions, and administrators; and sometimes they permit state or local governments to participate as well. Statutes similarly grant administrators a wide variety of powers — for example, the power to make rules, develop informal practices, investigate, adjudicate, impose sanctions, grant licenses, and provide goods, services, advice, and so forth.

The upshot is that today vast numbers of statutes governing vast numbers of subjects, concerned with vast numbers of different problems, provide for, or foresee, their execution or administration through the work of administrators organized within many different kinds of administrative structures, exercising different kinds of administrative authority, to achieve their legislatively mandated objectives. And, given the nature of the Government's work, it is not surprising that administrative units come in many different shapes and sizes.

The functional approach required by our precedents recognizes this administrative complexity and, more importantly, recognizes the various ways presidential power operates within this context—and the various ways in which a removal provision might affect that power. As human beings have known ever since Ulysses tied himself to the mast so as safely to hear the Sirens' song, sometimes it is necessary to disable oneself in order to achieve a broader objective. Thus, legally enforceable commitments—such as contracts, statutes that cannot instantly be changed, and, as in the case before us, the establishment of independent administrative institutions—hold the potential to empower precisely because of their ability to constrain. If the President seeks to regulate through impartial adjudication, then insulation of the adjudicator from removal at will can help him achieve that goal. And to free a technical decisionmaker from the fear of removal without cause can similarly help create legitimacy with respect to that official's regulatory actions by helping to insulate his technical decisions from nontechnical political pressure.

Neither is power always susceptible to the equations of elementary arithmetic. A rule that takes power from a President's friends and allies may weaken him. But a rule that takes power from the President's opponents may strengthen him. And what if the rule takes power from a functionally *neutral* independent authority? In that case, it is difficult to predict how the President's power is affected in the abstract.

These practical reasons not only support our precedents' determination that cases such as this should examine the specific functions and context at issue; they also indicate that judges should hesitate before second-guessing a "for cause" decision made by the other branches. See, e.g., *Chadha* (applying a "presumption that the challenged statute is valid"). Compared to Congress and the President, the Judiciary possesses an inferior understanding of the realities of administration, and the manner in which power, including and most especially political power, operates in context.

There is no indication that the two comparatively more expert branches were divided in their support for the "for cause" provision at issue here. In this case, the Act embodying the provision was passed by a vote of 423 to 3 in the House of Representatives and a by vote of 99 to 0 in the Senate. The creation of the Accounting Board was discussed at great length in both bodies without anyone finding in its structure any constitutional problem. [President Bush] signed the Act. And, when he did so, he issued a signing statement that critiqued multiple provisions of the Act but did not express any separation-of-powers concerns.

Thus, here, as in similar cases, we should decide the constitutional question in light of the provision's practical functioning in context. And our decision should take account of the Judiciary's comparative lack of institutional expertise.

II

To what extent then is the Act's "for cause" provision likely, as a practical matter, to limit the President's exercise of executive authority? In practical terms no "for cause" provision can, in isolation, define the full measure of executive power. This is because a legislative decision to place ultimate administrative authority in, say, the Secretary of Agriculture rather than the President, the way in which the statute defines the scope of the power the relevant administrator can exercise, the decision as to who controls the agency's budget requests and funding, the relationships between one agency or department and another, as well as more purely political factors (including Congress' ability to assert influence) are more likely to affect the President's power to get something done. . . . Indeed, notwithstanding the majority's assertion that the removal authority is "*the* key" mechanism by which the President oversees inferior officers in the independent agencies, it appears that no President has ever actually sought to exercise that power by testing the scope of a "for cause" provision.

But even if we put all these other matters to the side, we should still conclude that the "for cause" restriction before us will not restrict presidential power significantly. For one thing, the restriction directly limits, not the President's power, but the power of an already independent agency. The Court seems to have forgotten that fact when it identifies its central constitutional problem: According to the Court, the President "is powerless to intervene" if he has determined that the Board members' "conduct merit[s] removal" because "[t]hat decision is vested instead in other tenured officers — the Commissioners — none of whom is subject to the President's direct control." But so long as the President is *legitimately* foreclosed from removing the *Commissioners* except for cause (as the majority assumes), nullifying the Commission's power to remove Board members only for cause will not resolve the problem the Court has identified: The President will *still* be "powerless to intervene" by removing the Board members if the Commission reasonably decides not to do so.

In other words, the Court fails to show why *two* layers of "for cause" protection — Layer One insulating the Commissioners from the President, and Layer Two insulating the Board from the Commissioners — impose any more serious limitation upon the *President's* powers than *one* layer. Consider the four scenarios that might arise:

1. The President and the Commission both want to keep a Board member in office. Neither layer is relevant.
2. The President and the Commission both want to dismiss a Board member. Layer Two stops them both from doing so without cause. The President's ability to remove the Commission (Layer One) is irrelevant, for he and the Commission are in agreement.
3. The President wants to dismiss a Board member, but the Commission wants to keep the member. Layer One allows the Commission to make that determination notwithstanding the President's contrary view. Layer

Two is irrelevant because the Commission does not seek to remove the Board member.

4. The President wants to keep a Board member, but the Commission wants to dismiss the Board member. Here, Layer Two *helps the President*, for it hinders the Commission's ability to dismiss a Board member whom the President wants to keep in place.

Thus, the majority's decision to eliminate only *Layer Two* accomplishes virtually nothing. And that is because a removal restriction's effect upon presidential power depends not on the presence of a "double-layer" of for-cause removal, as the majority pretends, but rather on the real-world nature of the President's relationship with the Commission. If the President confronts a Commission that seeks to *resist* his policy preferences — a distinct possibility when, as here, a Commission's membership must reflect both political parties — the restriction on the *Commission's* ability to remove a Board member is either irrelevant (as in scenario 3) or may actually help the President (as in scenario 4). And if the President faces a Commission that seeks to *implement* his policy preferences, Layer One is irrelevant, for the President and Commission see eye to eye.

In order to avoid this elementary logic, the Court creates two alternative scenarios. In the first, the Commission and the President *both* want to remove a Board member, but have varying judgments as to whether they have good "cause" to do so — *i.e.*, the President and the Commission both conclude that a Board member should be removed, but disagree as to whether that conclusion (which they have both reached) is *reasonable*. In the second, the President wants to remove a Board member and the Commission disagrees; but, notwithstanding its freedom to make reasonable decisions independent of the President (afforded by Layer One), the Commission (while apparently telling the President that it agrees with him and would like to remove the Board member) uses Layer Two as an "excuse" to pursue its actual aims — an excuse which, given Layer One, it does not need.

Both of these circumstances seem unusual. I do not know if they have ever occurred. But I do not deny their logical possibility. I simply doubt their importance. And the fact that, with respect to the President's power, the double layer of for-cause removal sometimes might help, sometimes might hurt, leads me to conclude that its over all effect is at most indeterminate.

But once we leave the realm of hypothetical logic and view the removal provision at issue in the context of the entire Act, its lack of practical effect becomes readily apparent. That is because the statute provides the Commission with full authority and virtually comprehensive control over all of the Board's functions. . . . Everyone concedes that the President's control over the Commission is constitutionally sufficient. See [Humphrey's Executor v. United States (1935)]. And if the President's control over the Commission is sufficient, and the Commission's control over the Board is virtually absolute, then, as a practical matter, the President's control over the Board should prove sufficient as well.

At the same time, Congress and the President had good reason for enacting the challenged "for cause" provision. First and foremost, the Board adjudicates cases. This Court has long recognized the appropriateness of using "for cause" provisions to protect the personal independence of those who even only sometimes engage in adjudicatory functions. *Humphrey's Executor*. . . . Moreover, in addition to their adjudicative functions, the Accounting Board members supervise, and are themselves, technical professional experts. . . . This Court has recognized that the "difficulties involved in the preparation of" sound auditing reports require the application of "scientific accounting principles." United States v. Anderson (1926). And this Court has recognized the constitutional legitimacy of a justification that rests agency independence upon the need for technical expertise. See *Humphrey's Executor*. . . .

Congress and the President could reasonably have thought it prudent to insulate the adjudicative Board members from fear of purely politically based removal. And in a world in which we count on the Federal Government to regulate matters as complex as, say, nuclear-power production, the Court's assertion that we should simply learn to get by "without being" regulated "by experts" is, at best, unrealistic — at worst, dangerously so. . . .

* * *

In my view the Court's decision is wrong — very wrong. . . . [I]f the Court were to look to the proper functional and contextual considerations, it would find the Accounting Board provision constitutional. . . .

With respect I dissent.

ASSIGNMENT S-4

Because the next case considers the constitutionality of a congressional statute, it does not concern the scope of executive power. It concerns instead the scope of the writ of habeas corpus, and the power of Congress to provide an adequate substitute for its protections. The law governing habeas corpus is complex, and is not typically studied in either Con Law I or Con Law II courses. This lengthy excerpt is included to round out the topic of the treatment of detainees at Guantanamo.

Study Guide: *When reading the next case keep in mind that it involves (at least) two separate issues: (1) Does the writ of habeas corpus apply to the detainees at Guantanamo, and (2) if it does, has Congress provided an adequate substitute for the habeas corpus protections. If the answer to the first question is "no," there is no need to reach the second. Why would not the Court be more deferential to the decisions of the political branches? [Hint: does this case fall under any of the exceptions identified in Footnote Four?] With respect to the first question, has the Court been properly respectful of its precedents? Does its treatment of precedent suggest anything about the invocation of* stare decisis *in* *other cases? Does it matter that the issue here involves the war powers of Congress and the President?*

BOUMEDIENE v. BUSH

553 U.S. 723 (2008)

JUSTICE KENNEDY delivered the opinion of the Court.

Petitioners are aliens designated as enemy combatants and detained at the United States Naval Station at Guantanamo Bay, Cuba. There are others detained there, also aliens, who are not parties to this suit.

Petitioners present a question not resolved by our earlier cases relating to the detention of aliens at Guantanamo: whether they have the constitutional privilege of habeas corpus, a privilege not to be withdrawn except in conformance with the Suspension Clause, Art. I, §9, cl. 2. We hold these petitioners do have the habeas corpus privilege. Congress has enacted a statute, the Detainee Treatment Act of 2005 (DTA), 119 Stat. 2739, that provides certain procedures for review of the detainees' status. We hold that those procedures are not an adequate and effective substitute for habeas corpus. Therefore §7 of the Military Commissions Act of 2006 (MCA) operates as an unconstitutional suspension of the writ. We do not address whether the President has authority to detain these petitioners nor do we hold that the writ must issue. These and other questions regarding the legality of the detention are to be resolved in the first instance by the District Court. . . .

III

In deciding the constitutional questions now presented we must determine whether petitioners are barred from seeking the writ or invoking the protections of the Suspension Clause either because of their status, *i.e.*, petitioners' designation by the Executive Branch as enemy combatants, or their physical location, *i.e.*, their presence at Guantanamo Bay. The Government contends that noncitizens designated as enemy combatants and detained in territory located outside our Nation's borders have no constitutional rights and no privilege of habeas corpus. Petitioners contend they do have cognizable constitutional rights and that Congress, in seeking to eliminate recourse to habeas corpus as a means to assert those rights, acted in violation of the Suspension Clause.

We begin with a brief account of the history and origins of the writ. Our account proceeds from two propositions. First, protection for the privilege of habeas corpus was one of the few safeguards of liberty specified in a Constitution that, at the outset, had no Bill of Rights. In the system conceived by the Framers the writ had a centrality that must inform proper interpretation of the Suspension Clause. Second, to the extent there were settled precedents or legal commentaries in 1789 regarding the extraterritorial scope of the writ or its application to enemy aliens, those authorities can be instructive for the present cases.

A

The Framers viewed freedom from unlawful restraint as a fundamental precept of liberty, and they understood the writ of habeas corpus as a vital instrument to secure that freedom. Experience taught, however, that the common-law writ all too often had been insufficient to guard against the abuse of monarchial power. That history counseled the necessity for specific language in the Constitution to secure the writ and ensure its place in our legal system.

Magna Carta decreed that no man would be imprisoned contrary to the law of the land. Art. 39 ("No free man shall be taken or imprisoned or dispossessed, or outlawed, or banished, or in any way destroyed, nor will we go upon him, nor send upon him, except by the legal judgment of his peers or by the law of the land"). Important as the principle was, the Barons at Runnymede prescribed no specific legal process to enforce it. Holdsworth tells us, however, that gradually the writ of habeas corpus became the means by which the promise of Magna Carta was fulfilled. 9 W. Holdsworth, A History of English Law 112 (1926) (hereinafter Holdsworth).

The development was painstaking, even by the centuries-long measures of English constitutional history. The writ was known and used in some form at least as early as the reign of Edward I. Yet at the outset it was used to protect not the rights of citizens but those of the King and his courts. The early courts were considered agents of the Crown, designed to assist the King in the exercise of his power. Thus the writ, while it would become part of the foundation of liberty for the King's subjects, was in its earliest use a mechanism for securing compliance with the King's laws. Over time it became clear that by issuing the writ of habeas corpus common-law courts sought to enforce the King's prerogative to inquire into the authority of a jailer to hold a prisoner.

Even so, from an early date it was understood that the King, too, was subject to the law. As the writers said of Magna Carta, "it means this, that the king is and shall be below the law." 1 F. Pollock & F. Maitland, History of English Law 173 (2d ed. 1909). And, by the 1600's, the writ was deemed less an instrument of the King's power and more a restraint upon it.

Still, the writ proved to be an imperfect check. Even when the importance of the writ was well understood in England, habeas relief often was denied by the courts or suspended by Parliament. Denial or suspension occurred in times of political unrest, to the anguish of the imprisoned and the outrage of those in sympathy with them. . . .

This history was known to the Framers. It no doubt confirmed their view that pendular swings to and away from individual liberty were endemic to undivided, uncontrolled power. The Framers' inherent distrust of governmental power was the driving force behind the constitutional plan that allocated powers among three independent branches. This design serves not only to make Government accountable but also to secure individual liberty. Because the Constitution's separation-of-powers structure, like the substantive guarantees of the Fifth and Fourteenth Amendments, protects persons as well as citizens, foreign nationals who have the privilege of litigating in our courts can seek to enforce separation-of-powers principles.

That the Framers considered the writ a vital instrument for the protection of individual liberty is evident from the care taken to specify the limited grounds for its suspension: "The Privilege of the Writ of Habeas Corpus shall not be suspended, unless when in Cases of Rebellion or Invasion the public Safety may require it." Art. I, §9, cl. 2. The word "privilege" was used, perhaps, to avoid mentioning some rights to the exclusion of others. (Indeed, the only mention of the term "right" in the Constitution, as ratified, is in its clause giving Congress the power to protect the rights of authors and inventors. See Art. I, §8, cl. 8.)

Surviving accounts of the ratification debates provide additional evidence that the Framers deemed the writ to be an essential mechanism in the separation-of-powers scheme. In a critical exchange with Patrick Henry at the Virginia ratifying convention Edmund Randolph referred to the Suspension Clause as an "exception" to the "power given to Congress to regulate courts." A resolution passed by the New York ratifying convention made clear its understanding that the Clause not only protects against arbitrary suspensions of the writ but also guarantees an affirmative right to judicial inquiry into the causes of detention. Alexander Hamilton likewise explained that by providing the detainee a judicial forum to challenge detention, the writ preserves limited government. As he explained in The Federalist No. 84:

> [T]he practice of arbitrary imprisonments, have been, in all ages, the favorite and most formidable instruments of tyranny. The observations of the judicious Blackstone . . . are well worthy of recital: "To bereave a man of life . . . or by violence to confiscate his estate, without accusation or trial, would be so gross and notorious an act of despotism as must at once convey the alarm of tyranny throughout the whole nation; but confinement of the person, by secretly hurrying him to jail, where his sufferings are unknown or forgotten, is a less public, a less striking, and therefore a *more dangerous engine* of arbitrary government." And as a remedy for this fatal evil he is everywhere peculiarly emphatical in his encomiums on the *habeas corpus* act, which in one place he calls "the BULWARK of the British Constitution."

. . .

In our own system the Suspension Clause . . . protects the rights of the detained by a means consistent with the essential design of the Constitution. It ensures that, except during periods of formal suspension, the Judiciary will have a time-tested device, the writ, to maintain the "delicate balance of governance" that is itself the surest safeguard of liberty. [Hamdi v. Rumsfeld (2004)]. The Clause protects the rights of the detained by affirming the duty and authority of the Judiciary to call the jailer to account. The separation-of-powers doctrine, and the history that influenced its design, therefore must inform the reach and purpose of the Suspension Clause.

B

The broad historical narrative of the writ and its function is central to our analysis, but we seek guidance as well from founding-era authorities addressing the specific question before us: whether foreign nationals, apprehended and detained in distant countries during a time of serious threats to our Nation's security, may assert the privilege of the writ and seek its protection. . . . To support their arguments, the parties in these cases have examined historical sources to construct a view of the common-law writ as it existed in 1789. . . . The Government argues the common-law writ ran only to those territories over which the Crown was sovereign. Petitioners argue that jurisdiction followed the King's officers. Diligent search by all parties reveals no certain conclusions. In none of the cases cited do we find that a common-law court would or would not have granted, or refused to hear for lack of jurisdiction, a petition for a writ of habeas corpus brought by a prisoner deemed an enemy combatant, under a standard like the one the Department of Defense has used in these cases, and when held in a territory, like Guantanamo, over which the Government has total military and civil control. . . .

Each side in the present matter argues that the very lack of a precedent on point supports its position. The Government points out there is no evidence that a court sitting in England granted habeas relief to an enemy alien detained abroad; petitioners respond there is no evidence that a court refused to do so for lack of jurisdiction.

Both arguments are premised, however, upon the assumption that the historical record is complete and that the common law, if properly understood, yields a definite answer to the questions before us. There are reasons to doubt both assumptions. Recent scholarship points to the inherent shortcomings in the historical record. . . . And given the unique status of Guantanamo Bay and the particular dangers of terrorism in the modern age, the common-law courts simply may not have confronted cases with close parallels to this one. We decline, therefore, to infer too much, one way or the other, from the lack of historical evidence on point.

IV

Drawing from its position that at common law the writ ran only to territories over which the Crown was sovereign, the Government says the Suspension Clause affords petitioners no rights because the United States does not claim sovereignty over the place of detention.

Guantanamo Bay is not formally part of the United States. And under the terms of the lease between the United States and Cuba, Cuba retains "ultimate sovereignty" over the territory while the United States exercises "complete jurisdiction and control." Under the terms of the 1934 Treaty, however, Cuba effectively has no rights as a sovereign until the parties agree to modification of the 1903 Lease Agreement or the United States abandons the base.

The United States contends, nevertheless, that Guantanamo is not within its sovereign control. . . . We . . . do not question the Government's position that Cuba, not the United States, maintains sovereignty, in the legal and technical sense of the term, over Guantanamo Bay. But this does not end the analysis. Our cases do not hold it is improper for us to inquire into the objective degree of control the Nation asserts over foreign territory. . . . Accordingly, for purposes of our analysis, we accept the Government's position that Cuba, and not the United States, retains *de jure* sovereignty over Guantanamo Bay. . . . [H]owever, we take notice of the obvious and uncontested fact that the United States, by virtue of its complete jurisdiction and control over the base, maintains *de facto* sovereignty over this territory.

Were we to hold that the present cases turn on the political question doctrine, we would be required first to accept the Government's premise that *de jure* sovereignty is the touchstone of habeas corpus jurisdiction. This premise, however, is unfounded. For the reasons indicated above, the history of common-law habeas corpus provides scant support for this proposition; and, for the reasons indicated below, that position would be inconsistent with our precedents and contrary to fundamental separation-of-powers principles.

A

The Court has discussed the issue of the Constitution's extraterritorial application on many occasions. These decisions undermine the Government's argument that, at least as applied to noncitizens, the Constitution necessarily stops where *de jure* sovereignty ends.

The Framers foresaw that the United States would expand and acquire new territories. Save for a few notable (and notorious) exceptions, *e.g.*, Dred Scott v. Sandford (1857), throughout most of our history there was little need to explore the outer boundaries of the Constitution's geographic reach. When Congress exercised its power to create new territories, it guaranteed constitutional protections to the inhabitants by statute. In particular, there was no need to test the limits of the Suspension Clause because, as early as 1789, Congress extended the writ to the Territories. See Act of Aug. 7, 1789, 1 Stat. 52 (reaffirming Art. II of Northwest Ordinance of 1787, which provided that "[t]he inhabitants of the said territory, shall always be entitled to the benefits of the writ of habeas corpus").

Fundamental questions regarding the Constitution's geographic scope first arose at the dawn of the 20th century when the Nation acquired noncontiguous Territories: Puerto Rico, Guam, and the Philippines — ceded to the United States by Spain at the conclusion of the Spanish-American War — and Hawaii — annexed by the United States in 1898. At this point Congress chose to discontinue its previous practice of extending constitutional rights to the territories by statute.

In a series of opinions later known as the *Insular Cases*, the Court addressed whether the Constitution, by its own force, applies in any territory that is not a State. The Court held that the Constitution has independent force in these territories, a force not contingent upon acts of legislative grace. Yet it took note of the difficulties inherent in that position. . . . The Court thus was reluctant to risk the uncertainty and instability that could result from a rule that displaced altogether the existing legal systems in these newly acquired Territories.

These considerations resulted in the doctrine of territorial incorporation, under which the Constitution applies in full in incorporated Territories surely destined for statehood but only in part in unincorporated Territories. . . . [N]oting the inherent practical difficulties of enforcing all constitutional provisions "always and everywhere," the Court devised in the *Insular Cases* a doctrine that allowed it to use its power sparingly and where it would be most needed. This century-old doctrine informs our analysis in the present matter. . . .

Practical considerations weighed heavily as well in Johnson v. Eisentrager (1950), where the Court addressed whether habeas corpus jurisdiction extended to enemy aliens who had been convicted of violating the laws of war. The prisoners were detained at Landsberg Prison in Germany during the Allied Powers' postwar occupation. The Court stressed the difficulties of ordering the Government to produce the prisoners in a habeas corpus proceeding. It "would require allocation of shipping space, guarding personnel, billeting and rations" and would damage the prestige of military commanders at a sensitive time. In considering these factors the Court sought to balance the constraints of military occupation with constitutional necessities.

True, the Court in *Eisentrager* denied access to the writ, and it noted the prisoners "at no relevant time were within any territory over which the United States is sovereign, and [that] the scenes of their offense, their capture, their trial and their punishment were all beyond the territorial jurisdiction of any court of the United States." The Government seizes upon this language as proof positive that the *Eisentrager* Court adopted a formalistic, sovereignty-based test for determining the reach of the Suspension Clause. We reject this reading for three reasons.

First, we do not accept the idea that the above-quoted passage from *Eisentrager* is the only authoritative language in the opinion and that all the rest is dicta. The Court's further determinations, based on practical considerations, were integral to Part II of its opinion and came before the decision announced its holding.

Second, because the United States lacked both *de jure* sovereignty and plenary control over Landsberg Prison, it is far from clear that the *Eisentrager* Court used the term sovereignty only in the narrow technical sense and not to connote the degree of control the military asserted over the facility. The Justices who decided *Eisentrager* would have understood sovereignty as a multifaceted concept. See Black's Law Dictionary 1568 (4th ed. 1951) (defining "sovereignty" as "[t]he supreme, absolute, and uncontrollable power by which any independent state is governed"; "the international independence of a state, combined with the right and power of regulating its internal affairs without foreign dictation"; and "[t]he power to do everything in a state without accountability"). In its principal brief in *Eisentrager*, the Government advocated a bright-line test for determining the scope of the writ, similar to the one it advocates in these cases. Yet the Court mentioned the concept of territorial sovereignty only twice in its opinion. That the Court devoted a significant portion of Part II to a discussion of practical barriers to the running of the writ suggests that the Court was not concerned exclusively with the formal legal status of Landsberg Prison but also with the objective degree of control the United States asserted over it. Even if we assume the *Eisentrager* Court considered the United States' lack of formal legal sovereignty over Landsberg Prison as the decisive factor in that case, its holding is not inconsistent with a functional approach to questions of extraterritoriality. The formal legal status of a given territory affects, at least to some extent, the political branches' control over that territory. *De jure* sovereignty is a factor that bears upon which constitutional guarantees apply there.

Third, if the Government's reading of *Eisentrager* were correct, the opinion would have marked not only a change in, but a complete repudiation of, the *Insular Cases*' . . . functional approach to questions of extraterritoriality. We cannot accept the Government's view. Nothing in *Eisentrager* says that *de jure* sovereignty is or has ever been the only relevant consideration in determining the geographic reach of the Constitution or of habeas corpus. . . . A constricted reading of *Eisentrager* overlooks what we see as a common thread uniting the *Insular Cases* [and] *Eisentrager* . . . : the idea that questions of extraterritoriality turn on objective factors and practical concerns, not formalism.

B

The Government's formal sovereignty-based test raises troubling separation-of-powers concerns as well. The political history of Guantanamo illustrates the deficiencies of this approach. The United States has maintained complete and uninterrupted control of the bay for over 100 years. At the close of the Spanish-American War, Spain ceded control over the entire island of Cuba to the United States and specifically "relinquishe[d] all claim[s] of sovereignty . . . and title." From the date the treaty with Spain was signed until the Cuban Republic was established on May 20, 1902, the United States governed the territory "in trust" for the benefit of the Cuban people. And although it recognized, by entering into the 1903 Lease Agreement, that Cuba retained "ultimate sovereignty" over Guantanamo, the United States continued to maintain the same plenary control it had enjoyed since 1898. Yet the Government's view is that the Constitution had no effect there, at least as to noncitizens, because the United States disclaimed sovereignty in the formal sense of the term. The necessary implication of the argument is that by surrendering formal sovereignty over any unincorporated territory to a third party, while at the same time entering into a lease that grants total control over the territory back to the United States, it would be possible for the political branches to govern without legal constraint.

Our basic charter cannot be contracted away like this. The Constitution grants Congress and the President the power to acquire, dispose of, and govern territory, not the power to decide when and where its terms apply. Even when the United States acts outside its borders, its powers are not "absolute and unlimited" but are subject "to such restrictions as are expressed in the Constitution." Murphy v. Ramsey (1885). Abstaining from questions involving formal sovereignty and territorial governance is one thing. To hold the political branches have the power to switch the Constitution on or off at will is quite another. The former position reflects this Court's recognition that certain matters requiring political judgments are best left to the political branches. The latter would permit a striking anomaly in our tripartite system of government, leading to a regime in which Congress and the President, not this Court, say "what the law is." Marbury v. Madison (1803).

These concerns have particular bearing upon the Suspension Clause question in the cases now before us, for the writ of habeas corpus is itself an indispensable mechanism for monitoring the separation of powers. The test for determining the scope of this provision must not be subject to manipulation by those whose power it is designed to restrain.

C

[A]t least three factors are relevant in determining the reach of the Suspension Clause: (1) the citizenship and status of the detainee and the adequacy of the process through which that status determination was made; (2) the nature of the sites where apprehension and then detention took place; and (3) the practical obstacles inherent in resolving the prisoner's entitlement to the writ.

Applying this framework, we note at the onset that the status of these detainees is a matter of dispute. The petitioners, like those in *Eisentrager*, are not American citizens. But the petitioners in *Eisentrager* did not contest, it seems, the Court's assertion that they were "enemy alien[s]." In the instant cases, by contrast, the detainees deny they are enemy combatants. They have been afforded some process in CSRT proceedings to determine their status; but, unlike in *Eisentrager*, there has been no trial by military commission for violations of the laws of war. The difference is not trivial. The records from the *Eisentrager* trials suggest that, well before the petitioners brought their case to this Court, there had been a rigorous adversarial process to test the legality of their detention. The *Eisentrager* petitioners were charged by a bill of particulars that made detailed factual allegations against them. To rebut the accusations, they were entitled to representation by counsel, allowed to introduce evidence on their own behalf, and permitted to cross-examine the prosecution's witnesses.

In comparison the procedural protections afforded to the detainees in the CSRT hearings are far more limited, and, we conclude, fall well short of the procedures and adversarial mechanisms that would eliminate the need for habeas corpus review. Although the detainee is assigned a "Personal Representative" to assist him during CSRT proceedings, the Secretary of the Navy's memorandum makes clear that person is not the detainee's lawyer or even his "advocate." The Government's evidence is accorded a presumption of validity. The detainee is allowed to present "reasonably available" evidence, but his ability to rebut the Government's evidence against him is limited by the circumstances of his confinement and his lack of counsel at this stage. And although the detainee can seek review of his status determination in the Court of Appeals, that review process cannot cure all defects in the earlier proceedings.

As to the second factor relevant to this analysis, the detainees here are similarly situated to the *Eisentrager* petitioners in that the sites of their apprehension and detention are technically outside the sovereign territory of the United States. As noted earlier, this is a factor that weighs against finding they have rights under the Suspension Clause. But there are critical differences between Landsberg Prison, circa 1950, and the United States Naval Station at Guantanamo Bay in 2008. Unlike its present control over the naval station, the United States' control over the prison in Germany was neither absolute nor indefinite. Like all parts of occupied Germany, the prison was under the jurisdiction of the combined Allied Forces. The United States was therefore answerable to its Allies for all activities occurring there. The Allies had not planned a long-term occupation of Germany, nor did they intend to displace all German institutions even during the period of occupation. The Court's holding in *Eisentrager* was thus consistent with the *Insular Cases*, where it had held there was no need to extend full constitutional protections to territories the United States did not intend to govern indefinitely. Guantanamo Bay, on the other hand, is no transient possession. In every practical sense Guantanamo is not abroad; it is within the constant jurisdiction of the United States.

As to the third factor, we recognize, as the Court did in *Eisentrager*, that there are costs to holding the Suspension Clause applicable in a case of military detention abroad. Habeas corpus proceedings may require expenditure of funds by the Government and may divert the attention of military personnel from other pressing tasks. While we are sensitive to these concerns, we do not find them dispositive. Compliance with any judicial process requires some incremental expenditure of resources. Yet civilian courts and the Armed Forces have functioned along side each other at various points in our history. The Government presents no credible arguments that the military mission at Guantanamo would be compromised if habeas corpus courts had jurisdiction to hear the detainees' claims. And in light of the plenary control the United States asserts over the base, none are apparent to us.

The situation in *Eisentrager* was far different, given the historical context and nature of the military's mission in post-War Germany. When hostilities in the European Theater came to an end, the United States became responsible for an occupation zone encompassing over 57,000 square miles with a population of 18 million. In addition to supervising massive reconstruction and aid efforts the American forces stationed in Germany faced potential security threats from a defeated enemy. In retrospect the post-War occupation may seem uneventful. But at the time *Eisentrager* was decided, the Court was right to be concerned about judicial interference with the military's efforts to contain "enemy elements, guerilla fighters, and 'were-wolves.'"

Similar threats are not apparent here; nor does the Government argue that they are. The United States Naval Station at Guantanamo Bay consists of 45 square miles of land and water. The base has been used, at various points, to house migrants and refugees temporarily. At present, however, other than the detainees themselves, the only long-term residents are American military personnel, their families, and a small number of workers. The detainees have been deemed enemies of the United States. At present, dangerous as they may be if released, they are contained in a secure prison facility located on an isolated and heavily fortified military base. . . .

It is true that before today the Court has never held that noncitizens detained by our Government in territory over which another country maintains *de jure* sovereignty have any rights under our Constitution. But the cases before us lack any precise historical parallel. They involve individuals detained by executive order for the duration of a conflict that, if measured from September 11, 2001, to the present, is already among the longest wars in American history. The detainees, moreover, are held in a territory that, while technically not part of the United States, is under the complete and total control of our Government. Under these circumstances the lack of a precedent on point is no barrier to our holding.

We hold that Art. I, §9, cl. 2, of the Constitution has full effect at Guantanamo Bay. If the privilege of habeas corpus is to be denied to the detainees now before us, Congress must act in accordance with the requirements of the Suspension Clause. This Court may not impose a *de facto* suspension by abstaining from these controversies. The MCA does not purport to be a formal suspension of the writ; and the Government, in its submissions to us, has not argued that it is. Petitioners, therefore, are entitled to the privilege of habeas corpus to challenge the legality of their detention.

V

In light of this holding the question becomes whether the statute stripping jurisdiction to issue the writ avoids the Suspension Clause mandate because Congress has provided adequate substitute procedures for habeas corpus. . . . We do not endeavor to offer a comprehensive summary of the requisites for an adequate substitute for habeas corpus. We do consider it uncontroversial, however, that the privilege of habeas corpus entitles the prisoner to a meaningful opportunity to demonstrate that he is being held pursuant to "the erroneous application or interpretation" of relevant law. And the habeas court must have the power to order the conditional release of an individual unlawfully detained — though release need not be the exclusive remedy and is not the appropriate one in every case in which the writ is granted. These are the easily identified attributes of any constitutionally adequate habeas corpus proceeding. But, depending on the circumstances, more may be required. . . . What matters is the sum total of procedural protections afforded to the detainee at all stages, direct and collateral.

Petitioners identify what they see as myriad deficiencies in the CSRTs. The most relevant for our purposes are the constraints upon the detainee's ability to rebut the factual basis for the Government's assertion that he is an enemy combatant. As already noted, at the CSRT stage the detainee has limited means to find or present evidence to challenge the Government's case against him. He does not have the assistance of counsel and may not be aware of the most critical allegations that the

Government relied upon to order his detention. The detainee can confront witnesses that testify during the CSRT proceedings. But given that there are in effect no limits on the admission of hearsay evidence — the only requirement is that the tribunal deem the evidence "relevant and helpful," — the detainee's opportunity to question witnesses is likely to be more theoretical than real. . . .

[W]e agree with petitioners that, even when all the parties involved in this process act with diligence and in good faith, there is considerable risk of error in the tribunal's findings of fact. This is a risk inherent in any process that, in the words of the former Chief Judge of the Court of Appeals, is "closed and accusatorial." And given that the consequence of error may be detention of persons for the duration of hostilities that may last a generation or more, this is a risk too significant to ignore.

For the writ of habeas corpus, or its substitute, to function as an effective and proper remedy in this context, the court that conducts the habeas proceeding must have the means to correct errors that occurred during the CSRT proceedings. This includes some authority to assess the sufficiency of the Government's evidence against the detainee. It also must have the authority to admit and consider relevant exculpatory evidence that was not introduced during the earlier proceeding. Federal habeas petitioners long have had the means to supplement the record on review, even in the postconviction habeas setting. Here that opportunity is constitutionally required. . . .

The extent of the showing required of the Government in these cases is a matter to be determined. We need not explore it further at this stage. We do hold that when the judicial power to issue habeas corpus properly is invoked the judicial officer must have adequate authority to make a determination in light of the relevant law and facts and to formulate and issue appropriate orders for relief, including, if necessary, an order directing the prisoner's release.

C

We now consider whether the DTA allows the Court of Appeals to conduct a proceeding meeting these standards. . . .

Assuming the DTA can be construed to allow the Court of Appeals to review or correct the CSRT's factual determinations, as opposed to merely certifying that the tribunal applied the correct standard of proof, we see no way to construe the statute to allow what is also constitutionally required in this context: an opportunity for the detainee to present relevant exculpatory evidence that was not made part of the record in the earlier proceedings. . . .

We do not imply DTA review would be a constitutionally sufficient replacement for habeas corpus but for these limitations on the detainee's ability to present exculpatory evidence. For even if it were possible, as a textual matter, to read into the statute each of the necessary procedures we have identified, we could not overlook the cumulative effect of our doing so. To hold that the detainees at Guantanamo may, under the DTA, challenge the President's legal authority to detain them, contest the CSRT's findings of fact, supplement the record on review with exculpatory evidence, and request an order of release would come close to reinstating the §2241 habeas corpus process Congress sought to deny them. The language of the statute, read in light of Congress' reasons for enacting it, cannot bear this interpretation. Petitioners have met their burden of establishing that the DTA review process is, on its face, an inadequate substitute for habeas corpus. . . .

VI

In light of our conclusion that there is no jurisdictional bar to the District Court's entertaining petitioners' claims the question remains whether there are prudential barriers to habeas corpus review under these circumstances. . . . The real risks, the real threats, of terrorist attacks are constant and not likely soon to abate. The ways to disrupt our life and laws are so many and unforeseen that the Court should not attempt even some general catalogue of crises that might occur. Certain principles are apparent, however. Practical considerations and exigent circumstances inform the definition and reach of the law's writs, including habeas corpus. The cases and our tradition reflect this precept.

In cases involving foreign citizens detained abroad by the Executive, it likely would be both an impractical and unprecedented extension of judicial power to assume that habeas corpus would be available at the moment the prisoner is taken into custody. If and when habeas corpus jurisdiction applies, as it does in these cases, then proper deference can be accorded to reasonable procedures for screening and initial detention under lawful and proper conditions of confinement and treatment for a reasonable period of time. Domestic exigencies, furthermore, might also impose such onerous burdens on the Government that here, too, the Judicial Branch would be required to devise sensible rules for staying habeas corpus proceedings until the Government can comply with its requirements in a responsible way. Here, as is true with detainees apprehended abroad, a relevant consideration in determining the courts' role is whether there are suitable alternative processes in place to protect against the arbitrary exercise of governmental power.

The cases before us, however, do not involve detainees who have been held for a short period of time while awaiting their CSRT determinations. . . . In some of these cases six years have elapsed without the judicial oversight that habeas corpus or an adequate substitute demands. And there has been no showing that the Executive faces such onerous burdens that it cannot respond to habeas corpus actions. To require these detainees to complete DTA review before proceeding with their habeas corpus actions would be to require additional months, if not years, of delay. . . . While some delay in fashioning new procedures is unavoidable, the costs of delay can no longer be borne by those who are held in custody. The detainees in these cases are entitled to a prompt habeas corpus hearing.

Our decision today holds only that the petitioners before us are entitled to seek the writ; that the DTA review procedures are an inadequate substitute for habeas corpus; and that the petitioners in these cases need not exhaust the review procedures in the Court of Appeals before proceeding with their habeas actions in the District Court. . . . Accordingly, both the DTA and the CSRT process remain intact. Our holding with regard to exhaustion should not be read to imply that a habeas court should intervene the moment an enemy combatant steps foot in a territory where the writ runs. The Executive is entitled to a reasonable period of time to determine a detainee's status before a court entertains that detainee's habeas corpus petition. The CSRT process is the mechanism Congress and the President set up to deal with these issues. Except in cases of undue delay, federal courts should refrain from entertaining an enemy combatant's habeas corpus petition at least until after the Department, acting via the CSRT, has had a chance to review his status. . . .

***

In considering both the procedural and substantive standards used to impose detention to prevent acts of terrorism, proper deference must be accorded to the political branches. See United States v. Curtiss-Wright Export Corp. (1936). Unlike the President and some designated Members of Congress, neither the Members of this Court nor most federal judges begin the day with briefings that may describe new and serious threats to our Nation and its people. The law must accord the Executive substantial authority to apprehend and detain those who pose a real danger to our security.

Officials charged with daily operational responsibility for our security may consider a judicial discourse on the history of the Habeas Corpus Act of 1679 and like matters to be far removed from the Nation's present, urgent concerns. Established legal doctrine, however, must be consulted for its teaching. Remote in time it may be; irrelevant to the present it is not. Security depends upon a sophisticated intelligence apparatus and the ability of our Armed Forces to act and to interdict. There are further considerations, however. Security subsists, too, in fidelity to freedom's first principles. Chief among these are freedom from arbitrary and unlawful restraint and the personal liberty that is secured by adherence to the separation of powers. It is from these principles that the judicial authority to consider petitions for habeas corpus relief derives.

Our opinion does not undermine the Executive's powers as Commander in Chief. On the contrary, the exercise of those powers is vindicated, not eroded, when confirmed by the Judicial Branch. Within the Constitution's separation-of-powers structure, few exercises of judicial power are as legitimate or as necessary as the responsibility to hear challenges to the authority of the Executive to imprison a person. Some of these petitioners have been in custody for six years with no definitive judicial determination as to the legality of their detention. Their access to the writ is a necessity to determine the lawfulness of their status, even if, in the end, they do not obtain the relief they seek.

Because our Nation's past military conflicts have been of limited duration, it has been possible to leave the outer boundaries of war powers undefined. If, as some fear, terrorism continues to pose dangerous threats to us for years to come, the Court might not have this luxury. This result is not inevitable, however. The political branches, consistent with their independent obligations to interpret and uphold the Constitution, can engage in a genuine debate about how best to preserve constitutional values while protecting the Nation from terrorism.

It bears repeating that our opinion does not address the content of the law that governs petitioners' detention. That is a matter yet to be determined. We hold that petitioners may invoke the fundamental procedural protections of habeas corpus. The laws and Constitution are designed to survive, and remain in force, in extraordinary times. Liberty and security can be reconciled; and in our system they are reconciled within the framework of the law. The Framers decided that habeas corpus, a right of first importance, must be a part of that framework, a part of that law.

The determination by the Court of Appeals that the Suspension Clause and its protections are inapplicable to petitioners was in error. The judgment of the Court of Appeals is reversed. The cases are remanded to the Court of Appeals with instructions that it remand the cases to the District Court for proceedings consistent with this opinion.

It is so ordered.

CHIEF JUSTICE ROBERTS, with whom JUSTICE SCALIA, JUSTICE THOMAS, and JUSTICE ALITO join, dissenting.

Today the Court strikes down as inadequate the most generous set of procedural protections ever afforded aliens detained by this country as enemy combatants. The political branches crafted these procedures amidst an ongoing military conflict, after much careful investigation and thorough debate. The Court rejects them today out of hand, without bothering to say what due process rights the detainees possess, without explaining how the statute fails to vindicate those rights, and before a single petitioner has even attempted to avail himself of the law's operation. And to what effect? The majority merely replaces a review system designed by the people's representatives with a set of shapeless procedures to be defined by federal courts at some future date. One cannot help but think, after surveying the modest practical results of the majority's ambitious opinion, that this decision is not really about the detainees at all, but about control of federal policy regarding enemy combatants.

The majority is adamant that the Guantanamo detainees are entitled to the protections of habeas corpus—its opinion begins by deciding that question. I regard the issue as a difficult one, primarily because of the unique and unusual jurisdictional status of Guantanamo Bay. I nonetheless agree with JUSTICE SCALIA'S analysis of our precedents and the pertinent history of the writ, and accordingly join his dissent. The important point for me, however, is that the Court should have resolved these cases on other grounds. Habeas is most fundamentally a procedural right, a mechanism for contesting the legality of executive detention. The critical threshold question in these cases, prior to any inquiry about the writ's scope, is whether the system the political branches designed protects whatever rights the detainees may possess. If so, there is no need for any additional process, whether called "habeas" or something else.

Congress entrusted that threshold question in the first instance to the Court of Appeals for the District of Columbia Circuit, as the Constitution surely allows Congress to do. But before the D. C. Circuit has addressed the issue, the Court cashiers the statute, and without answering this critical threshold question itself. The Court does eventually get around to asking whether review under the DTA is, as the Court frames it, an "adequate substitute" for habeas, but even then its opinion fails to determine what rights the detainees possess and whether the DTA system satisfies them. The majority instead compares the undefined DTA process to an equally undefined habeas right—one that is to be given shape only in the future by district courts on a case-by-case basis. This whole approach is misguided.

It is also fruitless. How the detainees' claims will be decided now that the DTA is gone is anybody's guess. But the habeas process the Court mandates will most likely end up looking a lot like the DTA system it replaces, as the district court judges shaping it will have to reconcile review of the prisoners' detention with the undoubted need to protect the American people from the terrorist threat—precisely the challenge Congress undertook in drafting the DTA. All that today's opinion has done is shift responsibility for those sensitive foreign policy and national security decisions from the elected branches to the Federal Judiciary.

I believe the system the political branches constructed adequately protects any constitutional rights aliens captured abroad and detained as enemy combatants may enjoy. I therefore would dismiss these cases on that ground. With all respect for the contrary views of the majority, I must dissent. . . .

The majority's overreaching is particularly egregious given the weakness of its objections to the DTA. Simply put, the Court's opinion fails on its own terms. The majority strikes down the statute because it is not an "adequate substitute" for habeas review, but fails to show what rights the detainees have that cannot be vindicated by the DTA system.

Because the central purpose of habeas corpus is to test the legality of executive detention, the writ requires most fundamentally an Article III court able to hear the prisoner's claims and, when necessary, order release. Beyond that, the process a given prisoner is entitled to receive depends on the circumstances and the rights of the prisoner. After much hemming and hawing, the majority appears to concede that the DTA provides an Article III court competent to order release. The only issue in dispute is the process the Guantanamo prisoners are entitled to use to test the legality of their detention. *Hamdi* concluded that American citizens detained as enemy combatants are entitled to only limited process, and that much of that process could be supplied by a military tribunal, with review to follow in an Article III court. That is precisely the system we have here. It is adequate to vindicate whatever due process rights petitioners may have. . . .

The use of a military tribunal such as the CSRTs to review the aliens' detention should be familiar to this Court in light of the *Hamdi* plurality, which said that the due process rights enjoyed by American citizens detained as enemy combatants could be vindicated "by an appropriately authorized and properly constituted military tribunal." The DTA represents Congress' considered attempt to provide the accused alien combatants detained at Guantanamo a constitutionally adequate opportunity to contest their detentions before just such a tribunal.

But Congress went further in the DTA. CSRT review is just the first tier of collateral review in the DTA system. The statute provides additional review in an Article III court. Given the rationale of today's decision, it is well worth recalling exactly what the DTA provides in this respect. The statute directs the D. C. Circuit to consider whether a particular alien's status determination "was consistent with the standards and procedures specified by the Secretary of Defense" *and* "whether the use of such standards and procedures to make the determination is consistent with the Constitution and laws of the United States." That is, a *court* determines whether the CSRT procedures are constitutional, and a *court* determines whether those procedures were followed in a particular case.

In short, the *Hamdi* plurality concluded that this type of review would be enough to satisfy due process, even for citizens. Congress followed the Court's lead, only to find itself the victim of a constitutional bait and switch. . . .

Declaring that petitioners have a right to habeas in no way excuses the Court from explaining why the DTA does not protect whatever due process or statutory rights petitioners may have. Because if the DTA provides a means for vindicating petitioners' rights, it is necessarily an adequate substitute for habeas corpus. . . . Today's Court opines that the Suspension Clause guarantees prisoners such as the detainees "a meaningful opportunity to demonstrate that [they are] being held pursuant to the erroneous application or interpretation of relevant law." Further, the Court holds that to be an adequate substitute, any tribunal reviewing the detainees' cases "must have the power to order the conditional release of an individual unlawfully detained." The DTA system — CSRT review of the Executive's determination followed by D.C. Circuit review for sufficiency of the evidence and the constitutionality of the CSRT process — meets these criteria.

At the CSRT stage, every petitioner has the right to present evidence that he has been wrongfully detained. This includes the right to call witnesses who are reasonably available, question witnesses called by the tribunal, introduce documentary evidence, and testify before the tribunal.

While the Court concedes detainees may confront all witnesses called before the tribunal, it suggests this right is "more theoretical than real" because "there are in effect no limits on the admission of hearsay evidence." The Court further complains that petitioners lack "the assistance of counsel," and — given the limits on their access to classified information — "may not be aware of the most critical allegations" against them. None of these complaints is persuasive.

Detainees not only have the opportunity to confront any witness who appears before the tribunal, they may call witnesses of their own. The Implementation Memo requires only that detainees' witnesses be "reasonably available," a requirement entirely consistent with the Government's interest in avoiding "a futile search for evidence" that might burden warmaking responsibilities. The dangerous mission assigned to our forces abroad is to fight terrorists, not serve subpoenas. The Court is correct that some forms of hearsay evidence are admissible before the CSRT, but *Hamdi* expressly approved this use of hearsay by habeas courts. ("Hearsay, for example, may need to be accepted as the most reliable available evidence from the Government").

As to classified information, while detainees are not permitted access to it themselves, the Implementation Memo provides each detainee with a "Personal Representative" who may review classified documents at the CSRT stage and summarize them for the detainee. The prisoner's counsel enjoys the same privilege on appeal before the D.C. Circuit. That is more access to classified material for alleged alien enemy combatants than ever before provided. I am not aware of a single instance — and certainly the majority cites none — in which detainees such as petitioners have been provided access to classified material in *any* form. Indeed, prisoners of war who challenge their status determinations under the Geneva Convention are afforded no such access, and the prisoner-of-war model is the one *Hamdi* cited as consistent with the demands of due process for *citizens.*

What alternative does the Court propose? Allow free access to classified information and ignore the risk the prisoner may eventually convey what he learns to parties hostile to this country, with deadly consequences for those who helped apprehend the detainee? If the Court can design a better system for communicating to detainees the substance of any classified information relevant to their cases, without fatally compromising national security interests and sources, the majority should come forward with it. Instead, the majority fobs that vexing question off on district courts to answer down the road. . . .

Keep in mind that all this is just at the CSRT stage. Detainees receive additional process before the D. C. Circuit, including full access to appellate counsel and the right to challenge the factual and legal bases of their detentions. . . . These provisions permit detainees to dispute the sufficiency of the evidence against them. They allow detainees to challenge a CSRT panel's interpretation of any relevant law, and even the constitutionality of the CSRT proceedings themselves. This includes, as the Solicitor General acknowledges, the ability to dispute the Government's right to detain alleged combatants in the first place, and to dispute the Government's definition of "enemy combatant." All this before an Article III court — plainly a neutral decisionmaker.

All told, the DTA provides the prisoners held at Guantanamo Bay adequate opportunity to contest the bases of their detentions, which is all habeas corpus need allow. The DTA provides more opportunity and more process, in fact, than that afforded prisoners of war or any other alleged enemy combatants in history. . . .

The majority rests its decision on abstract and hypothetical concerns. Step back and consider what, in the real world, Congress and the Executive have actually granted aliens captured by our Armed Forces overseas and found to be enemy combatants:

- The right to hear the bases of the charges against them, including a summary of any classified evidence.

- The ability to challenge the bases of their detention before military tribunals modeled after Geneva Convention procedures. Some 38 detainees have been released as a result of this process.
- The right, before the CSRT, to testify, introduce evidence, call witnesses, question those the Government calls, and secure release, if and when appropriate.
- The right to the aid of a personal representative in arranging and presenting their cases before a CSRT.
- Before the D.C. Circuit, the right to employ counsel, challenge the factual record, contest the lower tribunal's legal determinations, ensure compliance with the Constitution and laws, and secure release, if any errors below establish their entitlement to such relief.

In sum, the DTA satisfies the majority's own criteria for assessing adequacy. This statutory scheme provides the combatants held at Guantanamo greater procedural protections than have ever been afforded alleged enemy detainees — whether citizens or aliens — in our national history.

***

So who has won? Not the detainees. The Court's analysis leaves them with only the prospect of further litigation to determine the content of their new habeas right, followed by further litigation to resolve their particular cases, followed by further litigation before the D.C. Circuit — where they could have started had they invoked the DTA procedure. Not Congress, whose attempt to "determine — through democratic means — how best" to balance the security of the American people with the detainees' liberty interests, see Hamdan v. Rumsfeld (2006) (BREYER, J., concurring), has been unceremoniously brushed aside. Not the Great Writ, whose majesty is hardly enhanced by its extension to a jurisdictionally quirky outpost, with no tangible benefit to anyone. Not the rule of law, unless by that is meant the rule of lawyers, who will now arguably have a greater role than military and intelligence officials in shaping policy for alien enemy combatants. And certainly not the American people, who today lose a bit more control over the conduct of this Nation's foreign policy to unelected, politically unaccountable judges.

I respectfully dissent.

JUSTICE SCALIA, with whom THE CHIEF JUSTICE, JUSTICE THOMAS, and JUSTICE ALITO join, dissenting.

Today, for the first time in our Nation's history, the Court confers a constitutional right to habeas corpus on alien enemies detained abroad by our military forces in the course of an ongoing war. The CHIEF JUSTICE'S dissent, which I join, shows that the procedures prescribed by Congress in the Detainee Treatment Act provide the essential protections that habeas corpus guarantees; there has thus been no suspension of the writ, and no basis exists for judicial intervention beyond what the Act allows. My problem with today's opinion is more fundamental still: The writ of habeas corpus does not, and never has, run in favor of aliens abroad; the Suspension Clause thus has no application, and the Court's intervention in this military matter is entirely *ultra vires.*

I shall devote most of what will be a lengthy opinion to the legal errors contained in the opinion of the Court. Contrary to my usual practice, however, I think it appropriate to begin with a description of the disastrous consequences of what the Court has done today.

I

America is at war with radical Islamists. The enemy began by killing Americans and American allies abroad: 241 at the Marine barracks in Lebanon, 19 at the Khobar Towers in Dhahran, 224 at our embassies in Dar es Salaam and Nairobi, and 17 on the USS Cole in Yemen. On September 11, 2001, the enemy brought the battle to American soil, killing 2,749 at the Twin Towers in New York City, 184 at the Pentagon in Washington, D.C., and 40 in Pennsylvania. It has threatened further attacks against our homeland; one need only walk about buttressed and barricaded Washington, or board a plane anywhere in the country, to know that the threat is a serious one. Our Armed Forces are now in the field against the enemy, in Afghanistan and Iraq. Last week, 13 of our countrymen in arms were killed.

The game of bait-and-switch that today's opinion plays upon the Nation's Commander in Chief will make the war harder on us. It will almost certainly cause more Americans to be killed. That consequence would be tolerable if necessary to preserve a time-honored legal principle vital to our constitutional Republic. But it is this Court's blatant *abandonment* of such a principle that produces the decision today. The President relied on our settled precedent in Johnson v. Eisentrager, (1950), when he established the prison at Guantanamo Bay for enemy aliens. Citing that case, the President's Office of Legal Counsel advised him "that the great weight of legal authority indicates that a federal district court could not properly exercise habeas jurisdiction over an alien detained at [Guantanamo Bay]." Memorandum from Patrick F. Philbin and John C. Yoo, Deputy Assistant Attorneys General, Office of Legal Counsel, to William J. Haynes II, General Counsel, Dept. of Defense (Dec. 28, 2001). Had the law been otherwise, the military surely would not have transported prisoners there, but would have kept them in Afghanistan, transferred them to another of our foreign military bases, or turned them over to allies for detention. Those other facilities might well have been worse for the detainees themselves.

In the long term, then, the Court's decision today accomplishes little, except perhaps to reduce the well-being of enemy combatants that the Court ostensibly seeks to protect. In the short term, however, the decision is devastating. At least 30 of those prisoners hitherto released from Guantanamo Bay have returned to the battlefield. But others have succeeded in carrying on their atrocities against innocent civilians. In one case, a detainee released from Guantanamo Bay masterminded the kidnapping of two Chinese dam workers, one of whom was later shot to death when used as a human shield against Pakistani commandoes. Another former detainee promptly resumed his post as a senior Taliban commander and murdered a United Nations engineer and three Afghan soldiers. Still another murdered an Afghan judge. It was reported only last month that a released detainee carried out a suicide bombing against Iraqi soldiers in Mosul, Iraq.

These, mind you, were detainees whom the *military* had concluded were not enemy combatants. Their return to the kill illustrates the incredible difficulty of assessing who is and who is not an enemy combatant in a foreign theater of operations where the environment does not lend itself to rigorous evidence collection. Astoundingly, the Court today raises the bar, requiring military officials to appear before civilian courts and defend their decisions under procedural and evidentiary rules that go beyond what Congress has specified. As The Chief Justice's dissent makes clear, we have no idea what those procedural and evidentiary rules are, but they will be determined by civil courts and (in the Court's contemplation at least) will be more detainee-friendly than those now applied, since otherwise there would be no reason to hold the congressionally prescribed procedures unconstitutional. If they impose a higher standard of proof (from foreign battlefields) than the current procedures require, the number of the enemy returned to combat will obviously increase.

But even when the military has evidence that it can bring forward, it is often foolhardy to release that evidence to the attorneys representing our enemies. And one escalation of procedures that the Court is clear about is affording the detainees increased access to witnesses (perhaps troops serving in Afghanistan?) and to classified information. During the 1995 prosecution of Omar Abdel Rahman, federal prosecutors gave the names of 200 unindicted co-conspirators to the "Blind Sheik's" defense lawyers; that information was in the hands of Osama Bin Laden within two weeks. In another case, trial testimony revealed to the enemy that the United States had been monitoring their cellular network, whereupon they promptly stopped using it, enabling more of them to evade capture and continue their atrocities.

And today it is not just the military that the Court elbows aside. A mere two Terms ago in Hamdan v. Rumsfeld (2006), when the Court held (quite amazingly) that the Detainee Treatment Act of 2005 had not stripped habeas jurisdiction over Guantanamo petitioners' claims, four Members of today's five-Justice majority joined an opinion saying the following:

> Nothing prevents the President from returning to Congress to seek the authority [for trial by military commission] he believes necessary.
>
> Where, as here, no emergency prevents consultation with Congress, judicial insistence upon that consultation does not weaken our Nation's ability to deal with danger. To the contrary, that insistence strengthens the Nation's ability to determine — through democratic means — how best to do so. The Constitution places its faith in those democratic means. (Breyer, J., concurring).

Turns out they were just kidding. For in response, Congress, at the President's request, quickly enacted the Military Commissions Act, emphatically reasserting that it did not want these prisoners filing habeas petitions. It is therefore clear that

Congress and the Executive—*both* political branches—have determined that limiting the role of civilian courts in adjudicating whether prisoners captured abroad are properly detained is important to success in the war that some 190,000 of our men and women are now fighting. As the Solicitor General argued, "the Military Commissions Act and the Detainee Treatment Act . . . represent an effort by the political branches to strike an appropriate balance between the need to preserve liberty and the need to accommodate the weighty and sensitive governmental interests in ensuring that those who have in fact fought with the enemy during a war do not return to battle against the United States."

But it does not matter. The Court today decrees that no good reason to accept the judgment of the other two branches is "apparent." "The Government," it declares, "presents no credible arguments that the military mission at Guantanamo would be compromised if habeas corpus courts had jurisdiction to hear the detainees' claims." What competence does the Court have to second-guess the judgment of Congress and the President on such a point? None whatever. But the Court blunders in nonetheless. Henceforth, as today's opinion makes unnervingly clear, how to handle enemy prisoners in this war will ultimately lie with the branch that knows least about the national security concerns that the subject entails.

II

. . . The Court purports to derive from our precedents a "functional" test for the extraterritorial reach of the writ, which shows that the Military Commissions Act unconstitutionally restricts the scope of habeas. That is remarkable because the most pertinent of those precedents, Johnson v. Eisentrager conclusively establishes the opposite. There we were confronted with the claims of 21 Germans held at Landsberg Prison, an American military facility located in the American Zone of occupation in postwar Germany. They had been captured in China, and an American military commission sitting there had convicted them of war crimes—collaborating with the Japanese after Germany's surrender. Like the petitioners here, the Germans claimed that their detentions violated the Constitution and international law, and sought a writ of habeas corpus. Writing for the Court, Justice Jackson held that American courts lacked habeas jurisdiction:

> We are cited to [*sic*] no instance where a court, in this or any other country where the writ is known, has issued it on behalf of an alien enemy who, at no relevant time and in no stage of his captivity, has been within its territorial jurisdiction. Nothing in the text of the Constitution extends such a right, nor does anything in our statutes.

Justice Jackson then elaborated on the historical scope of the writ:

> The alien, to whom the United States has been traditionally hospitable, has been accorded a generous and ascending scale of rights as he increases his identity with our society. . . .

> But, in extending constitutional protections beyond the citizenry, the Court has been at pains to point out that it was the alien's presence within its territorial jurisdiction that gave the Judiciary power to act.

. . . *Eisentrager* thus held—*held* beyond any doubt—that the Constitution does not ensure habeas for aliens held by the United States in areas over which our Government is not sovereign.

The Court would have us believe that *Eisentrager* rested on "[p]ractical considerations," such as the "difficulties of ordering the Government to produce the prisoners in a habeas corpus proceeding." Formal sovereignty, says the Court, is merely one consideration "that bears upon which constitutional guarantees apply" in a given location. This is a sheer rewriting of the case. *Eisentrager* mentioned practical concerns, to be sure—but not for the purpose of determining *under what circumstances* American courts could issue writs of habeas corpus for aliens abroad. It cited them to support *its holding* that the Constitution does not empower courts to issue writs of habeas corpus to aliens abroad *in any circumstances*. . . .

The Court also tries to change *Eisentrager* into a "functional" test by quoting a paragraph that lists the characteristics of the German petitioners:

> "To support [the] assumption [of a constitutional right to habeas corpus] we must hold that a prisoner of our military authorities is constitutionally entitled to the writ, even though he (a) is an enemy alien; (b) has never been or resided in the United States; (c) was captured outside of our territory and there held in military custody as a prisoner of war; (d) was tried and convicted by a Military Commission sitting outside the United States; (e) for offenses against laws of war committed outside the United States; (f) and is at all times imprisoned outside the United States."

But that paragraph is introduced by a sentence stating that "[t]he foregoing demonstrates *how much further* we must go if we are to invest these enemy aliens, resident, captured and imprisoned abroad, with standing to demand access to our courts." 339 U. S., at 777 (emphasis added). How much further than *what*? Further than the rule set forth in the prior section of the opinion, which said that "in extending constitutional protections beyond the citizenry, the Court has been at pains to point out that it was the alien's presence within its territorial jurisdiction that gave the Judiciary power to act." In other words, the characteristics of the German prisoners were set forth, not in application of some "functional" test, but to show that the case before the Court represented an *a fortiori* application of the ordinary rule. That is reaffirmed by the sentences that immediately follow the listing of the Germans' characteristics:

> We have pointed out that the privilege of litigation has been extended to aliens, whether friendly or enemy, only because permitting their presence in the country implied protection. No such basis can be invoked here, for these prisoners at no relevant time were within any territory over which the United States is sovereign, and the scenes of their offense, their capture, their trial and their punishment were all beyond the territorial jurisdiction of any court of the United States.

Eisentrager nowhere mentions a "functional" test, and the notion that it is based upon such a principle is patently false. . . .

The Court tries to reconcile Eisentrager with its holding today by pointing out that in postwar Germany, the United States was "answerable to its Allies" and did not "pla[n] a long-term occupation." Those factors were not mentioned in *Eisentrager.* Worse still, it is impossible to see how they relate to the Court's asserted purpose in creating this "functional" test—namely, to ensure a judicial inquiry into detention and prevent the political branches from acting with impunity. Can it possibly be that the Court trusts the political branches more when they are beholden to foreign powers than when they act alone?

After transforming the *a fortiori* elements discussed above into a "functional" test, the Court is still left with the difficulty that most of those elements exist here as well with regard to all the detainees. To make the application of the newly crafted "functional" test produce a different result in the present cases, the Court must rely upon factors (d) and (e): The Germans had been tried by a military commission for violations of the laws of war; the present petitioners, by contrast, have been tried by a Combatant Status Review Tribunal (CSRT) whose procedural protections, according to the Court's *ipse dixit,* "fall well short of the procedures and adversarial mechanisms that would eliminate the need for habeas corpus review." But no one looking for "functional" equivalents would put *Eisentrager* and the present cases in the same category, much less place the present cases in a preferred category. The difference between them cries out for lesser procedures in the present cases. The prisoners in *Eisentrager* were *prosecuted* for crimes after the cessation of hostilities; the prisoners here are enemy combatants *detained* during an ongoing conflict. See Hamdi v. Rumsfeld (plurality opinion) (suggesting, as an adequate substitute for habeas corpus, the use of a tribunal akin to a CSRT to authorize the detention of American citizens as enemy combatants during the course of the present conflict).

The category of prisoner comparable to these detainees are not the *Eisentrager* criminal defendants, but the more than 400,000 prisoners of war detained in the United States alone during World War II. Not a single one was accorded the right to have his detention validated by a habeas corpus action in federal court—and that despite the fact that they were present on U.S. soil. . . .

By blatantly distorting *Eisentrager,* the Court avoids the difficulty of explaining why it should be overruled. See Planned Parenthood of Southeastern Pa. v. Casey (1992) (identifying *stare decisis* factors). The rule that aliens abroad are not constitutionally entitled to habeas corpus has not proved unworkable in practice; if anything, it is the Court's "functional" test that does not (and never will) provide clear guidance for the future. *Eisentrager* forms a coherent whole with the accepted proposition that aliens abroad have no substantive rights under our Constitution. Since it was announced, no relevant factual premises have changed. It has engendered considerable reliance on the part of our military. And, as the Court acknowledges, text and history do not clearly compel a contrary ruling. It is a sad day for the rule of law when such an important constitutional precedent is discarded without an apologia, much less an apology. . . .

III

Putting aside the conclusive precedent of *Eisentrager*, it is clear that the original understanding of the Suspension Clause was that habeas corpus was not available to aliens abroad. . . .

The Suspension Clause reads: "The Privilege of the Writ of Habeas Corpus shall not be suspended, unless when in Cases of Rebellion or Invasion the public Safety may require it." U. S. Const., Art. I, §9, cl. 2. The proper course of constitutional interpretation is to give the text the meaning it was understood to have at the time of its adoption by the people. That course is especially demanded when (as here) the Constitution limits the power of Congress to infringe upon a pre-existing common-law right. The nature of the writ of habeas corpus that cannot be suspended must be defined by the common-law writ that was available at the time of the founding. . . .

[A]ll available historical evidence points to the conclusion that the writ would not have been available at common law for aliens captured and held outside the sovereign territory of the Crown. Despite three opening briefs, three reply briefs, and support from a legion of *amici*, petitioners have failed to identify a single case in the history of Anglo-American law that supports their claim to jurisdiction. The Court finds it significant that there is no recorded case *denying* jurisdiction to such prisoners either. But a case standing for the remarkable proposition that the writ could issue to a foreign land would surely have been reported, whereas a case denying such a writ for lack of jurisdiction would likely not. At a minimum, the absence of a reported case either way leaves unrefuted the voluminous commentary stating that habeas was confined to the dominions of the Crown.

What history teaches is confirmed by the nature of the limitations that the Constitution places upon suspension of the common-law writ. It can be suspended only "in Cases of Rebellion or Invasion." Art. I, §9, cl. 2. The latter case (invasion) is plainly limited to the territory of the United States; and while it is conceivable that a rebellion could be mounted by American citizens abroad, surely the overwhelming majority of its occurrences would be domestic. If the extraterritorial scope of habeas turned on flexible, "functional" considerations, as the Court holds, why would the Constitution limit its suspension almost entirely to instances of domestic crisis? Surely there is an even greater justification for suspension in foreign lands where the United States might hold prisoners of war during an ongoing conflict. And correspondingly, there is less threat to liberty when the Government suspends the writ's (supposed) application in foreign lands, where even on the most extreme view prisoners are entitled to fewer constitutional rights. It makes no sense, therefore, for the Constitution generally to forbid suspension of the writ abroad if indeed the writ has application there. . . .

In sum, because I conclude that the text and history of the Suspension Clause provide no basis for our jurisdiction, I would affirm the Court of Appeals even if *Eisentrager* did not govern these cases.

***

Today the Court warps our Constitution in a way that goes beyond the narrow issue of the reach of the Suspension Clause, invoking judicially brainstormed separation-of-powers principles to establish a manipulable "functional" test for the extraterritorial reach of habeas corpus (and, no doubt, for the extraterritorial reach of other constitutional protections as well). It blatantly misdescribes important precedents, most conspicuously Justice Jackson's opinion for the Court in Johnson v. Eisentrager. It breaks a chain of precedent as old as the common law that prohibits judicial inquiry into detentions of aliens abroad absent statutory authorization. And, most tragically, it sets our military commanders the impossible task of proving to a civilian court, under whatever standards this Court devises in the future, that evidence supports the confinement of each and every enemy prisoner.

The Nation will live to regret what the Court has done today. I dissent.

Chapter 14

Equal Protection

SECTION A: Racial Discrimination & Strict Scrutiny

ASSIGNMENT S-5

Study Guide: Do you agree with the "minimalist" manner with which Justice Kennedy resolves this dispute? How does he view Title VII's prohibition of both disparate treatment and disparate impact as "damned if they do, damned if they don't"? What is Justice Ginsburg's reply to this complaint? Although neither side invokes the concept of "invidious discrimination," is there a sense in which it, once again, underlies the disagreement of the Justices? Hint: if only "invidious discrimination" is illegal (either under Title VII or the Equal Protection Clause), does this eliminate the conflict perceived by the majority between disparate treatment and disparate impact, and help explain why the dissenters see no conflict? Does it matter whether a case like this arises during the "test-design phase," rather than after a test is administered? If Bolling *is not justified on textual or originalist grounds, what happens to Justice Scalia's constitutional concerns about what New Haven did in this case? What does the dispute between Justices Alito and Ginsburg say about the role that empathy or "sympathy" should play in judicial decisions? Also note the stress Justice Alito places on the allegedly pretextual justification for what New Haven did here. Should this concern for pretextual rationales be more widely employed by courts when evaluating legislation or executive actions? Finally, note that if the dissent contends that the case should have been remanded to consider the claims of pretext, as well as whether New Haven comported with the dissent's proposed standard, then the dissent appears to be implicitly rejecting the Second Circuit's affirmance of the District Court's summary judgment against the firefighters.*

RICCI v. DeSTEFANO

557 U.S. _____ (2009)

Justice Kennedy delivered the opinion of the Court, in which Chief Justice Roberts and Justices Scalia, Thomas, and Alito joined.

In the fire department of New Haven, Connecticut—as in emergency-service agencies throughout the Nation—firefighters prize their promotion to and within the officer ranks. An agency's officers command respect within the department and in the whole community; and, of course, added responsibilities command increased salary and benefits. Aware of the intense competition for promotions, New Haven, like many cities, relies on objective examinations to identify the best qualified candidates.

In 2003, 118 New Haven firefighters took examinations to qualify for promotion to the rank of lieutenant or captain. Promotion examinations in New Haven (or City) were infrequent, so the stakes were high. The results would determine which firefighters would be considered for promotions during the next two years, and the order in which they would be considered. Many firefighters studied for months, at considerable personal and financial cost.

When the examination results showed that white candidates had outperformed minority candidates, the mayor and other local politicians opened a public debate that turned rancorous. Some firefighters argued the tests should be discarded because the results showed the tests to be discriminatory. They threatened a discrimination lawsuit if the City made promotions based on the tests. Other firefighters said the exams were neutral and fair. And they, in turn, threatened a discrimination lawsuit if the City, relying on the statistical racial disparity, ignored the test results and denied promotions to the candidates who had performed well. In the end the City took the side of those who protested the test results. It threw out the examinations.

[Seventeen white and one Hispanic firefighter] who likely would have been promoted based on their good test performance sued the City and some of its officials. Theirs is the suit now before us. The suit alleges that, by discarding the test results, the City and the named officials discriminated against the plaintiffs based on their race, in violation of both Title VII of the Civil Rights Act of 1964 and the Equal Protection Clause of the Fourteenth Amendment. The City and the officials defended their actions, arguing that if they had certified the results, they could have faced liability under Title VII for adopting a practice that had a disparate impact on the minority firefighters. The District Court granted summary judgment for the defendants, and the Court of Appeals affirmed.

We conclude that race-based action like the City's in this case is impermissible under Title VII unless the employer can demonstrate a strong basis in evidence that, had it not taken the action, it would have been liable under the disparate-impact statute. The respondents, we further determine, cannot meet that threshold standard. As a result, the City's action in discarding the tests was a violation of Title VII. In light of our ruling under the statutes, we need not reach the question whether respondents' actions may have violated the Equal Protection Clause. . . .

II

Petitioners raise a statutory claim, under the disparate treatment prohibition of Title VII, and a constitutional claim, under the Equal Protection Clause of the Fourteenth Amendment. A decision for petitioners on their statutory claim would provide the relief sought, so we consider it first. See . . . . Escambia County v. McMillan (1984) (per curiam) ("[N]ormally the Court will not decide a constitutional question if there is some other ground upon which to dispose of the case").

A

Title VII of the Civil Rights Act of 1964 prohibits employment discrimination on the basis of race, color, religion, sex, or national origin. Title VII prohibits both intentional discrimination (known as "disparate treatment") as well as, in some cases, practices that are not intended to discriminate but in fact have a disproportionately adverse effect on minorities (known as "disparate impact").

As enacted in 1964, Title VII's principal nondiscrimination provision held employers liable only for disparate treatment. That section retains its original wording today. It makes it unlawful for an employer "to fail or refuse to hire or to discharge any individual, or otherwise to discriminate against any individual with respect to his compensation, terms, conditions, or privileges of employment, because of such individual's race, color, religion, sex, or national origin." Disparate-treatment cases present "the most easily understood type of discrimination," Teamsters v. United States (1977), and occur where an employer has "treated [a] particular person less favorably than others because of" a protected trait. Watson v. Fort Worth Bank & Trust (1988). A disparate-treatment plaintiff must establish "that the defendant had a discriminatory intent or motive" for taking a job-related action. *Id.*

The Civil Rights Act of 1964 did not include an express prohibition on policies or practices that produce a disparate impact. But in Griggs v. Duke Power Co. (1971), the Court interpreted the Act to prohibit, in some cases, employers' facially neutral practices that, in fact, are "discriminatory in operation." The *Griggs* Court stated that the "touchstone" for disparate-impact liability is the lack of "business necessity": "If an employment practice which operates to exclude [minorities] cannot be shown to be related to job performance, the practice is prohibited." . . . [I]f an employer met its burden by showing that its practice was job-related, the plaintiff was required to show a legitimate alternative that would have resulted in less discrimination.

Twenty years after *Griggs*, the Civil Rights Act of 1991 was enacted. The Act included a provision codifying the prohibition on disparate-impact discrimination. That provision is now in force along with the disparate-treatment section already noted. Under the disparate-impact statute, a plaintiff establishes a prima facie violation by showing that an employer uses "a particular employment practice that causes a disparate impact on the basis of race, color, religion, sex, or national origin." An employer may defend against liability by demonstrating that the practice is "job related for the position in question and consistent with business necessity." Even if the employer meets that burden, however, a plaintiff may still succeed by showing that the employer refuses to adopt an available alternative employment practice that has less disparate impact and serves the employer's legitimate needs.

B

Petitioners allege that when the [Civil Service Board (CSB or Board)] refused to certify the captain and lieutenant exam results based on the race of the successful candidates, it discriminated against them in violation of Title VII's disparate-treatment provision. The City counters that its decision was permissible because the tests "appear[ed] to violate Title VII's disparate-impact provisions."

Our analysis begins with this premise: The City's actions would violate the disparate-treatment prohibition of Title VII absent some valid defense. All the evidence demonstrates that the City chose not to certify the examination results because of the statistical disparity based on race — *i.e.*, how minority candidates had performed when compared to white candidates. As the District Court put it, the City rejected the test results because "too many whites and not enough minorities would be promoted were the lists to be certified." Without some other justification, this express, race-based decisionmaking violates Title VII's command that employers cannot take adverse employment actions because of an individual's race.

The District Court did not adhere to this principle, however. It held that respondents' "motivation to avoid making promotions based on a test with a racially disparate impact . . . does not, as a matter of law, constitute discriminatory intent." And the Government makes a similar argument in this Court. It contends that the "structure of Title VII belies any claim that an employer's intent to comply with Title VII's disparate-impact provisions constitutes prohibited discrimination on the basis of race." But both of those statements turn upon the City's objective — avoiding disparate-impact liability — while ignoring the City's conduct in the name of reaching that objective. Whatever the City's ultimate aim — however well intentioned or benevolent it might have seemed — the City made its employment decision because of race. The City rejected the test results solely because the higher scoring candidates were white. The question is not whether that conduct was discriminatory but whether the City had a lawful justification for its race-based action.

We consider, therefore, whether the purpose to avoid disparate-impact liability excuses what otherwise would be prohibited disparate-treatment discrimination. Courts often confront cases in which statutes and principles point in different directions. Our task is to provide guidance to employers and courts for situations when these two prohibitions could be in conflict absent a rule to reconcile them. In providing this guidance our decision must be consistent with the important purpose of Title VII — that the workplace be an environment free of discrimination, where race is not a barrier to opportunity.

With these principles in mind, we turn to the parties' proposed means of reconciling the statutory provisions. Petitioners take a strict approach, arguing that under Title VII, it cannot be permissible for an employer to take race-based adverse employment actions in order to avoid disparate-impact liability — even if the employer knows its practice violates the disparate-impact provision. Petitioners would have us hold that, under Title VII, avoiding unintentional discrimination cannot justify intentional discrimination. That assertion, however, ignores the fact that, by codifying the disparate-impact provision in 1991, Congress has expressly prohibited both types of discrimination. We must interpret the statute to give effect to both provisions where possible.

Petitioners next suggest that an employer in fact must be in violation of the disparate-impact provision before it can use compliance as a defense in a disparate-treatment suit. Again, this is overly simplistic and too restrictive of Title VII's purpose. . . . Forbidding employers to act unless they know, with certainty, that a practice violates the disparate-impact provision would bring compliance efforts to a near standstill. Even in the limited situations when this restricted standard could be met, employers likely would hesitate before taking voluntary action for fear of later being proven wrong in the course of litigation and then held to account for disparate treatment.

At the opposite end of the spectrum, respondents and the Government assert that an employer's good-faith belief that its actions are necessary to comply with Title VII's disparate-impact provision should be enough to justify race-conscious conduct. But the original, foundational prohibition of Title VII bars employers from taking adverse action "because of . . . race." And when Congress codified the disparate-impact provision in 1991, it made no exception to disparate-treatment liability for actions taken in a good-faith effort to comply with the new, disparate-impact provision. . . . Allowing employers to violate the disparate-treatment prohibition based on a mere good-faith fear of disparate-impact liability would encourage race-based action at the slightest hint of disparate impact. A minimal standard could cause employers to discard the results of lawful and beneficial promotional examinations even where there is little if any evidence of disparate-impact discrimination. That would amount to a *de facto* quota system, in which a "focus on statistics . . . could put undue pressure on employers to adopt inappropriate prophylactic measures." Watson [v. Fort Worth Bank & Trust (1988)]. Even worse, an employer could discard test results (or other employment practices) with the intent of obtaining the employer's preferred racial balance. That operational principle could not be justified, for Title VII is express in disclaiming any interpretation of its requirements as calling for outright racial balancing. The purpose of Title VII "is to promote hiring on the basis of job qualifications, rather than on the basis of race or color." *Griggs*.

In searching for a standard that strikes a more appropriate balance, we note that this Court has considered cases similar to this one, albeit in the context of the Equal Protection Clause of the Fourteenth Amendment. The Court has held that certain government actions to remedy past racial discrimination — actions that are themselves based on race — are constitutional only where there is a "'strong basis in evidence'" that the remedial actions were necessary. Richmond v. J. A. Croson Co. (1989) (quoting [Wygant v. Jackson Bd. of Ed. (1986)] (plurality opinion)). . . .

Writing for a plurality in *Wygant* and announcing the strong-basis-in-evidence standard, Justice Powell recognized the tension between eliminating segregation and discrimination on the one hand and doing away with all governmentally imposed discrimination based on race on the other. The plurality stated that those "related constitutional duties are not always harmonious," and that "reconciling them requires . . . employers to act with extraordinary care." The plurality required a strong basis in evidence because "[e]videntiary support for the conclusion that remedial action is warranted becomes crucial when the remedial program is challenged in court by nonminority employees." . . .

The same interests are at work in the interplay between the disparate-treatment and disparate-impact provisions of Title VII. Congress has imposed liability on employers for unintentional discrimination in order to rid the workplace of "practices that are fair in form, but discriminatory in operation." *Griggs*. But it has also prohibited employers from taking adverse employment actions "because of" race. Applying the strong-basis-in-evidence standard to Title VII gives effect to both the disparate-treatment and disparate-impact provisions, allowing violations of one in the name of compliance with the other only in certain, narrow circumstances. The standard leaves ample room for employers' voluntary compliance efforts, which are essential to the statutory scheme and to Congress's efforts to eradicate workplace discrimination. And the standard appropriately constrains employers' discretion in making race-based decisions: It limits that discretion to cases in which there is a strong basis in evidence of disparate-impact liability, but it is not so restrictive that it allows employers to act only when there is a provable, actual violation.

Resolving the statutory conflict in this way allows the disparate-impact prohibition to work in a manner that is consistent with other provisions of Title VII, including the prohibition on adjusting employment-related test scores on the basis of race. Examinations like those administered by the City create legitimate expectations on the part of those who took the tests. As is the case with any promotion exam, some of the firefighters here invested substantial time, money, and personal commitment in preparing for the tests. Employment tests can be an important part of a neutral selection system that safeguards against the very racial animosities Title VII was intended to prevent. Here, however, the firefighters saw their efforts invalidated by the City in sole reliance upon race-based statistics.

If an employer cannot rescore a test based on the candidates' race, then it follows *a fortiori* that it may not take the greater step of discarding the test altogether to achieve a more desirable racial distribution of promotion-eligible candidates — absent a strong basis in evidence that the test was deficient and that discarding the results is necessary to avoid violating the disparate-impact provision. Restricting an employer's ability to discard test results (and thereby discriminate against qualified candidates on the basis of their race) also is in keeping with Title VII's express protection of bona fide promotional examinations.

For the foregoing reasons, we adopt the strong-basis-in-evidence standard as a matter of statutory construction to resolve any conflict between the disparate-treatment and disparate-impact provisions of Title VII.

Our statutory holding does not address the constitutionality of the measures taken here in purported compliance with Title VII. We also do not hold that meeting the strong-basis-in-evidence standard would satisfy the Equal Protection Clause in a future case. As we explain below, because respondents have not met their burden under Title VII, we need not decide whether a legitimate fear of disparate impact is ever sufficient to justify discriminatory treatment under the Constitution.

Nor do we question an employer's affirmative efforts to ensure that all groups have a fair opportunity to apply for promotions and to participate in the process by which promotions will be made. But once that process has been established and employers have made clear their selection criteria, they may not then invalidate the test results, thus upsetting an employee's legitimate expectation not to be judged on the basis of race. Doing so, absent a strong basis in evidence of an impermissible disparate impact, amounts to the sort of racial preference that Congress has disclaimed, and is antithetical to the notion of a workplace where individuals are guaranteed equal opportunity regardless of race.

Title VII does not prohibit an employer from considering, before administering a test or practice, how to design that test or practice in order to provide a fair opportunity for all individuals, regardless of their race. And when, during the test-design stage, an employer invites comments to ensure the test is fair, that process can provide a common ground for open discussions toward that end. We hold only that, under Title VII, before an employer can engage in intentional discrimination for the asserted purpose of avoiding or remedying an unintentional disparate impact, the employer must have a strong basis in evidence to believe it will be subject to disparate-impact liability if it fails to take the race-conscious, discriminatory action.

C

The City argues that, even under the strong-basis-in-evidence standard, its decision to discard the examination results was permissible under Title VII. That is incorrect. Even if respondents were motivated as a subjective matter by a desire to avoid committing disparate-impact discrimination, the record makes clear there is no support for the conclusion that respondents had an objective, strong basis in evidence to find the tests inadequate, with some consequent disparate-impact liability in violation of Title VII. . . .

The racial adverse impact here was significant, and petitioners do not dispute that the City was faced with a prima facie case of disparate-impact liability. On the captain exam, the pass rate for white candidates was 64 percent but was 37.5 percent for both black and Hispanic candidates. On the lieutenant exam, the pass rate for white candidates was 58.1 percent; for black candidates, 31.6 percent; and for Hispanic candidates, 20 percent. The pass rates of minorities, which were approximately one-half the pass rates for white candidates, fall well below the 80-percent standard set by the EEOC to implement the disparate-impact provision of Title VII. . . .

Based on the degree of adverse impact reflected in the results, respondents were compelled to take a hard look at the examinations to determine whether certifying the results would have had an impermissible disparate impact. The problem for respondents is that a prima facie case of disparate-impact liability—essentially, a threshold showing of a significant statistical disparity and nothing more—is far from a strong basis in evidence that the City would have been liable under Title VII had it certified the results. That is because the City could be liable for disparate-impact discrimination only if the examinations were not job related and consistent with business necessity, or if there existed an equally valid, less-discriminatory alternative that served the City's needs but that the City refused to adopt. We conclude there is no strong basis in evidence to establish that the test was deficient in either of these respects. . . . [Discussion of evidence omitted.]

On the record before us, there is no genuine dispute that the City lacked a strong basis in evidence to believe it would face disparate-impact liability if it certified the examination results. In other words, there is no evidence — let alone the required strong basis in evidence — that the tests were flawed because they were not job-related or because other, equally valid and less discriminatory tests were available to the City. Fear of litigation alone cannot justify an employer's reliance on race to the detriment of individuals who passed the examinations and qualified for promotions. The City's discarding the test results was impermissible under Title VII, and summary judgment is appropriate for petitioners on their disparate-treatment claim. . . .

Our holding today clarifies how Title VII applies to resolve competing expectations under the disparate-treatment and disparate-impact provisions. If, after it certifies the test results, the City faces a disparate-impact suit, then in light of our holding today it should be clear that the City would avoid disparate-impact liability based on the strong basis in evidence that, had it not certified the results, it would have been subject to disparate-treatment liability.

Petitioners are entitled to summary judgment on their Title VII claim, and we therefore need not decide the underlying constitutional question. The judgment of the Court of Appeals is reversed, and the cases are remanded for further proceedings consistent with this opinion.

It is so ordered.

JUSTICE SCALIA concurring.

I join the Court's opinion in full, but write separately to observe that its resolution of this dispute merely postpones the evil day on which the Court will have to confront the question: Whether, or to what extent, are the disparate-impact provisions of Title VII of the Civil Rights Act of 1964 consistent with the Constitution's guarantee of equal protection? The question is not an easy one.

The difficulty is this: Whether or not Title VII's disparate-treatment provisions forbid "remedial" race-based actions when a disparate-impact violation would not otherwise result — the question resolved by the Court today — it is clear that Title VII not only permits but affirmatively *requires* such actions when a disparate-impact violation *would* otherwise result. But if the Federal Government is prohibited from discriminating on the basis of race, Bolling v. Sharpe (1954), then surely it is also prohibited from enacting laws mandating that third parties — *e.g.*, employers, whether private, State, or municipal — discriminate on the basis of race. As the facts of these cases illustrate, Title VII's disparate-impact provisions place a racial thumb on the scales, often requiring employers to evaluate the racial outcomes of their policies, and to make decisions based on (because of) those racial outcomes. That type of racial decisionmaking is, as the Court explains, discriminatory.

To be sure, the disparate-impact laws do not mandate imposition of quotas, but it is not clear why that should provide a safe harbor. Would a private employer not be guilty of unlawful discrimination if he refrained from establishing a racial hiring quota but intentionally designed his hiring practices to achieve the same end? Surely he would. Intentional discrimination is still occurring, just one step up the chain. Government compulsion of such design would therefore seemingly violate equal protection principles. . . .

It might be possible to defend the law by framing it as simply an evidentiary tool used to identify genuine, intentional discrimination — to "smoke out," as it were, disparate treatment. Disparate impact is sometimes (though not always) a signal of something illicit, so a regulator might allow statistical disparities to play some role in the evidentiary process. But arguably the disparate-impact provisions sweep too broadly to be fairly characterized in such a fashion — since they fail to provide an affirmative defense for good-faith (*i.e.*, nonracially motivated) conduct, or perhaps even for good faith plus hiring standards that are entirely reasonable. See (GINSBURG, J., dissenting) (describing the demanding nature of the "business necessity" defense). This is a question that this Court will have to consider in due course. It is one thing to free plaintiffs from proving an employer's illicit intent, but quite another to preclude the employer from proving that its motives were pure and its actions reasonable.

The Court's resolution of these cases makes it unnecessary to resolve these matters today. But the war between disparate impact and equal protection will be waged sooner or later, and it behooves us to begin thinking about how — and on what terms — to make peace between them.

JUSTICE ALITO, with whom JUSTICE SCALIA and JUSTICE THOMAS join, concurring.

I join the Court's opinion in full. I write separately only because the dissent . . . provides an incomplete description of the events that led to New Haven's decision to reject the results of its exam. The dissent's omissions are important because, when all of the evidence in the record is taken into account, it is clear that, even if the legal analysis . . . of the dissent were accepted, affirmance of the decision below is untenable.

I

When an employer in a disparate-treatment case under Title VII of the Civil Rights Act of 1964 claims that an employment decision, such as the refusal to promote, was based on a legitimate reason, two questions — one objective and one subjective — must be decided. The first, objective question is whether the reason given by the employer is one that is legitimate under Title VII. If the reason provided by the employer is not legitimate on its face, the employer is liable. The second, subjective question concerns the employer's intent. If an employer offers a facially legitimate reason for its decision but it turns out that this explanation was just a pretext for discrimination, the employer is again liable.

The question on which the opinion of the Court and the dissenting opinion disagree concerns the objective component of the determination that must be made when an employer justifies an employment decision, like the one made in this litigation, on the ground that a contrary decision would have created a risk of disparate-impact liability. The Court holds — and I entirely agree — that concern about disparate-impact liability is a legitimate reason for a decision of the type involved here only if there was a "substantial basis in evidence to find the tests inadequate." . . .

The dissent advocates a different objective component of the governing standard. According to the dissent, the objective component should be whether the evidence provided "good cause" for the decision, and the dissent argues — incorrectly, in my view — that no reasonable juror could fail to find that such evidence was present here. But even if the dissent were correct on this point, I assume that the dissent would not countenance summary judgment for respondents if respondents' professed concern about disparate-impact litigation was simply a pretext. Therefore, the decision below, which sustained the entry of summary judgment for respondents, cannot be affirmed unless no reasonable jury could find that the City's asserted reason for scrapping its test — concern about disparate-impact liability — was a pretext and that the City's real reason was illegitimate, namely, the desire to placate a politically important racial constituency.

II

As initially described by the dissent, the process by which the City reached the decision not to accept the test results was open, honest, serious, and deliberative. But even the District Court admitted that "a jury could rationally infer that city officials worked behind the scenes to sabotage the promotional examinations because they knew that, were the exams certified, the Mayor would incur the wrath of [Rev. Boise] Kimber and other influential leaders of New Haven's African-American community." This admission finds ample support in the record. . . .

Taking into account all the evidence in the summary judgment record, a reasonable jury could find the following. Almost as soon as the City disclosed the racial makeup of the list of firefighters who scored the highest on the exam, the City administration was lobbied by an influential community leader to scrap the test results, and the City administration decided on that course of action before making any real assessment of the possibility of a disparate-impact violation. To achieve that end, the City administration concealed its internal decision but worked — as things turned out, successfully — to persuade the CSB that acceptance of the test results would be illegal and would expose the City to disparate-impact liability. But in the event that the CSB was not persuaded, the Mayor, wielding ultimate decisionmaking authority, was prepared to overrule the CSB immediately. Taking this view of the evidence, a reasonable jury could easily find that the City's real reason for scrapping the test results was not a concern about violating the disparate-impact provision of Title VII but a simple desire to please a politically important racial constituency. . . .

* * *

Petitioners are firefighters who seek only a fair chance to move up the ranks in their chosen profession. In order to qualify for promotion, they made personal sacrifices. Petitioner Frank Ricci, who is dyslexic, found it necessary to "hir[e] someone, at considerable expense, to read onto audiotape the content of the books and study materials." He "studied an average of eight to thirteen hours a day . . . , even listening to audio tapes while driving his car." Petitioner Benjamin Vargas, who is Hispanic, had to "give up a part-time job," and his wife had to "take leave from her own job in order to take care of their three young children while Vargas studied." "Vargas devoted countless hours to study . . . , missed two of his children's birthdays and over two weeks of vacation time," and "incurred significant financial expense" during the three-month study period.

Petitioners were denied promotions for which they qualified because of the race and ethnicity of the firefighters who achieved the highest scores on the City's exam. The District Court threw out their case on summary judgment, even though that court all but conceded that a jury could find that the City's asserted justification was pretextual. The Court of Appeals then summarily affirmed that decision.

The dissent grants that petitioners' situation is "unfortunate" and that they "understandably attract this Court's sympathy." But "sympathy" is not what petitioners have a right to demand. What they have a right to demand is evenhanded enforcement of the law — of Title VII's prohibition against discrimination based on race. And that is what, until today's decision, has been denied them.

JUSTICE GINSBURG, with whom JUSTICE STEVENS, JUSTICE SOUTER, and JUSTICE BREYER join, dissenting.

In assessing claims of race discrimination, "[c]ontext matters." Grutter v. Bollinger (2003). In 1972, Congress extended Title VII of the Civil Rights Act of 1964 to cover public employment. At that time, municipal fire departments across the country, including New Haven's, pervasively discriminated against minorities. The extension of Title VII to cover jobs in firefighting effected no overnight change. It took decades of persistent effort, advanced by Title VII litigation, to open firefighting posts to members of racial minorities.

The white firefighters who scored high on New Haven's promotional exams understandably attract this Court's sympathy. But they had no vested right to promotion. Nor have other persons received promotions in preference to them. New Haven maintains that it refused to certify the test results because it believed, for good cause, that it would be vulnerable to a Title VII disparate-impact suit if it relied on those results. The Court today holds that New Haven has not demonstrated "a strong basis in evidence" for its plea. In so holding, the Court pretends that "[t]he City rejected the test results solely because the higher scoring candidates were white." That pretension, essential to the Court's disposition, ignores substantial evidence of multiple flaws in the tests New Haven used. The Court similarly fails to acknowledge the better tests used in other cities, which have yielded less racially skewed outcomes.[1]

By order of this Court, New Haven, a city in which African-Americans and Hispanics account for nearly 60 percent of the population, must today be served—as it was in the days of undisguised discrimination—by a fire department in which members of racial and ethnic minorities are rarely seen in command positions. In arriving at its order, the Court barely acknowledges the pathmarking decision in Griggs v. Duke Power Co. (1971) , which explained the centrality of the disparate-impact concept to effective enforcement of Title VII. The Court's order and opinion, I anticipate, will not have staying power.

I

A

The Court's recitation of the facts leaves out important parts of the story. Firefighting is a profession in which the legacy of racial discrimination casts an especially long shadow. In extending Title VII to state and local government employers in 1972, Congress took note of a U.S. Commission on Civil Rights (USCCR) report finding racial discrimination in municipal employment even "more pervasive than in the private sector." According to the report, overt racism was partly to blame, but so too was a failure on the part of municipal employers to apply merit-based employment principles. In making hiring and promotion decisions, public employers often "rel[ied] on criteria unrelated to job performance," including nepotism or political patronage. Such flawed selection methods served to entrench preexisting racial hierarchies. The USCCR report singled out police and fire departments for having "[b]arriers to equal employment . . . greater . . . than in any other area of State or local government," with African-Americans "hold[ing] almost no positions in the officer ranks."

The city of New Haven (City) was no exception. In the early 1970's, African-Americans and Hispanics composed 30 percent of New Haven's population, but only 3.6 percent of the City's 502 firefighters. The racial disparity in the officer ranks was even more pronounced: "[O]f the 107 officers in the Department only one was black, and he held the lowest rank above private." Firebird Soc. of New Haven, Inc. v. New Haven Bd. of Fire Comm'rs (Conn. 1975).

Following a lawsuit and settlement agreement, the City initiated efforts to increase minority representation in the New Haven Fire Department (Department). Those litigation-induced efforts produced some positive change. New Haven's population includes a greater proportion of minorities today than it did in the 1970's: Nearly 40 percent of the City's residents are African-American and more

1. Never mind the flawed tests New Haven used and the better selection methods used elsewhere, JUSTICE ALITO'S concurring opinion urges. Overriding all else, racial politics, fired up by a strident African-American pastor, were at work in New Haven. Even a detached and disinterested observer, however, would have every reason to ask: Why did such racially skewed results occur in New Haven, when better tests likely would have produced less disproportionate results?

than 20 percent are Hispanic. Among entry-level firefighters, minorities are still underrepresented, but not starkly so. As of 2003, African-Americans and Hispanics constituted 30 percent and 16 percent of the City's firefighters, respectively. In supervisory positions, however, significant disparities remain. Overall, the senior officer ranks (captain and higher) are nine percent African-American and nine percent Hispanic. Only one of the Department's 21 fire captains is African-American. It is against this backdrop of entrenched inequality that the promotion process at issue in this litigation should be assessed. . . .

II

A

Title VII became effective in July 1965. Employers responded to the law by eliminating rules and practices that explicitly barred racial minorities from "white" jobs. But removing overtly race-based job classifications did not usher in genuinely equal opportunity. More subtle—and sometimes unconscious—forms of discrimination replaced once undisguised restrictions.

In Griggs v. Duke Power Co. (1971), this Court responded to that reality and supplied important guidance on Title VII's mission and scope. Congress, the landmark decision recognized, aimed beyond "disparate treatment"; it targeted "disparate impact" as well. Title VII's original text, it was plain to the Court, "proscribe[d] not only overt discrimination but also practices that are fair in form, but discriminatory in operation." Only by ignoring *Griggs* could one maintain that intentionally disparate treatment alone was Title VII's "original, foundational prohibition," and disparate impact a mere afterthought. . . .

In response to *Wards Cove* and "a number of [other] recent decisions by the United States Supreme Court that sharply cut back on the scope and effectiveness of [civil rights] laws," Congress enacted the Civil Rights Act of 1991. H. R. Rep. No. 102–40 (1991). Among the 1991 alterations, Congress formally codified the disparate-impact component of Title VII. In so amending the statute, Congress made plain its intention to restore "the concepts of 'business necessity' and 'job related' enunciated by the Supreme Court in Griggs v. Duke Power Co. . . . and in other Supreme Court decisions prior to Wards Cove Packing Co. v. Atonio." Once a complaining party demonstrates that an employment practice causes a disparate impact, amended Title VII states, the burden is on the employer "to demonstrate that the challenged practice is job related for the position in question and consistent with business necessity." If the employer carries that substantial burden, the complainant may respond by identifying "an alternative employment practice" which the employer "refuses to adopt."

B

Neither Congress' enactments nor this Court's Title VII precedents (including the now-discredited decision in *Wards Cove*) offer even a hint of "conflict" between an employer's obligations under the statute's disparate-treatment and disparate-impact provisions. Standing on an equal footing, these twin pillars of Title VII advance the same objectives: ending workplace discrimination and promoting genuinely equal opportunity.

Yet the Court today sets at odds the statute's core directives. When an employer changes an employment practice in an effort to comply with Title VII's disparate-impact provision, the Court reasons, it acts "because of race"—something Title VII's disparate-treatment provision generally forbids. Ante, at 20. This characterization of an employer's compliance-directed action shows little attention to Congress' design or to the *Griggs* line of cases Congress recognized as pathmarking. . . .

Congress declared unambiguously that selection criteria operating to the disadvantage of minority group members can be retained only if justified by business necessity. In keeping with Congress' design, employers who reject such criteria due to reasonable doubts about their reliability can hardly be held to have engaged in discrimination "because of" race. A reasonable endeavor to comply with the law and to ensure that qualified candidates of all races have a fair opportunity to compete is simply not what Congress meant to interdict. I would therefore hold that an employer who jettisons a selection device when its disproportionate racial impact becomes apparent does not violate Title VII's disparate-treatment bar automatically or at all, subject to this key condition: The employer must have good cause to believe the device would not withstand examination for business necessity. . . .

III

A

Applying what I view as the proper standard to the record thus far made, I would hold that New Haven had ample cause to believe its selection process was flawed and not justified by business necessity. Judged by that standard, petitioners have not shown that New Haven's failure to certify the exam results violated Title VII's disparate-treatment provision.

The City, all agree, "was faced with a prima facie case of disparate-impact liability": The pass rate for minority candidates was half the rate for nonminority candidates, and virtually no minority candidates would have been eligible for promotion had the exam results been certified. Alerted to this stark disparity, the CSB heard expert and lay testimony, presented at public hearings, in an endeavor to ascertain whether the exams were fair and consistent with business necessity. Its investigation revealed grave cause for concern about the exam process itself and the City's failure to consider alternative selection devices.

Chief among the City's problems was the very nature of the tests for promotion. In choosing to use written and oral exams with a 60/40 weighting, the City simply adhered to the union's preference and apparently gave no consideration to whether the weighting was likely to identify the most qualified fire-officer candidates. There is strong reason to think it was not.

Relying heavily on written tests to select fire officers is a questionable practice, to say the least. Successful fire officers, the City's description of the position makes clear, must have the "[a]bility to lead personnel effectively, maintain discipline, promote harmony, exercise sound judgment, and cooperate with other officials." CA2 App. A432. These qualities are not well measured by written tests. Testifying before the CSB, Christopher Hornick, an exam-design expert with more than two decades of relevant experience, was emphatic on this point: Leadership skills, command presence, and the like "could have been identified and evaluated in a much more appropriate way." . . .

[M]ost municipal employers do not evaluate their fire-officer candidates as New Haven does. Although comprehensive statistics are scarce, a 1996 study found that nearly two-thirds of surveyed municipalities used assessment centers ("simulations of the real world of work") as part of their promotion processes. P. Lowry, A Survey of the Assessment Center Process in the Public Sector, 25 Public Personnel Management 307, 315 (1996). That figure represented a marked increase over the previous decade, so the percentage today may well be even higher. Among municipalities still relying in part on written exams, the median weight assigned to them was 30 percent—half the weight given to New Haven's written exam. . . . Considering the prevalence of these proven alternatives, New Haven was poorly positioned to argue that promotions based on its outmoded and exclusionary selection process qualified as a business necessity.

Ignoring the conceptual and other defects in New Haven's selection process, the Court describes the exams as "painstaking[ly]" developed to test "relevant" material and on that basis finds no substantial risk of disparate-impact liability. Perhaps such reasoning would have sufficed under *Wards Cove*, which permitted exclusionary practices as long as they advanced an employer's "legitimate" goals. But Congress repudiated *Wards Cove* and reinstated the "business necessity" rule attended by a "manifest relationship" requirement. Like the chess player who tries to win by sweeping the opponent's pieces off the table, the Court simply shuts from its sight the formidable obstacles New Haven would have faced in defending against a disparate-impact suit. . . .

In sum, the record solidly establishes that the City had good cause to fear disparate-impact liability. . . .

B

Concurring in the Court's opinion, Justice Alito asserts that summary judgment for respondents would be improper even if the City had good cause for its noncertification decision. A reasonable jury, he maintains, could have found that respondents were not actually motivated by concern about disparate-impact litigation, but instead sought only "to placate a politically important [African-American] constituency." . . . I would not oppose a remand for further proceedings fair to both sides. It is the Court that has chosen to short-circuit this litigation based on its pretension that the City has shown, and can show, nothing more than a statistical disparity. Justice Alito compounds the Court's error. . . .

Justice Alito's analysis contains a . . . fundamental flaw: It equates political considerations with unlawful discrimination. As Justice Alito sees it, if the mayor and his staff were motivated by their desire "to placate a . . . racial constituency," then they engaged in unlawful discrimination against petitioners. But JUSTICE ALITO fails to ask a vital question: "[P]lacate" how? That political officials would have politics in mind is hardly extraordinary, and there are many ways in which a politician can attempt to win over a constituency—including a racial constituency—without engaging in unlawful discrimination. . . .

The real issue, then, is not whether the mayor and his staff were politically motivated; it is whether their attempt to score political points was legitimate (*i.e.*, nondiscriminatory). Were they seeking to exclude white firefighters from promotion (unlikely, as a fair test would undoubtedly result in the addition of white firefighters to the officer ranks), or did they realize, at least belatedly, that their tests could be toppled in a disparate-impact suit? In the latter case, there is no disparate-treatment violation. JUSTICE ALITO, I recognize, would disagree. In his view, an employer's action to avoid Title VII disparate-impact liability qualifies as a presumptively improper race-based employment decision. I reject that construction of Title VII. As I see it, when employers endeavor to avoid exposure to disparate-impact liability, they do not thereby encounter liability for disparate treatment. . . .

It is indeed regrettable that the City's noncertification decision would have required all candidates to go through another selection process. But it would have been more regrettable to rely on flawed exams to shut out candidates who may well have the command presence and other qualities needed to excel as fire officers. Yet that is the choice the Court makes today. It is a choice that breaks the promise of *Griggs* that groups long denied equal opportunity would not be held back by tests "fair in form, but discriminatory in operation."

This case presents an unfortunate situation, one New Haven might well have avoided had it utilized a better selection process in the first place. But what this case does not present is race-based discrimination in violation of Title VII. I dissent from the Court's judgment, which rests on the false premise that respondents showed "a significant statistical disparity," but "nothing more."

Chapter 16

Freedoms of Speech and Press

ASSIGNMENT S-6

STUDY GUIDE: *What does Justice Alito identify as the "compelling interest" that was previously held to justify spending and contributions limits? Why does the "Millionaire's Amendment" not serve this interest? How did Congress and the government justify this scheme? Why does Justice Alito reject their theory? What difference is there between the majority and Justice Stevens's analysis that produces a different outcome?*

DAVIS v. FEDERAL ELECTION COMMISSION

554 U.S. 724 (2008)

JUSTICE ALITO delivered the opinion of the Court. . . .

In this appeal, we consider the constitutionality of federal election law provisions that, under certain circumstances, impose different campaign contribution limits on candidates competing for the same congressional seat.

Federal law limits the amount of money that a candidate for the House of Representatives and the candidate's authorized committee may receive from an individual, as well as the amount that the candidate's party may devote to coordinated campaign expenditures. Under the usual circumstances, the same restrictions apply to all the competitors for a seat and their authorized committees. Contributions from individual donors during a 2-year election cycle are subject to a cap, which is currently set at $2,300. In addition, no funds may be accepted from an individual whose aggregate contributions to candidates and their committees during the election cycle have reached the legal limit, currently $42,700. A candidate also may not accept general election coordinated expenditures by national or state political party committees that exceed an imposed limit. Currently, the limit for candidates in States with more than one House seat is $40,900.

Section 319(a) of the Bipartisan Campaign Reform Act of 2002 (BCRA), part of the so-called "Millionaire's Amendment," fundamentally alters this scheme when, as a result of a candidate's expenditure of personal funds, the "opposition personal funds amount" (OPFA) exceeds $350,000. The OPFA, in simple terms, is a statistic that compares the expenditure of personal funds by competing candidates and also takes into account to some degree certain other fundraising. When a candidate's expenditure of personal funds causes the OPFA to pass the $350,000 mark (for convenience, such candidates will be referred to as "self-financing"), a new, asymmetrical regulatory scheme comes into play. The self-financing candidate remains subject to the limitations noted above, but the candidate's opponent (the "non-self-financing" candidate) may receive individual contributions at treble the normal limit (*e.g.*, $6,900 rather than the current $2,300), even from individuals who have reached the normal aggregate contributions cap, and may accept coordinated party expenditures without limit. Once the non-self-financing candidate's receipts exceed the OPFA, the prior limits are revived. A candidate who does not spend the contributions received under the asymmetrical limits must return them. . . .

Appellant Jack Davis was the Democratic candidate for the House of Representatives from New York's 26th Congressional District in 2004 and 2006. In both elections, he lost to the incumbent. In his brief, Davis discloses having spent $1.2 million, principally his own funds, on his 2004 campaign. He reports spending $2.3 million in 2006, all but $126,000 of which came from personal funds. . . . Davis' 2006 candidacy began in March 2006, when he filed with the FEC a "Statement of Candidacy" and, in compliance with §319(b), declared that he intended to spend $1 million in personal funds during the general election. Two months later, in anticipation of this expenditure and its §319 consequences, Davis filed suit against the FEC, requesting that §319 be declared unconstitutional and that the FEC be enjoined from enforcing it during the 2006 election. . . .

We turn to the merits of Davis' claim that the First Amendment is violated by the contribution limits that apply when §319(a) comes into play. Under this scheme, as previously noted, when a candidate spends more than $350,000 in personal funds and creates what the statute apparently regards as a financial imbalance, that candidate's opponent may qualify to receive both larger individual contributions than would otherwise be allowed and unlimited coordinated party expenditures. Davis contends that §319(a) unconstitutionally burdens his exercise of his First Amendment right to make unlimited expenditures of his personal funds because making expenditures that create the imbalance has the effect of enabling his opponent to raise more money and to use that money to finance speech that counteracts and thus diminishes the effectiveness of Davis' own speech.

If §319(a) simply raised the contribution limits for all candidates, Davis' argument would plainly fail. This Court has previously sustained the facial constitutionality of limits on discrete and aggregate individual contributions and on coordinated party expenditures. Buckley v. Valeo (1976) (*per curiam*). At the same time, the Court has recognized that such limits implicate First Amendment interests and that they cannot stand unless they are "closely drawn" to serve a "sufficiently important interest," such as preventing corruption and the appearance of corruption. See, e.g., McConnell v. Federal Election Comm'n (2003). When contribution limits are challenged as too restrictive, we have extended a measure of deference to the judgment of the legislative body that enacted the law. But we have held that limits that are too low cannot stand.

There is, however, no constitutional basis for attacking contribution limits on the ground that they are too high. Congress has no constitutional obligation to limit contributions at all; and if Congress concludes that allowing contributions of a certain amount does not create an undue risk of corruption or the appearance of corruption, a candidate who wishes to restrict an opponent's fundraising cannot argue that the Constitution demands that contributions be regulated more strictly. Consequently, if §319(a)'s elevated contribution limits applied across the board, Davis would not have any basis for challenging those limits.

Section 319(a), however, does not raise the contribution limits across the board. Rather, it raises the limits only for the non-self-financing candidate and does so only when the self-financing candidate's expenditure of personal funds causes the OPFA threshold to be exceeded. We have never upheld the constitutionality of a law that imposes different contribution limits for candidates who are competing against each other, and we agree with Davis that this scheme impermissibly burdens his First Amendment right to spend his own money for campaign speech.

In *Buckley*, we soundly rejected a cap on a candidate's expenditure of personal funds to finance campaign speech. We held that a "candidate . . . has a First Amendment right to engage in the discussion of public issues and vigorously and tirelessly to advocate his own election" and that a cap on personal expenditures imposes "a substantial," "clea[r]" and "direc[t]" restraint on that right. We found that the cap at issue was not justified by "[t]he primary governmental interest" proffered in its defense, *i.e.*, "the prevention of actual and apparent corruption of the political process." Far from preventing these evils, "the use of personal funds," we observed, "reduces the candidate's dependence on outside contributions and thereby counteracts the coercive pressures and attendant risks of abuse to which . . . contribution limitations are directed." *Ibid.* We also rejected the argument that the expenditure cap could be justified on the ground that it served "[t]he ancillary interest in equalizing the relative financial resources of candidates competing for elective office." This putative interest, we noted, was "clearly not sufficient to justify the . . . infringement of fundamental First Amendment rights."

Buckley's emphasis on the fundamental nature of the right to spend personal funds for campaign speech is instructive. While BCRA does not impose a cap on a candidate's expenditure of personal funds, it imposes an unprecedented penalty on any candidate who robustly exercises that First Amendment right. Section 319(a) requires a candidate to choose between the First Amendment right to engage in unfettered political speech and subjection to discriminatory fundraising limitations. Many candidates who can afford to make large personal expenditures to support their campaigns may choose to do so despite §319(a), but they must shoulder a special and potentially significant burden if they make that choice. Under §319(a), the vigorous exercise of the right to use personal funds to finance campaign speech produces fundraising advantages for opponents in the competitive context of electoral politics.

The resulting drag on First Amendment rights is not constitutional simply because it attaches as a consequence of a statutorily imposed choice. In *Buckley*, we held that Congress "may engage in public financing of election campaigns and may condition acceptance of public funds on an agreement by the candidate to abide by specified expenditure limitations" even though we found an independent limit on overall campaign expenditures to be unconstitutional. But the choice involved in *Buckley* was quite different from the choice imposed by §319(a).

In *Buckley*, a candidate, by forgoing public financing, could retain the unfettered right to make unlimited personal expenditures. Here, §319(a) does not provide any way in which a candidate can exercise that right without abridgment. Instead, a candidate who wishes to exercise that right has two choices: abide by a limit on personal expenditures or endure the burden that is placed on that right by the activation of a scheme of discriminatory contribution limits. The choice imposed by §319(a) is not remotely parallel to that in *Buckley*.

Because §319(a) imposes a substantial burden on the exercise of the First Amendment right to use personal funds for campaign speech, that provision cannot stand unless it is "justified by a compelling state interest." No such justification is present here.

The burden imposed by §319(a) on the expenditure of personal funds is not justified by any governmental interest in eliminating corruption or the perception of corruption. The *Buckley* Court reasoned that reliance on personal funds *reduces* the threat of corruption, and therefore §319(a), by discouraging use of personal funds, disserves the anticorruption interest. Similarly, given Congress' judgment that liberalized limits for non-self-financing candidates do not unduly imperil anticorruption interests, it is hard to imagine how the denial of liberalized limits to self-financing candidates can be regarded as serving anticorruption goals sufficiently to justify the resulting constitutional burden.

The Government maintains that §319(a)'s asymmetrical limits are justified because they "level electoral opportunities for candidates of different personal wealth." "Congress enacted Section 319," the Government writes," "to reduce *the natural advantage* that wealthy individuals possess in campaigns for federal office." (emphasis added). Our prior decisions, however, provide no support for the proposition that this is a legitimate government objective. On the contrary, in *Buckley*, we held that "[t]he interest in equalizing the financial resources of candidates" did not provide a "justification for restricting" candidates' overall campaign expenditures, particularly where equalization "might serve . . . to handicap a candidate who lacked substantial name recognition or exposure of his views before the start of the campaign." We have similarly held that the interest "in equalizing the relative ability of individuals and groups to influence the outcome of elections" cannot support a cap on expenditures for "express advocacy of the election or defeat of candidates," as "the concept that government may restrict the speech of some elements of our society in order to enhance the relative voice of others is wholly foreign to the First Amendment."

The argument that a candidate's speech may be restricted in order to "level electoral opportunities" has ominous implications because it would permit Congress to arrogate the voters' authority to evaluate the strengths of candidates competing for office. Different candidates have different strengths. Some are wealthy; others have wealthy supporters who are willing to make large contributions. Some are celebrities; some have the benefit of a well-known family name. Leveling electoral opportunities means making and implementing judgments about which strengths should be permitted to contribute to the outcome of an election. The Constitution, however, confers upon voters, not Congress, the power to choose the Members of the House of Representatives, Art. I, §2, and it is a dangerous business for Congress to use the election laws to influence the voters' choices.

Finally, the Government contends that §319(a) is justified because it ameliorates the deleterious effects that result from the tight limits that federal election law places on individual campaign contributions and coordinated party expenditures. These limits, it is argued, make it harder for candidates who are not wealthy to raise funds and therefore provide a substantial advantage for wealthy candidates. Accordingly, §319(a) can be seen, not as a legislative effort to interfere with the natural operation of the electoral process, but as a legislative effort to mitigate the untoward consequences of Congress' own handiwork and restore "the normal relationship between a candidate's financial resources and the level of popular support for his candidacy."

Whatever the merits of this argument as an original matter, it is fundamentally at war with the analysis of expenditure and contributions limits that this Court adopted in *Buckley* and has applied in subsequent cases. The advantage that wealthy candidates now enjoy and that §319(a) seeks to reduce is an advantage that flows directly from *Buckley*'s disparate treatment of expenditures and contributions. If that approach is sound—and the Government does not urge us to hold otherwise—it is hard to see how undoing the consequences of that decision can be viewed as a compelling interest. If the normally applicable limits on individual contributions and coordinated party contributions are seriously distorting the electoral process, if they are feeding a "public perception that wealthy people can buy seats in Congress," and if those limits are not needed in order to combat corruption, then the obvious remedy is to raise or eliminate those limits. But the unprecedented step of imposing different contribution and coordinated party expenditure limits on candidates vying for the same seat is antithetical to the First Amendment. . . .

In sum, we hold that §§319(a) . . . violate[s] the First Amendment. The judgment of the District Court is reversed, and the case is remanded for proceedings consistent with this opinion.

It is so ordered.

JUSTICE STEVENS, with whom JUSTICE SOUTER, JUSTICE GINSBURG, and JUSTICE BREYER join as to Part II . . . dissenting. . . .

II

. . . The thrust of Davis' First Amendment challenge is that by relaxing the contribution limits applicable to the opponent of a self-funding candidate, the Millionaire's Amendment punishes the candidate who chooses to self-fund. Extrapolating from the zero-sum nature of a political race, Davis insists that any benefit conferred upon a self-funder's opponent thereby works a detriment to the self-funding candidate. Accordingly, he argues, the scheme burdens the self-funding candidate's First Amendment right to speak freely and to participate fully in the political process.

But Davis cannot show that the Millionaire's Amendment causes him — or any other self-funding candidate — any First Amendment injury whatsoever. The Millionaire's Amendment quiets no speech at all. On the contrary, it does no more than assist the opponent of a self-funding candidate in his attempts to make his voice heard; this amplification in no way mutes the voice of the millionaire, who remains able to speak as loud and as long as he likes in support of his campaign. Enhancing the speech of the millionaire's opponent, far from contravening the First Amendment, actually advances its core principles. If only one candidate can make himself heard, the voter's ability to make an informed choice is impaired. And the self-funding candidate's ability to engage meaningfully in the political process is in no way undermined by this provision.

Even were we to credit Davis' view that the benefit conferred on the self-funding candidate's opponent burdens the self-funder's First Amendment rights, the purposes of the Amendment surely justify its effects. The Court is simply wrong when it suggests that the "governmental interest in eliminating corruption or the perception of corruption," is the sole governmental interest sufficient to support campaign finance regulations. It is true, of course, that in upholding the Federal Election Campaign Act of 1971's (FECA) limits on the size of contributions to political campaigns, the *Buckley* Court held that preventing both actual corruption and the appearance of corruption were Government interests of sufficient weight that they justified any infringement upon First Amendment freedoms that resulted from FECA's contribution limits; the Court explained that, "[t]o the extent that large contributions are given to secure a political *quid pro quo* from current and potential office holders, the integrity of our system of representative democracy is undermined. . . . Of almost equal concern . . . is the impact of the appearance of corruption stemming from public awareness of the opportunities for abuse inherent in a regime of large individual financial contributions." It is also true that the Court found that same interest insufficient to justify FECA's expenditure limitations. But it does not follow that the *Buckley* Court concluded that *only* the interest in combating corruption and the appearance of corruption can justify congressional regulation of campaign financing.

Indeed, we have long recognized the strength of an independent governmental interest in reducing both the influence of wealth on the outcomes of elections, and the appearance that wealth alone dictates those results. In case after case, we have held that statutes designed to protect against the undue influence of aggregations of wealth on the political process — where such statutes are responsive to the identified evil — do not contravene the First Amendment. . . . *cf.* Red Lion Broadcasting Co. v. FCC (1969) (upholding constitutionality of several components of the FCC's "fair coverage" requirements, and explaining that "[i]t is the purpose of the First Amendment to preserve an uninhibited marketplace of ideas in which truth will ultimately prevail, rather than to countenance monopolization of that market").

Although the focus of our cases has been on aggregations of corporate rather than individual wealth, there is no reason that their logic — specifically, their concerns about the corrosive and distorting effects of wealth on our political process — is not equally applicable in the context of individual wealth. . . .

Minimizing the effect of concentrated wealth on our political process, and the concomitant interest in addressing the dangers that attend the perception that political power can be purchased, are, therefore, sufficiently weighty objectives to justify significant congressional action. And, not only was Congress motivated by proper and weighty goals in crafting the Millionaire's Amendment, the details of the scheme it devised are genuinely responsive to the problems it identified. The statute's "Opposition Personal Funds Amount" formula permits a self-funding candidate to spend as much money as he wishes, while taking into account fundraising by the relevant campaigns; it thereby ensures that a candidate who happens to enjoy a significant fundraising advantage against a self-funding opponent does not reap a windfall as a result of the enhanced contribution limits. Rather, the self-funder's opponent may avail himself of the enhanced contribution limits only until parity is achieved, at which point he becomes again ineligible for contributions above the normal maximum.

It seems uncontroversial that "there is no good reason to allow disparities in wealth to be translated into disparities in political power. A well-functioning democracy distinguishes between market processes of purchase and sale on the one hand and political processes of voting and reason-giving on the other." Sunstein, Political Equality and Unintended Consequences, 94 Colum. L. Rev. 1390 (1994). In light of that clear truth, Congress' carefully crafted attempt to reduce the distinct advantages enjoyed by wealthy candidates for congressional office does not offend the First Amendment. . . .

ASSIGNMENT S-7

In his State of the Union Address in January, 2010, with six justices of the Supreme Court in attendance, President Obama stated the following:

> With all due deference to separation of powers, last week, the Supreme Court reversed a century of law that I believe will open the floodgates for special interests, including foreign corporations, to spend without limit in our elections. (APPLAUSE.) I don't think American elections should be bankrolled by America's most powerful interests or, worse, by foreign entities. They should be decided by the American people. And I urge Democrats and Republicans to pass a bill that helps correct some of these problems.

As Democratic members of Congress and the administration surrounding the seated justices rose to applaud, cameras showed Justice Alito responding by mouthing the words, "That's not true."

Study Guide: *Is the President's characterization a fair one? On what might he have been basing his claim? How can you best summarize the difference between the majority's approach to the First Amendment and that of the dissenters? What justifications for regulating political speech are accepted by the majority? By* *the dissent? Why these? One of the questions that concerned the justices in oral argument was whether the statute permitted the government from prohibiting* books. *(The United States was represented by then-Solicitor General Elena Kagan.) What was the government's response and why did it not satisfy Justice Kennedy? What is special about books? How would you characterize the interpretive methodology of the majority? Notice the debate between Justices Scalia and Stevens about "original understandings," as well as Justice Stevens's distinction between "original expectation" and "original meaning." The decision below affects unions as well as corporations. Why is this issue all but ignored in all the opinions? How do you think the Court would or should respond to proposed legislation that imposes disclosure requirements on corporate political advertising but not on unions? Finally, notice Justice Thomas's continued objection to the constitutionality of disclosure requirements.*

CITIZENS UNITED v. FEDERAL ELECTION COMMISSION

558 U.S. _____ (2010)

JUSTICE KENNEDY delivered the opinion of the Court.

Federal law prohibits corporations and unions from using their general treasury funds to make independent expenditures for speech defined as an "electioneering communication" or for speech expressly advocating the election or defeat of a candidate. Limits on electioneering communications were upheld in McConnell v. Federal Election Comm'n (2003). The holding of *McConnell* rested to a large extent on an earlier case, Austin v. Michigan Chamber of Commerce (1990). *Austin* had held that political speech may be banned based on the speaker's corporate identity.

In this case we are asked to reconsider *Austin* and, in effect, *McConnell*. It has been noted that "*Austin* was a significant departure from ancient First Amendment principles," Federal Election Comm'n v. Wisconsin Right to Life, Inc. (2007) (WRTL) (SCALIA, J., concurring in part and concurring in judgment). We agree with that conclusion and hold that *stare decisis* does not compel the continued acceptance of *Austin*. The Government may regulate corporate political speech through disclaimer and disclosure requirements, but it may not suppress that speech altogether. We turn to the case now before us.

I

Citizens United is a nonprofit corporation [with] an annual budget of about $12 million. Most of its funds are from donations by individuals; but, in addition, it accepts a small portion of its funds from for-profit corporations.

In January 2008, Citizens United released a film entitled *Hillary: The Movie*. We refer to the film as *Hillary*. It is a 90-minute documentary about then-Senator Hillary Clinton, who was a candidate in the Democratic Party's 2008 Presidential primary elections. *Hillary* mentions Senator Clinton by name and depicts interviews with political commentators and other persons, most of them quite critical of Senator Clinton. *Hillary* was released in theaters and on DVD, but Citizens United wanted to increase distribution by making it available through video-on-demand.

Video-on-demand allows digital cable subscribers to select programming from various menus, including movies, television shows, sports, news, and music. The viewer can watch the program at any time and can elect to rewind or pause the program. In December 2007, a cable company offered, for a payment of $1.2 million, to make *Hillary* available on a video-on-demand channel called "Elections '08." Some video-on-demand services require viewers to pay a small fee to view a selected program, but here the proposal was to make *Hillary* available to viewers free of charge.

To implement the proposal, Citizens United was prepared to pay for the video-on-demand; and to promote the film, it produced two 10-second ads and one 30-second ad for *Hillary*. Each ad includes a short (and, in our view, pejorative) statement about Senator Clinton, followed by the name of the movie and the movie's Website address. Citizens United desired to promote the video-on-demand offering by running advertisements on broadcast and cable television.

Before the Bipartisan Campaign Reform Act of 2002 (BCRA), federal law prohibited—and still does prohibit—corporations and unions from using general treasury funds to make direct contributions to candidates or independent expenditures that expressly advocate the election or defeat of a candidate, through any form of media, in connection with certain qualified federal elections. BCRA §203 amended §441b to prohibit any "electioneering communication" as well. An electioneering communication is defined as "any broadcast, cable, or satellite communication" that "refers to a clearly identified candidate for Federal office" and is made within 30 days of a primary or 60 days of a general election. The Federal Election Commission's (FEC) regulations further define an electioneering communication as a communication that is "publicly distributed." "In the case of a candidate for nomination for President . . . *publicly distributed* means" that the communication "[c]an be received by 50,000 or more persons in a State where a primary election . . . is being held within 30 days." Corporations and unions are barred from using their general treasury funds for express advocacy or electioneering communications. They may establish, however, a "separate segregated fund" (known as a political action committee, or PAC) for these purposes. The moneys received by the segregated fund are limited to donations from stockholders and employees of the corporation or, in the case of unions, members of the union.

Citizens United wanted to make *Hillary* available through video-on-demand within 30 days of the 2008 primary elections. It feared, however, that both the film and the ads would be covered by §441b's ban on corporate-funded independent expenditures, thus subjecting the corporation to civil and criminal penalties. . . . In December 2007, Citizens United sought declaratory and injunctive relief against the FEC. It argued that (1) §441b is unconstitutional as applied to *Hillary*; and (2) BCRA's disclaimer and disclosure requirements are unconstitutional as applied to *Hillary* and to the three ads for the movie. . . .

III

The First Amendment provides that "Congress shall make no law . . . abridging the freedom of speech." Laws enacted to control or suppress speech may operate at different points in the speech process. . . . The law before us is an outright ban, backed by criminal sanctions. Section 441b makes it a felony for all corporations — including nonprofit advocacy corporations — either to expressly advocate the election or defeat of candidates or to broadcast electioneering communications within 30 days of a primary election and 60 days of a general election. Thus, the following acts would all be felonies under §441b: The Sierra Club runs an ad, within the crucial phase of 60 days before the general election, that exhorts the public to disapprove of a Congressman who favors logging in national forests; the National Rifle Association publishes a book urging the public to vote for the challenger because the incumbent U. S. Senator supports a handgun ban; and the American Civil Liberties Union creates a Web site telling the public to vote for a Presidential candidate in light of that candidate's defense of free speech. These prohibitions are classic examples of censorship.

Section 441b is a ban on corporate speech notwithstanding the fact that a PAC created by a corporation can still speak. A PAC is a separate association from the corporation. So the PAC exemption from §441b's expenditure ban, §441b(b)(2), does not allow corporations to speak. Even if a PAC could somehow allow a corporation to speak — and it does not — the option to form PACs does not alleviate the First Amendment problems with §441b. PACs are burdensome alternatives; they are expensive to administer and subject to extensive regulations. For example, every PAC must appoint a treasurer, forward donations to the treasurer promptly, keep detailed records of the identities of the persons making donations, preserve receipts for three years, and file an organization statement and report changes to this information within 10 days.

And that is just the beginning. PACs must file detailed monthly reports with the FEC, which are due at different times depending on the type of election that is about to occur. . . . PACs have to comply with these regulations just to speak. This might explain why fewer than 2,000 of the millions of corporations in this country have PACs. PACs, furthermore, must exist before they can speak. Given the onerous restrictions, a corporation may not be able to establish a PAC in time to make its views known regarding candidates and issues in a current campaign.

Section 441b's prohibition on corporate independent expenditures is thus a ban on speech. As a "restriction on the amount of money a person or group can spend on political communication during a campaign," that statute "necessarily reduces the quantity of expression by restricting the number of issues discussed, the depth of their exploration, and the size of the audience reached." Buckley v. Valeo (1976) (*per curiam*). Were the Court to uphold these restrictions, the Government could repress speech by silencing certain voices at any of the various points in the speech process. If §441b applied to individuals, no one would believe that it is merely a time, place, or manner restriction on speech. Its purpose and effect are to silence entities whose voices the Government deems to be suspect.

Speech is an essential mechanism of democracy, for it is the means to hold officials accountable to the people. The right of citizens to inquire, to hear, to speak, and to use information to reach consensus is a precondition to enlightened self-government and a necessary means to protect it. The First Amendment "'has its fullest and most urgent application' to speech uttered during a campaign for political office." Eu v. San Francisco County Democratic Central Comm. (1989).

For these reasons, political speech must prevail against laws that would suppress it, whether by design or inadvertence. Laws that burden political speech are "subject to strict scrutiny," which requires the Government to prove that the restriction "furthers a compelling interest and is narrowly tailored to achieve that interest." WRTL (opinion of Roberts, C. J.). While it might be maintained that political speech simply cannot be banned or restricted as a categorical matter, the quoted language from WRTL provides a sufficient framework for protecting the relevant First Amendment interests in this case. We shall employ it here.

Premised on mistrust of governmental power, the First Amendment stands against attempts to disfavor certain subjects or viewpoints. See, *e.g.*, United States v. Playboy Entertainment Group, Inc. (striking down content-based restriction). Prohibited, too, are restrictions distinguishing among different speakers, allowing speech by some but not others. See First Nat. Bank of Boston v. Bellotti (1978). As instruments to censor, these categories are interrelated: Speech restrictions based on the identity of the speaker are all too often simply a means to control content.

Quite apart from the purpose or effect of regulating content, moreover, the Government may commit a constitutional wrong when by law it identifies certain preferred speakers. By taking the right to speak from some and giving it to others, the Government deprives the disadvantaged person or class of the right to use speech to strive to establish worth, standing, and respect for the speaker's voice. The Government may not by these means deprive the public of the right and privilege to determine for itself what speech and speakers are worthy of consideration. The First Amendment protects speech and speaker, and the ideas that flow from each.

The Court has upheld a narrow class of speech restrictions that operate to the disadvantage of certain persons, but these rulings were based on an interest in allowing governmental entities to perform their functions. The corporate independent expenditures at issue in this case, however, would not interfere with governmental functions, so these cases are inapposite. These precedents stand only for the proposition that there are certain governmental functions that cannot operate without some restrictions on particular kinds of speech. By contrast, it is inherent in the nature of the political process that voters must be free to obtain information from diverse sources in order to determine how to cast their votes. At least before *Austin*, the Court had not allowed the exclusion of a class of speakers from the general public dialogue.

We find no basis for the proposition that, in the context of political speech, the Government may impose restrictions on certain disfavored speakers. Both history and logic lead us to this conclusion.

A

The Court has recognized that First Amendment protection extends to corporations. [21 citations omitted.] This protection has been extended by explicit holdings to the context of political speech. Under the rationale of these precedents, political speech does not lose First Amendment protection "simply because its source is a corporation." *Bellotti*. The Court has thus rejected the argument that political speech of corporations or other associations should be treated differently under the First Amendment simply because such associations are not "natural persons."

At least since the latter part of the 19th century, the laws of some States and of the United States imposed a ban on corporate direct contributions to candidates. Yet not until 1947 did Congress first prohibit independent expenditures by corporations and labor unions in §304 of the Labor Management Relations Act 1947. In passing this Act Congress overrode the veto of President Truman, who warned that the expenditure ban was a "dangerous intrusion on free speech." For almost three decades thereafter, the Court did not reach the question whether restrictions on corporate and union expenditures are constitutional . . . .

In *Buckley*, the Court addressed various challenges to the Federal Election Campaign Act of 1971 (FECA) as amended in 1974. These amendments created an independent expenditure ban separate from that applied to individuals as well as corporations and labor unions. Before addressing the constitutionality of [the] independent expenditure ban, *Buckley* first upheld [the] FECA's limits on direct contributions to candidates. The *Buckley* Court recognized a "sufficiently important" governmental interest in "the prevention of corruption and the appearance of corruption." This followed from the Court's concern that large contributions could be given "to secure a political *quid pro quo*."

The *Buckley* Court explained that the potential for *quid pro quo* corruption distinguished direct contributions to candidates from independent expenditures. The Court emphasized that "the independent expenditure ceiling . . . fails to serve any substantial governmental interest in stemming the reality or appearance of corruption in the electoral process," because "[t]he absence of prearrangement and coordination . . . alleviates the danger that expenditures will be given as a *quid pro quo* for improper commitments from the candidate." *Buckley* invalidated [the] restrictions on independent expenditures, with only one Justice dissenting. . . . Notwithstanding this precedent, Congress recodified [the] corporate and union expenditure ban at §441b four months after *Buckley* was decided. Section 441b is the independent expenditure restriction challenged here.

Less than two years after *Buckley*, *Bellotti* reaffirmed the First Amendment principle that the Government cannot restrict political speech based on the speaker's corporate identity. *Bellotti* could not have been clearer when it struck down a state-law prohibition on corporate independent expenditures related to referenda issues:

> "We thus find no support in the First . . . Amendment, or in the decisions of this Court, for the proposition that speech that otherwise would be within the protection

> of the First Amendment loses that protection simply because its source is a corporation that cannot prove, to the satisfaction of a court, a material effect on its business or property. . . . [That proposition] amounts to an impermissible legislative prohibition of speech based on the identity of the interests that spokesmen may represent in public debate over controversial issues and a requirement that the speaker have a sufficiently great interest in the subject to justify communication. . . .
>
> "In the realm of protected speech, the legislature is constitutionally disqualified from dictating the subjects about which persons may speak and the speakers who may address a public issue."

It is important to note that the reasoning and holding of *Bellotti* did not rest on the existence of a viewpoint-discriminatory statute. It rested on the principle that the Government lacks the power to ban corporations from speaking.

Bellotti did not address the constitutionality of the State's ban on corporate independent expenditures to support candidates. In our view, however, that restriction would have been unconstitutional under *Bellotti*'s central principle: that the First Amendment does not allow political speech restrictions based on a speaker's corporate identity.

Thus the law stood until *Austin*. *Austin* "uph[eld] a direct restriction on the independent expenditure of funds for political speech for the first time in [this Court's] history." (KENNEDY, J., dissenting). There, the Michigan Chamber of Commerce sought to use general treasury funds to run a newspaper ad supporting a specific candidate. Michigan law, however, prohibited corporate independent expenditures that supported or opposed any candidate for state office. A violation of the law was punishable as a felony. The Court sustained the speech prohibition.

To bypass *Buckley* and *Bellotti*, the *Austin* Court identified a new governmental interest in limiting political speech: an antidistortion interest. *Austin* found a compelling governmental interest in preventing "the corrosive and distorting effects of immense aggregations of wealth that are accumulated with the help of the corporate form and that have little or no correlation to the public's support for the corporation's political ideas."

B

The Court is thus confronted with conflicting lines of precedent: a pre-*Austin* line that forbids restrictions on political speech based on the speaker's corporate identity and a post-*Austin* line that permits them. No case before *Austin* had held that Congress could prohibit independent expenditures for political speech based on the speaker's corporate identity. . . .

In its defense of the corporate-speech restrictions in §441b, the Government notes the antidistortion rationale on which *Austin* and its progeny rest in part, yet it all but abandons reliance upon it. It argues instead that two other compelling interests support *Austin*'s holding that corporate expenditure restrictions are constitutional: an anticorruption interest, and a shareholder-protection interest. We consider the three points in turn.

1

As for *Austin*'s antidistortion rationale, the Government does little to defend it. And with good reason, for the rationale cannot support §441b.

If the First Amendment has any force, it prohibits Congress from fining or jailing citizens, or associations of citizens, for simply engaging in political speech. If the antidistortion rationale were to be accepted, however, it would permit Government to ban political speech simply because the speaker is an association that has taken on the corporate form. The Government contends that *Austin* permits it to ban corporate expenditures for almost all forms of communication stemming from a corporation. If *Austin* were correct, the Government could prohibit a corporation from expressing political views in media beyond those presented here, such as by printing books. The Government responds "that the FEC has never applied this statute to a book," and if it did, "there would be quite [a] good as-applied challenge." Tr. of Oral Arg. 65 (Sept. 9, 2009). This troubling assertion of brooding governmental power cannot be reconciled with the confidence and stability in civic discourse that the First Amendment must secure.

Political speech is "indispensable to decisionmaking in a democracy, and this is no less true because the speech comes from a corporation rather than an individual." *Bellotti*; see *ibid.* (the worth of speech "does not depend upon the identity of its source, whether corporation, association, union, or individual"); *Buckley* ("[T]he concept that government may restrict the speech of some elements of our society in order to enhance the relative voice of others is wholly foreign to the First Amendment"). This protection for speech is inconsistent with *Austin*'s antidistortion rationale. *Austin* sought to defend the antidistortion rationale as a means to prevent corporations from obtaining "'an unfair advantage in the political marketplace'" by using "'resources amassed in the economic marketplace.'" But *Buckley* rejected the premise that the Government has an interest "in equalizing the relative ability of individuals and groups to influence the outcome of elections." *Buckley* was specific in stating that "the skyrocketing cost of political campaigns" could not sustain the governmental prohibition. The First Amendment's protections do not depend on the speaker's "financial ability to engage in public discussion."

The Court reaffirmed these conclusions when it invalidated the BCRA provision that increased the cap on contributions to one candidate if the opponent made certain expenditures from personal funds. See Davis v. Federal Election Comm'n (2008) ("Leveling electoral opportunities means making and implementing judgments about which strengths should be permitted to contribute to the outcome of an election. The Constitution, however, confers upon voters, not Congress, the power to choose the Members of the House of Representatives, Art. I, §2, and it is a dangerous business for Congress to use the election laws to influence the voters' choices"). The rule that political speech cannot be limited based on a speaker's wealth is a necessary consequence of the premise that the First Amendment generally prohibits the suppression of political speech based on the speaker's identity.

Either as support for its antidistortion rationale or as a further argument, the *Austin* majority undertook to distinguish wealthy individuals from corporations on the ground that "[s]tate law grants corporations special advantages — such as limited liability, perpetual life, and favorable treatment of the accumulation and distribution of assets." This does not suffice, however, to allow laws prohibiting speech. "It is rudimentary that the State cannot exact as the price of those special advantages the forfeiture of First Amendment rights." *Id.* (SCALIA , J., dissenting).

It is irrelevant for purposes of the First Amendment that corporate funds may "have little or no correlation to the public's support for the corporation's political ideas." *Id.* (majority opinion). All speakers, including individuals and the media, use money amassed from the economic marketplace to fund their speech. The First Amendment protects the resulting speech, even if it was enabled by economic transactions with persons or entities who disagree with the speaker's ideas.

Austin's antidistortion rationale would produce the dangerous, and unacceptable, consequence that Congress could ban political speech of media corporations. See *McConnell* (opinion of THOMAS, J.) ("The chilling endpoint of the Court's reasoning is not difficult to foresee: outright regulation of the press"). Media corporations are now exempt from §441b's ban on corporate expenditures. Yet media corporations accumulate wealth with the help of the corporate form, the largest media corporations have "immense aggregations of wealth," and the views expressed by media corporations often "have little or no correlation to 'the public's support" for those views. *Austin.* Thus, under the Government's reasoning, wealthy media corporations could have their voices diminished to put them on par with other media entities. There is no precedent for permitting this under the First Amendment.

The media exemption discloses further difficulties with the law now under consideration. There is no precedent supporting laws that attempt to distinguish between corporations which are deemed to be exempt as media corporations and those which are not. "We have consistently rejected the proposition that the institutional press has any constitutional privilege beyond that of other speakers." *Id.* (SCALIA, J., dissenting) With the advent of the Internet and the decline of print and broadcast media, moreover, the line between the media and others who wish to comment on political and social issues becomes far more blurred.

The law's exception for media corporations is, on its own terms, all but an admission of the invalidity of the antidistortion rationale. And the exemption results in a further, separate reason for finding this law invalid: Again by its own terms, the law exempts some corporations but covers others, even though both have the need or the motive to communicate their views. The exemption applies to media corporations owned or controlled by corporations that have diverse and substantial investments and participate in endeavors other than news. So even assuming the most doubtful proposition that a news organization has a right to speak when others do not, the exemption would allow a conglomerate that owns both a media business and an unrelated business to influence or control the media in order to advance its overall business interest. At the same time, some other corporation, with an identical business interest but no media outlet in its ownership structure, would be forbidden to speak or inform the public about the same issue. This differential treatment cannot be squared with the First Amendment.

There is simply no support for the view that the First Amendment, as originally understood, would permit the suppression of political speech by media corporations. The Framers may not have anticipated modern business and media corporations. Yet television networks and major newspapers owned by media corporations have become the most important means of mass communication in modern times. The First Amendment was certainly not understood to condone the suppression of political speech in society's most salient media. It was understood as a response to the repression of speech and the press that had existed in England and the heavy taxes on the press that were imposed in the colonies. The great debates between the Federalists and the Anti-Federalists over our founding document were published and expressed in the most important means of mass communication of that era — newspapers owned by individuals. At the founding, speech was open, comprehensive, and vital to society's definition of itself; there were no limits on the sources of speech and knowledge. The Framers may have been unaware of certain types of speakers or forms of communication, but that does not mean that those speakers and media are entitled to less First Amendment protection than those types of speakers and media that provided the means of communicating political ideas when the Bill of Rights was adopted.

Austin interferes with the "open marketplace" of ideas protected by the First Amendment. It permits the Government to ban the political speech of millions of associations of citizens. See Statistics of Income (5.8 million for-profit corporations filed 2006 tax returns). Most of these are small corporations without large amounts of wealth. See Supp. Brief for Chamber of Commerce of the United States of America (96% of the 3 million businesses that belong to the U. S. Chamber of Commerce have fewer than 100 employees); M. Keightley, Congressional Research Service Report for Congress, Business Organizational Choices: Taxation and Responses to Legislative Changes (2009) (more than 75% of corporations whose income is taxed under federal law have less than $1 million in receipts per year). This fact belies the Government's argument that the statute is justified on the ground that it prevents the "distorting effects of immense aggregations of wealth." *Austin*. It is not even aimed at amassed wealth.

The censorship we now confront is vast in its reach. . . . By suppressing the speech of manifold corporations, both for-profit and nonprofit, the Government prevents their voices and viewpoints from reaching the public and advising voters on which persons or entities are hostile to their interests. Factions will necessarily form in our Republic, but the remedy of "destroying the liberty" of some factions is "worse than the disease." The Federalist No. 10 (J. Madison). Factions should be checked by permitting them all to speak and by entrusting the people to judge what is true and what is false . . . .

Even if §441b's expenditure ban were constitutional, wealthy corporations could still lobby elected officials, although smaller corporations may not have the resources to do so. And wealthy individuals and unincorporated associations can spend unlimited amounts on independent expenditures. Yet certain disfavored associations of citizens — those that have taken on the corporate form — are penalized for engaging in the same political speech.

When Government seeks to use its full power, including the criminal law, to command where a person may get his or her information or what distrusted source he or she may not hear, it uses censorship to control thought. This is unlawful. The First Amendment confirms the freedom to think for ourselves.

2

What we have said also shows the invalidity of other arguments made by the Government. For the most part relinquishing the antidistortion rationale, the Government falls back on the argument that corporate political speech can be banned in order to prevent corruption or its appearance. In *Buckley*, the Court found this interest "sufficiently important" to allow limits on contributions but did not extend that reasoning to expenditure limits. When *Buckley* examined an expenditure ban, it found "that the governmental interest in preventing corruption and the appearance of corruption [was] inadequate to justify [the ban] on independent expenditures."

With regard to large direct contributions, *Buckley* reasoned that they could be given "to secure a political *quid pro quo*," and that "the scope of such pernicious practices can never be reliably ascertained." The practices *Buckley* noted would be covered by bribery laws if a *quid pro quo* arrangement were proved. The Court, in consequence, has noted that restrictions on direct contributions are preventative, because few if any contributions to candidates will involve *quid pro quo* arrangements. The *Buckley* Court, nevertheless, sustained limits on direct contributions in order to ensure against the reality or appearance of corruption. That case did not extend this rationale to independent expenditures, and the Court does not do so here.

"The absence of prearrangement and coordination of an expenditure with the candidate or his agent not only undermines the value of the expenditure to the candidate, but also alleviates the danger that expenditures will be given as a *quid pro quo* for improper commitments from the candidate." *Buckley*. Limits on independent expenditures, such as §441b, have a chilling effect extending well beyond the Government's interest in preventing *quid pro quo* corruption. The anticorruption interest is not sufficient to displace the speech here in question. . . .

When *Buckley* identified a sufficiently important governmental interest in preventing corruption or the appearance of corruption, that interest was limited to *quid pro quo* corruption. The fact that speakers may have influence over or access to elected officials does not mean that these officials are corrupt:

> "Favoritism and influence are not . . . avoidable in representative politics. It is in the nature of an elected representative to favor certain policies, and, by necessary corollary, to favor the voters and contributors who support those policies. It is well understood that a substantial and legitimate reason, if not the only reason, to cast a vote for, or to make a contribution to, one candidate over another is that the can-

didate will respond by producing those political outcomes the supporter favors. Democracy is premised on responsiveness." *McConnell* (opinion of KENNEDY, J.).

Reliance on a "generic favoritism or influence theory . . . is at odds with standard First Amendment analyses because it is unbounded and susceptible to no limiting principle."

The appearance of influence or access, furthermore, will not cause the electorate to lose faith in our democracy. By definition, an independent expenditure is political speech presented to the electorate that is not coordinated with a candidate. The fact that a corporation, or any other speaker, is willing to spend money to try to persuade voters presupposes that the people have the ultimate influence over elected officials. This is inconsistent with any suggestion that the electorate will refuse "to take part in democratic governance" because of additional political speech made by a corporation or any other speaker. *McConnell*. . . .

We must give weight to attempts by Congress to seek to dispel either the appearance or the reality of these influences. The remedies enacted by law, however, must comply with the First Amendment; and, it is our law and our tradition that more speech, not less, is the governing rule. An outright ban on corporate political speech during the critical preelection period is not a permissible remedy. Here Congress has created categorical bans on speech that are asymmetrical to preventing *quid pro quo* corruption.

3

The Government contends further that corporate independent expenditures can be limited because of its interest in protecting dissenting shareholders from being compelled to fund corporate political speech. This asserted interest, like *Austin*'s antidistortion rationale, would allow the Government to ban the political speech even of media corporations. Assume, for example, that a shareholder of a corporation that owns a newspaper disagrees with the political views the newspaper expresses. Under the Government's view, that potential disagreement could give the Government the authority to restrict the media corporation's political speech. The First Amendment does not allow that power. There is, furthermore, little evidence of abuse that cannot be corrected by shareholders "through the procedures of corporate democracy." *Bellotti*.

Those reasons are sufficient to reject this shareholder-protection interest; and, moreover, the statute is both underinclusive and overinclusive. As to the first, if Congress had been seeking to protect dissenting shareholders, it would not have banned corporate speech in only certain media within 30 or 60 days before an election. A dissenting shareholder's interests would be implicated by speech in any media at any time. As to the second, the statute is overinclusive because it covers all corporations, including nonprofit corporations and for-profit corporations with only single shareholders. As to other corporations, the remedy is not to restrict speech but to consider and explore other regulatory mechanisms.

The regulatory mechanism here, based on speech, contravenes the First Amendment.

4

We need not reach the question whether the Government has a compelling interest in preventing foreign individuals or associations from influencing our Nation's political process. Section 441b is not limited to corporations or associations that were created in foreign countries or funded predominately by foreign shareholders. Section 441b therefore would be overbroad even if we assumed, *arguendo*, that the Government has a compelling interest in limiting foreign influence over our political process. . . .

C

Our precedent is to be respected unless the most convincing of reasons demonstrates that adherence to it puts us on a course that is sure error. . . . For the reasons above, it must be concluded that *Austin* was not well reasoned. . . .

Due consideration leads to this conclusion: *Austin* should be and now is overruled. We return to the principle established in *Buckley* and *Bellotti* that the Government may not suppress political speech on the basis of the speaker's corporate identity. No sufficient governmental interest justifies limits on the political speech of nonprofit or for-profit corporations. . . . Given our conclusion we are further required to overrule the part of *McConnell* that upheld BCRA §203's extension of §441b's restrictions on corporate independent expenditures. The *McConnell* Court relied on the antidistortion interest recognized in *Austin* to uphold a greater restriction on speech than the restriction upheld in *Austin* and we have found this interest unconvincing and insufficient. This part of *McConnell* is now overruled.

IV[1]

Citizens United next challenges BCRA's disclaimer and disclosure provisions as applied to *Hillary* and the three advertisements for the movie. Under BCRA §311, televised electioneering communications funded by anyone other than a candidate must include a disclaimer that "_____ is responsible for the content of this advertising." The required statement must be made in a "clearly spoken manner," and displayed on the screen in a "clearly readable manner" for at least four seconds. It must state that the communication "is not authorized by any candidate or candidate's committee"; it must also display the name and address (or Web site address) of the person or group that funded the advertisement. Under BCRA §201, any person who spends more than $10,000 on electioneering communications within a calendar year must file a disclosure statement with the FEC. That statement must identify the person making the expenditure, the

1. [Justice Thomas dissented from this portion of the Court's opinion. — Ed.]

amount of the expenditure, the election to which the communication was directed, and the names of certain contributors.

Disclaimer and disclosure requirements may burden the ability to speak, but they "impose no ceiling on campaign-related activities," *Buckley*, and "do not prevent anyone from speaking," *McConnell*. The Court has subjected these requirements to "exacting scrutiny," which requires a "substantial relation" between the disclosure requirement and a "sufficiently important" governmental interest.

In *Buckley*, the Court explained that disclosure could be justified based on a governmental interest in "provid[ing] the electorate with information" about the sources of election-related spending. The *McConnell* Court applied this interest in rejecting facial challenges to BCRA §§201 and 311. There was evidence in the record that independent groups were running election-related advertisements "while hiding behind dubious and misleading names." The Court therefore upheld BCRA §§201 and 311 on the ground that they would help citizens "make informed choices in the political marketplace." Although both provisions were facially upheld, the Court acknowledged that as-applied challenges would be available if a group could show a "'reasonable probability'" that disclosure of its contributors' names "will subject them to threats, harassment, or reprisals from either Government officials or private parties." . . .

Citizens United argues that disclosure requirements can chill donations to an organization by exposing donors to retaliation. Some *amici* point to recent events in which donors to certain causes were blacklisted, threatened, or otherwise targeted for retaliation. See Brief for Institute for Justice; Brief for Alliance Defense Fund. In *McConnell*, the Court recognized that §201 would be unconstitutional as applied to an organization if there were a reasonable probability that the group's members would face threats, harassment, or reprisals if their names were disclosed. The examples cited by *amici* are cause for concern. Citizens United, however, has offered no evidence that its members may face similar threats or reprisals. To the contrary, Citizens United has been disclosing its donors for years and has identified no instance of harassment or retaliation. . . .

With the advent of the Internet, prompt disclosure of expenditures can provide shareholders and citizens with the information needed to hold corporations and elected officials accountable for their positions and supporters. . . . The First Amendment protects political speech; and disclosure permits citizens and shareholders to react to the speech of corporate entities in a proper way. This transparency enables the electorate to make informed decisions and give proper weight to different speakers and messages.

For the same reasons we uphold the application of BCRA §§201 and 311 to the ads, we affirm their application to *Hillary*. We find no constitutional impediment to the application of BCRA's disclaimer and disclosure requirements to a movie broadcast via video-on-demand. And there has been no showing that, as applied in this case, these requirements would impose a chill on speech or expression.

V

When word concerning the plot of the movie *Mr. Smith Goes to Washington* reached the circles of Government, some officials sought, by persuasion, to discourage its distribution. Under *Austin*, though, officials could have done more than discourage its distribution—they could have banned the film. After all, it, like *Hillary*, was speech funded by a corporation that was critical of Members of Congress. *Mr. Smith Goes to Washington* may be fiction and caricature; but fiction and caricature can be a powerful force.

Modern day movies, television comedies, or skits on Youtube.com might portray public officials or public policies in unflattering ways. Yet if a covered transmission during the blackout period creates the background for candidate endorsement or opposition, a felony occurs solely because a corporation, other than an exempt media corporation, has made the "purchase, payment, distribution, loan, advance, deposit, or gift of money or anything of value" in order to engage in political speech. Speech would be suppressed in the realm where its necessity is most evident: in the public dialogue preceding a real election. Governments are often hostile to speech, but under our law and our tradition it seems stranger than fiction for our Government to make this political speech a crime. Yet this is the statute's purpose and design.

Some members of the public might consider *Hillary* to be insightful and instructive; some might find it to be neither high art nor a fair discussion on how to set the Nation's course; still others simply might suspend judgment on these points but decide to think more about issues and candidates. Those choices and assessments, however, are not for the Government to make. "The First Amendment underwrites the freedom to experiment and to create in the realm of thought and speech. Citizens must be free to use new forms, and new forums, for the expression of ideas. The civic discourse belongs to the people, and the Government may not prescribe the means used to conduct it." *McConnell* (opinion of KENNEDY, J.).

The judgment of the District Court is reversed with respect to the constitutionality of §441b's restrictions on corporate independent expenditures. The judgment is affirmed with respect to BCRA's disclaimer and disclosure requirements. The case is remanded for further proceedings consistent with this opinion.

It is so ordered.

CHIEF JUSTICE ROBERTS, with whom JUSTICE ALITO joins, concurring.

. . . I write separately to address the important principles of judicial restraint and *stare decisis* implicated in this case. . . . Fidelity to precedent—the policy of *stare decisis*—is vital to the proper exercise of the judicial function. "*Stare decisis* is the preferred course because it promotes the evenhanded, predictable, and consistent development of legal principles, fosters reliance on judicial decisions, and contributes to the actual and perceived integrity of the judicial process." Payne v. Tennessee (1991). For these reasons, we have long recognized that departures from precedent are inappropriate in the absence of a "special justification." Arizona v. Rumsey (1984).

At the same time, *stare decisis* is neither an "inexorable command," Lawrence v. Texas (2003), nor "a mechanical formula of adherence to the latest decision," Helvering v. Hallock (1940), especially in constitutional cases. If it were, segregation would be legal, minimum wage laws would be unconstitutional, and the Government could wiretap ordinary criminal suspects without first obtaining warrants. See Plessy v. Ferguson (1896), overruled by Brown v. Board of Education (1954); Adkins v. Children's Hospital of D. C. (1923), overruled by West Coast Hotel Co. v. Parrish (1937); Olmstead v. United States (1928), overruled by Katz v. United States (1967). . . .

Stare decisis is instead a "principle of policy." *Helvering*. When considering whether to reexamine a prior erroneous holding, we must balance the importance of having constitutional questions *decided* against the importance of having them *decided right*. . . . In conducting this balancing, we must keep in mind that *stare decisis* is not an end in itself. It is instead "the means by which we ensure that the law will not merely change erratically, but will develop in a principled and intelligible fashion." Vasquez v. Hillery (1986). Its greatest purpose is to serve a constitutional ideal — the rule of law. It follows that in the unusual circumstance when fidelity to any particular precedent does more to damage this constitutional ideal than to advance it, we must be more willing to depart from that precedent. . . .

[T]he *Austin* decision is uniquely destabilizing because it threatens to subvert our Court's decisions even outside the particular context of corporate express advocacy. The First Amendment theory underlying *Austin*'s holding is extraordinarily broad. *Austin*'s logic would authorize government prohibition of political speech by a category of speakers in the name of equality — a point that most scholars acknowledge (and many celebrate), but that the dissent denies.

It should not be surprising, then, that Members of the Court have relied on *Austin*'s expansive logic to justify greater incursions on the First Amendment, even outside the original context of corporate advocacy on behalf of candidates running for office. . . .

To the extent that the Government's case for reaffirming *Austin* depends on radically reconceptualizing its reasoning, that argument is at odds with itself. *Stare decisis* is a doctrine of preservation, not transformation. It counsels deference to past mistakes, but provides no justification for making new ones. There is therefore no basis for the Court to give precedential sway to reasoning that it has never accepted, simply because that reasoning happens to support a conclusion reached on different grounds that have since been abandoned or discredited.

Doing so would undermine the rule-of-law values that justify *stare decisis* in the first place. It would effectively license the Court to invent and adopt new principles of constitutional law solely for the purpose of rationalizing its past errors, without a proper analysis of whether those principles have merit on their own. This approach would allow the Court's past missteps to spawn future mistakes, undercutting the very rule-of-law values that *stare decisis* is designed to protect.

None of this is to say that the Government is barred from making new arguments to support the outcome in *Austin*. On the contrary, it is free to do so. And of course the Court is free to accept them. But the Government's new arguments must stand or fall on their own; they are not entitled to receive the special deference we accord to precedent. . . .

JUSTICE SCALIA, with whom JUSTICE ALITO joins, and with whom JUSTICE THOMAS joins in part, concurring.

I join the opinion of the Court.[2]

I write separately to address JUSTICE STEVENS' discussion of "Original Understandings," (hereinafter referred to as the dissent). This section of the dissent purports to show that today's decision is not supported by the original understanding of the First Amendment. The dissent attempts this demonstration, however, in splendid isolation from the text of the First Amendment. It never shows why "the freedom of speech" that was the right of Englishmen did not include the freedom to speak in association with other individuals, including association in the corporate form. To be sure, in 1791 (as now) corporations could pursue only the objectives set forth in their charters; but the dissent provides no evidence that their speech in the pursuit of those objectives could be censored.

Instead of taking this straightforward approach to determining the Amendment's meaning, the dissent embarks on a detailed exploration of the Framers' views about the "role of corporations in society." The Framers didn't like corporations, the dissent concludes, and therefore it follows (as night the day) that corporations had no rights of free speech. Of course the Framers' personal affection or disaffection for corporations is relevant only insofar as it can be thought to be reflected in the understood meaning of the text they enacted — not, as the dissent suggests, as a freestanding substitute for that text. But the dissent's distortion of proper analysis is even worse than that. Though faced with a constitutional text that makes no distinction between types of speakers, the dissent feels no necessity to provide even an isolated statement from the founding era to the effect that corporations are not covered, but places the burden on petitioners to bring forward statements showing that they are ("there is not a scintilla of evidence to support the notion that anyone believed [the First Amendment] would preclude regulatory distinctions based on the corporate form.").

Despite the corporation-hating quotations the dissent has dredged up, it is far from clear that by the end of the 18th century corporations were despised. If so, how came there to be so many of them? . . . As I have previously noted, "[b]y the end of the eighteenth century the corporation was a familiar figure in American economic life." McConnell v. Federal Election Comm'n (2003)

2. JUSTICE THOMAS does not join Part IV of the Court's opinion.

(SCALIA, J., concurring in part, concurring in judgment in part, and dissenting in part).

Even if we thought it proper to apply the dissent's approach of excluding from First Amendment coverage what the Founders disliked, and even if we agreed that the Founders disliked founding-era corporations; modern corporations might not qualify for exclusion. Most of the Founders' resentment towards corporations was directed at the state-granted monopoly privileges that individually chartered corporations enjoyed. Modern corporations do not have such privileges, and would probably have been favored by most of our enterprising Founders—excluding, perhaps, Thomas Jefferson and others favoring perpetuation of an agrarian society. Moreover, if the Founders' specific intent with respect to corporations is what matters, why does the dissent ignore the Founders' views about other legal entities that have more in common with modern business corporations than the founding-era corporations? At the time of the founding, religious, educational, and literary corporations were incorporated under general incorporation statutes, much as business corporations are today. There were also small unincorporated business associations, which some have argued were the "'true progenitors'" of today's business corporations. [L. Friedman, A History of American Law (2d ed. 1985)] Were all of these silently excluded from the protections of the First Amendment?

The lack of a textual exception for speech by corporations cannot be explained on the ground that such organizations did not exist or did not speak. To the contrary, colleges, towns and cities, religious institutions, and guilds had long been organized as corporations at common law and under the King's charter, and as I have discussed, the practice of incorporation only expanded in the United States. Both corporations and voluntary associations actively petitioned the Government and expressed their views in newspapers and pamphlets. For example: An antislavery Quaker corporation petitioned the First Congress, distributed pamphlets, and communicated through the press in 1790. The New York Sons of Liberty sent a circular to colonies farther south in 1766. And the Society for the Relief and Instruction of Poor Germans circulated a biweekly paper from 1755 to 1757. The dissent offers no evidence—none whatever—that the First Amendment 's unqualified text was originally understood to exclude such associational speech from its protection.

Historical evidence relating to the textually similar clause "the freedom of . . . the press" also provides no support for the proposition that the First Amendment excludes conduct of artificial legal entities from the scope of its protection. The freedom of "the press" was widely understood to protect the publishing activities of individual editors and printers. But these individuals often acted through newspapers, which (much like corporations) had their own names, outlived the individuals who had founded them, could be bought and sold, were sometimes owned by more than one person, and were operated for profit. Their activities were not stripped of First Amendment protection simply because they were carried out under the banner of an artificial legal entity. And the notion which follows from the dissent's view, that modern newspapers, since they are incorporated, have free-speech rights only at the sufferance of Congress, boggles the mind. . . .

The dissent says that when the Framers "constitutionalized the right to free speech in the First Amendment , it was the free speech of individual Americans that they had in mind." That is no doubt true. All the provisions of the Bill of Rights set forth the rights of individual men and women — not, for example, of trees or polar bears. But the individual person's right to speak includes the right to speak *in association with other individual persons*. Surely the dissent does not believe that speech by the Republican Party or the Democratic Party can be censored because it is not the speech of "an individual American." It is the speech of many individual Americans, who have associated in a common cause, giving the leadership of the party the right to speak on their behalf. The association of individuals in a business corporation is no different — or at least it cannot be denied the right to speak on the simplistic ground that it is not "an individual American."[3]

But to return to, and summarize, my principal point, which is the conformity of today's opinion with the original meaning of the First Amendment. The Amendment is written in terms of "speech," not speakers. Its text offers no foothold for excluding any category of speaker, from single individuals to partnerships of individuals, to unincorporated associations of individuals, to incorporated associations of individuals — and the dissent offers no evidence about the original meaning of the text to support any such exclusion. We are therefore simply left with the question whether the speech at issue in this case is "speech" covered by the First Amendment. No one says otherwise. A documentary film critical of a potential Presidential candidate is core political speech, and its nature as such does not change simply because it was funded by a corporation. Nor does the character of that funding produce any reduction whatever in the "inherent worth of the speech" and "its capacity for informing the public," First Nat. Bank of Boston v. Bellotti (1978). Indeed, to exclude or impede corporate speech is to muzzle the principal agents of the modern free economy. We should celebrate rather than condemn the addition of this speech to the public debate.

JUSTICE STEVENS, with whom JUSTICE GINSBURG, JUSTICE BREYER, and JUSTICE SOTOMAYOR join, concurring in part and dissenting in part.

The real issue in this case concerns how, not if, the appellant may finance its electioneering. Citizens United is a wealthy nonprofit corporation that runs a political action committee (PAC) with millions of dollars in assets. Under the

3. The dissent says that "speech" refers to oral communications of human beings, and since corporations are not human beings they cannot speak. This is sophistry. The authorized spokesman of a corporation is a human being, who speaks on behalf of the human beings who have formed that association — just as the spokesman of an unincorporated association speaks on behalf of its members. The power to publish thoughts, no less than the power to speak thoughts, belongs only to human beings, but the dissent sees no problem with a corporation's enjoying the freedom of the press. . . .

Bipartisan Campaign Reform Act of 2002 (BCRA), it could have used those assets to televise and promote *Hillary: The Movie* wherever and whenever it wanted to. It also could have spent unrestricted sums to broadcast *Hillary* at any time other than the 30 days before the last primary election. Neither Citizens United's nor any other corporation's speech has been "banned." All that the parties dispute is whether Citizens United had a right to use the funds in its general treasury to pay for broadcasts during the 30-day period. The notion that the First Amendment dictates an affirmative answer to that question is, in my judgment, profoundly misguided. Even more misguided is the notion that the Court must rewrite the law relating to campaign expenditures by *for-profit* corporations and unions to decide this case.

The basic premise underlying the Court's ruling is its iteration, and constant reiteration, of the proposition that the First Amendment bars regulatory distinctions based on a speaker's identity, including its "identity" as a corporation. While that glittering generality has rhetorical appeal, it is not a correct statement of the law. Nor does it tell us when a corporation may engage in electioneering that some of its shareholders oppose. It does not even resolve the specific question whether Citizens United may be required to finance some of its messages with the money in its PAC. The conceit that corporations must be treated identically to natural persons in the political sphere is not only inaccurate but also inadequate to justify the Court's disposition of this case.

In the context of election to public office, the distinction between corporate and human speakers is significant. Although they make enormous contributions to our society, corporations are not actually members of it. They cannot vote or run for office. Because they may be managed and controlled by nonresidents, their interests may conflict in fundamental respects with the interests of eligible voters. The financial resources, legal structure, and instrumental orientation of corporations raise legitimate concerns about their role in the electoral process. Our lawmakers have a compelling constitutional basis, if not also a democratic duty, to take measures designed to guard against the potentially deleterious effects of corporate spending in local and national races. . . .

III

[The Court's] ruling on the merits. . . . rests on several premises. First, the Court claims that *Austin* and *McConnell* have "banned" corporate speech. Second, it claims that the First Amendment precludes regulatory distinctions based on speaker identity, including the speaker's identity as a corporation. Third, it claims that *Austin* and *McConnell* were radical outliers in our First Amendment tradition and our campaign finance jurisprudence. Each of these claims is wrong.

The So-Called "Ban"

Pervading the Court's analysis is the ominous image of a "categorical ba[n]" on corporate speech. Indeed, the majority invokes the specter of a "ban" on nearly every page of its opinion. This characterization is highly misleading, and needs to be corrected. . . .

Under BCRA, any corporation's "stockholders and their families and its executive or administrative personnel and their families" can pool their resources to finance electioneering communications. A significant and growing number of corporations avail themselves of this option; during the most recent election cycle, corporate and union PACs raised nearly a billion dollars. Administering a PAC entails some administrative burden, but so does complying with the disclaimer, disclosure, and reporting requirements that the Court today upholds, and no one has suggested that the burden is severe for a sophisticated for-profit corporation. . . .

At the time Citizens United brought this lawsuit, the only types of speech that could be regulated under §203 were: (1) broadcast, cable, or satellite communications; (2) capable of reaching at least 50,000 persons in the relevant electorate; (3) made within 30 days of a primary or 60 days of a general federal election; (4) by a labor union or a non-MCFL, nonmedia corporation; (5) paid for with general treasury funds; and (6) "susceptible of no reasonable interpretation other than as an appeal to vote for or against a specific candidate." The category of communications meeting all of these criteria is not trivial, but the notion that corporate political speech has been "suppress[ed] . . . altogether," that corporations have been "exclu[ded] . . . from the general public dialogue," or that a work of fiction such as *Mr. Smith Goes to Washington* might be covered, is nonsense. Even the plaintiffs in *McConnell*, who had every incentive to depict BCRA as negatively as possible, declined to argue that §203's prohibition on certain uses of general treasury funds amounts to a complete ban.

In many ways, then, §203 functions as a source restriction or a time, place, and manner restriction. It applies in a viewpoint-neutral fashion to a narrow subset of advocacy messages about clearly identified candidates for federal office, made during discrete time periods through discrete channels. In the case at hand, all Citizens United needed to do to broadcast *Hillary* right before the primary was to abjure business contributions or use the funds in its PAC, which by its own account is "one of the most active conservative PACs in America."

So let us be clear: Neither *Austin* nor *McConnell* held or implied that corporations may be silenced; the FEC is not a "censor"; and in the years since these cases were decided, corporations have continued to play a major role in the national dialogue. Laws such as §203 target a class of communications that is especially likely to corrupt the political process, that is at least one degree removed from the views of individual citizens, and that may not even reflect the views of those who pay for it. Such laws burden political speech, and that is always a serious matter, demanding careful scrutiny. But the majority's incessant talk of a "ban" aims at a straw man.

Identity-Based Distinctions

The second pillar of the Court's opinion is its assertion that "the Government cannot restrict political speech based on the speaker's . . . identity." The case on which it relies for this proposition is First Nat. Bank of Boston v. Bellotti (1978). . . . Like its paeans to unfettered discourse, the Court's denunciation of identity-based distinctions may have rhetorical appeal but it obscures reality. . . .

In a variety of contexts, we have held that speech can be regulated differentially on account of the speaker's identity, when identity is understood in categorical or institutional terms. The Government routinely places special restrictions on the speech rights of students, prisoners, members of the Armed Forces, foreigners, and its own employees. When such restrictions are justified by a legitimate governmental interest, they do not necessarily raise constitutional problems. In contrast to the blanket rule that the majority espouses, our cases recognize that the Government's interests may be more or less compelling with respect to different classes of speakers. . . . It is fair to say that our First Amendment doctrine has "frowned on" certain identity-based distinctions, particularly those that may reflect invidious discrimination or preferential treatment of a politically powerful group. But it is simply incorrect to suggest that we have prohibited all legislative distinctions based on identity or content. Not even close. . . .

We have not reviewed them directly, we have never cast doubt on laws that place special restrictions on campaign spending by foreign nationals. And we have consistently approved laws that bar Government employees, but not others, from contributing to or participating in political activities. These statutes burden the political expression of one class of speakers, namely, civil servants. Yet we have sustained them on the basis of longstanding practice and Congress' reasoned judgment that certain regulations which leave "untouched full participation . . . in political decisions at the ballot box," Civil Service Comm'n v. Letter Carriers (1973), help ensure that public officials are "sufficiently free from improper influences," and that "confidence in the system of representative Government is not eroded . . . to a disastrous extent."

The same logic applies to this case with additional force because it is the identity of corporations, rather than individuals, that the Legislature has taken into account. . . . Not only has the distinctive potential of corporations to corrupt the electoral process long been recognized, but within the area of campaign finance, corporate spending is also "furthest from the core of political expression, since corporations' First Amendment speech and association interests are derived largely from those of their members and of the public in receiving information," [FEC v. Beaumont (2003)]. . . .

If taken seriously, our colleagues' assumption that the identity of a speaker has *no* relevance to the Government's ability to regulate political speech would lead to some remarkable conclusions. Such an assumption would have accorded the propaganda broadcasts to our troops by "Tokyo Rose" during World War II the same protection as speech by Allied commanders. More pertinently, it would appear to afford the same protection to multinational corporations controlled by foreigners as to individual Americans: To do otherwise, after all, could "enhance the relative voice" of some (*i.e.*, humans) over others (*i.e.*, nonhumans). Under the majority's view, I suppose it may be a First Amendment problem that corporations are not permitted to vote, given that voting is, among other things, a form of speech.

In short, the Court dramatically overstates its critique of identity-based distinctions, without ever explaining why corporate identity demands the same treatment as individual identity. Only the most wooden approach to the First Amendment could justify the unprecedented line it seeks to draw.

Our First Amendment Tradition

A third fulcrum of the Court's opinion is the idea that *Austin* and *McConnell* are radical outliers, "aberration[s]," in our First Amendment tradition. The Court has it exactly backwards. It is today's holding that is the radical departure from what had been settled First Amendment law. To see why, it is useful to take a long view.

1. *Original Understandings*

Let us start from the beginning. The Court invokes "ancient First Amendment principles," and original understandings to defend today's ruling, yet it makes only a perfunctory attempt to ground its analysis in the principles or understandings of those who drafted and ratified the Amendment. Perhaps this is because there is not a scintilla of evidence to support the notion that anyone believed it would preclude regulatory distinctions based on the corporate form. To the extent that the Framers' views are discernible and relevant to the disposition of this case, they would appear to cut strongly against the majority's position.

This is not only because the Framers and their contemporaries conceived of speech more narrowly than we now think of it, see Bork, Neutral Principles and Some First Amendment Problems, 47 Ind. L. J. 1 (1971), but also because they held very different views about the nature of the First Amendment right and the role of corporations in society. Those few corporations that existed at the founding were authorized by grant of a special legislative charter. Corporate sponsors would petition the legislature, and the legislature, if amenable, would issue a charter that specified the corporation's powers and purposes and "authoritatively fixed the scope and content of corporate organization," including "the internal structure of the corporation." J. Hurst, The Legitimacy of the Business Corporation in the Law of the United States 1780–1970 (1970). Corporations were created, supervised, and conceptualized as quasi-public entities, "designed to serve a social function for the state." Handlin & Handlin, Origin of the American Business Corporation, 5 J. Econ. Hist. 1, 22 (1945). It was "assumed that [they] were legally privileged organizations that had to be closely scrutinized by the legislature because their purposes had to be made consistent with public welfare." R. Seavoy, Origins of the American Business Corporation, 1784–1855 (1982).

The individualized charter mode of incorporation reflected the "cloud of disfavor under which corporations labored" in the early years of this Nation. 1

W. Fletcher, Cyclopedia of the Law of Corporations §2 (rev. ed. 2006). Thomas Jefferson famously fretted that corporations would subvert the Republic. General incorporation statutes, and widespread acceptance of business corporations as socially useful actors, did not emerge until the 1800's.

The Framers thus took it as a given that corporations could be comprehensively regulated in the service of the public welfare. Unlike our colleagues, they had little trouble distinguishing corporations from human beings, and when they constitutionalized the right to free speech in the First Amendment, it was the free speech of individual Americans that they had in mind.[4] While individuals might join together to exercise their speech rights, business corporations, at least, were plainly not seen as facilitating such associational or expressive ends. Even "the notion that business corporations could invoke the First Amendment would probably have been quite a novelty," given that "at the time, the legitimacy of every corporate activity was thought to rest entirely in a concession of the sovereign." Shelledy, Autonomy, Debate, and Corporate Speech, 18 Hastings Const. L. Q. 541 (1991). In light of these background practices and understandings, it seems to me implausible that the Framers believed "the freedom of speech" would extend equally to all corporate speakers, much less that it would preclude legislatures from taking limited measures to guard against corporate capture of elections.

The Court observes that the Framers drew on diverse intellectual sources, communicated through newspapers, and aimed to provide greater freedom of speech than had existed in England. From these (accurate) observations, the Court concludes that "[t]he First Amendment was certainly not understood to condone the suppression of political speech in society's most salient media." This conclusion is far from certain, given that many historians believe the Framers were focused on prior restraints on publication and did not understand the First Amendment to "prevent the subsequent punishment of such [publications] as may be deemed contrary to the public welfare." Near v. Minnesota ex rel. Olson (1931). Yet, even if the majority's conclusion were correct, it would tell us only that the First Amendment was understood to protect political speech *in* certain media. It would tell us little about whether the Amendment was understood to protect general treasury electioneering expenditures by corporations, *and to what extent*.

As a matter of original expectations, then, it seems absurd to think that the First Amendment prohibits legislatures from taking into account the corporate identity of a sponsor of electoral advocacy. As a matter of original meaning, it likewise seems baseless—unless one evaluates the First Amendment's

4. In normal usage then, as now, the term "speech" referred to oral communications by individuals. See, e.g., 2 S. Johnson, Dictionary of the English Language 1853–1854 (4th ed. 1773) (listing as primary definition of "speech": "The power of articulate utterance; the power of expressing thoughts by vocal words"). . . . Given that corporations were conceived of as artificial entities and do not have the technical capacity to "speak," the burden of establishing that the Framers and ratifiers understood "the freedom of speech" to encompass corporate speech is, I believe, far heavier than the majority acknowledges.

"principles," or its "purpose" (opinion of ROBERTS, C. J.) at such a high level of generality that the historical understandings of the Amendment cease to be a meaningful constraint on the judicial task. This case sheds a revelatory light on the assumption of some that an impartial judge's application of an originalist methodology is likely to yield more determinate answers, or to play a more decisive role in the decisional process, than his or her views about sound policy.

JUSTICE SCALIA criticizes the foregoing discussion for failing to adduce statements from the founding era showing that corporations were understood to be excluded from the First Amendment's free speech guarantee. Of course, JUSTICE SCALIA adduces no statements to suggest the contrary proposition, or even to suggest that the contrary proposition better reflects the kind of right that the drafters and ratifiers of the Free Speech Clause thought they were enshrining. Although JUSTICE SCALIA makes a perfectly sensible argument that an individual's right to speak entails a right to speak with others for a common cause, he does not explain why those two rights must be precisely identical, or why that principle applies to electioneering by corporations that serve no "common cause." Nothing in his account dislodges my basic point that members of the founding generation held a cautious view of corporate power and a narrow view of corporate rights (not that they "despised" corporations), and that they conceptualized speech in individualistic terms. If no prominent Framer bothered to articulate that corporate speech would have lesser status than individual speech, that may well be because the contrary proposition—if not also the very notion of "corporate speech"—was inconceivable.

JUSTICE SCALIA also emphasizes the unqualified nature of the First Amendment text. Yet he would seemingly read out the Free Press Clause: How else could he claim that my purported views on newspapers must track my views on corporations generally? Like virtually all modern lawyers, JUSTICE SCALIA presumably believes that the First Amendment restricts the Executive, even though its language refers to Congress alone. In any event, the text only leads us back to the questions who or what is guaranteed "the freedom of speech," and, just as critically, what that freedom consists of and under what circumstances it may be limited. JUSTICE SCALIA appears to believe that because corporations are created and utilized by individuals, it follows (as night the day) that their electioneering must be equally protected by the First Amendment and equally immunized from expenditure limits. That conclusion certainly does not follow as a logical matter, and JUSTICE SCALIA fails to explain why the original public meaning leads it to follow as a matter of interpretation.

The truth is we cannot be certain how a law such as BCRA §203 meshes with the original meaning of the First Amendment. I have given several reasons why I believe the Constitution would have been understood then, and ought to be understood now, to permit reasonable restrictions on corporate electioneering, and I will give many more reasons in the pages to come. The Court enlists the Framers in its defense without seriously grappling with their understandings of corporations or the free speech right, or with the republican principles that underlay those understandings.

In fairness, our campaign finance jurisprudence has never attended very closely to the views of the Framers, whose political universe differed profoundly from that of today. We have long since held that corporations are covered by the First Amendment, and many legal scholars have long since rejected the concession theory of the corporation. But "historical context is usually relevant," [Randall v. Sorrell (2006) (STEVENS, J., dissenting)] in light of the Court's effort to cast itself as guardian of ancient values, it pays to remember that nothing in our constitutional history dictates today's outcome. To the contrary, this history helps illuminate just how extraordinarily dissonant the decision is.

2. *Legislative and Judicial Interpretation*

A century of more recent history puts to rest any notion that today's ruling is faithful to our First Amendment tradition. At the federal level, the express distinction between corporate and individual political spending on elections stretches back to 1907, when Congress passed the Tillman Act, banning all corporate contributions to candidates. The Senate Report on the legislation observed that "[t]he evils of the use of [corporate] money in connection with political elections are so generally recognized that the committee deems it unnecessary to make any argument in favor of the general purpose of this measure. It is in the interest of good government and calculated to promote purity in the selection of public officials." (1906). President Roosevelt, in his 1905 annual message to Congress, declared:

> "All contributions by corporations to any political committee or for any political purpose should be forbidden by law; directors should not be permitted to use stockholders' money for such purposes; and, moreover, a prohibition of this kind would be, as far as it went, an effective method of stopping the evils aimed at in corrupt practices acts."

The Court has surveyed the history leading up to the Tillman Act several times and I will refrain from doing so again. It is enough to say that the Act was primarily driven by two pressing concerns: first, the enormous power corporations had come to wield in federal elections, with the accompanying threat of both actual corruption and a public perception of corruption; and second, a respect for the interest of shareholders and members in preventing the use of their money to support candidates they opposed.

Over the years, the limitations on corporate political spending have been modified in a number of ways, as Congress responded to changes in the American economy and political practices that threatened to displace the commonweal. . . . By the time Congress passed FECA in 1971, the bar on corporate contributions and expenditures had become such an accepted part of federal campaign finance regulation that when a large number of plaintiffs, including several nonprofit corporations, challenged virtually every aspect of the Act in *Buckley*, no one even bothered to argue that the bar as such was unconstitutional. *Buckley* famously (or infamously) distinguished direct contributions from independent expenditures, but its silence on corporations only reinforced the understanding that corporate expenditures could be treated differently from individual expenditures. . . .

3. Buckley *and* Bellotti

Against this extensive background of congressional regulation of corporate campaign spending, and our repeated affirmation of this regulation as constitutionally sound, the majority dismisses *Austin* as "a significant departure from ancient First Amendment principles." How does the majority attempt to justify this claim? Selected passages from two cases, *Buckley* and *Bellotti*, do all of the work. In the Court's view, *Buckley* and *Bellotti* decisively rejected the possibility of distinguishing corporations from natural persons in the 1970's; it just so happens that in every single case in which the Court has reviewed campaign finance legislation in the decades since, the majority failed to grasp this truth. The Federal Congress and dozens of state legislatures, we now know, have been similarly deluded.

The majority emphasizes *Buckley*'s statement that "[t]he concept that government may restrict the speech of some elements of our society in order to enhance the relative voice of others is wholly foreign to the First Amendment." But this elegant phrase cannot bear the weight that our colleagues have placed on it. For one thing, the Constitution does, in fact, permit numerous "restrictions on the speech of some in order to prevent a few from drowning out the many": for example, restrictions on ballot access and on legislators' floor time. Nixon v. Shrink Missouri Government PAC (2000) (BREYER, J., concurring). For another, the *Buckley* Court used this line in evaluating "the ancillary governmental interest in equalizing the relative ability of individuals and groups to influence the outcome of elections." It is not apparent why this is relevant to the case before us. The majority suggests that *Austin* rests on the foreign concept of speech equalization, but we made it clear in *Austin* (as in several cases before and since) that a restriction on the way corporations spend their money is no mere exercise in disfavoring the voice of some elements of our society in preference to others. . . .

The case on which the majority places even greater weight than *Buckley*, however, is *Bellotti*, claiming it "could not have been clearer" that *Bellotti*'s holding forbade distinctions between corporate and individual expenditures like the one at issue here. The Court's reliance is odd. The only thing about *Bellotti* that could not be clearer is that it declined to adopt the majority's position. *Bellotti* ruled, in an explicit limitation on the scope of its holding, that "our consideration of a corporation's right to speak on issues of general public interest implies no comparable right in the quite different context of participation in a political campaign for election to public office." *Bellotti*, in other words, did not touch the question presented in *Austin* and *McConnell*, and the opinion squarely disavowed the proposition for which the majority cites it. . . .

Austin and *McConnell*, then, sit perfectly well with *Bellotti*. . . . The only thing new about *Austin* was the dissent, with its stunning failure to appreciate the legitimacy of interests recognized in the name of democratic integrity since the days of the Progressives.

IV

Having explained why this is not an appropriate case in which to revisit *Austin* and *McConnell* and why these decisions sit perfectly well with "First Amendment principles," I come at last to the interests that are at stake. . . . Corporations, as a class, tend to be more attuned to the complexities of the legislative process and more directly affected by tax and appropriations measures that receive little public scrutiny; they also have vastly more money with which to try to buy access and votes. Business corporations must engage the political process in instrumental terms if they are to maximize shareholder value. The unparalleled resources, professional lobbyists, and single-minded focus they bring to this effort . . . make *quid pro quo* corruption and its appearance inherently more likely when they (or their conduits or trade groups) spend unrestricted sums on elections . . .

Just as the majority gives short shrift to the general societal interests at stake in campaign finance regulation, it also overlooks the distinctive considerations raised by the regulation of *corporate* expenditures. The majority fails to appreciate that *Austin*'s antidistortion rationale is itself an anticorruption rationale tied to the special concerns raised by corporations. Understood properly, "antidistortion" is simply a variant on the classic governmental interest in protecting against improper influences on officeholders that debilitate the democratic process. It is manifestly not just an "equalizing" ideal in disguise.

1. *Antidistortion*

The fact that corporations are different from human beings might seem to need no elaboration, except that the majority opinion almost completely elides it. *Austin* set forth some of the basic differences. Unlike natural persons, corporations have "limited liability" for their owners and managers, "perpetual life," separation of ownership and control, "and favorable treatment of the accumulation and distribution of assets . . . that enhance their ability to attract capital and to deploy their resources in ways that maximize the return on their shareholders' investments." Unlike voters in U. S. elections, corporations may be foreign controlled. Unlike other interest groups, business corporations have been "effectively delegated responsibility for ensuring society's economic welfare"; they inescapably structure the life of every citizen. "[T]he resources in the treasury of a business corporation," furthermore, "are not an indication of popular support for the corporation's political ideas." "They reflect instead the economically motivated decisions of investors and customers. The availability of these resources may make a corporation a formidable political presence, even though the power of the corporation may be no reflection of the power of its ideas."

It might also be added that corporations have no consciences, no beliefs, no feelings, no thoughts, no desires. Corporations help structure and facilitate the activities of human beings, to be sure, and their "personhood" often serves as a useful legal fiction. But they are not themselves members of "We the People" by whom and for whom our Constitution was established.

These basic points help explain why corporate electioneering is not only more likely to impair compelling governmental interests, but also why restrictions on that electioneering are less likely to encroach upon First Amendment freedoms. . . . Corporate speech . . . is derivative speech, speech by proxy. A regulation such as BCRA §203 may affect the way in which individuals disseminate certain messages through the corporate form, but it does not prevent anyone from speaking in his or her own voice. . . .

It is an interesting question "who" is even speaking when a business corporation places an advertisement that endorses or attacks a particular candidate. Presumably it is not the customers or employees, who typically have no say in such matters. It cannot realistically be said to be the shareholders, who tend to be far removed from the day-to-day decisions of the firm and whose political preferences may be opaque to management. Perhaps the officers or directors of the corporation have the best claim to be the ones speaking, except their fiduciary duties generally prohibit them from using corporate funds for personal ends. Some individuals associated with the corporation must make the decision to place the ad, but the idea that these individuals are thereby fostering their self-expression or cultivating their critical faculties is fanciful. It is entirely possible that the corporation's electoral message will *conflict* with their personal convictions. Take away the ability to use general treasury funds for some of those ads, and no one's autonomy, dignity, or political equality has been impinged upon in the least. . . .

Austin recognized that there are substantial reasons why a legislature might conclude that unregulated general treasury expenditures will give corporations "unfai[r] influence" in the electoral process and distort public debate in ways that undermine rather than advance the interests of listeners. The legal structure of corporations allows them to amass and deploy financial resources on a scale few natural persons can match. . . .

In addition to this immediate drowning out of noncorporate voices, there may be deleterious effects that follow soon thereafter. Corporate "domination" of electioneering, *Austin*, can generate the impression that corporations dominate our democracy. When citizens turn on their televisions and radios before an election and hear only corporate electioneering, they may lose faith in their capacity, as citizens, to influence public policy. A Government captured by corporate interests, they may come to believe, will be neither responsive to their needs nor willing to give their views a fair hearing. The predictable result is cynicism and disenchantment: an increased perception that large spenders "call the tune" and a reduced "willingness of voters to take part in democratic governance." *McConnell*. To the extent that corporations are allowed to exert undue influence in electoral races, the speech of the eventual winners of those races may also be chilled. Politicians who fear that a certain corporation can make or break their reelection chances may be cowed into silence about that corporation. . . . At the least, I stress again, a legislature is entitled to credit these concerns and to take tailored measures in response. . . .

The Court's blinkered and aphoristic approach to the First Amendment may well promote corporate power at the cost of the individual and collective self-expression the Amendment was meant to serve. It will undoubtedly cripple the ability of ordinary citizens, Congress, and the States to adopt even limited measures to protect against corporate domination of the electoral process. Americans may be forgiven if they do not feel the Court has advanced the cause of self-government today.

2. *Shareholder Protection*

. . . When corporations use general treasury funds to praise or attack a particular candidate for office, it is the shareholders, as the residual claimants, who are effectively footing the bill. Those shareholders who disagree with the corporation's electoral message may find their financial investments being used to undermine their political convictions. . . . Recognizing the limits of the shareholder protection rationale, the *Austin* Court did not hold it out as an adequate and independent ground for sustaining the statute in question. Rather, the Court applied it to reinforce the antidistortion rationale, in two main ways. First, the problem of dissenting shareholders shows that even if electioneering expenditures can advance the political views of some members of a corporation, they will often compromise the views of others. Second, it provides an additional reason, beyond the distinctive legal attributes of the corporate form, for doubting that these "expenditures reflect actual public support for the political ideas espoused." The shareholder protection rationale, in other words, bolsters the conclusion that restrictions on corporate electioneering can serve both speakers' and listeners' interests, as well as the anticorruption interest. And it supplies yet another reason why corporate expenditures merit less protection than individual expenditures.

V

. . . In a democratic society, the longstanding consensus on the need to limit corporate campaign spending should outweigh the wooden application of judge-made rules. The majority's rejection of this principle "elevate[s] corporations to a level of deference which has not been seen at least since the days when substantive due process was regularly used to invalidate regulatory legislation thought to unfairly impinge upon established economic interests." *Bellotti* (WHITE, J., dissenting). At bottom, the Court's opinion is thus a rejection of the common sense of the American people, who have recognized a need to prevent corporations from undermining self-government since the founding, and who have fought against the distinctive corrupting potential of corporate electioneering since the days of Theodore Roosevelt. It is a strange time to repudiate that common sense. While American democracy is imperfect, few outside the majority of this Court would have thought its flaws included a dearth of corporate money in politics.

I would affirm the judgment of the District Court.

JUSTICE THOMAS, concurring in part and dissenting in part.

I join all but Part IV of the Court's opinion . . . because the Court's constitutional analysis does not go far enough. The disclosure, disclaimer, and reporting requirements in BCRA §§201 and 311 are also unconstitutional. Congress may not abridge the "right to anonymous speech" based on the "simple interest in providing voters with additional relevant information" [*McConnell* (THOMAS, J., concurring in part, concurring in judgment in part, and dissenting in part)].

In continuing to hold otherwise, the Court misapprehends the import of "recent events" that some *amici* describe "in which donors to certain causes were blacklisted, threatened, or otherwise targeted for retaliation." The Court properly recognizes these events as "cause for concern," but fails to acknowledge their constitutional significance. In my view, *amici*'s submissions show why the Court's insistence on upholding §§201 and 311 will ultimately prove as misguided (and ill fated) as was its prior approval of §203.

Amici's examples relate principally to Proposition 8, a state ballot proposition that California voters narrowly passed in the 2008 general election. Proposition 8 amended California's constitution to provide that "[o]nly marriage between a man and a woman is valid or recognized in California." Any donor who gave more than $100 to any committee supporting or opposing Proposition 8 was required to disclose his full name, street address, occupation, employer's name (or business name, if self-employed), and the total amount of his contributions. The California Secretary of State was then required to post this information on the Internet.

Some opponents of Proposition 8 compiled this information and created Web sites with maps showing the locations of homes or businesses of Proposition 8 supporters. Many supporters (or their customers) suffered property damage, or threats of physical violence or death, as a result. They cited these incidents in a complaint they filed after the 2008 election, seeking to invalidate California's mandatory disclosure laws. Supporters recounted being told: "Consider yourself lucky. If I had a gun I would have gunned you down along with each and every other supporter," or, "we have plans for you and your friends." Proposition 8 opponents also allegedly harassed the measure's supporters by defacing or damaging their property. Two religious organizations supporting Proposition 8 reportedly received through the mail envelopes containing a white powdery substance.

Those accounts are consistent with media reports describing Proposition 8-related retaliation. The director of the nonprofit California Musical Theater gave $1,000 to support the initiative; he was forced to resign after artists complained to his employer. Lott & Smith, Donor Disclosure Has Its Downsides, Wall Street Journal, Dec. 26, 2008 [hereinafter *Donor Disclosure*]. The director of the Los Angeles Film Festival was forced to resign after giving $1,500 because opponents threatened to boycott and picket the next festival. And a woman who had managed her popular, family-owned restaurant for 26 years was forced to resign after she gave $100, because "throngs of [angry] protesters" repeatedly arrived at the restaurant and "shout[ed] 'shame on you' at customers." Lopez, Prop. 8 Stance Upends Her Life, Los Angeles Times, Dec. 14, 2008. The police even had to "arriv[e] in riot gear one night to quell the angry mob" at the restaurant. Some supporters of Proposition 8 engaged in similar tactics; one real estate businessman in San Diego who had donated to a group opposing Proposition 8 "received a letter from the Prop. 8 Executive Committee threatening to publish his company's name if he didn't also donate to the 'Yes on 8' campaign." *Donor Disclosure.*

The success of such intimidation tactics has apparently spawned a cottage industry that uses forcibly disclosed donor information to *pre-empt* citizens' exercise of their First Amendment rights. Before the 2008 Presidential election, a "newly formed nonprofit group . . . plann[ed] to confront donors to conservative groups, hoping to create a chilling effect that will dry up contributions." Luo, Group Plans Campaign Against G.O.P. Donors, N. Y. Times, Aug. 8, 2008. Its leader, "who described his effort as 'going for the jugular,'" detailed the group's plan to send a "warning letter . . . alerting donors who might be considering giving to right-wing groups to a variety of potential dangers, including legal trouble, public exposure and watchdog groups digging through their lives."

These instances of retaliation sufficiently demonstrate why this Court should invalidate mandatory disclosure and reporting requirements. But *amici* present evidence of yet another reason to do so — the threat of retaliation from *elected officials.* As *amici*'s submissions make clear, this threat extends far beyond a single ballot proposition in California. For example, a candidate challenging an incumbent state attorney general reported that some members of the State's business community feared donating to his campaign because they did not want to cross the incumbent; in his words, "I go to so many people and hear the same thing: 'I sure hope you beat [the incumbent], but I can't afford to have my name on your records. He might come after me next.'" Strassel, Challenging Spitzerism at the Polls, Wall Street Journal, Aug. 1, 2008. The incumbent won reelection in 2008.

My point is not to express any view on the merits of the political controversies I describe. Rather, it is to demonstrate — using real-world, recent examples — the fallacy in the Court's conclusion that "[d]isclaimer and disclosure requirements . . . impose no ceiling on campaign-related activities, and do not prevent anyone from speaking." Of course they do. Disclaimer and disclosure requirements enable private citizens and elected officials to implement political strategies *specifically calculated* to curtail campaign-related activity and prevent the lawful, peaceful exercise of First Amendment rights. . . .

[T]he Court's promise that as-applied challenges will adequately protect speech is a hollow assurance. Now more than ever, §§201 and 311 will chill protected speech because — as California voters can attest — "the advent of the Internet" enables "prompt disclosure of expenditures," which "provide[s]" political opponents "with the information needed" to intimidate and retaliate against their foes. Thus, "disclosure permits citizens . . . to react to the speech of [their political opponents] in a proper" — or undeniably *improper* — "way" long before a plaintiff could prevail on an as-applied challenge.

I cannot endorse a view of the First Amendment that subjects citizens of this Nation to death threats, ruined careers, damaged or defaced property, or pre-emptive and threatening warning letters as the price for engaging in "core political speech, the 'primary object of First Amendment protection.'" *McConnell* (THOMAS, J., concurring in part, concurring in judgment in part, and dissenting in part) Accordingly, I respectfully dissent from the Court's judgment upholding BCRA §§201 and 311.

ASSIGNMENT S-8

STUDY GUIDE: *When combined with* Davis *and* Citizens United, *does this case suggest any trajectory for the Court's treatment of campaign finance regulations? What is left of* Buckley *after these latest cases? Are there any deeper jurisprudential issues accounting for the division of the justices on this issue? Does Justice Kagan's characterization of the operation of existing public financing systems unintentionally undercut* their *claim to constitutionality? Is Justice Kagan's reliance upon "First Amendment values" different than reliance on the First Amendment itself?*

ARIZONA FREE ENTERPRISE CLUB'S FREEDOM CLUB PAC v. BENNETT

564 U.S. _____ (2011)

CHIEF JUSTICE ROBERTS delivered the opinion of the Court.

Under Arizona law, candidates for state office who accept public financing can receive additional money from the State in direct response to the campaign activities of privately financed candidates and independent expenditure groups. Once a set spending limit is exceeded, a publicly financed candidate receives roughly one dollar for every dollar spent by an opposing privately financed candidate. The publicly financed candidate also receives roughly one dollar for every dollar spent by independent expenditure groups to support the privately financed candidate, or to oppose the publicly financed candidate. We hold that Arizona's matching funds scheme substantially burdens protected political speech without serving a compelling state interest and therefore violates the First Amendment.

I

The Arizona Citizens Clean Elections Act, passed by initiative in 1998, created a voluntary public financing system to fund the primary and general election campaigns of candidates for state office. All eligible candidates for

Governor, secretary of state, attorney general, treasurer, superintendent of public instruction, the corporation commission, mine inspector, and the state legislature (both the House and Senate) may opt to receive public funding. Eligibility is contingent on the collection of a specified number of five-dollar contributions from Arizona voters, and the acceptance of certain campaign restrictions and obligations. Publicly funded candidates must agree, among other things, to limit their expenditure of personal funds to $500, participate in at least one public debate, adhere to an overall expenditure cap, and return all unspent public moneys to the State.

In exchange for accepting these conditions, participating candidates are granted public funds to conduct their campaigns. In many cases, this initial allotment may be the whole of the State's financial backing of a publicly funded candidate. But when certain conditions are met, publicly funded candidates are granted additional "equalizing" or matching funds.

Matching funds are available in both primary and general elections. In a primary, matching funds are triggered when a privately financed candidate's expenditures, combined with the expenditures of independent groups made in support of the privately financed candidate or in opposition to a publicly financed candidate, exceed the primary election allotment of state funds to the publicly financed candidate. During the general election, matching funds are triggered when the amount of money a privately financed candidate receives in contributions, combined with the expenditures of independent groups made in support of the privately financed candidate or in opposition to a publicly financed candidate, exceed the general election allotment of state funds to the publicly financed candidate. A privately financed candidate's expenditures of his personal funds are counted as contributions for purposes of calculating matching funds during a general election. . . .

During a general election, every dollar that a candidate receives in contributions — which includes any money of his own that a candidate spends on his campaign — results in roughly one dollar in additional state funding to his publicly financed opponent. In an election where a privately funded candidate faces multiple publicly financed candidates, one dollar raised or spent by the privately financed candidate results in an almost one dollar increase in public funding to each of the publicly financed candidates.

Once the public financing cap is exceeded, additional expenditures by independent groups can result in dollar-for-dollar matching funds as well. Spending by independent groups on behalf of a privately funded candidate, or in opposition to a publicly funded candidate, results in matching funds. Independent expenditures made in support of a publicly financed candidate can result in matching funds for other publicly financed candidates in a race. The matching funds provision is not activated, however, when independent expenditures are made in opposition to a privately financed candidate. Matching funds top out at two times the initial authorized grant of public funding to the publicly financed candidate.

Under Arizona law, a privately financed candidate may raise and spend unlimited funds, subject to state-imposed contribution limits and disclosure requirements. Contributions to candidates for statewide office are limited to $840 per contributor per election cycle and contributions to legislative candidates are limited to $410 per contributor per election cycle. . . . [1]

II

. . . Although the speech of the candidates and independent expenditure groups that brought this suit is not directly capped by Arizona's matching funds provision, those parties contend that their political speech is substantially burdened by the state law in the same way that speech was burdened by the law we recently found invalid in Davis v. Federal Election Comm'n (2008). . . .

A

1

The logic of *Davis* largely controls our approach to this case. Much like the burden placed on speech in *Davis,* the matching funds provision "imposes an unprecedented penalty on any candidate who robustly exercises [his] First Amendment right[s]." Under that provision, "the vigorous exercise of the right to use personal funds to finance campaign speech" leads to "advantages for opponents in the competitive context of electoral politics." Once a privately financed candidate has raised or spent more than the State's initial grant to a publicly financed candidate, each personal dollar spent by the privately financed candidate results in an award of almost one additional dollar to his opponent. That plainly forces the privately financed candidate to "shoulder a special and potentially significant burden" when choosing to exercise his First Amendment right to spend funds on behalf of his candidacy. If the law at issue in *Davis* imposed a burden on candidate speech, the Arizona law unquestionably does so as well.

The penalty imposed by Arizona's matching funds provision is different in some respects from the penalty imposed by the law we struck down in *Davis.* But those differences make the Arizona law *more* constitutionally problematic, not less. First, the penalty in *Davis* consisted of raising the contribution limits for one of the candidates. The candidate who benefited from the increased limits still had to go out and raise the funds. He may or may not have been able to do so. The other candidate, therefore, faced merely the possibility that his opponent would be able to raise additional funds, through contribution limits that remained subject to a cap. And still the Court held that this was an "unprecedented penalty," a "special and potentially significant burden" that had to be justified by a compelling state interest — a rigorous First Amendment hurdle. Here the

1. Maine and North Carolina have both passed matching funds statutes that resemble Arizona's law. Minnesota, Connecticut, and Florida have also adopted matching funds provisions, but courts have enjoined the enforcement of those schemes after concluding that their operation violates the First Amendment.

benefit to the publicly financed candidate is the direct and automatic release of public money. That is a far heavier burden than in *Davis*.

Second, depending on the specifics of the election at issue, the matching funds provision can create a multiplier effect. In the Arizona Fourth District House election previously discussed, if the spending cap were exceeded, each dollar spent by the privately funded candidate would result in an additional dollar of campaign funding to each of that candidate's publicly financed opponents. In such a situation, the matching funds provision forces privately funded candidates to fight a political hydra of sorts. Each dollar they spend generates two adversarial dollars in response. Again, a markedly more significant burden than in *Davis*.

Third, unlike the law at issue in *Davis,* all of this is to some extent out of the privately financed candidate's hands. Even if that candidate opted to spend less than the initial public financing cap, any spending by independent expenditure groups to promote the privately financed candidate's election — regardless whether such support was welcome or helpful — could trigger matching funds. What is more, that state money would go directly to the publicly funded candidate to use as he saw fit. That disparity in control — giving money directly to a publicly financed candidate, in response to independent expenditures that cannot be coordinated with the privately funded candidate — is a substantial advantage for the publicly funded candidate. That candidate can allocate the money according to his own campaign strategy, which the privately financed candidate could not do with the independent group expenditures that triggered the matching funds. Cf. *Citizens United* ("'The absence of prearrangement and coordination of an expenditure with the candidate or his agent . . . undermines the value of the expenditure to the candidate'" (quoting *Buckley*)).

The burdens that this regime places on independent expenditure groups are akin to those imposed on the privately financed candidates themselves. Just as with the candidate the independent group supports, the more money spent on that candidate's behalf or in opposition to a publicly funded candidate, the more money the publicly funded candidate receives from the State. And just as with the privately financed candidate, the effect of a dollar spent on election speech is a guaranteed financial payout to the publicly funded candidate the group opposes. Moreover, spending one dollar can result in the flow of dollars to multiple candidates the group disapproves of, dollars directly controlled by the publicly funded candidate or candidates.

In some ways, the burden the Arizona law imposes on independent expenditure groups is worse than the burden it imposes on privately financed candidates, and thus substantially worse than the burden we found constitutionally impermissible in *Davis*. If a candidate contemplating an electoral run in Arizona surveys the campaign landscape and decides that the burdens imposed by the matching funds regime make a privately funded campaign unattractive, he at least has the option of taking public financing. Independent expenditure groups, of course, do not.

Once the spending cap is reached, an independent expenditure group that wants to support a particular candidate — because of that candidate's stand on an issue of concern to the group—can only avoid triggering matching funds in one of two ways. The group can either opt to change its message from one addressing the merits of the candidates to one addressing the merits of an issue, or refrain from speaking altogether. Presenting independent expenditure groups with such a choice makes the matching funds provision particularly burdensome to those groups. And forcing that choice—trigger matching funds, change your message, or do not speak—certainly contravenes "the fundamental rule of protection under the First Amendment, that a speaker has the autonomy to choose the content of his own message." Hurley v. Irish–American Gay, Lesbian and Bisexual Group of Boston, Inc., (1995).[2]

2

. . . Arizona contends that the matching funds provision is distinguishable from the law we invalidated in *Davis*. The State correctly points out that our decision in *Davis* focused on the asymmetrical contribution limits imposed by the Millionaire's Amendment. But that is not because—as the State asserts—the reach of that opinion is limited to asymmetrical contribution limits. It is because that was the particular burden on candidate speech we faced in *Davis*. And whatever the significance of the distinction in general, there can be no doubt that the burden on speech is significantly greater in this case than in *Davis*: That means that the law here—like the one in *Davis*—must be justified by a compelling state interest.

The State argues that the matching funds provision actually results in more speech by "increas[ing] debate about issues of public concern" in Arizona elections and "promot[ing] the free and open debate that the First Amendment was intended to foster." In the State's view, this promotion of First Amendment ideals offsets any burden the law might impose on some speakers.

Not so. Any increase in speech resulting from the Arizona law is of one kind and one kind only—that of publicly financed candidates. The burden imposed on privately financed candidates and independent expenditure groups reduces their speech; "restriction[s] on the amount of money a person or group can spend on political communication during a campaign necessarily reduces the quantity of expression." *Buckley*. Thus, even if the matching funds provision did result in more speech by publicly financed candidates and more speech in general, it would do so at the expense of impermissibly burdening (and thus reducing) the speech of privately financed candidates and independent expenditure groups. This sort of "beggar thy neighbor" approach to free speech— "restrict[ing] the

2. The dissent sees "chutzpah" in candidates exercising their right not to participate in the public financing scheme, while objecting that the system violates their First Amendment rights. The charge is unjustified, but, in any event, it certainly cannot be leveled against the independent expenditure groups. The dissent barely mentions such groups in its analysis, and fails to address not only the distinctive burdens imposed on these groups—as set forth above—but also the way in which privately financed candidates are particularly burdened when matching funds are triggered by independent group speech.

speech of some elements of our society in order to enhance the relative voice of others" — is "wholly foreign to the First Amendment."

We have rejected government efforts to increase the speech of some at the expense of others outside the campaign finance context. In Miami Herald Publishing Co. v. Tornillo (1974), we held unconstitutional a Florida law that required any newspaper assailing a political candidate's character to allow that candidate to print a reply. We have explained that while the statute in that case "purported to advance free discussion, . . . its effect was to deter newspapers from speaking out in the first instance" because it "penalized the newspaper's own expression." Pacific Gas & Elec. Co. v. Public Util. Comm'n of Cal. (1986) (plurality opinion). Such a penalty, we concluded, could not survive First Amendment scrutiny. The Arizona law imposes a similar penalty: The State grants funds to publicly financed candidates as a direct result of the speech of privately financed candidates and independent expenditure groups. The argument that this sort of burden promotes free and robust discussion is no more persuasive here than it was in *Tornillo*. . . .

In disagreeing with our conclusion, the dissent relies on cases in which we have upheld government subsidies against First Amendment challenge, and asserts that "[w]e have never, not once, understood a viewpoint-neutral subsidy given to one speaker to constitute a First Amendment burden on another." But none of those cases — not one — involved a subsidy given in direct response to the political speech of another, to allow the recipient to counter that speech. And nothing in the analysis we employed in those cases suggests that the challenged subsidies would have survived First Amendment scrutiny if they were triggered by someone else's political speech.[3]

The State also argues, and the Court of Appeals concluded, that any burden on privately financed candidates and independent expenditure groups is more analogous to the burden placed on speakers by the disclosure and disclaimer requirements we recently upheld in *Citizens United* than to direct restrictions on candidate and independent expenditures. This analogy is not even close. A political candidate's disclosure of his funding resources does not result in a cash windfall to his opponent, or affect their respective disclosure obligations. . . .

The dissent's disagreement is little more than disagreement with *Davis*. . . .

B

Because the Arizona matching funds provision imposes a substantial burden on the speech of privately financed candidates and independent expenditure groups, "that provision cannot stand unless it is 'justified by a compelling state interest,'"

3. The dissent cites *Buckley* in response, but the funding in *Buckley* was of course not triggered by the speech of a publicly funded candidate's political opponent, or the speech of anyone else for that matter. Whether Arizona's matching funds provision comports with the First Amendment is not simply a question of whether the State can give a subsidy to a candidate to fund that candidate's election, but whether that subsidy can be triggered by the speech of another candidate or independent group.

id. There is a debate between the parties in this case as to what state interest is served by the matching funds provision. The privately financed candidates and independent expenditure groups contend that the provision works to "level [] electoral opportunities" by equalizing candidate "resources and influence." The State and the Clean Elections Institute counter that the provision "furthers Arizona's interest in preventing corruption and the appearance of corruption."

1

There is ample support for the argument that the matching funds provision seeks to "level the playing field" in terms of candidate resources. The clearest evidence is of course the very operation of the provision: It ensures that campaign funding is equal, up to three times the initial public funding allotment. The text of the Citizens Clean Elections Act itself confirms this purpose. The statutory provision setting up the matching funds regime is titled "Equal funding of candidates." The Act refers to the funds doled out after the Act's matching mechanism is triggered as "equalizing funds." And the regulations implementing the matching funds provision refer to those funds as "equalizing funds" as well. . . .

We have repeatedly rejected the argument that the government has a compelling state interest in "leveling the playing field" that can justify undue burdens on political speech. In *Davis,* we stated that discriminatory contribution limits meant to "level electoral opportunities for candidates of different personal wealth" did not serve "a legitimate government objective," let alone a compelling one. And in *Buckley,* we held that limits on overall campaign expenditures could not be justified by a purported government "interest in equalizing the financial resources of candidates." After all, equalizing campaign resources "might serve not to equalize the opportunities of all candidates, but to handicap a candidate who lacked substantial name recognition or exposure of his views before the start of the campaign."

"Leveling electoral opportunities means making and implementing judgments about which strengths should be permitted to contribute to the outcome of an election," *Davis* — a dangerous enterprise and one that cannot justify burdening protected speech. The dissent essentially dismisses this concern, but it needs to be taken seriously; we have, as noted, held that it is not legitimate for the government to attempt to equalize electoral opportunities in this manner. And such basic intrusion by the government into the debate over who should govern goes to the heart of First Amendment values.

"Leveling the playing field" can sound like a good thing. But in a democracy, campaigning for office is not a game. It is a critically important form of speech. The First Amendment embodies our choice as a Nation that, when it comes to such speech, the guiding principle is freedom — the "unfettered interchange of ideas" — not whatever the State may view as fair. *Buckley.*

2

[E]ven if the ultimate objective of the matching funds provision is to combat corruption — and not "level the playing field" — the burdens that the matching funds provision imposes on protected political speech are not justified.

Burdening a candidate's expenditure of his own funds on his own campaign does not further the State's anticorruption interest. Indeed, we have said that "reliance on personal funds *reduces* the threat of corruption" and that "discouraging [the] use of personal funds[ ] disserves the anticorruption interest." *Davis*. That is because "the use of personal funds reduces the candidate's dependence on outside contributions and thereby counteracts the coercive pressures and attendant risks of abuse" of money in politics. *Buckley*. The matching funds provision counts a candidate's expenditures of his own money on his own campaign as contributions, and to that extent cannot be supported by any anticorruption interest.

We have also held that "independent expenditures . . . do not give rise to corruption or the appearance of corruption." *Citizens United*. "By definition, an independent expenditure is political speech presented to the electorate that is not coordinated with a candidate." *Id.* The candidate-funding circuit is broken. The separation between candidates and independent expenditure groups negates the possibility that independent expenditures will result in the sort of *quid pro quo* corruption with which our case law is concerned. Including independent expenditures in the matching funds provision cannot be supported by any anticorruption interest. . . .

Perhaps recognizing that the burdens the matching funds provision places on speech cannot be justified in and of themselves, either as a means of leveling the playing field or directly fighting corruption, the State and the Clean Elections Institute offer another argument: They contend that the provision indirectly serves the anticorruption interest, by ensuring that enough candidates participate in the State's public funding system, which in turn helps combat corruption. . . .

The flaw in the State's argument is apparent in what its reasoning would allow. By the State's logic it could grant a publicly funded candidate five dollars in matching funds for every dollar his privately financed opponent spent, or force candidates who wish to run on private funds to pay a $10,000 fine in order to encourage participation in the public funding regime. Such measures might well promote participation in public financing, but would clearly suppress or unacceptably alter political speech. How the State chooses to encourage participation in its public funding system matters, and we have never held that a State may burden political speech — to the extent the matching funds provision does — to ensure adequate participation in a public funding system. Here the State's chosen method is unduly burdensome and not sufficiently justified to survive First Amendment scrutiny.

III

We do not today call into question the wisdom of public financing as a means of funding political candidacy. That is not our business. But determining whether laws governing campaign finance violate the First Amendment is very much our business. In carrying out that responsibility over the past 35 years, we have upheld some restrictions on speech and struck down others. We have said that governments "may engage in public financing of election campaigns" and that doing so can further "significant governmental interest[s]," such as the state interest in preventing corruption. *Buckley*. But the goal of creating a viable public financing scheme can only be pursued in a manner consistent with the First Amendment. The dissent criticizes the Court for standing in the way of what the people of Arizona want. But the whole point of the First Amendment is to protect speakers against unjustified government restrictions on speech, even when those restrictions reflect the will of the majority. When it comes to protected speech, the speaker is sovereign.

Arizona's program gives money to a candidate in direct response to the campaign speech of an opposing candidate or an independent group. It does this when the opposing candidate has chosen not to accept public financing, and has engaged in political speech above a level set by the State. The professed purpose of the state law is to cause a sufficient number of candidates to sign up for public financing, which subjects them to the various restrictions on speech that go along with that program. This goes too far; Arizona's matching funds provision substantially burdens the speech of privately financed candidates and independent expenditure groups without serving a compelling state interest. . . . Laws like Arizona's matching funds provision that inhibit robust and wide-open political debate without sufficient justification cannot stand.

The judgment of the Court of Appeals for the Ninth Circuit is reversed.

It is so ordered.

JUSTICE KAGAN, with Whom JUSTICE GINSBURG, JUSTICE BREYER, and JUSTICE SOTOMAYOR Join, Dissenting.

Imagine two States, each plagued by a corrupt political system. In both States, candidates for public office accept large campaign contributions in exchange for the promise that, after assuming office, they will rank the donors' interests ahead of all others. As a result of these bargains, politicians ignore the public interest, sound public policy languishes, and the citizens lose confidence in their government. Recognizing the cancerous effect of this corruption, voters of the first State, acting through referendum, enact several campaign finance measures previously approved by this Court. They cap campaign contributions; require disclosure of substantial donations; and create an optional public financing program that gives candidates a fixed public subsidy if they refrain from private fundraising. But these measures do not work. Individuals who "bundle" campaign contributions become indispensable to candidates in need of money. Simple disclosure fails to prevent shady dealing. And candidates choose not to participate in the public financing system because the sums provided do not make them competitive with their privately financed opponents. So the State remains afflicted with corruption.

Voters of the second State, having witnessed this failure, take an ever-so-slightly different tack to cleaning up their political system. They too enact contribution limits and disclosure requirements. But they believe that the greatest hope of eliminating corruption lies in creating an effective public financing program, which will break candidates' dependence on large donors and bundlers. These voters realize, based on the first State's experience, that such a program will not work unless candidates agree to participate in it. And candidates will participate only if they know that they will receive sufficient funding to run competitive races. So the voters enact a program that carefully adjusts the money given to would-be officeholders, through the use of a matching funds mechanism, in order to provide this assurance. The program does not discriminate against any candidate or point of view, and it does not restrict any person's ability to speak. In fact, by providing resources to many candidates, the program creates more speech and thereby broadens public debate. And just as the voters had hoped, the program accomplishes its mission of restoring integrity to the political system. The second State rids itself of corruption.

A person familiar with our country's core values—our devotion to democratic self-governance, as well as to "uninhibited, robust, and wide-open" debate, New York Times Co. v. Sullivan (1964)—might expect this Court to celebrate, or at least not to interfere with, the second State's success. But today, the majority holds that the second State's system—the system that produces honest government, working on behalf of all the people—clashes with our Constitution. The First Amendment, the majority insists, requires us all to rely on the measures employed in the first State, even when they have failed to break the stranglehold of special interests on elected officials.

I disagree. The First Amendment's core purpose is to foster a healthy, vibrant political system full of robust discussion and debate. Nothing in Arizona's anticorruption statute, the Arizona Citizens Clean Elections Act, violates this constitutional protection. To the contrary, the Act promotes the values underlying both the First Amendment and our entire Constitution by enhancing the "opportunity for free political discussion to the end that government may be responsive to the will of the people." *Id.* I therefore respectfully dissent.

I

A

Campaign finance reform over the last century has focused on one key question: how to prevent massive pools of private money from corrupting our political system. If an officeholder owes his election to wealthy contributors, he may act for their benefit alone, rather than on behalf of all the people. As we recognized in Buckley v. Valeo (1976) *(per curiam),* our seminal campaign finance case, large private contributions may result in "political *quid pro quo[s],*" which undermine the integrity of our democracy. And even if these contributions are not converted into corrupt bargains, they still may weaken confidence in our political system because the public perceives "the opportunities for abuse[s]." *Id.* To prevent both corruption and the appearance of corruption—and so to protect our democratic system of governance—citizens have implemented reforms designed to curb the power of special interests. Among these measures, public financing of elections has emerged as a potentially potent mechanism to preserve elected officials' independence. . . .

Public financing can achieve its goals only if a meaningful number of candidates receive the state subsidy, rather than raise private funds. But a public funding program must be voluntary to pass constitutional muster, because of its restrictions on contributions and expenditures. See *Buckley*. And candidates will choose to sign up only if the subsidy provided enables them to run competitive races. If the grant is pegged too low, it puts the participating candidate at a disadvantage: Because he has agreed to spend no more than the amount of the subsidy, he will lack the means to respond if his privately funded opponent spends over that threshold. So when lump-sum grants do not keep up with campaign expenditures, more and more candidates will choose not to participate. But if the subsidy is set too high, it may impose an unsustainable burden on the public fisc. At the least, hefty grants will waste public resources in the many state races where lack of competition makes such funding unnecessary.

The difficulty, then, is in finding the Goldilocks solution — not too large, not too small, but just right. . . .

B

The people of Arizona had every reason to try to develop effective anti-corruption measures. Before turning to public financing, Arizonans voted by referendum to establish campaign contribution limits. But that effort to abate corruption, standing alone, proved unsuccessful. Five years after the enactment of these limits, the State suffered "the worst public corruption scandal in its history." Brief for State Respondents. In that scandal, known as "AzScam," nearly 10% of the State's legislators were caught accepting campaign contributions or bribes in exchange for supporting a piece of legislation. Following that incident, the voters of Arizona decided that further reform was necessary. Acting once again by referendum, they adopted the public funding system at issue here.

The hallmark of Arizona's program is its inventive approach to the challenge that bedevils all public financing schemes: fixing the amount of the subsidy. For each electoral contest, the system calibrates the size of the grant automatically to provide sufficient — but no more than sufficient — funds to induce voluntary participation. In effect, the program's designers found the Goldilocks solution, which produces the "just right" grant to ensure that a participant in the system has the funds needed to run a competitive race.

As the Court explains, Arizona's matching funds arrangement responds to the shortcoming of the lump-sum model by adjusting the public subsidy in each race to reflect the expenditures of a privately financed candidate and the independent groups that support him. . . . The question here is whether this modest adjustment to the public financing program that we approved in *Buckley* makes the Arizona law unconstitutional. The majority contends that the matching funds provision "substantially burdens protected political speech" and does not "serv[e] a compelling state interest." But the Court is wrong on both counts.

II

Arizona's statute does not impose a "restriction," or "substantia[l] burde[n]," on expression. The law has quite the opposite effect: It subsidizes and so produces *more* political speech. We recognized in *Buckley* that, for this reason, public financing of elections "facilitate[s] and enlarge[s] public discussion," in support of First Amendment values. And what we said then is just as true today. Except in a world gone topsy-turvy, additional campaign speech and electoral competition is not a First Amendment injury.

A

At every turn, the majority tries to convey the impression that Arizona's matching fund statute is of a piece with laws prohibiting electoral speech. . . . There is just one problem. Arizona's matching funds provision does not restrict, but instead subsidizes, speech. The law "impose[s] no ceiling on [speech] and do[es] not prevent anyone from speaking." Citizens United v. Federal Election Comm'n (2010); see *Buckley* (holding that a public financing law does not "abridge, restrict, or censor" expression). The statute does not tell candidates or their supporters how much money they can spend to convey their message, when they can spend it, or what they can spend it on. Rather, the Arizona law, like the public financing statute in *Buckley,* provides funding for political speech, thus "facilitat[ing] communication by candidates with the electorate." *Id.* By enabling participating candidates to respond to their opponents'expression, the statute expands public debate, in adherence to "our tradition that more speech, not less, is the governing rule." *Citizens United.* What the law does — all the law does — is fund more speech.[4]

And under the First Amendment, that makes all the difference. In case after case, year upon year, we have distinguished between speech restrictions and speech subsidies. That is because subsidies, by definition and contra the majority, do not restrict any speech.

No one can claim that Arizona's law discriminates against particular ideas, and so violates the First Amendment's sole limitation on speech subsidies. The State throws open the doors of its public financing program to all candidates who meet minimal eligibility requirements and agree not to raise private funds. Republicans and Democrats, conservatives and liberals may participate; so too, the law applies equally to independent expenditure groups across the political spectrum. Arizona disburses funds based not on a candidate's (or supporter's) ideas, but on the candidate's decision to sign up for public funding. So under our precedent, Arizona's subsidy statute should easily survive First Amendment scrutiny.[5]

4. And the law appears to do that job well. Between 1998 (when the statute was enacted) and 2006, overall candidate expenditures increased between 29% and 67%; overall independent expenditures rose by a whopping 253%; and average candidate expenditures grew by 12% to 40%.

5. The majority claims that none of our subsidy cases involved the funding of "respons[ive]" expression. But the majority does not explain why this distinction, created to fit the facts of this case, should matter so long as the government is not discriminating on the basis of viewpoint. Indeed, the difference the majority highlights should cut in the opposite direction, because facilitating responsive speech fosters "uninhibited, robust, and wide-open" public debate. New York Times Co. v. Sullivan, (1964). In any event, the majority is wrong to say that we have never approved funding to "allow the recipient to counter" someone else's political speech. That is exactly what we approved in Buckley

This suit, in fact, may merit less attention than any challenge to a speech subsidy ever seen in this Court. In the usual First Amendment subsidy case, a person complains that the government declined to finance his speech, while bankrolling someone else's; we must then decide whether the government differentiated between these speakers on a prohibited basis — because it preferred one speaker's ideas to another's. But the candidates bringing this challenge do not make that claim — because they were never denied a subsidy. Arizona, remember, offers to support any person running for state office. Petitioners here *refused* that assistance. So they are making a novel argument: that Arizona violated *their* First Amendment rights by disbursing funds to *other* speakers even though they could have received (but chose to spurn) the same financial assistance. Some people might call that *chutzpah.*

Indeed, what petitioners demand is essentially a right to quash others' speech through the prohibition of a (universally available) subsidy program. Petitioners are able to convey their ideas without public financing — and they would prefer the field to themselves, so that they can speak free from response. To attain that goal, they ask this Court to prevent Arizona from funding electoral speech — even though that assistance is offered to every state candidate, on the same (entirely unobjectionable) basis. And this Court gladly obliges.

If an ordinary citizen, without the hindrance of a law degree, thought this result an upending of First Amendment values, he would be correct. That Amendment protects no person's, nor any candidate's, "right to be free from vigorous debate." Pacific Gas & Elec. Co. v. Public Util. Comm'n of Cal. (1986) (plurality opinion). Indeed, the Amendment exists so that this debate can occur — robust, forceful, and contested. It is the theory of the Free Speech Clause that "falsehood and fallacies" are exposed through "discussion," "education," and "more speech." Whitney v. California (1927) (Brandeis, J., concurring). Or once again from *Citizens United:* "[M]ore speech, not less, is the governing rule." And this is no place more true than in elections, where voters' ability to choose the best representatives depends on debate — on charge and countercharge, call and response. So to invalidate a statute that restricts no one's speech and discriminates against no idea — that only provides more voices, wider discussion, and greater competition in elections — is to undermine, rather than to enforce, the First Amendment.[6]

---

v. Valeo (1976) (per curiam). The majority notes that the public financing scheme in *Buckley* lacked the trigger mechanism used in the Arizona law. But again, that is just to describe a difference, not to say why it matters. As I will show, the trigger is constitutionally irrelevant — as we made clear in the very case (Davis v. Federal Election Commn (2008)) on which the majority principally relies.

6. The majority argues that more speech will quickly become "less speech," as candidates switch to public funding. But that claim misunderstands how a voluntary public financing system works. Candidates with significant financial resources will likely decline public funds, so that they can spend in excess of the system's expenditure caps. Other candidates accept public financing because they believe it will enhance their communication with voters. So the system continually pushes toward more speech. That is exactly what has happened in Arizona and the majority offers no counter-examples.

We said all this in *Buckley,* when we upheld the presidential public financing system—a ruling this Court has never since questioned. . . . We should be saying the same today.

B

The majority has one, and only one, way of separating this case from *Buckley* and our other, many precedents involving speech subsidies. According to the Court, the special problem here lies in Arizona's matching funds mechanism, which the majority claims imposes a "substantia[l] burde[n]" on a privately funded candidate's speech . . . [But] the majority is wrong to see a substantial burden on expression.[7]

Most important, and as just suggested, the very notion that additional speech constitutes a "burden" is odd and unsettling. Here is a simple fact: Arizona imposes nothing remotely resembling a coercive penalty on privately funded candidates. The State does not jail them, fine them, or subject them to any kind of lesser disability. (So the majority's analogies to a fine on speech are inapposite.) The only "burden" in this case comes from the grant of a subsidy to another person, and the opportunity that subsidy allows for responsive speech. But that means the majority cannot get out from under our subsidy precedents. Once again: We have never, not once, understood a viewpoint-neutral subsidy given to one speaker to constitute a First Amendment burden on another. (And that is so even when the subsidy is not open to all, as it is here.) Yet in this case, the majority says that the prospect of more speech—responsive speech, competitive speech, the kind of speech that drives public debate—counts as a constitutional injury. That concept, for all the reasons previously given, is "wholly foreign to the First Amendment." *Buckley.*

But put to one side this most fundamental objection to the majority's argument; even then, has the majority shown that the burden resulting from the Arizona statute is "substantial"? I will not quarrel with the majority's assertion that responsive speech by one candidate may make another candidate's speech less effective; that, after all, is the whole idea of the First Amendment, and a *benefit* of having more responsive speech. And I will assume that the operation of this statute may on occasion deter a privately funded candidate from spending money, and conveying ideas by that means. My guess is that this does not happen often: Most political candidates, I suspect, have enough faith in the power of their ideas to prefer speech on both sides of an issue to speech on neither. But I will take on faith that the matching funds provision may lead one

7. The majority's error on this score extends both to candidates and to independent expenditure groups. Contrary to the majority's suggestion, nearly all of my arguments showing that the Clean Elections Act does not impose a substantial burden apply to both sets of speakers (and apply regardless of whether independent or candidate expenditures trigger the matching funds). That is also true of every one of my arguments demonstrating the State's compelling interest in this legislation. But perhaps the best response to the majority's view that the Act inhibits independent expenditure groups lies in an empirical fact already noted: Expenditures by these groups have risen by 253% since Arizona's law was enacted.

or another privately funded candidate to stop spending at one or another moment in an election. Still, does that effect count as a severe burden on expression? By the measure of our prior decisions — which have upheld campaign reforms with an equal or greater impact on speech — the answer is no.

Number one: *Any* system of public financing, including the lump-sum model upheld in *Buckley*, imposes a similar burden on privately funded candidates. Suppose Arizona were to do what all parties agree it could under *Buckley* — provide a single upfront payment (say, $150,000) to a participating candidate, rather than an initial payment (of $50,000) plus 94% of whatever his privately funded opponent spent, up to a ceiling (the same $150,000). That system would "diminis[h] the effectiveness" of a privately funded candidate's speech at least as much, and in the same way: It would give his opponent, who presumably would not be able to raise that sum on his own, more money to spend. And so too, a lump-sum system may deter speech. A person relying on private resources might well choose not to enter a race at all, because he knows he will face an adequately funded opponent. And even if he decides to run, he likely will choose to speak in different ways — for example, by eschewing dubious, easy-to-answer charges — because his opponent has the ability to respond. Indeed, privately funded candidates may well find the lump-sum system *more* burdensome than Arizona's (assuming the lump is big enough). Pretend you are financing your campaign through private donations. Would you prefer that your opponent receive a guaranteed, upfront payment of $150,000, or that he receive only $50,000, with the *possibility* — a possibility that you mostly get to control — of collecting another $100,000 somewhere down the road? Me too. That's the first reason the burden on speech cannot command a different result in this case than in *Buckley*.

Number two: Our decisions about disclosure and disclaimer requirements show the Court is wrong. Starting in *Buckley* and continuing through last Term, the Court has repeatedly declined to view these requirements as a substantial First Amendment burden, even though they discourage some campaign speech. . . . So too here. Like a disclosure rule, the matching funds provision may occasionally deter, but "impose[s] no ceiling" on electoral expression. [*Citizens United*].

The majority breezily dismisses this comparison, labeling the analogy "not even close" because disclosure requirements result in no payment of money to a speaker's opponent. That is indeed the factual distinction: A matching fund provision, we can all agree, is not a disclosure rule. But the majority does not tell us why this difference matters. Nor could it. The majority strikes down the matching funds provision because of its ostensible *effect* — most notably, that it may deter a person from spending money in an election. But this Court has acknowledged time and again that disclosure obligations have the selfsame effect. If that consequence does not trigger the most stringent judicial review in the one case, it should not do so in the other.

Number three: Any burden that the Arizona law imposes does not exceed the burden associated with contribution limits, which we have also repeatedly upheld. . . . Rather than potentially deterring or "diminish [ing] the effectiveness" of expressive activity [*Davis*], these limits stop it cold. Yet we have never subjected these restrictions to the most stringent review. I doubt I have to reiterate that the Arizona statute imposes no restraints on any expressive activity. So the majority once again has no reason here to reach a different result

In this way, our campaign finance cases join our speech subsidy cases in supporting the constitutionality of Arizona's law. Both sets of precedents are in accord that a statute funding electoral speech in the way Arizona's does imposes no First Amendment injury.

C

The majority thinks it has one case on its side—Davis v. Federal Election Comm'n—and it pegs everything on that decision. But *Davis* relies on principles that fit securely within our First Amendment law and tradition—most unlike today's opinion. . . .

Under the First Amendment, the similarity between *Davis* and this case matters far less than the differences. Here is the similarity: In both cases, one candidate's campaign expenditure triggered . . . something. Now here are the differences: In *Davis,* the candidate's expenditure triggered a discriminatory speech restriction, which Congress could not otherwise have imposed consistent with the First Amendment; by contrast, in this case, the candidate's expenditure triggers a non-discriminatory speech subsidy, which all parties agree Arizona could have provided in the first instance. In First Amendment law, that difference makes a difference—indeed, it makes *all* the difference. . . .

[T]wo great fault lines run through our First Amendment doctrine: one, between speech restrictions and speech subsidies, and the other, between discriminatory and neutral government action. The Millionaire's Amendment fell on the disfavored side of both divides: To reiterate, it imposed a discriminatory speech restriction. The Arizona Clean Elections Act lands on the opposite side of both: It grants a non-discriminatory speech subsidy.[8] So to say that *Davis* "largely controls" this case, is to decline to take our First Amendment doctrine seriously. . . .

But what of the trigger mechanism—in *Davis,* as here, a candidate's campaign expenditures? That, after all, is the only thing that this case and *Davis* share. If *Davis* had held that the trigger mechanism itself violated the First Amendment, then the case would support today's holding. But *Davis* said nothing of the kind. It made clear that the trigger mechanism could not *rescue* the discriminatory contribution limits from constitutional invalidity; that the limits went into effect only after a candidate spent substantial personal resources

8. Of course, only publicly funded candidates receive the subsidy. But that is because only those candidates have agreed to abide by stringent spending caps (which privately funded candidates can exceed by any amount). And *Buckley* specifically approved that exchange as consistent with the First Amendment. By contrast, *Davis* involved a scheme in which one candidate in a race received concrete fundraising advantages, in the form of asymmetrical contribution limits, just because his opponent had spent a certain amount of his own money.

rendered them no more permissible under the First Amendment. But *Davis* did not call into question the trigger mechanism itself. Indeed, *Davis* explained that Congress could have used that mechanism to activate a *non-discriminatory* (*i.e.*, across-the-board) increase in contribution limits; in that case, the Court stated, "Davis' argument would plainly fail." The constitutional infirmity in *Davis* was not the trigger mechanism, but rather what lay on the other side of it—a discriminatory speech restriction.

The Court's response to these points is difficult to fathom. The majority concedes that "our decision in *Davis* focused on the asymmetrical contribution limits imposed by the Millionaire's Amendment." That was because, the majority explains, *Davis* presented only that issue. And yet, the majority insists (without explaining how this can be true), the reach of *Davis* is not so limited. And in any event, the majority claims, the burden on speech is "greater in this case than in *Davis*." But for reasons already stated, that is not so. The burden on speech in *Davis*—the penalty that campaign spending triggered—*was* the discriminatory contribution restriction, which Congress could not otherwise have imposed. By contrast, the thing triggered here is a non-discriminatory subsidy, of a kind this Court has approved for almost four decades. Maybe the majority is saying today that it had something like this case in mind all the time. But nothing in the logic of *Davis* controls this decision.[9]

III

For all these reasons, the Court errs in holding that the government action in this case substantially burdens speech and so requires the State to offer a compelling interest. But in any event, Arizona has come forward with just such an interest, explaining that the Clean Elections Act attacks corruption and the appearance of corruption in the State's political system. The majority's denigration of this interest—the suggestion that it either is not real or does not matter—wrongly prevents Arizona from protecting the strength and integrity of its democracy.

A

Our campaign finance precedents leave no doubt: Preventing corruption or the appearance of corruption is a compelling government interest. And so too, these precedents are clear: Public financing of elections serves this interest. . . . When

9. The majority also briefly relies on Miami Herald Publishing Co. v. Tornillo (1974), but that case is still wider of the mark. There, we invalidated a law compelling newspapers (by threat of criminal sanction) to print a candidate's rejoinder to critical commentary. That law, we explained, overrode the newspaper's own editorial judgment and forced the paper both to pay for and to convey a message with which it disagreed. An analogy might be if Arizona forced privately funded candidates to purchase their opponents' posters, and then to display those posters in their own campaign offices. But that is very far from this case. The Arizona statute does not require petitioners to disseminate or fund any opposing speech; nor does it in any way associate petitioners with that speech.

private contributions fuel the political system, candidates may make corrupt bargains to gain the money needed to win election. And voters, seeing the dependence of candidates on large contributors (or on bundlers of smaller contributions), may lose faith that their representatives will serve the public's interest. Public financing addresses these dangers by minimizing the importance of private donors in elections. Even the majority appears to agree with this premise. . . .

And that interest justifies the matching funds provision at issue because it is a critical facet of Arizona's public financing program. The provision is no more than a disbursement mechanism; but it is also the thing that makes the whole Clean Elections Act work. As described earlier, public financing has an Achilles heel—the difficulty of setting the subsidy at the right amount. Too small, and the grant will not attract candidates to the program; and with no participating candidates, the program can hardly decrease corruption. Too large, and the system becomes unsustainable, or at the least an unnecessary drain on public resources. But finding the sweet-spot is near impossible because of variation, across districts and over time, in the political system. Enter the matching funds provision, which takes an ordinary lump-sum amount, divides it into thirds, and disburses the last two of these (to the extent necessary) via a self-calibrating mechanism. That provision is just a fine-tuning of the lump-sum program approved in *Buckley*—a fine-tuning, it bears repeating, that prevents no one from speaking and discriminates against no message. But that fine-tuning can make the difference between a wholly ineffectual program and one that removes corruption from the political system.[10] If public financing furthers a compelling interest—and according to this Court, it does—then so too does the disbursement formula that Arizona uses to make public financing effective. The one conclusion follows directly from the other. . . .

Assuming (against reason and precedent) that the matching funds provision substantially burdens speech, the question becomes whether the State has offered a sufficient justification for imposing that burden. Arizona has made a forceful argument on this score, based on the need to establish an effective public financing system. The majority does not even engage that reasoning.

B

The majority instead devotes most of its energy to trying to show that "level [ing] the playing field," not fighting corruption, was the State's real goal. . . . But . . . so long as Arizona had a compelling interest in eliminating political

10. For this reason, the majority is quite wrong to say that the State's interest in combating corruption does not support the matching fund provision's application to a candidates expenditure of his own money or to an independent expenditure. The point is not that these expenditures themselves corrupt the political process. Rather, Arizona includes these, as well as all other, expenditures in the program to ensure that participating candidates receive the funds necessary to run competitive races—and so to attract those candidates in the first instance. That is in direct service of the State's anti-corruption interest.

corruption (which it clearly did) . . . , any interest of the State in "leveling" should be irrelevant. That interest could not support Arizona's law (assuming the law burdened speech), but neither would the interest invalidate the legislation. . . . This Court, after all, has never said that a law restricting speech (or any other constitutional right) demands two compelling interests. One is enough. And this statute has one: preventing corruption. So it does not matter that equalizing campaign speech is an insufficient interest. The statute could violate the First Amendment only if "equalizing" qualified as a forbidden motive — a motive that itself could annul an otherwise constitutional law. But we have never held that to be so. And that should not be surprising: It is a "fundamental principle of constitutional adjudication," from which we have deviated only in exceptional cases, "that this Court will not strike down an otherwise constitutional statute on the basis of an alleged illicit legislative motive." United States v. O'Brien (1968). When a law is otherwise constitutional — when it either does not restrict speech or rests on an interest sufficient to justify any such restriction — that is the end of the story.

That proposition disposes of this case, even if Arizona had an adjunct interest here in equalizing electoral opportunities. No special rule of automatic invalidation applies to statutes having some connection to equality; like any other laws, they pass muster when supported by an important enough government interest. Here, Arizona has demonstrated in detail how the matching funds provision is necessary to serve a compelling interest in combating corruption. So the hunt for evidence of "leveling" is a waste of time; Arizona's law survives constitutional scrutiny no matter what that search would uncover.

IV

This case arose because Arizonans wanted their government to work on behalf of all the State's people. On the heels of a political scandal involving the near-routine purchase of legislators' votes, Arizonans passed a law designed to sever political candidates' dependence on large contributors. They wished, as many of their fellow Americans wish, to stop corrupt dealing — to ensure that their representatives serve the public, and not just the wealthy donors who helped put them in office. The legislation that Arizona's voters enacted was the product of deep thought and care. It put into effect a public financing system that attracted large numbers of candidates at a sustainable cost to the State's taxpayers. The system discriminated against no ideas and prevented no speech. Indeed, by increasing electoral competition and enabling a wide range of candidates to express their views, the system "further[ed] . . . First Amendment values." *Buckley*. Less corruption, more speech. Robust campaigns leading to the election of representatives not beholden to the few, but accountable to the many. The people of Arizona might have expected a decent respect for those objectives.

Today, they do not get it. The Court invalidates Arizonans' efforts to ensure that in their State, "'[t]he people . . . possess the absolute sovereignty.'" *Id.* (quoting James Madison in 4 Elliot's Debates on the Federal Constitution 569–570 (1876)). No precedent compels the Court to take this step; to the contrary, today's decision is in tension with broad swaths of our First Amendment doctrine. No fundamental principle of our Constitution backs the Court's ruling; to the contrary, it is the law struck down today that fostered both the vigorous competition of ideas and its ultimate object—a government responsive to the will of the people. Arizonans deserve better. Like citizens across this country, Arizonans deserve a government that represents and serves them all. And no less, Arizonans deserve the chance to reform their electoral system so as to attain that most American of goals.

Truly, democracy is not a game. I respectfully dissent.

ASSIGNMENT S-9

STUDY GUIDE: *As in New York Times v. Sullivan, the next case raises the issue of when and why "wrongful" speech—as defined by the state law of torts—should be any more constitutionally protected from state "infringement" any other wrongful acts. Could part of the problem lie in the "dignitary" nature of the torts of defamation or intentional infliction of emotional distress themselves? In other words, do these torts raise First Amendment concerns and, if so, how should they be reconciled? Should it make any difference whether the offending speech was aimed specifically at the plantiff, or simply disturbed the peace of a private funeral ceremony (if indeed it did)?*

SNYDER v. PHELPS

564 U.S. _____ (2011)

CHIEF JUSTICE ROBERTS delivered the opinion of the Court.

A jury held members of the Westboro Baptist Church liable for millions of dollars in damages for picketing near a soldier's funeral service. The picket signs reflected the church's view that the United States is overly tolerant of sin and that God kills American soldiers as punishment. The question presented is whether the First Amendment shields the church members from tort liability for their speech in this case.

I

A

Fred Phelps founded the Westboro Baptist Church in Topeka, Kansas, in 1955. The church's congregation believes that God hates and punishes the United States for its tolerance of homosexuality, particularly in America's military. The church frequently communicates its views by picketing, often at military funerals. In the more than 20 years that the members of Westboro Baptist have publicized their message, they have picketed nearly 600 funerals. Marine Lance Corporal Matthew Snyder was killed in Iraq in the line of duty. Lance Corporal Snyder's father selected the Catholic church in the Snyders' hometown of Westminster, Maryland, as the site for his son's funeral. Local newspapers provided notice of the time and location of the service.

Phelps became aware of Matthew Snyder's funeral and decided to travel to Maryland with six other Westboro Baptist parishioners (two of his daughters and four of his grandchildren) to picket. On the day of the memorial service, the Westboro congregation members picketed on public land adjacent to public streets near the Maryland State House, the United States Naval Academy, and Matthew Snyder's funeral. The Westboro picketers carried signs that were largely the same at all three locations. . . .

The church had notified the authorities in advance of its intent to picket at the time of the funeral, and the picketers complied with police instructions in staging their demonstration. The picketing took place within a 10-by 25-foot plot of public land adjacent to a public street, behind a temporary fence. That plot was approximately 1,000 feet from the church where the funeral was held. Several buildings separated the picket site from the church. The Westboro picketers displayed their signs for about 30 minutes before the funeral began and sang hymns and recited Bible verses. None of the picketers entered church property or went to the cemetery. They did not yell or use profanity, and there was no violence associated with the picketing.

The funeral procession passed within 200 to 300 feet of the picket site. Although Snyder testified that he could see the tops of the picket signs as he drove to the funeral, he did not see what was written on the signs until later that night, while watching a news broadcast covering the event.

B

Snyder filed suit against Phelps, Phelps's daughters, and the Westboro Baptist Church (collectively Westboro or the church) in the United States District Court for the District of Maryland under that court's diversity jurisdiction. Snyder alleged five state tort law claims: defamation, publicity given to private life, intentional infliction of emotional distress, intrusion upon seclusion, and civil conspiracy. . . . The District Court awarded Westboro summary judgment on Snyder's claims for defamation and publicity given to private life, concluding that Snyder could not prove the necessary elements of those torts. A trial was held on the remaining claims. At trial, Snyder described the severity of his emotional injuries. He testified that he is unable to separate the thought of his dead son from his thoughts of Westboro's picketing, and that he often becomes tearful, angry, and physically ill when he thinks about it. . . .

A jury found for Snyder on the intentional infliction of emotional distress, intrusion upon seclusion, and civil conspiracy claims, and held Westboro liable for $2.9 million in compensatory damages and $8 million in punitive damages. Westboro filed several post-trial motions, including a motion contending that the jury verdict was grossly excessive and a motion seeking judgment as a matter of law on all claims on First Amendment grounds. The District Court remitted the punitive damages award to $2.1 million, but left the jury verdict otherwise intact.

In the Court of Appeals, Westboro's primary argument was that the church was entitled to judgment as a matter of law because the First Amendment fully protected Westboro's speech. The Court of Appeals agreed. . . . We granted certiorari.

II

To succeed on a claim for intentional infliction of emotional distress in Maryland, a plaintiff must demonstrate that the defendant intentionally or recklessly engaged in extreme and outrageous conduct that caused the plaintiff to suffer severe emotional distress. The Free Speech Clause of the First Amendment— "Congress shall make no law . . . abridging the freedom of speech" —can serve as a defense in state tort suits, including suits for intentional infliction of emotional distress. See, e.g., Hustler Magazine, Inc. v. Falwell (1988).

Whether the First Amendment prohibits holding Westboro liable for its speech in this case turns largely on whether that speech is of public or private concern, as determined by all the circumstances of the case. . . . "[S]peech on 'matters of public concern' . . . is 'at the heart of the First Amendment's protection.'" Dun & Bradstreet, Inc. v. Greenmoss Builders, Inc. (1985) (opinion of Powell, J.)). The First Amendment reflects "a profound national commitment to the principle that debate on public issues should be uninhibited, robust, and wide-open." New York Times Co. v. Sullivan (1964). That is because "speech concerning public affairs is more than self-expression; it is the essence of self-government." Garrison v. Louisiana (1964). Accordingly, "speech on public issues occupies the highest rung of the hierarchy of First Amendment values, and is entitled to special protection." Connick v. Myers (1983).

"'[N]ot all speech is of equal First Amendment importance,'" however, and where matters of purely private significance are at issue, First Amendment protections are often less rigorous. *Hustler*. That is because restricting speech on purely private matters does not implicate the same constitutional concerns as limiting speech on matters of public interest: "[T]here is no threat to the free and robust debate of public issues; there is no potential interference with a meaningful dialogue of ideas"; and the "threat of liability" does not pose the risk of "a reaction of self-censorship" on matters of public import. *Dun & Bradstreet*. . . .

Speech deals with matters of public concern when it can "be fairly considered as relating to any matter of political, social, or other concern to the community," *Connick*, or when it "is a subject of legitimate news interest; that is, a subject of general interest and of value and concern to the public," [San Diego v. Roe (2004) (*per curiam*)] The arguably "inappropriate or controversial character of a statement is irrelevant to the question whether it deals with a matter of public concern." Rankin v. McPherson (1987).

Our opinion in *Dun & Bradstreet,* on the other hand, provides an example of speech of only private concern. In that case we held, as a general matter, that information about a particular individual's credit report "concerns no public issue." The content of the report, we explained, "was speech solely in the individual interest of the speaker and its specific business audience." That was confirmed by the fact that the particular report was sent to only five subscribers to the reporting service, who were bound not to disseminate it further. To cite another example, we concluded in San Diego v. Roe that, in the context of a government employer regulating the speech of its employees, videos of an employee engaging in sexually explicit acts did not address a public concern; the videos "did nothing to inform the public about any aspect of the [employing agency's] functioning or operation." . . .

The "content" of Westboro's signs plainly relates to broad issues of interest to society at large, rather than matters of "purely private concern." *Dun & Bradstreet*. The placards read "God Hates the USA/Thank God for 9/11," "America is Doomed," "Don't Pray for the USA," "Thank God for IEDs," "Fag Troops," "Semper Fi Fags," "God Hates Fags," "Maryland Taliban," "Fags Doom Nations," "Not Blessed Just Cursed," "Thank God for Dead Soldiers," "Pope in Hell," "Priests Rape Boys," "You're Going to Hell," and "God Hates You." While these messages may fall short of refined social or political commentary, the issues they highlight—the political and moral conduct of the United States and its citizens, the fate of our Nation, homosexuality in the military, and scandals involving the Catholic clergy—are matters of public import. The signs certainly convey Westboro's position on those issues, in a manner designed, unlike the private speech in *Dun & Bradstreet,* to reach as broad a public audience as possible. And even if a few of the signs—such as "You're Going to Hell" and "God Hates You"—were viewed as containing messages related to Matthew Snyder or the Snyders specifically, that would not change the fact that the overall thrust and dominant theme of Westboro's demonstration spoke to broader public issues.

Apart from the content of Westboro's signs, Snyder contends that the "context" of the speech—its connection with his son's funeral—makes the speech a matter of private rather than public concern. The fact that Westboro spoke in connection with a funeral, however, cannot by itself transform the nature of Westboro's speech. Westboro's signs, displayed on public land next to a public street, reflect the fact that the church finds much to condemn in modern society. Its speech is "fairly characterized as constituting speech on a matter of public concern," *Connick,* and the funeral setting does not alter that conclusion.

Snyder argues that the church members in fact mounted a personal attack on Snyder and his family, and then attempted to "immunize their conduct by claiming that they were actually protesting the United States' tolerance of homosexuality or the supposed evils of the Catholic Church." We are not concerned in this case that Westboro's speech on public matters was in any way contrived to insulate speech on a private matter from liability. Westboro had been actively engaged in speaking on the subjects addressed in its picketing long before it became aware of Matthew Snyder, and there can be no serious claim that Westboro's picketing did not represent its "honestly believed" views on public issues. *Garrison*. There was no pre-existing relationship or conflict between Westboro and Snyder that might suggest Westboro's speech on public matters was intended to mask an attack on Snyder over a private matter. Contrast *Connick* (finding public employee speech a matter of private concern when it was "no coincidence that [the speech] followed upon the heels of [a] transfer notice" affecting the employee).

Snyder goes on to argue that Westboro's speech should be afforded less than full First Amendment protection "not only because of the words" but also because the church members exploited the funeral "as a platform to bring their message to a broader audience." There is no doubt that Westboro chose to stage its picketing at the Naval Academy, the Maryland State House, and Matthew Snyder's funeral to increase publicity for its views and because of the relation between those sites and its views — in the case of the military funeral, because Westboro believes that God is killing American soldiers as punishment for the Nation's sinful policies.

Westboro's choice to convey its views in conjunction with Matthew Snyder's funeral made the expression of those views particularly hurtful to many, especially to Matthew's father. The record makes clear that the applicable legal term — "emotional distress" — fails to capture fully the anguish Westboro's choice added to Mr. Snyder's already incalculable grief. But Westboro conducted its picketing peacefully on matters of public concern at a public place adjacent to a public street. Such space occupies a "special position in terms of First Amendment protection." United States v. Grace (1983). "[W]e have repeatedly referred to public streets as the archetype of a traditional public forum," noting that " '[t]ime out of mind' public streets and sidewalks have been used for public assembly and debate." Frisby v. Schultz (1988).

That said, . . . Westboro's choice of where and when to conduct its picketing is not beyond the Government's regulatory reach — it is "subject to reasonable time, place, or manner restrictions" that are consistent with the standards announced in this Court's precedents. Clark v. Community for Creative Non-Violence (1984). Maryland now has a law imposing restrictions on funeral picketing, as do 43 other States and the Federal Government. To the extent these laws are content neutral, they raise very different questions from the tort verdict at issue in this case. Maryland's law, however, was not in effect at the time of the events at issue here, so we have no occasion to consider how it might apply to facts such as those before us, or whether it or other similar regulations are constitutional.[11]

We have identified a few limited situations where the location of targeted picketing can be regulated under provisions that the Court has determined to be content neutral. In *Frisby,* for example, we upheld a ban on such picketing "before or about" a particular residence. In Madsen v. Women's Health Center, Inc. [1994], we approved an injunction requiring a buffer zone between protesters and an abortion clinic entrance. The facts here are obviously quite different, both with respect to the activity being regulated and the means of restricting those activities.

11. The Maryland law prohibits picketing within 100 feet of a funeral service or funeral procession; Westboro's picketing would have complied with that restriction.

Simply put, the church members had the right to be where they were. Westboro alerted local authorities to its funeral protest and fully complied with police guidance on where the picketing could be staged. The picketing was conducted under police supervision some 1,000 feet from the church, out of the sight of those at the church. The protest was not unruly; there was no shouting, profanity, or violence.

The record confirms that any distress occasioned by Westboro's picketing turned on the content and viewpoint of the message conveyed, rather than any interference with the funeral itself. A group of parishioners standing at the very spot where Westboro stood, holding signs that said "God Bless America" and "God Loves You," would not have been subjected to liability. It was what Westboro said that exposed it to tort damages.

Given that Westboro's speech was at a public place on a matter of public concern, that speech is entitled to "special protection" under the First Amendment. Such speech cannot be restricted simply because it is upsetting or arouses contempt. "If there is a bedrock principle underlying the First Amendment, it is that the government may not prohibit the expression of an idea simply because society finds the idea itself offensive or disagreeable." Texas v. Johnson (1989). Indeed, "the point of all speech protection . . . is to shield just those choices of content that in someone's eyes are misguided, or even hurtful." Hurley v. Irish-American Gay, Lesbian and Bisexual Group of Boston, Inc. (1995).

The jury here was instructed that it could hold Westboro liable for intentional infliction of emotional distress based on a finding that Westboro's picketing was "outrageous." "Outrageousness," however, is a highly malleable standard with "an inherent subjectiveness about it which would allow a jury to impose liability on the basis of the jurors' tastes or views, or perhaps on the basis of their dislike of a particular expression." *Hustler*. In a case such as this, a jury is "unlikely to be neutral with respect to the content of [the] speech," posing "a real danger of becoming an instrument for the suppression of . . . 'vehement, caustic, and sometimes unpleasan[t]'" expression. [Bose Corp. v. Consumers Union of United States, Inc. (1984)]. Such a risk is unacceptable; "in public debate [we] must tolerate insulting, and even outrageous, speech in order to provide adequate 'breathing space' to the freedoms protected by the First Amendment." *Boos v. Barry* (1988). What Westboro said, in the whole context of how and where it chose to say it, is entitled to "special protection" under the First Amendment, and that protection cannot be overcome by a jury finding that the picketing was outrageous.

For all these reasons, the jury verdict imposing tort liability on Westboro for intentional infliction of emotional distress must be set aside. . . .

IV

Our holding today is narrow. We are required in First Amendment cases to carefully review the record, and the reach of our opinion here is limited by the particular facts before us. . . . Westboro believes that America is morally flawed;

many Americans might feel the same about Westboro. Westboro's funeral picketing is certainly hurtful and its contribution to public discourse may be negligible. But Westboro addressed matters of public import on public property, in a peaceful manner, in full compliance with the guidance of local officials. The speech was indeed planned to coincide with Matthew Snyder's funeral, but did not itself disrupt that funeral, and Westboro's choice to conduct its picketing at that time and place did not alter the nature of its speech.

Speech is powerful. It can stir people to action, move them to tears of both joy and sorrow, and—as it did here—inflict great pain. On the facts before us, we cannot react to that pain by punishing the speaker. As a Nation we have chosen a different course-to protect even hurtful speech on public issues to ensure that we do not stifle public debate. That choice requires that we shield Westboro from tort liability for its picketing in this case.

The judgment of the United States Court of Appeals for the Fourth Circuit is affirmed.

It is so ordered.

JUSTICE ALITO, dissenting.

Our profound national commitment to free and open debate is not a license for the vicious verbal assault that occurred in this case. Petitioner Albert Snyder is not a public figure. He is simply a parent whose son, Marine Lance Corporal Matthew Snyder, was killed in Iraq. Mr. Snyder wanted what is surely the right of any parent who experiences such an incalculable loss: to bury his son in peace. But respondents, members of the Westboro Baptist Church, deprived him of that elementary right. . . .

In this case, respondents brutally attacked Matthew Snyder, and this attack, which was almost certain to inflict injury, was central to respondents' well-practiced strategy for attracting public attention. On the morning of Matthew Snyder's funeral, respondents could have chosen to stage their protest at countless locations. They could have picketed the United States Capitol, the White House, the Supreme Court, the Pentagon, or any of the more than 5,600 military recruiting stations in this country. They could have returned to the Maryland State House or the United States Naval Academy, where they had been the day before. They could have selected any public road where pedestrians are allowed. (There are more than 4,000,000 miles of public roads in the United States.) They could have staged their protest in a public park. (There are more than 20,000 public parks in this country.) They could have chosen any Catholic church where no funeral was taking place. (There are nearly 19,000 Catholic churches in the United States.) But of course, a small group picketing at any of these locations would have probably gone unnoticed.

The Westboro Baptist Church, however, has devised a strategy that remedies this problem. As the Court notes, church members have protested at nearly 600 military funerals. They have also picketed the funerals of police officers, fire-fighters, and the victims of natural disasters, accidents, and shocking crimes. And in advance of these protests, they issue press releases to ensure that their protests will attract public attention.

This strategy works because it is expected that respondents' verbal assaults will wound the family and friends of the deceased and because the media is irresistibly drawn to the sight of persons who are visibly in grief. The more outrageous the funeral protest, the more publicity the Westboro Baptist Church is able to obtain. Thus, when the church recently announced its intention to picket the funeral of a 9-year-old girl killed in the shooting spree in Tucson—proclaiming that she was "better off dead"—their announcement was national news, and the church was able to obtain free air time on the radio in exchange for canceling its protest. Similarly, in 2006, the church got air time on a talk radio show in exchange for canceling its threatened protest at the funeral of five Amish girls killed by a crazed gunman.

In this case, respondents implemented the Westboro Baptist Church's publicity-seeking strategy. Their press release stated that they were going "to picket the funeral of Lance Cpl. Matthew A. Snyder" because "God Almighty killed Lance Cpl. Snyder. He died in shame, not honor—for a fag nation cursed by God. . . . Now in Hell—sine die." This announcement guaranteed that Matthew's funeral would be transformed into a raucous media event and began the wounding process. It is well known that anticipation may heighten the effect of a painful event.

On the day of the funeral, respondents, true to their word, displayed placards that conveyed the message promised in their press release. Signs stating "God Hates You" and "Thank God for Dead Soldiers" reiterated the message that God had caused Matthew's death in retribution for his sins. Others, stating "You're Going to Hell" and "Not Blessed Just Cursed," conveyed the message that Matthew was "in Hell—sine die." . . .

Other signs would most naturally have been understood as suggesting—falsely—that Matthew was gay. Homosexuality was the theme of many of the signs. There were signs reading "God Hates Fags," "Semper Fi Fags," "Fags Doom Nations," and "Fag Troops." Another placard depicted two men engaging in anal intercourse. A reasonable bystander seeing those signs would have likely concluded that they were meant to suggest that the deceased was a homosexual.

After the funeral, the Westboro picketers reaffirmed the meaning of their protest. They posted an online account entitled "The Burden of Marine Lance Cpl. Matthew A. Snyder. The Visit of Westboro Baptist Church to Help the Inhabitants of Maryland Connect the Dots!" Belying any suggestion that they had simply made general comments about homosexuality, the Catholic Church, and the United States military, the "epic" addressed the Snyder family directly:

> "God blessed you, Mr. and Mrs. Snyder, with a resource and his name was Matthew. He was an arrow in your quiver! In thanks to God for the comfort the child could bring you, you had a DUTY to prepare that child to serve the LORD his GOD-PERIOD! You did JUST THE OPPOSITE—you raised him for the devil.
>
> . . .
>
> "Albert and Julie RIPPED that body apart and taught Matthew to defy his Creator, to divorce, and to commit adultery. They taught him how to support the largest

> pedophile machine in the history of the entire world, the Roman Catholic monstrosity. Every dime they gave the Roman Catholic monster they condemned their own souls. They also, in supporting satanic Catholicism, taught Matthew to be an idolater.
>
> . . .
>
> "Then after all that they sent him to fight for the United States of Sodom, a filthy country that is in lock step with his evil, wicked, and sinful manner of life, putting him in the cross hairs of a God that is so mad He has smoke coming from his nostrils and fire from his mouth! How dumb was that?"

In light of this evidence, it is abundantly clear that respondents, going far beyond commentary on matters of public concern, specifically attacked Matthew Snyder because (1) he was a Catholic and (2) he was a member of the United States military. Both Matthew and petitioner were private figures, and this attack was not speech on a matter of public concern. While commentary on the Catholic Church or the United States military constitutes speech on matters of public concern, speech regarding Matthew Snyder's purely private conduct does not. . . .

This captures what respondents did in this case. Indeed, this is the strategy that they have routinely employed—and that they will now continue to employ—inflicting severe and lasting emotional injury on an ever growing list of innocent victims. . . .

The Court concludes that respondents' speech was protected by the First Amendment for essentially three reasons, but none is sound. First—and most important—the Court finds that "the overall thrust and dominant theme of [their] demonstration spoke to" broad public issues. As I have attempted to show, this portrayal is quite inaccurate; respondents' attack on Matthew was of central importance. But in any event, I fail to see why actionable speech should be immunized simply because it is interspersed with speech that is protected. The First Amendment allows recovery for defamatory statements that are interspersed with nondefamatory statements on matters of public concern, and there is no good reason why respondents' attack on Matthew Snyder and his family should be treated differently.

Second, the Court suggests that respondents' personal attack on Matthew Snyder is entitled to First Amendment protection because it was not motivated by a private grudge, but I see no basis for the strange distinction that the Court appears to draw. Respondents' motivation—"to increase publicity for its views,"—did not transform their statements attacking the character of a private figure into statements that made a contribution to debate on matters of public concern. Nor did their publicity-seeking motivation soften the sting of their attack. And as far as culpability is concerned, one might well think that wounding statements uttered in the heat of a private feud are less, not more, blameworthy than similar statements made as part of a cold and calculated strategy to slash a stranger as a means of attracting public attention.

Third, the Court finds it significant that respondents' protest occurred on a public street, but this fact alone should not be enough to preclude IIED liability. To be sure, statements made on a public street may be less likely to satisfy the elements of the IIED tort than statements made on private property, but there is no reason why a public street in close proximity to the scene of a funeral should be regarded as a free-fire zone in which otherwise actionable verbal attacks are shielded from liability. If the First Amendment permits the States to protect their residents from the harm inflicted by such attacks — and the Court does not hold otherwise — then the location of the tort should not be dispositive. A physical assault may occur without trespassing; it is no defense that the perpetrator had "the right to be where [he was]." And the same should be true with respect to unprotected speech. Neither classic "fighting words" nor defamatory statements are immunized when they occur in a public place, and there is no good reason to treat a verbal assault based on the conduct or character of a private figure like Matthew Snyder any differently.

One final comment about the opinion of the Court is in order. The Court suggests that the wounds inflicted by vicious verbal assaults at funerals will be prevented or at least mitigated in the future by new laws that restrict picketing within a specified distance of a funeral. It is apparent, however, that the enactment of these laws is no substitute for the protection provided by the established IIED tort; according to the Court, the verbal attacks that severely wounded petitioner in this case complied with the new Maryland law regulating funeral picketing. And there is absolutely nothing to suggest that Congress and the state legislatures, in enacting these laws, intended them to displace the protection provided by the well-established IIED tort.

The real significance of these new laws is not that they obviate the need for IIED protection. Rather, their enactment dramatically illustrates the fundamental point that funerals are unique events at which special protection against emotional assaults is in order. At funerals, the emotional well-being of bereaved relatives is particularly vulnerable. Exploitation of a funeral for the purpose of attracting public attention "intrud[es] upon their . . . grief," and may permanently stain their memories of the final moments before a loved one is laid to rest. Allowing family members to have a few hours of peace without harassment does not undermine public debate. I would therefore hold that, in this setting, the First Amendment permits a private figure to recover for the intentional infliction of emotional distress caused by speech on a matter of private concern. . . .

Hustler did involve an IIED claim, but the plaintiff there was a public figure, and the Court did not suggest that its holding would also apply in a case involving a private figure. Nor did the Court suggest that its holding applied across the board to all types of IIED claims. Instead, the holding was limited to "publications such as the one here at issue," namely, a caricature in a magazine. Unless a caricature of a public figure can reasonably be interpreted as stating facts that may be proved to be wrong, the caricature does not have the same potential to wound as a personal verbal assault on a vulnerable private figure. . . .

Respondents' outrageous conduct caused petitioner great injury, and the Court now compounds that injury by depriving petitioner of a judgment that acknowledges the wrong he suffered. In order to have a society in which public issues can be openly and vigorously debated, it is not necessary to allow the brutalization of innocent victims like petitioner. I therefore respectfully dissent.

ASSIGNMENT S-10

STUDY GUIDE: *How does the Court distinguish the statute in this case from the statute invalidated in Ashcroft v. Free Speech Coalition? Why does Justice Souter think that, in the future, the government will no longer prosecute defendants for selling child pornography but will prosecute for merely proposing a child-pornography transaction? If he is correct, of what relevance is this to the constitutionality of the statute?*

UNITED STATES v. WILLIAMS

553 U.S. 28 (2008)

JUSTICE SCALIA delivered the opinion of the Court.

Section 2252A(a)(3)(B) of Title 18, United States Code, criminalizes, in certain specified circumstances, the pandering or solicitation of child pornography. This case presents the question whether that statute is overbroad under the First Amendment or impermissibly vague under the Due Process Clause of the Fifth Amendment.

I

A

We have long held that obscene speech—sexually explicit material that violates fundamental notions of decency—is not protected by the First Amendment. See Roth v. United States (1957). But to protect explicit material that has social value, we have limited the scope of the obscenity exception, and have overturned convictions for the distribution of sexually graphic but non-obscene material. See Miller v. California (1973).

Over the last 25 years, we have confronted a related and overlapping category of proscribable speech: child pornography. See Ashcroft v. Free Speech Coalition (2002); New York v. Ferber (1982). This consists of sexually explicit visual portrayals that feature children. We have held that a statute which proscribes the distribution of all child pornography, even material that does not qualify as obscenity, does not on its face violate the First Amendment. Moreover, we have held that the government may criminalize the possession of child pornography, even though it may not criminalize the mere possession of obscene material involving adults.

The broad authority to proscribe child pornography is not, however, unlimited. Four Terms ago, we held facially overbroad two provisions of the federal Child Pornography Protection Act of 1996 (CPPA). *Free Speech Coalition.* The first of these banned the possession and distribution of "any visual depiction" that "is, or appears to be, of a minor engaging in sexually explicit conduct," even if it contained only youthful-looking adult actors or virtual images of children generated by a computer. This was invalid, we explained, because the child-protection rationale for speech restriction does not apply to materials produced without children. The second provision at issue in *Free Speech Coalition* criminalized the possession and distribution of material that had been pandered as child pornography, regardless of whether it actually was that. A person could thus face prosecution for possessing unobjectionable material that someone else had pandered. We held that this prohibition, which did "more than prohibit pandering," was also facially overbroad.

After our decision in *Free Speech Coalition*, Congress went back to the drawing board and produced legislation with the unlikely title of the Prosecutorial Remedies and Other Tools to end the Exploitation of Children Today Act of 2003. We shall refer to it as the Act. Section 503 of the Act amended 18 U. S. C. §2252A to add a new pandering and solicitation provision, relevant portions of which now read as follows:

> (a) Any person who—
> (3) knowingly— . . .
> (B) advertises, promotes, presents, distributes, or solicits through the mails, or in interstate or foreign commerce by any means, including by computer, any material or purported material in a manner that reflects the belief, or that is intended to cause another to believe, that the material or purported material is, or contains—
> (i) an obscene visual depiction of a minor engaging in sexually explicit conduct; or
> (ii) a visual depiction of an actual minor engaging in sexually explicit conduct, . . .
> shall be punished as provided in subsection (b).

Section 2256(2)(A) defines "sexually explicit conduct" as

> actual or simulated—
> (i) sexual intercourse, including genital-genital, oral-genital, anal-genital, or oral-anal, whether between persons of the same or opposite sex;
> (ii) bestiality;
> (iii) masturbation;
> (iv) sadistic or masochistic abuse; or
> (v) lascivious exhibition of the genitals or pubic area of any person.

Violation of §2252A(a)(3)(B) incurs a minimum sentence of 5 years imprisonment and a maximum of 20 years. 18 U. S. C. §2252A(b)(1).

The Act's express findings indicate that Congress was concerned that limiting the child-pornography prohibition to material that could be proved to feature actual children, as our decision in *Free Speech Coalition* required, would enable many child pornographers to evade conviction. The emergence of new technology and the repeated retransmission of picture files over the Internet could make it nearly impossible to prove that a particular image was produced using real children—even though "[t]here is no substantial evidence that any of the child pornography images being trafficked today were made other than by the abuse of real children," virtual imaging being prohibitively expensive.

B

The following facts appear in the opinion of the Eleventh Circuit, 444 F. 3d 1286, 1288 (2006). On April 26, 2004, respondent Michael Williams, using a sexually explicit screen name, signed in to a public Internet chat room. A Secret Service agent had also signed in to the chat room under the moniker "Lisa n Miami." The agent noticed that Williams had posted a message that read: "Dad of toddler has 'good' pics of her an [sic] me for swap of your toddler pics, or live cam." The agent struck up a conversation with Williams, leading to an electronic exchange of nonpornographic pictures of children. (The agent's picture was in fact a doctored photograph of an adult.) Soon thereafter, Williams messaged that he had photographs of men molesting his 4-year-old daughter. Suspicious that "Lisa n Miami" was a law-enforcement agent, before proceeding further Williams demanded that the agent produce additional pictures. When he did not, Williams posted the following public message in the chat room: "HERE ROOM; I CAN PUT UPLINK CUZ IM FOR REAL—SHE CANT." Appended to this declaration was a hyperlink that, when clicked, led to seven pictures of actual children, aged approximately 5 to 15, engaging in sexually explicit conduct and displaying their genitals. The Secret Service then obtained a search warrant for Williams's home, where agents seized two hard drives containing at least 22 images of real children engaged in sexually explicit conduct, some of it sadomasochistic.

Williams was charged with one count of pandering child pornography under §2252A(a)(3)(B) and one count of possessing child pornography under §2252A(a)(5)(B). He pleaded guilty to both counts but reserved the right to challenge the constitutionality of the pandering conviction. The District Court rejected his challenge, and sentenced him to concurrent 60-month sentences on the two counts. The United States Court of Appeals for the Eleventh Circuit reversed the pandering conviction, holding that the statute was both overbroad and impermissibly vague.

We granted certiorari.

II

A

According to our First Amendment overbreadth doctrine, a statute is facially invalid if it prohibits a substantial amount of protected speech. The doctrine seeks to strike a balance between competing social costs. On the one hand, the threat of enforcement of an overbroad law deters people from engaging in constitutionally protected speech, inhibiting the free exchange of ideas. On the other hand, invalidating a law that in some of its applications is perfectly constitutional—particularly a law directed at conduct so antisocial that it has been made criminal—has obvious harmful effects. In order to maintain an appropriate balance, we have vigorously enforced the requirement that a statute's overbreadth be *substantial*, not only in an absolute sense, but also relative to the statute's plainly legitimate sweep. . . .

The first step in overbreadth analysis is to construe the challenged statute; it is impossible to determine whether a statute reaches too far without first knowing what the statute covers. Generally speaking, §2252A(a)(3)(B) prohibits offers to provide and requests to obtain child pornography. The statute does not require the actual existence of child pornography. In this respect, it differs from the statutes in *Ferber* . . . and *Free Speech Coalition*, which prohibited the possession or distribution of child pornography. Rather than targeting the underlying material, this statute bans the collateral speech that introduces such material into the child-pornography distribution network. Thus, an Internet user who solicits child pornography from an undercover agent violates the statute, even if the officer possesses no child pornography. Likewise, a person who advertises virtual child pornography as depicting actual children also falls within the reach of the statute.

The statute's definition of the material or purported material that may not be pandered or solicited precisely tracks the material held constitutionally proscribable in *Ferber* and *Miller*: obscene material depicting (actual or virtual) children engaged in sexually explicit conduct, and any other material depicting actual children engaged in sexually explicit conduct. See *Free Speech Coalition* (stating that the First Amendment does not protect obscenity or pornography produced with actual children).

A number of features of the statute are important to our analysis: . . .

[T]he phrase "in a manner that reflects the belief" includes both subjective and objective components. "[A] manner that reflects the belief" is quite different from "a manner that would give one cause to believe." The first formulation suggests that the defendant must actually have held the subjective "belief" that the material or purported material was child pornography. Thus, a misdescription that leads the listener to believe the defendant is offering child pornography, when the defendant in fact does not believe the material is child pornography, does not violate this prong of the statute. (It may, however, violate the "manner . . . that is intended to cause another to believe" prong if the misdescription is intentional.) There is also an objective component to the phrase "manner that reflects the belief." The statement or action must objectively manifest a belief that the material is child pornography; a mere belief, without an accompanying statement or action that would lead a reasonable person to understand that the defendant holds that belief, is insufficient. . . .

[T]he other key phrase, "in a manner . . . that is intended to cause another to believe," contains only a subjective element: The defendant must "intend" that the listener believe the material to be child pornography, and must select a manner of "advertising, promoting, presenting, distributing, or soliciting" the material that he thinks will engender that belief—whether or not a reasonable person would think the same. (Of course in the ordinary case the proof of the defendant's intent will be the fact that, as an objective matter, the manner of "advertising, promoting, presenting, distributing, or soliciting" plainly sought to convey that the material was child pornography.) . . .

B

We now turn to whether the statute, as we have construed it, criminalizes a substantial amount of protected expressive activity.

Offers to engage in illegal transactions are categorically excluded from First Amendment protection. . . . Many long established criminal proscriptions—such as laws against conspiracy, incitement, and solicitation—criminalize speech (commercial or not) that is intended to induce or commence illegal activities. Offers to provide or requests to obtain unlawful material, whether as part of a commercial exchange or not, are similarly undeserving of First Amendment protection. . . .

To be sure, there remains an important distinction between a proposal to engage in illegal activity and the abstract advocacy of illegality. See Brandenburg v. Ohio (1969) (*per curiam*). The Act before us does not prohibit advocacy of child pornography, but only offers to provide or requests to obtain it. There is no doubt that this prohibition falls well within constitutional bounds. The constitutional defect we found in the pandering provision at issue in *Free Speech Coalition* was that it went *beyond* pandering to prohibit possession of material that could not otherwise be proscribed.

In sum, we hold that offers to provide or requests to obtain child pornography are categorically excluded from the First Amendment. . . .

Amici contend that some advertisements for mainstream Hollywood movies that depict underage characters having sex violate the statute. Brief for Free Speech Coalition et al. as Amici Curiae 9–18. We think it implausible that a reputable distributor of Hollywood movies, such as Amazon.com, believes that one of these films contains *actual* children engaging in *actual* or *simulated* sex on camera; and even more implausible that Amazon.com would *intend* to make its customers believe such a thing. The average person understands that sex scenes in mainstream movies use nonchild actors, depict sexual activity in a way that would not rise to the explicit level necessary under the statute, or, in most cases, both. . . .

Finally, the dissent accuses us of silently overruling our prior decisions in *Ferber* and *Free Speech Coalition*. According to the dissent, Congress has made an end-run around the First Amendment's protection of virtual child pornography by prohibiting proposals to transact in such images rather than prohibiting the images themselves. But an offer to provide or request to receive virtual child pornography is not prohibited by the statute. A crime is committed only when the speaker believes or intends the listener to believe that the subject of the proposed transaction depicts *real* children. It is simply not true that this means "a protected category of expression [will] inevitably be suppressed." Simulated child pornography will be as available as ever, so long as it is offered and sought *as such*, and not as real child pornography. The dissent would require an exception from the statute's prohibition when, unbeknownst to one or both of the parties to the proposal, the completed transaction would not have been unlawful because it is (we have said) protected by the First Amendment. We fail to see what First Amendment interest would be served by drawing a distinction between two defendants who attempt to acquire contraband, one of whom happens to be mistaken about the contraband nature of what he would acquire. Is Congress forbidden from punishing those who attempt to acquire what they believe to be national-security documents, but which are actually fakes? To ask is to answer. There is no First Amendment exception from the general principle of criminal law that a person attempting to commit a crime need not be exonerated because he has a mistaken view of the facts. . . .

* * *

Child pornography harms and debases the most defenseless of our citizens. Both the State and Federal Governments have sought to suppress it for many years, only to find it proliferating through the new medium of the Internet. This Court held unconstitutional Congress's previous attempt to meet this new threat, and Congress responded with a carefully crafted attempt to eliminate the First Amendment problems we identified. As far as the provision at issue in this case is concerned, that effort was successful.

The judgment of the Eleventh Circuit is reversed.

JUSTICE SOUTER, with whom JUSTICE GINSBURG joins, dissenting.

Dealing in obscenity is penalized without violating the First Amendment, but as a general matter pornography lacks the harm to justify prohibiting it. If, however, a photograph (to take the kind of image in this case) shows an actual minor child as a pornographic subject, its transfer and even its possession may be made criminal. New York v. Ferber (1982). The exception to the general rule rests not on the content of the picture but on the need to foil the exploitation of child subjects, and the justification limits the exception: only pornographic photographs of actual children may be prohibited; Ashcroft v. Free Speech Coalition (2002). Thus, just six years ago the Court struck down a statute outlawing particular material merely represented to be child pornography, but not necessarily depicting actual children.

The Prosecutorial Remedies and Other Tools to end the Exploitation of Children Today Act of 2003 (Act), was enacted in the wake of *Free Speech Coalition*. The Act responds by avoiding any direct prohibition of transactions in child pornography when no actual minors may be pictured; instead, it prohibits proposals for transactions in pornography when a defendant manifestly believes or would induce belief in a prospective party that the subject of an exchange or exhibition is or will be an actual child, not an impersonated, simulated or "virtual" one, or the subject of a composite created from lawful photos spliced together. . . .

The tension with existing constitutional law is obvious. *Free Speech Coalition* reaffirmed that non-obscene virtual pornographic images are protected, because they fail to trigger the concern for child safety that disentitles child pornography to First Amendment protection. The case thus held that pictures without real minors (but only simulations, or young-looking adults) may not be the subject of a non-obscenity pornography crime, and it has reasonably been taken to mean that transactions in pornographic pictures featuring children may not be punished without proof of real children. The Act, however, punishes proposals regarding images when the inclusion of actual children is not established by the prosecution, as well as images that show no real children at all; and this, despite the fact that, under *Free Speech Coalition*, the first proposed transfer could not be punished without the very proof the Act is meant to dispense with, and the second could not be made criminal at all.

What justification can there be for making independent crimes of proposals to engage in transactions that may include protected materials? The Court gives three answers, none of which comes to grips with the difficulty raised by the question. The first says it is simply wrong to say that the Act makes it criminal to propose a lawful transaction, since an element of the forbidden proposal must express a belief or inducement to believe that the subject of the proposed transaction shows actual children. But this does not go to the point. The objection is not that the Act criminalizes a proposal for a transaction described as being in virtual (that is, protected) child pornography. The point is that some proposals made criminal, because they express a belief that they refer to real child pornography, will relate to extant material that does not, or cannot be, demonstrated to show real children and so may not be prohibited. When a proposal covers existing photographs, the Act does not require that the requisite belief (manifested or encouraged) in the reality of the subjects be a correct belief. Prohibited proposals may relate to transactions in lawful, as well as unlawful, pornography.

Much the same may be said about the Court's second answer, that a proposal to commit a crime enjoys no speech protection. For the reason just given, that answer does not face up to the source of the difficulty: the action actually contemplated in the proposal, the transfer of the particular image, is not criminal if it turns out that an actual child is not shown in the photograph. If *Ferber* and *Free Speech Coalition* are good law, the facts sufficient for conviction under the Act do not suffice to show that the image (perhaps merely simulated), and thus a transfer of that image, are outside the bounds of constitutional protection. For this reason, it is not enough just to say that the First Amendment does not protect proposals to commit crimes. For that rule rests on the assumption that the proposal is actually to commit a crime, not to do an act that may turn out to be no crime at all. Why should the general rule of unprotected criminal proposals cover a case like the proposal to transfer what may turn out to be fake child pornography?

The Court's third answer analogizes the proposal to an attempt to commit a crime, and relies on the rule of criminal law that an attempt is criminal even when some impediment makes it impossible to complete the criminal act (the possible impediment here being the advanced age, say, or simulated character of the child-figure). Although the actual transfer the speaker has in mind may not turn out to be criminal, the argument goes, the transfer intended by the speaker is criminal, because the speaker believes that the contemplated transfer will be of real child pornography, and transfer of real child pornography is criminal. The fact that the circumstances are not as he believes them to be, because the material does not depict actual minors, is no defense to his attempt to engage in an unlawful transaction.

But invoking attempt doctrine to dispense with *Free Speech Coalition*'s real-child requirement in the circumstances of this case is incoherent with the Act, and it fails to fit the paradigm of factual impossibility or qualify for an extended version of that rule. The incoherence of the Court's answer with the scheme of the Act appears from §2252A(b)(1), which criminalizes attempting or conspiring to violate the Act's substantive prohibitions, including the pandering provision of §2252A(a)(3)(B). Treating pandering itself as a species of attempt would thus mean that there is a statutory, inchoate offense of attempting to attempt to commit a substantive child pornography crime. A metaphysician could imagine a system like this, but the universe of inchoate crimes is not expandable indefinitely under the actual principles of criminal law, let alone when First Amendment protection is threatened. See 2 W. LaFave, Substantive Criminal Law §11.2(a), p. 208 (2d ed. 2003) ("[W]here a certain crime is actually defined in terms of either doing or attempting a certain crime, then the argument that there is no crime of attempting this attempt is persuasive").

The more serious failure of the attempt analogy, however, is its unjustifiable extension of the classic factual frustration rule, under which the action specifically intended would be a criminal act if completed. The intending killer who mistakenly grabs the pistol loaded with blanks would have committed homicide if bullets had been in the gun; it was only the impossibility of completing the very intended act of shooting bullets that prevented the completion of the crime. This is not so, however, in the proposed transaction in an identified pornographic image without the showing of a real child; no matter what the parties believe, and no matter how exactly a defendant's actions conform to his intended course of conduct in completing the transaction he has in mind, if there turns out to be reasonable doubt that a real child was used to make the photos, or none was, there could be, respectively, no conviction and no crime. Thus, in the classic impossibility example, there is attempt liability when the course of conduct intended cannot be completed owing to some fact which the defendant was mistaken about, and which precludes completing the intended physical acts. But on the Court's reasoning there would be attempt liability even when the contemplated acts had been completed exactly as intended, but no crime had been committed. Why should attempt liability be recognized here (thus making way for "proposal" liability, under the Court's analogy)?

The Court's first response is to demur, with its example of the drug dealer who sells something else. (A package of baking powder, not powder cocaine, would be an example.) No one doubts the dealer may validly be convicted of an attempted drug sale even if he didn't know it was baking powder he was selling. Yet selling baking powder is no more criminal than selling virtual child pornography.

This response does not suffice, however, because it overlooks a difference between the lawfulness of selling baking powder and the lawful character of virtual child pornography. Powder sales are lawful but not constitutionally privileged. Any justification within the bounds of rationality would suffice for limiting baking powder transactions, just as it would for regulating the discharge of blanks from a pistol. Virtual pornography, however, has been held to fall within the First Amendment speech privilege, and thus is affirmatively protected, not merely allowed as a matter of course. The question stands: why should a proposal that may turn out to cover privileged expression be subject to standard attempt liability?

The Court's next response deals with the privileged character of the underlying material. It gives another example of attempt that presumably could be made criminal, in the case of the mistaken spy, who passes national security documents thinking they are classified and secret, when in fact they have been declassified and made subject to public inspection. Publishing unclassified documents is subject to the First Amendment privilege and can claim a value that fake child pornography cannot. The Court assumes that the document publication may be punished as an attempt to violate state-secret restrictions (and I assume so too); then why not attempt-proposals based on a mistaken belief that the underlying material is real child pornography? As the Court looks at it, the deterrent value that justifies prosecuting the mistaken spy (like the mistaken drug dealer and the intending killer) would presumably validate prosecuting those who make proposals about fake child pornography. But it would not, for there are significant differences between the cases of security documents and pornography without real children.

Where Government documents, blank cartridges, and baking powder are involved, deterrence can be promoted without compromising any other important policy, which is not true of criminalizing mistaken child pornography proposals. There are three dispositive differences. As for the first, if the law can criminalize proposals for transactions in fake as well as true child pornography as if they were like attempts to sell cocaine that turned out to be baking powder, constitutional law will lose something sufficiently important to have made it into multiple holdings of this Court, and that is the line between child pornography that may be suppressed and fake child pornography that falls within First Amendment protection. No one can seriously assume that after today's decision the Government will go on prosecuting defendants for selling child pornography (requiring a showing that a real child is pictured, under *Free Speech Coalition*); it will prosecute for merely proposing a pornography transaction manifesting or inducing the belief that a photo is real child pornography, free of any need to demonstrate that any extant underlying photo does show a real child. If the Act can be enforced, it will function just as it was meant to do, by merging the whole subject of child pornography into the offense of proposing a transaction, dispensing with the real-child element in the underlying subject. And eliminating the need to prove a real child will be a loss of some consequence. This is so not because there will possibly be less pornography available owing to the greater ease of prosecuting, but simply because there must be a line between what the Government may suppress and what it may not, and a segment of that line will be gone. This Court went to great pains to draw it in *Ferber* and *Free Speech Coalition*; it was worth drawing and it is worth respecting now in facing the attempt to end-run that line through the provisions of the Act.

The second reason for treating child pornography differently follows from the first. If the deluded drug dealer is held liable for an attempt crime there is no risk of eliminating baking powder from trade in lawful commodities. Likewise, if the mistaken spy is convicted of attempting to disclose classified national security documents there will be no worry that lawful speech will be suppressed as a consequence; any unclassified documents in question can be quoted in the newspaper, other unclassified documents will circulate, and analysts of politics and foreign policy will be able to rely on them. But if the Act can effectively eliminate the real-child requirement when a proposal relates to extant material, a class of protected speech will disappear. True, what will be lost is short on merit, but intrinsic value is not the reason for protecting unpopular expression.

Finally, if the Act stands when applied to identifiable, extant pornographic photographs, then in practical terms *Ferber* and *Free Speech Coalition* fall. They are left as empty as if the Court overruled them formally, and when a case as well considered and as recently decided as *Free Speech Coalition* is put aside (after a mere six years) there ought to be a very good reason. . . . Attempts with baking powder and unclassified documents can be punished without damage to confidence in precedent; suppressing protected pornography cannot be.

These differences should be dispositive. Eliminating the line between protected and unprotected speech, guaranteeing the suppression of a category of expression previously protected, and reducing recent and carefully considered First Amendment precedents to empty shells are heavy prices, not to be paid without a substantial offset, which is missing from this case. Hence, my answer that there is no justification for saving the Act's attempt to get around our holdings. We should hold that a transaction in what turns out to be fake pornography is better understood, not as an incomplete attempt to commit a crime, but as a completed series of intended acts that simply do not add up to a crime, owing to the privileged character of the material the parties were in fact about to deal in.

The upshot is that there ought to be no absolute rule on the relationship between attempt liability and a frustrating mistake. Not all attempts frustrated by mistake should be punishable, and not all mistaken assumptions that expressive material is unprotected should bar liability for attempts to commit a crime. The legitimacy of attempt liability should turn on its consequences for protected expression and the law that protects it. When, as here, a protected category of expression would inevitably be suppressed and its First Amendment safeguard left pointless, the Government has the burden to justify this damage to free speech. . . .

Untethering the power to suppress proposals about extant pornography from any assessment of the likely effects the proposals might have has an unsettling significance well beyond the subject of child pornography. For the Court is going against the grain of pervasive First Amendment doctrine that tolerates speech restriction not on mere general tendencies of expression, or the private understandings of speakers or listeners, but only after a critical assessment of practical consequences. Thus, one of the milestones of American political liberty is Brandenburg v. Ohio (1969) (*per curiam*), which is seen as the culmination of a half century's development that began with Justice Holmes's dissent in Abrams v. United States (1919). In place of the rule that dominated the First

World War sedition and espionage cases, allowing suppression of speech for its tendency and the intent behind it, see Schenck v. United States (1919), *Brandenburg* insisted that

> the constitutional guarantees of free speech and free press do not permit a State to forbid or proscribe advocacy of the use of force or of law violation except where such advocacy is directed to inciting or producing imminent lawless action and is likely to incite or produce such action.

Brandenburg unmistakably insists that any limit on speech be grounded in a realistic, factual assessment of harm. This is a far cry from the Act before us now, which rests criminal prosecution for proposing transactions in expressive material on nothing more than a speaker's statement about the material itself, a statement that may disclose no more than his own belief about the subjects represented or his desire to foster belief in another. . . .

Perhaps I am wrong, but without some demonstration that juries have been rendering exploitation of children unpunishable, there is no excuse for cutting back on the First Amendment and no alternative to finding overbreadth in this Act. I would hold it unconstitutional on the authority of *Ferber* and *Free Speech Coalition.*

ASSIGNMENT S-11

Other Offensive Forms of Speech

The next two cases involve efforts to extend the rationales by which obscene and sexually explicit speech can be prohibited to other forms of offensive speech—in particular, speech involving the depiction of violence.

STUDY GUIDE: *In this case the Court considers extending the rationale of* Ferber *governing child pornography to other offensive types of video. Much of what the majority and dissent are disagreeing about concerns whether circumstances support "facial" challenge to the statute, or whether the defendant is limited to bringing an "as-applied" challenge. The discussion of this issue is largely omitted from the excerpt in favor of the portions discussing the proper meaning and application of* Ferber*—in particular, how Chief Justice Roberts and seven justices approached the problem of distinguishing "protected" from "unprotected" speech. Because he thinks the statute is facially constitutional, Justice Alito's solo dissent also evaluates whether the conduct for which the defendant was charged is protected speech under* Ferber*. He must then discuss the particular facts that make this opinion difficult to read. Does the majority deny that the conduct that concerns Justice Alito* could *be criminalized? If not, why exactly does it invalidate the statute as unconstitutional?*

UNITED STATES v. STEVENS

559 U.S. _____ (2010)

CHIEF JUSTICE ROBERTS delivered the opinion of the Court.

Congress enacted 18 U. S. C. §48 to criminalize the commercial creation, sale, or possession of certain depictions of animal cruelty. The statute does not address underlying acts harmful to animals, but only portrayals of such conduct. The question presented is whether the prohibition in the statute is consistent with the freedom of speech guaranteed by the First Amendment.

I

Section 48 establishes a criminal penalty of up to five years in prison for anyone who knowingly "creates, sells, or possesses a depiction of animal cruelty," if done "for commercial gain" in interstate or foreign commerce. A depiction of "animal cruelty" is defined as one "in which a living animal is intentionally maimed, mutilated, tortured, wounded, or killed," if that conduct violates federal or state law where "the creation, sale, or possession takes place." In what is referred to as the "exceptions clause," the law exempts from prohibition any depiction "that has serious religious, political, scientific, educational, journalistic, historical, or artistic value."

The legislative background of §48 focused primarily on the interstate market for "crush videos." According to the House Committee Report on the bill, such videos feature the intentional torture and killing of helpless animals, including cats, dogs, monkeys, mice, and hamsters. Crush videos often depict women slowly crushing animals to death "with their bare feet or while wearing high heeled shoes," sometimes while "talking to the animals in a kind of dominatrix patter" over "[t]he cries and squeals of the animals, obviously in great pain." Apparently these depictions "appeal to persons with a very specific sexual fetish who find them sexually arousing or otherwise exciting." The acts depicted in crush videos are typically prohibited by the animal cruelty laws enacted by all 50 States and the District of Columbia. But crush videos rarely disclose the participants' identities, inhibiting prosecution of the underlying conduct.

This case, however, involves an application of §48 to depictions of animal fighting. Dogfighting, for example, is unlawful in all 50 States and the District of Columbia and has been restricted by federal law since 1976. Respondent Robert J. Stevens ran a business, "Dogs of Velvet and Steel," and an associated Web site, through which he sold videos of pit bulls engaging in dogfights and attacking other animals. Among these videos were *Japan Pit Fights* and *Pick-A-Winna: A Pit Bull Documentary*, which include contemporary footage of dogfights in Japan (where such conduct is allegedly legal) as well as footage of American dogfights from the 1960's and 1970's. A third video, *Catch Dogs and Country Living*, depicts the use of pit bulls to hunt wild boar, as well as a "gruesome" scene of a pit bull attacking a domestic farm pig. On the basis of these videos, Stevens was indicted on three counts of violating §48. . . . The jury convicted Stevens on all counts, and the District Court sentenced him to three concurrent sentences of 37 months' imprisonment, followed by three years of supervised release. The *en banc* Third Circuit, over a three-judge dissent, declared §48 facially unconstitutional and vacated Stevens's conviction. . . .

II

The Government's primary submission is that §48 necessarily complies with the Constitution because the banned depictions of animal cruelty, as a class, are categorically unprotected by the First Amendment. We disagree.

The First Amendment provides that "Congress shall make no law . . . abridging the freedom of speech." "[A]s a general matter, the First Amendment means that government has no power to restrict expression because of its message, its ideas, its subject matter, or its content." Ashcroft v. American Civil Liberties Union (2002). Section 48 explicitly regulates expression based on content: The statute restricts "visual [and] auditory depiction[s]," such as photographs, videos, or sound recordings, depending on whether they depict conduct in which a living animal is intentionally harmed. As such, §48 is "'presumptively invalid,' and the Government bears the burden to rebut that presumption." United States v. Playboy Entertainment Group, Inc. (2000) (quoting R. A. V. v. St. Paul (1992)).

"From 1791 to the present," however, the First Amendment has "permitted restrictions upon the content of speech in a few limited areas," and has never "include[d] a freedom to disregard these traditional limitations." *Id.* These "historic and traditional categories long familiar to the bar," Simon & Schuster, Inc. v. Members of N. Y. State Crime Victims Bd. (1991) (Kennedy, J., concurring in judgment) — including obscenity, Roth v. United States (1957), defamation, Beauharnais v. Illinois (1952), fraud, Virginia Bd. of Pharmacy v. Virginia Citizens Consumer Council (1976), incitement, Brandenburg v. Ohio (1969), and speech integral to criminal conduct, Giboney v. Empire Storage & Ice Co. (1949) — are "well-defined and narrowly limited classes of speech, the prevention and punishment of which have never been thought to raise any Constitutional problem." Chaplinsky v. New Hampshire (1942).

The Government argues that "depictions of animal cruelty" should be added to the list. It contends that depictions of "illegal acts of animal cruelty" that are "made, sold, or possessed for commercial gain" necessarily "lack expressive value," and may accordingly "be regulated as *unprotected* speech." Brief for United States (emphasis added). The claim is not just that Congress may regulate depictions of animal cruelty subject to the First Amendment, but that these depictions are outside the reach of that Amendment altogether — that they fall into a "First Amendment Free Zone." Board of Airport Comm'rs of Los Angeles v. Jews for Jesus, Inc. (1987).

As the Government notes, the prohibition of animal cruelty itself has a long history in American law, starting with the early settlement of the Colonies. But we are unaware of any similar tradition excluding *depictions* of animal cruelty from "the freedom of speech" codified in the First Amendment, and the Government points us to none.

The Government contends that "historical evidence" about the reach of the First Amendment is not "a necessary prerequisite for regulation today," and that categories of speech may be exempted from the First Amendment's protection without any long-settled tradition of subjecting that speech to regulation. Instead, the Government points to Congress's "legislative judgment that . . . depictions of animals being intentionally tortured and killed [are] of such minimal redeeming value as to render [them] unworthy of First Amendment protection," and asks the Court to uphold the ban on the same basis. The Government thus proposes that a claim of categorical exclusion should be considered under a simple balancing test: "Whether a given category of speech enjoys First Amendment protection depends upon a categorical balancing of the value of the speech against its societal costs."

As a free-floating test for First Amendment coverage, that sentence is startling and dangerous. The First Amendment's guarantee of free speech does not extend only to categories of speech that survive an ad hoc balancing of relative social costs and benefits. The First Amendment itself reflects a judgment by the American people that the benefits of its restrictions on the Government outweigh the costs. Our Constitution forecloses any attempt to revise that judgment simply on the basis that some speech is not worth it. The Constitution is not a document "prescribing limits, and declaring that those limits may be passed at pleasure." Marbury v. Madison (1803).

To be fair to the Government, its view did not emerge from a vacuum. As the Government correctly notes, this Court has often *described* historically unprotected categories of speech as being "of such slight social value as a step to truth that any benefit that may be derived from them is clearly outweighed by the social interest in order and morality." *R.A.V.* (quoting *Chaplinsky*). In New York v. Ferber (1982), we noted that within these categories of unprotected speech, "the evil to be restricted so overwhelmingly outweighs the expressive interests, if any, at stake, that no process of case-by-case adjudication is required," because "the balance of competing interests is clearly struck." The Government derives its proposed test from these descriptions in our precedents.

But such descriptions are just that—descriptive. They do not set forth a test that may be applied as a general matter to permit the Government to imprison any speaker so long as his speech is deemed valueless or unnecessary, or so long as an ad hoc calculus of costs and benefits tilts in a statute's favor.

When we have identified categories of speech as fully outside the protection of the First Amendment, it has not been on the basis of a simple cost-benefit analysis. In *Ferber*, for example, we classified child pornography as such a category. We noted that the State of New York had a compelling interest in protecting children from abuse, and that the value of using children in these works (as opposed to simulated conduct or adult actors) was *de minimis*. But our decision did not rest on this "balance of competing interests" alone. We made clear that *Ferber* presented a special case: The market for child pornography was "intrinsically related" to the underlying abuse, and was therefore "an integral part of the production of such materials, an activity illegal throughout the Nation." As we noted, "[i]t rarely has been suggested that the constitutional freedom for speech and press extends its immunity to speech or writing used as an integral part of conduct in violation of a valid criminal statute." *Ferber* thus grounded its analysis in a previously recognized, long-established category of unprotected speech, and our subsequent decisions have shared this understanding.

Our decisions in *Ferber* and other cases cannot be taken as establishing a freewheeling authority to declare new categories of speech outside the scope of the First Amendment. Maybe there are some categories of speech that have been historically unprotected, but have not yet been specifically identified or discussed as such in our case law. But if so, there is no evidence that "depictions of animal cruelty" is among them. We need not foreclose the future recognition of such additional categories to reject the Government's highly manipulable balancing test as a means of identifying them.

III

Because we decline to carve out from the First Amendment any novel exception for §48, we review Stevens's First Amendment challenge under our existing doctrine. . . .

The only thing standing between defendants who sell such depictions and five years in federal prison—other than the mercy of a prosecutor—is the statute's exceptions clause. Subsection (b) exempts from prohibition "any depiction that has serious religious, political, scientific, educational, journalistic, historical, or artistic value." The Government argues that this clause substantially narrows the statute's reach: News reports about animal cruelty have "journalistic" value; pictures of bullfights in Spain have "historical" value; and instructional hunting videos have "educational" value. Thus, the Government argues, §48 reaches only crush videos, depictions of animal fighting (other than Spanish bullfighting), and perhaps other depictions of "extreme acts of animal cruelty."

The Government's attempt to narrow the statutory ban, however, requires an unrealistically broad reading of the exceptions clause. As the Government reads the clause, any material with "redeeming societal value," "at least some minimal value," or anything more than "scant social value," is excluded under §48(b). But the text says "serious" value, and "serious" should be taken seriously. We decline the Government's invitation—advanced for the first time in this Court—to regard as "serious" anything that is not "scant." (Or, as the dissent puts it, "trifling.") . . .

Quite apart from the requirement of "serious" value in §48(b), the excepted speech must also fall within one of the enumerated categories. Much speech does not. Most hunting videos, for example, are not obviously instructional in nature, except in the sense that all life is a lesson. According to Safari Club International and the Congressional Sportsmen's Foundation, many popular videos "have primarily entertainment value" and are designed to "entertai[n] the viewer, marke[t] hunting equipment, or increas[e] the hunting community." The National Rifle Association agrees that "much of the content of hunting media . . . is merely *recreational* in nature." The Government offers no principled explanation why these depictions of hunting or depictions of Spanish bullfights would be *inherently* valuable while those of Japanese dogfights are not. The dissent contends that hunting depictions must have serious value because hunting has serious value, in a way that dogfights presumably do not. But § 48(b) addresses the value of the *depictions*, not of the underlying activity." There is simply no adequate reading of the exceptions clause that results in the statute's banning only the depictions the Government would like to ban.

The Government explains that the language of §48(b) was largely drawn from our opinion in Miller v. California (1973), which excepted from its definition of obscenity any material with "serious literary, artistic, political, or scientific value," According to the Government, this incorporation of the *Miller* standard into §48 is therefore surely enough to answer any First Amendment objection.

In *Miller* we held that "serious" value shields depictions of sex from regulation as obscenity. Limiting *Miller*'s exception to "serious" value ensured that "[a] quotation from Voltaire in the flyleaf of a book [would] not constitutionally redeem an otherwise obscene publication." We did not, however, determine that serious value could be used as a general precondition to protecting *other* types of speech in the first place. *Most* of what we say to one another lacks "religious, political, scientific, educational, journalistic, historical, or artistic value" (let alone serious value), but it is still sheltered from government regulation. . . .

Thus, the protection of the First Amendment presumptively extends to many forms of speech that do not qualify for the serious-value exception of §48(b), but nonetheless fall within the broad reach of §48(c).

Not to worry, the Government says: The Executive Branch construes §48 to reach only "extreme" cruelty, Brief for United States, and it "neither has brought nor will bring a prosecution for anything less." The Government hits this theme hard, invoking its prosecutorial discretion several times. But the First Amendment protects against the Government; it does not leave us at the mercy of *noblesse oblige*. We would not uphold an unconstitutional statute merely because the Government promised to use it responsibly.

This prosecution is itself evidence of the danger in putting faith in government representations of prosecutorial restraint. When this legislation was enacted, the Executive Branch announced that it would interpret §48 as covering only depictions "of wanton cruelty to animals designed to appeal to a prurient interest in sex." See Statement by President William J. Clinton upon Signing H. R. 1887 (Dec. 9, 1999). No one suggests that the videos in this case fit that description. The Government's assurance that it will apply §48 far more restrictively than its language provides is pertinent only as an implicit acknowledgment of the potential constitutional problems with a more natural reading. . . .

* * *

Our construction of §48 decides the constitutional question; the Government makes no effort to defend the constitutionality of §48 as applied beyond crush videos and depictions of animal fighting. It argues that those particular depictions are intrinsically related to criminal conduct or are analogous to obscenity (if not themselves obscene), and that the ban on such speech is narrowly tailored to reinforce restrictions on the underlying conduct, prevent additional crime arising from the depictions, or safeguard public mores. But the Government nowhere attempts to extend these arguments to depictions of any other activities—depictions that are presumptively protected by the First Amendment but that remain subject to the criminal sanctions of §48.

Nor does the Government seriously contest that the presumptively impermissible applications of §48 (properly construed) far outnumber any permissible ones. However "growing" and "lucrative" the markets for crush videos and dogfighting depictions might be, they are dwarfed by the market for other depictions, such as hunting magazines and videos, that we have determined to be within the scope of §48. We therefore need not and do not decide whether a statute limited to crush videos or other depictions of extreme animal cruelty would be constitutional. We hold only that §48 is not so limited but is instead substantially overbroad, and therefore invalid under the First Amendment.

The judgment of the United States Court of Appeals for the Third Circuit is affirmed.

It is so ordered.

JUSTICE ALITO, dissenting.

The Court strikes down in its entirety a valuable statute that was enacted not to suppress speech, but to prevent horrific acts of animal cruelty—in particular, the creation and commercial exploitation of "crush videos," a form of depraved entertainment that has no social value. The Court's approach, which has the practical effect of legalizing the sale of such videos and is thus likely to spur a resumption of their production, is unwarranted. . . . Instead of applying the doctrine of overbreadth, I would vacate the decision below and instruct the Court of Appeals on remand to decide whether the videos that respondent sold are constitutionally protected. . . .

The First Amendment protects freedom of speech, but it most certainly does not protect violent criminal conduct, even if engaged in for expressive purposes. Crush videos present a highly unusual free speech issue because they are so closely linked with violent criminal conduct. The videos record the commission of violent criminal acts, and it appears that these crimes are committed for the sole purpose of creating the videos. In addition, as noted above, Congress was presented with compelling evidence that the only way of preventing these crimes was to target the sale of the videos. Under these circumstances, I cannot believe that the First Amendment commands Congress to step aside and allow the underlying crimes to continue.

The most relevant of our prior decisions is *Ferber*, which concerned child pornography. The Court there held that child pornography is not protected speech, and I believe that *Ferber*'s reasoning dictates a similar conclusion here.

In *Ferber*, an important factor—I would say the most important factor—was that child pornography involves the commission of a crime that inflicts severe personal injury to the "children who are made to engage in sexual conduct for commercial purposes." The *Ferber* Court repeatedly described the production of child pornography as child "abuse," "molestation," or "exploitation."

Second, *Ferber* emphasized the fact that these underlying crimes could not be effectively combated without targeting the distribution of child pornography. As the Court put it, "the distribution network for child pornography must be closed if the production of material which requires the sexual exploitation of children is to be effectively controlled." . . .

Third, the *Ferber* Court noted that the value of child pornography "is exceedingly modest, if not *de minimis*," and that any such value was "overwhelmingly outweigh[ed]" by "the evil to be restricted."

All three of these characteristics are shared by §48, as applied to crush videos. First, the conduct depicted in crush videos is criminal in every State and the District of Columbia. Thus, any crush video made in this country records the actual commission of a criminal act that inflicts severe physical injury and excruciating pain and ultimately results in death. Those who record the underlying criminal acts are likely to be criminally culpable, either as aiders and abettors or conspirators. And in the tight and secretive market for these videos, some who sell the videos or possess them with the intent to make a profit may be similarly culpable. (For example, in some cases, crush videos were commissioned by purchasers who specified the details of the acts that they wanted to see performed.). To the extent that §48 reaches such persons, it surely does not violate the First Amendment.

Second, the criminal acts shown in crush videos cannot be prevented without targeting the conduct prohibited by §48 — the creation, sale, and possession for sale of depictions of animal torture with the intention of realizing a commercial profit. The evidence presented to Congress posed a stark choice: Either ban the commercial exploitation of crush videos or tolerate a continuation of the criminal acts that they record. Faced with this evidence, Congress reasonably chose to target the lucrative crush video market.

Finally, the harm caused by the underlying crimes vastly outweighs any minimal value that the depictions might conceivably be thought to possess. Section 48 reaches only the actual recording of acts of animal torture; the statute does not apply to verbal descriptions or to simulations. And, unlike the child pornography statute in *Ferber* or its federal counterpart, provides an exception for depictions having any "serious religious, political, scientific, educational, journalistic, historical, or artistic value."

It must be acknowledged that §48 differs from a child pornography law in an important respect: preventing the abuse of children is certainly much more important than preventing the torture of the animals used in crush videos. . . . But while protecting children is unquestionably *more* important than protecting animals, the Government also has a compelling interest in preventing the torture depicted in crush videos.

The animals used in crush videos are living creatures that experience excruciating pain. Our society has long banned such cruelty, which is illegal throughout the country. . . . Section 48's ban on trafficking in crush videos also helps to enforce the criminal laws and to ensure that criminals do not profit from their crimes. We have already judged that taking the profit out of crime is a compelling interest. See Simon & Schuster, Inc. v. Members of N. Y. State Crime Victims Bd. (1991).

In short, *Ferber* is the case that sheds the most light on the constitutionality of Congress' effort to halt the production of crush videos. Applying the principles set forth in *Ferber*, I would hold that crush videos are not protected by the First Amendment.

Application of the *Ferber* framework also supports the constitutionality of §48 as applied to depictions of brutal animal fights. (For convenience, I will focus on videos of dogfights, which appear to be the most common type of animal fight videos.)

First, such depictions, like crush videos, record the actual commission of a crime involving deadly violence. Dogfights are illegal in every State and the District of Columbia, and under federal law constitute a felony punishable by imprisonment for up to five years.

Second, Congress had an ample basis for concluding that the crimes depicted in these videos cannot be effectively controlled without targeting the videos. Like crush videos and child pornography, dogfight videos are very often produced as part of a "low-profile, clandestine industry," and "the need to market the resulting products requires a visible apparatus of distribution." *Ferber*. In such circumstances, Congress had reasonable grounds for concluding that it would be "difficult, if not impossible, to halt" the underlying exploitation of dogs by pursuing only those who stage the fights.

The commercial trade in videos of dogfights is "an integral part of the production of such materials," *Ferber*. As the Humane Society explains, "[v]ideotapes memorializing dogfights are integral to the success of this criminal industry" for a variety of reasons. Humane Society Brief. For one thing, some dogfighting videos are made "solely for the purpose of selling the video (and not for a live audience)." In addition, those who stage dogfights profit not just from the sale of the videos themselves, but from the gambling revenue they take in from the fights; the videos "encourage [such] gambling activity because they allow those reluctant to attend actual fights for fear of prosecution to still bet on the outcome." Moreover, "[v]ideo documentation is vital to the criminal enterprise because it provides *proof* of a dog's fighting prowess—proof demanded by potential buyers and critical to the underground market." Such recordings may also serve as "'training' videos for other fight organizers." In short, because videos depicting live dogfights are essential to the success of the criminal dogfighting subculture, the commercial sale of such videos helps to fuel the market for, and thus to perpetuate the perpetration of, the criminal conduct depicted in them.

Third, depictions of dogfights that fall within §48's reach have by definition no appreciable social value. As noted, §48(b) exempts depictions having any appreciable social value, and thus the mere inclusion of a depiction of a live fight in a larger work that aims at communicating an idea or a message with a modicum of social value would not run afoul of the statute.

Finally, the harm caused by the underlying criminal acts greatly outweighs any trifling value that the depictions might be thought to possess. As the Humane Society explains:

> "The abused dogs used in fights endure physical torture and emotional manipulation throughout their lives to predispose them to violence; common tactics include feeding the animals hot peppers and gunpowder, prodding them with sticks, and electrocution. Dogs are conditioned never to give up a fight, even if they will be gravely hurt or killed. As a result, dogfights inflict horrific injuries on the participating animals, including lacerations, ripped ears, puncture wounds and broken bones. Losing dogs are routinely refused treatment, beaten further as 'punishment' for the loss, and executed by drowning, hanging, or incineration."

For these dogs, unlike the animals killed in crush videos, the suffering lasts for years rather than minutes. As with crush videos, moreover, the statutory ban on commerce in dogfighting videos is also supported by compelling governmental interests in effectively enforcing the Nation's criminal laws and preventing criminals from profiting from their illegal activities.

In sum, §48 may validly be applied to at least two broad real-world categories of expression covered by the statute: crush videos and dogfighting videos. Thus, the statute has a substantial core of constitutionally permissible applications. Moreover, for the reasons set forth above, the record does not show that §48, properly interpreted, bans a substantial amount of protected speech in absolute terms. . . . Accordingly, I would reject respondent's claim that §48 is facially unconstitutional under the overbreadth doctrine.

For these reasons, I respectfully dissent.

ASSIGNMENT S-12

STUDY GUIDE: Here is another case about regulating speech concerning violence — in particular, simulated violence against humans — rather than sex. Why shouldn't offensive speech involving depictions of violence be treated the same way as offensive speech involving sex? Whose speech is being restricted by this statute? Do adults have a constitutional right to speak to other people's children? If freedom of speech is a "natural right," is there a natural right to speak to minors? Is the majority's analysis affected by the established view that the First Amendment protects the rights of the public to hear the speech of others as well as to speak? What is the difference "in kind" that Justice Alito raises and Justice Scalia dismisses? Should this alleged difference make any legal difference? Does Justice Thomas identify any historical examples of legal restrictions on speaking to minors? Is he relying on the original public meaning of the First Amendment? If not, upon what is he relying?

BROWN v. ENTERTAINMENT MERCHANTS ASS'N

564 U.S. _____ (2011)

JUSTICE SCALIA delivered the opinion of the Court.

We consider whether a California law imposing restrictions on violent video games comports with the First Amendment.

I

California Assembly Bill 1179 (2005) (Act), prohibits the sale or rental of "violent video games" to minors, and requires their packaging to be labeled "18." The Act covers games "in which the range of options available to a player includes killing, maiming, dismembering, or sexually assaulting an image of a human being, if those acts are depicted" in a manner that "[a] reasonable person, considering the game as a whole, would find appeals to a deviant or morbid interest of minors," that is "patently offensive to prevailing standards in the community as to what is suitable for minors," and that "causes the game, as a whole, to lack serious literary, artistic, political, or scientific value for minors." Violation of the Act is punishable by a civil fine of up to $1,000. Respondents, representing the video-game and software industries, brought a preenforcement challenge to the Act in the United States District Court for the Northern District of California. That court concluded that the Act violated the First Amendment and permanently enjoined its enforcement. The Court of Appeals affirmed, and we granted certiorari.

II

California correctly acknowledges that video games qualify for First Amendment protection. The Free Speech Clause exists principally to protect discourse on public matters, but we have long recognized that it is difficult to distinguish politics from entertainment, and dangerous to try. . . . "Everyone is familiar with instances of propaganda through fiction. What is one man's amusement, teaches another's doctrine." Winters v. New York (1948). Like the protected books, plays, and movies that preceded them, video games communicate ideas—and even social messages—through many familiar literary devices (such as characters, dialogue, plot, and music) and through features distinctive to the medium (such as the player's interaction with the virtual world). That suffices to confer First Amendment protection. Under our Constitution, "esthetic and moral judgments about art and literature . . . are for the individual to make, not for the Government to decree, even with the mandate or approval of a majority." United States v. Playboy Entertainment Group, Inc. (2000). And whatever the challenges of applying the Constitution to ever-advancing technology, "the basic principles of freedom of speech and the press, like the First Amendment's command, do not vary" when a new and different medium for communication appears. Joseph Burstyn, Inc. v. Wilson (1952).

The most basic of those principles is this: "[A]s a general matter, . . . government has no power to restrict expression because of its message, its ideas, its subject matter, or its content." Ashcroft v. American Civil Liberties Union (2002). There are of course exceptions. "'From 1791 to the present,' . . . the First Amendment has 'permitted restrictions upon the content of speech in a few limited areas,' and has never 'include[d] a freedom to disregard these traditional limitations.'" United States v. Stevens (2010) (quoting R.A.V. v. St. Paul (1992)). These limited areas — such as obscenity, Roth v. United States (1957), incitement, Brandenburg v. Ohio (1969) *(per curiam),* and fighting words, Chaplinsky v. New Hampshire (1942) — represent "well-defined and narrowly limited classes of speech, the prevention and punishment of which have never been thought to raise any Constitutional problem," *id.*

Last Term, in *Stevens,* we held that new categories of unprotected speech may not be added to the list by a legislature that concludes certain speech is too harmful to be tolerated. *Stevens* concerned a federal statute purporting to criminalize the creation, sale, or possession of certain depictions of animal cruelty. The statute covered depictions "in which a living animal is intentionally maimed, mutilated, tortured, wounded, or killed" if that harm to the animal was illegal where the "the creation, sale, or possession t[ook] place." A saving clause largely borrowed from our obscenity jurisprudence, see Miller v. California (1973), exempted depictions with "serious religious, political, scientific, educational, journalistic, historical, or artistic value." We held that statute to be an impermissible content-based restriction on speech. There was no American tradition of forbidding the *depiction of* animal cruelty — though States have long had laws against *committing* it. . . .

That holding controls this case. As in *Stevens,* California has tried to make violent-speech regulation look like obscenity regulation by appending a saving clause required for the latter. That does not suffice. Our cases have been clear that the obscenity exception to the First Amendment does not cover whatever a legislature finds shocking, but only depictions of "sexual conduct," *Miller.*

Stevens was not the first time we have encountered and rejected a State's attempt to shoehorn speech about violence into obscenity. In *Winters,* we considered a New York criminal statute "forbid[ding] the massing of stories of bloodshed and lust in such a way as to incite to crime against the person." The New York Court of Appeals upheld the provision as a law against obscenity. "[T]here can be no more precise test of written indecency or obscenity," it said, "than the continuing and changeable experience of the community as to what types of books are likely to bring about the corruption of public morals or other analogous injury to the public order." *Id.* That is of course the same expansive view of governmental power to abridge the freedom of speech based on interest-balancing that we rejected in *Stevens*. Our opinion in *Winters* . . . made clear that violence is not part of the obscenity that the Constitution permits to be regulated. The speech reached by the statute contained "no indecency or obscenity in any sense heretofore known to the law." *Id.*

Because speech about violence is not obscene, it is of no consequence that California's statute mimics the New York statute regulating obscenity-for-minors that we upheld in Ginsberg v. New York (1968). That case approved a prohibition on the sale to minors of *sexual* material that would be obscene from the perspective of a child. We held that the legislature could "adjus[t] the definition of obscenity 'to social realities by permitting the appeal of this type of material to be assessed in terms of the sexual interests . . . ' of . . . minors." *Id.* . . .

The California Act is something else entirely. It does not adjust the boundaries of an existing category of unprotected speech to ensure that a definition designed for adults is not uncritically applied to children. California does not argue that it is empowered to prohibit selling offensively violent works *to adults*—and it is wise not to, since that is but a hair's breadth from the argument rejected in *Stevens*. Instead, it wishes to create a wholly new category of content-based regulation that is permissible only for speech directed at children.

That is unprecedented and mistaken. "[M]inors are entitled to a significant measure of First Amendment protection, and only in relatively narrow and well-defined circumstances may government bar public dissemination of protected materials to them." Erznoznik v. Jacksonville (1975). No doubt a State possesses legitimate power to protect children from harm, but that does not include a free-floating power to restrict the ideas to which children may be exposed. "Speech that is neither obscene as to youths nor subject to some other legitimate proscription cannot be suppressed solely to protect the young from ideas or images that a legislative body thinks unsuitable for them." *Erznoznik*.[1]

California's argument would fare better if there were a longstanding tradition in this country of specially restricting children's access to depictions of violence, but there is none. Certainly the *books* we give children to read—or read to them

1. Justice Thomas ignores the holding of *Erznoznik*, and denies that persons under 18 have any constitutional right to speak or be spoken to without their parents' consent. He cites no case, state or federal, supporting this view, and to our knowledge there is none. Most of his dissent is devoted to the proposition that parents have traditionally had the power to control what their children hear and say. This is true enough. And it perhaps follows from this that the state has the power to enforce parental prohibitions—to require, for example, that the promoters of a rock concert exclude those minors whose parents have advised the promoters that their children are forbidden to attend. But it does not follow that the state has the power to prevent children from hearing or saying anything without their parents' prior consent. The latter would mean, for example, that it could be made criminal to admit persons under 18 to a political rally without their parents' prior written consent—even a political rally in support of laws against corporal punishment of children, or laws in favor of greater rights for minors. And what is good for First Amendment rights of speech must be good for First Amendment rights of religion as well: It could be made criminal to admit a person under 18 to church, or to give a person under 18 a religious tract, without his parents' prior consent. Our point is not, as Justice Thomas believes, merely that such laws are "undesirable." They are obviously an infringement upon the religious freedom of young people and those who wish to proselytize young people. Such laws do not enforce parental authority over children's speech and religion; they impose governmental authority, subject only to a parental veto. In the absence of any precedent for state control, uninvited by the parents, over a child's speech and religion (Justice Thomas cites none), and in the absence of any justification for such control that would satisfy strict scrutiny, those laws must be unconstitutional. This argument is not, as Justice Thomas asserts, "circular." It is the absence of any historical warrant or compelling justification for such restrictions, not our ipse dixit, that renders them invalid.

when they are younger—contain no shortage of gore. Grimm's Fairy Tales, for example, are grim indeed. As her just deserts for trying to poison Snow White, the wicked queen is made to dance in red hot slippers "till she fell dead on the floor, a sad example of envy and jealousy." Cinderella's evil stepsisters have their eyes pecked out by doves. And Hansel and Gretel (children!) kill their captor by baking her in an oven.

High-school reading lists are full of similar fare. Homer's Odysseus blinds Polyphemus the Cyclops by grinding out his eye with a heated stake. The Odyssey of Homer, Book IX ("Even so did we seize the fiery-pointed brand and whirled it round in his eye, and the blood flowed about the heated bar. And the breath of the flame singed his eyelids and brows all about, as the ball of the eye burnt away, and the roots thereof crackled in the flame"). In the Inferno, Dante and Virgil watch corrupt politicians struggle to stay submerged beneath a lake of boiling pitch, lest they be skewered by devils above the surface. And Golding's Lord of the Flies recounts how a schoolboy called Piggy is savagely murdered *by other children* while marooned on an island. W. Golding, Lord of the Flies (1997 ed.).[2]

This is not to say that minors' consumption of violent entertainment has never encountered resistance. In the 1800's, dime novels depicting crime and "penny dreadfuls" (named for their price and content) were blamed in some quarters for juvenile delinquency. See Brief for Cato Institute as *Amicus Curiae* 6–7. When motion pictures came along, they became the villains instead. "The days when the police looked upon dime novels as the most dangerous of textbooks in the school for crime are drawing to a close .... They say that the moving picture machine ... tends even more than did the dime novel to turn the thoughts of the easily influenced to paths which sometimes lead to prison." Moving Pictures as Helps to Crime, N.Y. Times, Feb. 21, 1909, quoted in Brief for Cato Institute. For a time, our Court did permit broad censorship of movies because of their capacity to be "used for evil," see Mutual Film Corp. v. Industrial Comm'n of Ohio (1915), but we eventually reversed course, *Joseph Burstyn, Inc.*; see also *Erznoznik* (invalidating a drive-in movies restriction designed to protect children). Radio dramas were next, and then came comic books. Brief for Cato Institute. Many in the late 1940's and early 1950's blamed comic books for fostering a "preoccupation with violence and horror" among the young, leading to a rising juvenile crime rate. See Note, Regulation of Comic Books, 68 Harv. L. Rev. 489, 490 (1955). But efforts to convince Congress to restrict comic

2. Justice Alito accuses us of pronouncing that playing violent video games "is not different in 'kind'" from reading violent literature. Well of course it is different in kind, but not in a way that causes the provision and viewing of violent video games, unlike the provision and reading of books, not to be expressive activity and hence not to enjoy First Amendment protection. Reading Dante is unquestionably more cultured and intellectually edifying than playing Mortal Kombat. But these cultural and intellectual differences are not constitutional ones. Crudely violent video games, tawdry TV shows, and cheap novels and magazines are no less forms of speech than The Divine Comedy, and restrictions upon them must survive strict scrutiny. . . . Even if we can see in them "nothing of any possible value to society . . . , they are as much entitled to the protection of free speech as the best of literature." Winters v. New York (1948).

books failed. Brief for Comic Book Legal Defense Fund as *Amicus Curiae*.[3] And, of course, after comic books came television and music lyrics.

California claims that video games present special problems because they are "interactive," in that the player participates in the violent action on screen and determines its outcome. The latter feature is nothing new: Since at least the publication of The Adventures of You: Sugarcane Island in 1969, young readers of choose-your-own-adventure stories have been able to make decisions that determine the plot by following instructions about which page to turn to. As for the argument that video games enable participation in the violent action, that seems to us more a matter of degree than of kind. As Judge Posner has observed, all literature is interactive. "[T]he better it is, the more interactive. Literature when it is successful draws the reader into the story, makes him identify with the characters, invites him to judge them and quarrel with them, to experience their joys and sufferings as the reader's own." American Amusement Machine Assn. v. Kendrick (C.A.7 2001) (striking down a similar restriction on violent video games).

JUSTICE ALITO has done considerable independent research to identify video games in which "the violence is astounding." "Victims are dismembered, decapitated, disemboweled, set on fire, and chopped into little pieces. . . . Blood gushes, splatters, and pools." JUSTICE ALITO recounts all these disgusting video games in order to disgust us—but disgust is not a valid basis for restricting expression. And the same is true of JUSTICE ALITO'S description of those video games he has discovered that have a racial or ethnic motive for their violence—"'ethnic cleansing' [of] . . . African Americans, Latinos, or Jews." To what end does he relate this? Does it somehow increase the "aggressiveness" that California wishes to suppress? Who knows? But it does arouse the reader's ire, and the reader's desire to put an end to this horrible message. Thus, ironically, JUSTICE ALITO'S argument highlights the precise danger posed by the California Act: that the *ideas* expressed by speech—whether it be violence, or gore, or racism—and not its objective effects, may be the real reason for governmental proscription.

III

Because the Act imposes a restriction on the content of protected speech, it is invalid unless California can demonstrate that it passes strict scrutiny—that is, unless it is justified by a compelling government interest and is narrowly drawn to serve that interest. *R.A.V.* The State must specifically identify an "actual

3. The crusade against comic books was led by a psychiatrist, Frederic Wertham, who told the Senate Judiciary Committee that "as long as the crime comic books industry exists in its present forms there are no secure homes." Juvenile Delinquency (Comic Books): Hearings before the Subcommittee to Investigate Juvenile Delinquency, 83d Cong., 2d Sess., 84 (1954). Wertham's objections extended even to Superman comics, which he described as "particularly injurious to the ethical development of children." Wertham's crusade did convince the New York Legislature to pass a ban on the sale of certain comic books to minors, but it was vetoed by Governor Thomas Dewey on the ground that it was unconstitutional given our opinion in *Winters*.

problem" in need of solving, and the curtailment of free speech must be actually necessary to the solution. That is a demanding standard. "It is rare that a regulation restricting speech because of its content will ever be permissible." *Playboy.*

California cannot meet that standard. At the outset, it acknowledges that it cannot show a direct causal link between violent video games and harm to minors. Rather, relying upon our decision in Turner Broadcasting System, Inc. v. FCC (1994), the State claims that it need not produce such proof because the legislature can make a predictive judgment that such a link exists, based on competing psychological studies. But reliance on *Turner Broadcasting* is misplaced. That decision applied *intermediate scrutiny* to a content-neutral regulation. California's burden is much higher, and because it bears the risk of uncertainty, ambiguous proof will not suffice.

The State's evidence is not compelling. California relies primarily on the research of Dr. Craig Anderson and a few other research psychologists whose studies purport to show a connection between exposure to violent video games and harmful effects on children. These studies have been rejected by every court to consider them, and with good reason: They do not prove that violent video games *cause* minors to *act* aggressively (which would at least be a beginning). Instead, "[n]early all of the research is based on correlation, not evidence of causation, and most of the studies suffer from significant, admitted flaws in methodology." [Video Software Dealers Assn. v. Schwarzenegger (C.A.9 2009)]. They show at best some correlation between exposure to violent entertainment and minuscule real-world effects, such as children's feeling more aggressive or making louder noises in the few minutes after playing a violent game than after playing a nonviolent game.

Even taking for granted Dr. Anderson's conclusions that violent video games produce some effect on children's feelings of aggression, those effects are both small and indistinguishable from effects produced by other media. In his testimony in a similar lawsuit, Dr. Anderson admitted that the "effect sizes" of children's exposure to violent video games are "about the same" as that produced by their exposure to violence on television. And he admits that the *same* effects have been found when children watch cartoons starring Bugs Bunny or the Road Runner, or when they play video games like Sonic the Hedgehog that are rated "E" (appropriate for all ages), or even when they "vie[w] a picture of a gun."[4]

4. JUSTICE ALITO is mistaken in thinking that we fail to take account of "new and rapidly evolving technology." The studies in question pertain to that new and rapidly evolving technology, and fail to show, with the degree of certitude that strict scrutiny requires, that this subject-matter restriction on speech is justified. Nor is Justice Alito correct in attributing to us the view that "violent video games really present no serious problem." Perhaps they do present a problem, and perhaps none of us would allow our own children to play them. But there are all sorts of "problems" — some of them surely more serious than this one — that cannot be addressed by governmental restriction of free expression: for example, the problem of encouraging anti-Semitism (National Socialist Party of America v. Skokie (1977)(per curiam)), the problem of spreading a political philosophy hostile to the Constitution (Noto v. United States (1961)), or the problem of encouraging disrespect for the Nation's flag (Texas v. Johnson (1989)). . . .

Of course, California has (wisely) declined to restrict Saturday morning cartoons, the sale of games rated for young children, or the distribution of pictures of guns. The consequence is that its regulation is wildly underinclusive when judged against its asserted justification, which in our view is alone enough to defeat it. Underinclusiveness raises serious doubts about whether the government is in fact pursuing the interest it invokes, rather than disfavoring a particular speaker or viewpoint. Here, California has singled out the purveyors of video games for disfavored treatment—at least when compared to booksellers, cartoonists, and movie producers—and has given no persuasive reason why.

The Act is also seriously underinclusive in another respect—and a respect that renders irrelevant the contentions of the concurrence and the dissents that video games are qualitatively different from other portrayals of violence. The California Legislature is perfectly willing to leave this dangerous, mind-altering material in the hands of children so long as one parent (or even an aunt or uncle) says it's OK. And there are not even any requirements as to how this parental or avuncular relationship is to be verified; apparently the child's or putative parent's, aunt's, or uncle's say-so suffices. That is not how one addresses a serious social problem. . . .

And finally, the Act's purported aid to parental authority is vastly overinclusive. Not all of the children who are forbidden to purchase violent video games on their own have parents who *care* whether they purchase violent video games. While some of the legislation's effect may indeed be in support of what some parents of the restricted children actually want, its entire effect is only in support of what the State thinks parents *ought* to want. This is not the narrow tailoring to "assisting parents" that restriction of First Amendment rights requires.

***

California's effort to regulate violent video games is the latest episode in a long series of failed attempts to censor violent entertainment for minors. While we have pointed out above that some of the evidence brought forward to support the harmfulness of video games is unpersuasive, we do not mean to demean or disparage the concerns that underlie the attempt to regulate them—concerns that may and doubtless do prompt a good deal of parental oversight. We have no business passing judgment on the view of the California Legislature that violent video games (or, for that matter, any other forms of speech) corrupt the young or harm their moral development. Our task is only to say whether or not such works constitute a "well-defined and narrowly limited clas[s] of speech, the prevention and punishment of which have never been thought to raise any Constitutional problem," *Chaplinsky* (the answer plainly is no); and if not, whether the regulation of such works is justified by that high degree of necessity we have described as a compelling state interest (it is not). Even where the protection of children is the object, the constitutional limits on governmental action apply.

California's legislation straddles the fence between (1) addressing a serious social problem and (2) helping concerned parents control their children. Both ends are legitimate, but when they affect First Amendment rights they must be pursued by means that are neither seriously underinclusive nor seriously overinclusive. See Church of Lukumi Babalu Aye, Inc. v. Hialeah (1993). As a means of protecting children from portrayals of violence, the legislation is seriously underinclusive, not only because it excludes portrayals other than video games, but also because it permits a parental or avuncular veto. And as a means of assisting concerned parents it is seriously overinclusive because it abridges the First Amendment rights of young people whose parents (and aunts and uncles) think violent video games are a harmless pastime. And the overbreadth in achieving one goal is not cured by the underbreadth in achieving the other. Legislation such as this, which is neither fish nor fowl, cannot survive strict scrutiny.

We affirm the judgment below.

It is so ordered.

JUSTICE ALITO, with whom THE CHIEF JUSTICE joins, concurring in the judgment.

The California statute that is before us in this case represents a pioneering effort to address what the state legislature and others regard as a potentially serious social problem: the effect of exceptionally violent video games on impressionable minors, who often spend countless hours immersed in the alternative worlds that these games create. Although the California statute is well intentioned, its terms are not framed with the precision that the Constitution demands, and I therefore agree with the Court that this particular law cannot be sustained.

I disagree, however, with the approach taken in the Court's opinion. In considering the application of unchanging constitutional principles to new and rapidly evolving technology, this Court should proceed with caution. We should make every effort to understand the new technology. We should take into account the possibility that developing technology may have important societal implications that will become apparent only with time. We should not jump to the conclusion that new technology is fundamentally the same as some older thing with which we are familiar. And we should not hastily dismiss the judgment of legislators, who may be in a better position than we are to assess the implications of new technology. The opinion of the Court exhibits none of this caution.

In the view of the Court, all those concerned about the effects of violent video games—federal and state legislators, educators, social scientists, and parents—are unduly fearful, for violent video games really present no serious problem. Spending hour upon hour controlling the actions of a character who guns down scores of innocent victims is not different in "kind" from reading a description of violence in a work of literature.

The Court is sure of this; I am not. There are reasons to suspect that the experience of playing violent video games just might be very different from reading a book, listening to the radio, or watching a movie or a television show.

I

Respondents in this case, representing the video-game industry, ask us to strike down the California law on two grounds: The broad ground adopted by the Court and the narrower ground that the law's definition of "violent video game," is impermissibly vague. Because I agree with the latter argument, I see no need to reach the broader First Amendment issues addressed by the Court. . . .

Due process requires that laws give people of ordinary intelligence fair notice of what is prohibited. The lack of such notice in a law that regulates expression "raises special First Amendment concerns because of its obvious chilling effect on free speech." Reno v. American Civil Liberties Union (1997). Vague laws force potential speakers to "'steer far wider of the unlawful zone' . . . than if the boundaries of the forbidden areas were clearly marked." Baggett v. Bullitt (1964) (quoting Speiser v. Randall (1958)). While "perfect clarity and precise guidance have never been required even of regulations that restrict expressive activity," Ward v. Rock Against Racism (1989), "government may regulate in the area" of First Amendment freedoms "only with narrow specificity," NAACP v. Button (1963). These principles apply to laws that regulate expression for the purpose of protecting children.

Here, the California law does not define "violent video games" with the "narrow specificity" that the Constitution demands. . . . [T]he work of providing fair notice is left in large part to the three requirements that follow, but those elements are also not up to the task. . . . One of the three elements at issue here refers expressly to "prevailing standards in the community as to what is suitable for minors." Another element points in the same direction, asking whether "[a] reasonable person, considering [a] game as a whole," would find that it "appeals to a *deviant* or *morbid* interest of minors."

The terms "deviant" and "morbid" are not defined in the statute, and California offers no reason to think that its courts would give the terms anything other than their ordinary meaning. I therefore assume that "deviant" and "morbid" carry the meaning that they convey in ordinary speech. The adjective "deviant" ordinarily means "deviating . . . from some accepted norm," and the term "morbid" means "of, relating to, or characteristic of disease." Webster's. A "deviant or morbid interest" in violence, therefore, appears to be an interest that deviates from what is regarded—presumably in accordance with some generally accepted standard—as normal and healthy. Thus, the application of the California law is heavily dependent on the identification of generally accepted standards regarding the suitability of violent entertainment for minors.

The California Legislature seems to have assumed that these standards are sufficiently well known so that a person of ordinary intelligence would have fair notice as to whether the kind and degree of violence in a particular game is enough to qualify the game as "violent." . . . As the Court notes, [however,] classic literature contains descriptions of great violence, and even children's stories sometimes depict very violent scenes. Although our society does not generally regard all depictions of violence as suitable for children or adolescents, the prevalence of violent depictions in children's literature and entertainment creates numerous opportunities for reasonable people to disagree about which depictions may excite "deviant" or "morbid" impulses.

Finally, the difficulty of ascertaining the community standards incorporated into the California law is compounded by the legislature's decision to lump all minors together. The California law draws no distinction between young children and adolescents who are nearing the age of majority. . . .

For these reasons, I conclude that the California violent video game law fails to provide the fair notice that the Constitution requires. And I would go no further. I would not express any view on whether a properly drawn statute would or would not survive First Amendment scrutiny. We should address that question only if and when it is necessary to do so.

II

Having outlined how I would decide this case, I will now briefly elaborate on my reasons for questioning the wisdom of the Court's approach. . . .

[T]he Court is far too quick to dismiss the possibility that the experience of playing video games (and the effects on minors of playing violent video games) may be very different from anything that we have seen before. Any assessment of the experience of playing video games must take into account certain characteristics of the video games that are now on the market and those that are likely to be available in the near future. Today's most advanced video games create realistic alternative worlds in which millions of players immerse themselves for hours on end. These games feature visual imagery and sounds that are strikingly realistic, and in the near future video-game graphics may be virtually indistinguishable from actual video footage. Many of the games already on the market can produce high definition images, and it is predicted that it will not be long before video-game images will be seen in three dimensions. It is also forecast that video games will soon provide sensory feedback. By wearing a special vest or other device, a player will be able to experience physical sensations supposedly felt by a character on the screen. Some *amici* who support respondents foresee the day when "'virtual-reality shoot-em-ups'" will allow children to "'actually feel the splatting blood from the blown-off head'" of a victim.

Persons who play video games also have an unprecedented ability to participate in the events that take place in the virtual worlds that these games create. Players can create their own video-game characters and can use photos to produce characters that closely resemble actual people. A person playing a sophisticated game can make a multitude of choices and can thereby alter the course of the action in the game. In addition, the means by which players control the action in video games now bear a closer relationship to the means by which people control action in the real world. While the action in older games was often directed with buttons or a joystick, players dictate the action in newer games by engaging in the same motions that they desire a character in the game to perform. For example, a player who wants a video-game character to swing a baseball bat—either to hit a ball or smash a skull—could bring that about by simulating the motion of actually swinging a bat.

These present-day and emerging characteristics of video games must be considered together with characteristics of the violent games that have already been marketed.

In some of these games, the violence is astounding. Victims by the dozens are killed with every imaginable implement, including machine guns, shotguns, clubs, hammers, axes, swords, and chainsaws. Victims are dismembered, decapitated, disemboweled, set on fire, and chopped into little pieces. They cry out in agony and beg for mercy. Blood gushes, splatters, and pools. Severed body parts and gobs of human remains are graphically shown. In some games, points are awarded based, not only on the number of victims killed, but on the killing technique employed.

It also appears that there is no antisocial theme too base for some in the video-game industry to exploit. There are games in which a player can take on the identity and reenact the killings carried out by the perpetrators of the murders at Columbine High School and Virginia Tech. The objective of one game is to rape a mother and her daughters; in another, the goal is to rape Native American women. There is a game in which players engage in "ethnic cleansing" and can choose to gun down African–Americans, Latinos, or Jews. In still another game, players attempt to fire a rifle shot into the head of President Kennedy as his motorcade passes by the Texas School Book Depository.

If the technological characteristics of the sophisticated games that are likely to be available in the near future are combined with the characteristics of the most violent games already marketed, the result will be games that allow troubled teens to experience in an extraordinarily personal and vivid way what it would be like to carry out unspeakable acts of violence.

The Court is untroubled by this possibility. According to the Court, the "interactive" nature of video games is "nothing new" because "all literature is interactive." Disagreeing with this assessment, the International Game Developers Association (IGDA)—a group that presumably understands the nature of video games and that supports respondents—tells us that video games are "far more concretely interactive." And on this point, the game developers are surely correct.

It is certainly true, as the Court notes, that "'[l]iterature, when it is successful draws the reader into the story, makes him identify with the characters, invites him to judge them and quarrel with them, to experience their joys and sufferings as the reader's own.'" But only an extraordinarily imaginative reader who reads a description of a killing in a literary work will experience that event as vividly as he might if he played the role of the killer in a video game. To take an example, think of a person who reads the passage in Crime and Punishment in which Raskolnikov kills the old pawn broker with an axe. Compare that reader with a video-game player who creates an avatar that bears his own image; who sees a realistic image of the victim and the scene of the killing in high definition and in three dimensions; who is forced to decide whether or not to kill the victim and decides to do so; who then pretends to grasp an axe, to raise it above the head of the victim, and then to bring it down; who hears the thud of the axe hitting her head and her cry of pain; who sees her split skull and feels the sensation of blood on his face and hands. For most people, the two experiences will not be the same.[5]

When all of the characteristics of video games are taken into account, there is certainly a reasonable basis for thinking that the experience of playing a video game may be quite different from the experience of reading a book, listening to a radio broadcast, or viewing a movie. And if this is so, then for at least some minors, the effects of playing violent video games may also be quite different. The Court acts prematurely in dismissing this possibility out of hand.

***

For all these reasons, I would hold only that the particular law at issue here fails to provide the clear notice that the Constitution requires. I would not squelch legislative efforts to deal with what is perceived by some to be a significant and developing social problem. If differently framed statutes are enacted by the States or by the Federal Government, we can consider the constitutionality of those laws when cases challenging them are presented to us.

JUSTICE THOMAS, dissenting.

The Court's decision today does not comport with the original public understanding of the First Amendment. The majority strikes down, as facially unconstitutional, a state law that prohibits the direct sale or rental of certain video games to minors because the law "abridg[es] the freedom of speech." U.S. Const., Amdt. 1. But I do not think the First Amendment stretches that far. The practices and beliefs of the founding generation establish that "the freedom of speech," as originally understood, does not include a right to speak to minors (or a right of minors to access speech) without going through the minors' parents or guardians. I would hold that the law at issue is not facially unconstitutional under the First Amendment, and reverse and remand for further proceedings.

I[6]

When interpreting a constitutional provision, "the goal is to discern the most likely public understanding of [that] provision at the time it was adopted." McDonald v. Chicago (2010) (THOMAS, J., concurring in part and concurring in judgment). Because the Constitution is a written instrument, "its meaning does not alter." McIntyre v. Ohio Elections Comm'n (1995) (Thomas, J., concurring in judgment) (internal quotation marks omitted). "That which it meant when adopted, it means now." *Ibid.*

5. As the Court notes, there are a few children's books that ask young readers to step into the shoes of a character and to make choices that take the stories along one of a very limited number of possible lines. But the very nature of the print medium makes it impossible for a book to offer anything like the same number of choices as those provided by a video game.

6. [Extensive supporting authorities have been omitted due to space constraints. — ED.]

As originally understood, the First Amendment's protection against laws "abridging the freedom of speech" did not extend to *all* speech. "There are certain well-defined and narrowly limited classes of speech, the prevention and punishment of which have never been thought to raise any Constitutional problem." Chaplinsky v. New Hampshire (1942). Laws regulating such speech do not "abridg[e] the freedom of speech" because such speech is understood to fall outside "the freedom of speech."

In my view, the "practices and beliefs held by the Founders" reveal another category of excluded speech: speech to minor children bypassing their parents. The historical evidence shows that the founding generation believed parents had absolute authority over their minor children and expected parents to use that authority to direct the proper development of their children. It would be absurd to suggest that such a society understood "the freedom of speech" to include a right to speak to minors (or a corresponding right of minors to access speech) without going through the minors' parents. The founding generation would not have considered it an abridgment of "the freedom of speech" to support parental authority by restricting speech that bypasses minors' parents.

Attitudes toward children were in a state of transition around the time that the States ratified the Bill of Rights. A complete understanding of the founding generation's views on children and the parent-child relationship must therefore begin roughly a century earlier, in colonial New England. In the Puritan tradition common in the New England Colonies, fathers ruled families with absolute authority. . . .

Part of the father's absolute power was the right and duty "to fill his children's minds with knowledge and . . . make them apply their knowledge in right action." E. Morgan, The Puritan Family (rev. ed. 1966). Puritans thought children were "innately sinful and that parents' primary task was to suppress their children's natural depravity." S. Mintz & S. Kellogg, Domestic Revolutions (1988). Accordingly, parents were not to let their children read "vain Books, profane Ballads, and filthy Songs" or "fond and amorous Romances, . . . fabulous Histories of Giants, the bombast Achievements of Knight Errantry, and the like." The History of Genesis (3d ed. corrected 1708).

This conception of parental authority was reflected in laws at that time. In the Massachusetts Colony, for example, it was unlawful for tavern keepers (or anyone else) to entertain children without their parents' consent. And a "stubborn or rebellious son" of 16 years or more committed a capital offense if he disobeyed "the voice of his Father, or the voice of his Mother." The Laws and Liberties of Massachusetts (1648).

In the decades leading up to and following the Revolution, attitudes towards children changed. Children came to be seen less as innately sinful and more as blank slates requiring careful and deliberate development. But the same overarching principles remained. Parents continued to have both the right and duty to ensure the proper development of their children. They exercised significant authority over their children, including control over the books that children read. And laws at the time continued to reflect strong support for parental authority and the sense that children were not fit to govern themselves.

The works of John Locke and Jean-Jacques Rousseau were a driving force behind the changed understanding of children and childhood. Locke taught that children's minds were blank slates and that parents therefore had to be careful and deliberate about what their children were told and observed. Parents had only themselves to blame if, "by humouring and cockering" their children, they "poison'd the fountain" and later "taste[d] the bitter waters." Some Thoughts Concerning Education (1692). All vices, he explained, were sowed by parents and "those about children." Significantly, Locke did not suggest circumscribing parental authority but rather articulated a new basis for it. Rousseau disagreed with Locke in important respects, but his philosophy was similarly premised on parental control over a child's development. Although Rousseau advocated that children should be allowed to develop naturally, he instructed that the environment be directed by "a tutor who is given total control over the child and who removes him from society, from all competing sources of authority and influence." J. Fliegelman, Prodigals and Pilgrims (1982). Locke's *An Essay Concerning Human Understanding* and his *Some Thoughts Concerning Education* were significantly more popular than his *Two Treatises of Government*, according to a study of 92 colonial libraries between 1700 and 1776. And Rousseau's *Emile*, a treatise on education, was more widely advertised and distributed than his political work, *The Social Contract*. In general, the most popular books in the Colonies on the eve of the American Revolution were not political discourses but ones concerned with child rearing.

Locke's and Rousseau's writings fostered a new conception of childhood. Children were increasingly viewed as malleable creatures, and childhood came to be seen as an important period of growth, development, and preparation for adulthood. . . . This conception of childhood led to great concern about influences on children. . . . As a result, it was widely accepted that children needed close monitoring and carefully planned development. . . . The Revolution only amplified these concerns. The Republic would require virtuous citizens, which necessitated proper training from childhood.

Based on these views of childhood, the founding generation understood parents to have a right and duty to govern their children's growth. Parents were expected to direct the development and education of their children and ensure that bad habits did not take root. . . . This conception of parental rights and duties was exemplified by Thomas Jefferson's approach to raising children. He wrote letters to his daughters constantly and often gave specific instructions about what the children should do. . . . Jefferson's rigorous management of his charges was not uncommon. . . . For their part, children were expected to be dutiful and obedient.

Society's concern with children's development extended to the books they read. "Vice always spreads by being published," Noah Webster observed. . . . Prominent children's authors harshly criticized fairy tales and the use of anthropomorphic animals. . . . Adults carefully controlled what they published for children. Stories written for children were dedicated to moral instruction and were relatively austere, lacking details that might titillate children's minds. John Newbery, the publisher often credited with creating the genre of children's literature, removed traditional folk characters, like Tom Thumb, from their original stories and placed them in new morality tales in which good children were rewarded and disobedient children punished. Parents had total authority over what their children read.

The law at the time reflected the founding generation's understanding of parent-child relations. According to Sir William Blackstone, parents were responsible for maintaining, protecting, and education their children, and therefore had "power" over their children. Chancellor James Kent agreed. The law entitled parents to "the custody of their [children]," "the value of th[e] [children's] labor and services," and the "right to the exercise of such discipline as may be requisite for the discharge of their sacred trust." Children, in turn, were charged with "obedience and assistance during their own minority, and gratitude and reverance during the rest of their lives." Thus, in case after case, courts made clear that parents had a right to the child's labor and services until the child reached majority. . . .

Relatedly, boys could not enlist in the military without parental consent. Many of those who did so during the Revolutionary War found, afterwards, that their fathers were entitled to their military wages. And after the war, minors who enlisted without parental consent in violation of federal law could find themselves returned home on writs of habeas corpus issued at their parents' request.

Laws also set age limits restricting marriage without parental consent. . . . Indeed, the law imposed age limits on all manner of activities that required judgment and reason. Children could not vote, could not serve on juries, and generally could not be witnesses in criminal cases unless they were older than 14. Nor could they swear loyalty to a State. Early federal laws granting aliens the ability to become citizens provided that those under 21 were deemed citizens if their fathers chose to naturalize.

The history clearly shows a founding generation that believed parents to have complete authority over their minor children and expected parents to direct the development of those children. The Puritan tradition in New England laid the foundation of American parental authority and duty. In the decades leading up to and following the Revolution, the conception of the child's mind evolved but the duty and authority of parents remained. Indeed, society paid closer attention to potential influences on children than before. Teachers and schools came under scrutiny, and children's reading material was carefully supervised. Laws reflected these concerns and often supported parental authority with the coercive power of the state.

II

In light of this history, the Framers could not possibly have understood "the freedom of speech" to include an unqualified right to speak to minors. Specifically, I am sure that the founding generation would not have understood "the freedom of speech" to include a right to speak to children without going through their parents. As a consequence, I do not believe that laws limiting such speech—for example, by requiring parental consent to speak to a minor—"abridg[e] the freedom of speech" within the original meaning of the First

Amendment.We have recently noted that this Court does not have "freewheeling authority to declare new categories of speech outside the scope of the First Amendment." [United States v. Stevens (2010)]. But we also recognized that there may be "some categories of speech that have been historically unprotected [and] have not yet been specifically identified or discussed as such in our case law." In my opinion, the historical evidence here plainly reveals one such category.[7]

Admittedly, the original public understanding of a constitutional provision does not always comport with modern sensibilities. It may also be inconsistent with precedent. This, however, is not such a case. Although much has changed in this country since the Revolution, the notion that parents have authority over their children and that the law can support that authority persists today. For example, at least some States make it a crime to lure or entice a minor away from the minor's parent. Every State in the Union still establishes a minimum age for marriage without parental or judicial consent. Individuals less than 18 years old cannot enlist in the military without parental consent. And minors remain subject to curfew laws across the country, and cannot unilaterally consent to most medical procedures.

Moreover, there are many things minors today cannot do at all, whether they have parental consent or not. State laws set minimum ages for voting and jury duty. In California (the State at issue here), minors cannot drive for hire or drive a school bus, purchase tobacco, play bingo for money, or execute a will.

My understanding of "the freedom of speech" is also consistent with this Court's precedents. To be sure, the Court has held that children are entitled to the protection of the First Amendment, see, e.g., Erznoznik v. Jacksonville (1975), and the government may not unilaterally dictate what children can say or hear. But this Court has never held, until today, that "the freedom of speech" includes a right to speak to minors (or a right of minors to access speech) without going through the minors' parents. To the contrary, "[i]t is well settled that a State or municipality can adopt more stringent controls on communicative materials available to youths than on those available to adults." *Erznoznik*. . . .

7. The majority responds that "it does not follow" from the historical evidence "that the state has the power to prevent children from hearing . . . anything without their parents' prior consent." Such a conclusion, the majority asserts, would lead to laws that, in its view, would be undesirable and "obviously" unconstitutional.

The majority's circular argument misses the point. The question is the majority's circular argument misses the point. The question is not whether certain laws might make sense to judges or legislators today, but rather what the public likely understood "the freedom of speech" to mean when the First Amendment was adopted. See District of Columbia v. Heller (2008). I believe it is clear that the founding public would not have understood "the freedom of speech" to include speech to minor children bypassing their parents. It follows that the First Amendment imposes no restriction on state regulation of such speech. To note that there may not be "precedent for [such] state control," ante, "is not to establish that [there] is a constitutional right," McIntyre v. Ohio Elections Comm'n (1995) (Scalia, J., dissenting).

III

The California law at issue here prohibits the sale or rental of "violent video game[s]" to minors, defined as anyone "under 18 years of age." A violation of the law is punishable by a civil fine of up to $1,000. Critically, the law does not prohibit adults from buying or renting violent video games for a minor or prohibit minors from playing such games. The law also does not restrict a "minor's parent, grandparent, aunt, uncle, or legal guardian" from selling or renting him a violent video game. . . .

Even assuming that video games are speech, in most applications the California law does not implicate the First Amendment. All that the law does is prohibit the direct sale or rental of a violent video game to a minor by someone other than the minor's parent, grandparent, aunt, uncle, or legal guardian. Where a minor has a parent or guardian, as is usually true, the law does not prevent that minor from obtaining a violent video game with his parent's or guardian's help. In the typical case, the only speech affected is speech that bypasses a minor's parent or guardian. Because such speech does not fall within "the freedom of speech" as originally understood, California's law does not ordinarily implicate the First Amendment and is not facially unconstitutional.[8] . . .

I respectfully dissent.

JUSTICE BREYER, dissenting. . . .

California's law imposes no more than a modest restriction on expression. The statute prevents no one from playing a video game, it prevents no adult from buying a video game, and it prevents no child or adolescent from obtaining a game provided a parent is willing to help. All it prevents is a child or adolescent from buying, without a parent's assistance, a gruesomely violent video game of a kind that the industry *itself* tells us it wants to keep out of the hands of those under the age of 17. Nor is the statute, if upheld, likely to create a precedent that would adversely affect other media, say films, or videos, or books. A typical video game involves a significant amount of physical activity. And pushing buttons that achieve an interactive, virtual form of target practice (using images of human beings as targets), while containing an expressive component, is not just like watching a typical movie.

The interest that California advances in support of the statute is compelling. As this Court has previously described that interest, it consists of both (1) the "basic" parental claim "to authority in their own household to direct the rearing of their children," which makes it proper to enact "laws designed to aid discharge of [parental] responsibility," and (2) the State's "independent interest in the well-being of its youth." [Ginsberg v. New York (1968)]. And where these interests work in tandem, it is not fatally "underinclusive" for a State to advance its interests in protecting children against the special harms present in an

8. Whether the statute would survive an as-applied challenge in the unusual case of an emancipated minor is a question for another day. To decide this case, it is enough that the statute is not unconstitutional on its face.

interactive video game medium through a default rule that still allows parents to provide their children with what their parents wish. Both interests are present here. As to the need to help parents guide their children, the Court noted in 1968 that "'parental control or guidance cannot always be provided.'" Today, 5.3 million grade-school-age children of working parents are routinely home alone. Thus, it has, if anything, become more important to supplement parents' authority to guide their children's development. . . .

At the same time, there is considerable evidence that California's statute significantly furthers this compelling interest. That is, in part, because video games are excellent teaching tools. Learning a practical task often means developing habits, becoming accustomed to performing the task, and receiving positive reinforcement when performing that task well. Video games can help develop habits, accustom the player to performance of the task, and reward the player for performing that task well. Why else would the Armed Forces incorporate video games into its training?

When the military uses video games to help soldiers train for missions, it is using this medium for a beneficial purpose. But California argues that when the teaching features of video games are put to less desirable ends, harm can ensue. In particular, extremely violent games can harm children by rewarding them for being violently aggressive in play, and thereby often teaching them to be violently aggressive in life. And video games can cause more harm in this respect than can typically passive media, such as books or films or television programs.

There are many scientific studies that support California's views. . . .

The upshot is that California's statute, as applied to its heartland of applications (*i.e.,* buyers under 17; extremely violent, realistic video games), imposes a restriction on speech that is modest at most. That restriction is justified by a compelling interest (supplementing parents' efforts to prevent their children from purchasing potentially harmful violent, interactive material). And there is no equally effective, less restrictive alternative. California's statute is consequently constitutional on its face — though litigants remain free to challenge the statute as applied in particular instances, including any effort by the State to apply it to minors aged 17.

I add that the majority's different conclusion creates a serious anomaly in First Amendment law. *Ginsberg* makes clear that a State can prohibit the sale to minors of depictions of nudity; today the Court makes clear that a State cannot prohibit the sale to minors of the most violent interactive video games. But what sense does it make to forbid selling to a 13-year-old boy a magazine with an image of a nude woman, while protecting a sale to that 13-year-old of an interactive video game in which he actively, but virtually, binds and gags the woman, then tortures and kills her? What kind of First Amendment would permit the government to protect children by restricting sales of that extremely violent video game *only* when the woman — bound, gagged, tortured, and killed — is also topless?

This anomaly is not compelled by the First Amendment. It disappears once one recognizes that extreme violence, where interactive, and *without literary, artistic, or similar justification,* can prove at least as, if not more, harmful to children as photographs of nudity. And the record here is more than adequate to support such a view. That is why I believe that *Ginsberg* controls the outcome here *a fortiori*. And it is why I believe California's law is constitutional on its face.

This case is ultimately less about censorship than it is about education. Our Constitution cannot succeed in securing the liberties it seeks to protect unless we can raise future generations committed cooperatively to making our system of government work. Education, however, is about choices. Sometimes, children need to learn by making choices for themselves. Other times, choices are made for children—by their parents, by their teachers, and by the people acting democratically through their governments. In my view, the First Amendment does not disable government from helping parents make such a choice here—a choice not to have their children buy extremely violent, interactive video games, which they more than reasonably fear pose only the risk of harm to those children.

For these reasons, I respectfully dissent.

Chapter 20

The Right to Keep and Bear Arms

SECTION A: DOES THE SECOND AMENDMENT PROTECT AN INDIVIDUAL RIGHT?

ASSIGNMENT S-13

STUDY GUIDE: *What methods of interpretation are employed in* Heller? *Does Justice Scalia use the same interpretive approach here that he used in other cases, for example the Establishment Clause Cases? Does Justice Stevens' reliance on the "legislative history" signal a difference in his interpretive methodology than that of the majority? In assessing how the Constitution ought to be interpreted, does it matter whether* Miller *decided the nature of the right protected by the Second Amendment? On what basis does Justice Scalia limit the scope of the individual right he identifies? Does he use the same method as he does to identify the right itself? Should he? Justice Stevens says that the Amendment protects an individual right. Try writing out the individual right he has in mind. To what sort of case would it apply? Does the disagreement between Justices Scalia and Breyer about the appropriate "level of scrutiny" signal a deeper disagreement? Notice Justice Scalia's treatment of the Ninth Amendment as protecting an individual right. Can this be reconciled with his dissenting opinion in Troxel v. Granville (Chapter 15)? Finally, note that, long as it is, the following is excerpted from 157 pages of opinions, so much of interest and importance has been omitted.*

DISTRICT OF COLUMBIA v. HELLER

554 U.S. 570 (2008)

JUSTICE SCALIA delivered the opinion of the Court.

We consider whether a District of Columbia prohibition on the possession of usable handguns in the home violates the Second Amendment to the Constitution.

I

The District of Columbia generally prohibits the possession of handguns. It is a crime to carry an unregistered firearm, and the registration of handguns is prohibited. See D. C. Code §§7-2501.01(12), 7-2502.01(a), 7-2502.02(a)(4) (2001).... District of Columbia law also requires residents to keep their lawfully owned firearms, such as registered long guns, "unloaded and dissembled or bound by a trigger lock or similar device" unless they are located in a place of business or are being used for lawful recreational activities.

Respondent Dick Heller is a D. C. special police officer authorized to carry a handgun while on duty at the Federal Judicial Center. He applied for a registration certificate for a handgun that he wished to keep at home, but the District refused. He thereafter filed a lawsuit in the Federal District Court for the District of Columbia seeking, on Second Amendment grounds, to enjoin the city from enforcing the bar on the registration of handguns, the licensing requirement insofar as it prohibits the carrying of a firearm in the home without a license, and the trigger-lock requirement insofar as it prohibits the use of "functional firearms within the home." The District Court dismissed respondent's complaint. The Court of Appeals for the District of Columbia Circuit ... reversed. It held that the Second Amendment protects an individual right to possess firearms and that the city's total ban on handguns, as well as its requirement that firearms in the home be kept nonfunctional even when necessary for self-defense, violated that right.

We granted certiorari.

II

We turn first to the meaning of the Second Amendment.

A

The Second Amendment provides: "A well regulated Militia, being necessary to the security of a free State, the right of the people to keep and bear Arms, shall not be infringed." In interpreting this text, we are guided by the principle that "[t]he Constitution was written to be understood by the voters; its words and phrases were used in their normal and ordinary as distinguished from technical meaning." United States v. Sprague (1931); see also Gibbons v. Ogden (1824). Normal meaning may of course include an idiomatic meaning, but it excludes secret or technical meanings that would not have been known to ordinary citizens in the founding generation.

The two sides in this case have set out very different interpretations of the Amendment. Petitioners and today's dissenting Justices believe that it protects only the right to possess and carry a firearm in connection with militia service. Respondent argues that it protects an individual right to possess a firearm unconnected with service in a militia, and to use that arm for traditionally lawful purposes, such as self-defense within the home.

The Second Amendment is naturally divided into two parts: its prefatory clause and its operative clause. The former does not limit the latter grammatically, but rather announces a purpose. The Amendment could be rephrased, "Because a well regulated Militia is necessary to the security of a free State, the right of the people to keep and bear Arms shall not be infringed." Although this structure of the Second Amendment is unique in our Constitution, other legal documents of the founding era, particularly individual-rights provisions of state constitutions, commonly included a prefatory statement of purpose. See generally Volokh, The Commonplace Second Amendment, 73 N.Y.U. L. Rev. 793, 814-821 (1998).

Logic demands that there be a link between the stated purpose and the command. The Second Amendment would be nonsensical if it read, "A well regulated Militia, being necessary to the security of a free State, the right of the people to petition for redress of grievances shall not be infringed." That requirement of logical connection may cause a prefatory clause to resolve an ambiguity in the operative clause ("The separation of church and state being an important objective, the teachings of canons shall have no place in our jurisprudence." The preface makes clear that the operative clause refers not to canons of interpretation but to clergymen.) But apart from that clarifying function, a prefatory clause does not limit or expand the scope of the operative clause.[1] . . . Therefore, while we will begin our textual analysis with the operative clause, we will return to the prefatory clause to ensure that our reading of the operative clause is consistent with the announced purpose.[2]

1. Operative Clause

a. "Right of the People." The first salient feature of the operative clause is that it codifies a "right of the people." The unamended Constitution and the Bill of Rights use the phrase "right of the people" two other times, in the First Amendment's Assembly-and-Petition Clause and in the Fourth Amendment's Search-and-Seizure Clause. The Ninth Amendment uses very similar terminology ("The enumeration in the Constitution, of certain rights, shall not be construed to deny or disparage others retained by the people"). All three of these instances unambiguously refer to individual rights, not "collective" rights, or

1. . . . JUSTICE STEVENS says that we violate the general rule that every clause in a statute must have effect. But where the text of a clause itself indicates that it does not have operative effect, such as "whereas" clauses in federal legislation or the Constitution's preamble, a court has no license to make it do what it was not designed to do. Or to put the point differently, operative provisions should be given effect as operative provisions, and prologues as prologues.

2. JUSTICE STEVENS criticizes us for discussing the prologue last. But if a prologue can be used only to clarify an ambiguous operative provision, surely the first step must be to determine whether the operative provision is ambiguous. It might be argued, we suppose, that the prologue itself should be one of the factors that go into the determination of whether the operative provision is ambiguous — but that would cause the prologue to be used to produce ambiguity rather than just to resolve it. . . .

rights that may be exercised only through participation in some corporate body.[3]

Three provisions of the Constitution refer to "the people" in a context other than "rights"—the famous preamble ("We the people"), §2 of Article I (providing that "the people" will choose members of the House), and the Tenth Amendment (providing that those powers not given the Federal Government remain with "the States" or "the people"). Those provisions arguably refer to "the people" acting collectively—but they deal with the exercise or reservation of powers, not rights. Nowhere else in the Constitution does a "right" attributed to "the people" refer to anything other than an individual right.

What is more, in all six other provisions of the Constitution that mention "the people," the term unambiguously refers to all members of the political community, not an unspecified subset. As we said in United States v. Verdugo-Urquidez (1990):

> "'[T]he people' seems to have been a term of art employed in select parts of the Constitution. . . . [Its uses] sugges[t] that 'the people' protected by the Fourth Amendment, and by the First and Second Amendments, and to whom rights and powers are reserved in the Ninth and Tenth Amendments, refers to a class of persons who are part of a national community or who have otherwise developed sufficient connection with this country to be considered part of that community."

This contrasts markedly with the phrase "the militia" in the prefatory clause. As we will describe below, the "militia" in colonial America consisted of a subset of "the people"—those who were male, able bodied, and within a certain age range. Reading the Second Amendment as protecting only the right to "keep and bear Arms" in an organized militia therefore fits poorly with the operative clause's description of the holder of that right as "the people."

We start therefore with a strong presumption that the Second Amendment right is exercised individually and belongs to all Americans.

b. "Keep and bear Arms." We move now from the holder of the right—"the people"—to the substance of the right: "to keep and bear Arms."

Before addressing the verbs "keep" and "bear," we interpret their object: "Arms." The 18th-century meaning is no different from the meaning today. The 1773 edition of Samuel Johnson's dictionary defined "arms" as "weapons of offence, or armour of defence." 1 Dictionary of the English Language 107 (4th ed.) (hereinafter Johnson). Timothy Cunningham's important 1771 legal dictionary defined "arms" as "any thing that a man wears for his defence, or takes into his hands, or useth in wrath to cast at or strike another." 1 A New and

3. Justice Stevens is of course correct that the right to assemble cannot be exercised alone, but it is still an individual right, and not one conditioned upon membership in some defined "assembly," as he contends the right to bear arms is conditioned upon membership in a defined militia. And Justice Stevens is dead wrong to think that the right to petition is "primarily collective in nature." See McDonald v. Smith (1985) (describing historical origins of right to petition).

Complete Law Dictionary (1771); see also N. Webster, American Dictionary of the English Language (1828) (hereinafter Webster) (similar).

The term was applied, then as now, to weapons that were not specifically designed for military use and were not employed in a military capacity. For instance, Cunningham's legal dictionary gave as an example of usage: "Servants and labourers shall use bows and arrows on *Sundays,* &c. and not bear other arms." Although one founding-era thesaurus limited "arms" (as opposed to "weapons") to "instruments of offence *generally* made use of in war," even that source stated that all firearms constituted "arms." 1 J. Trusler, The Distinction Between Words Esteemed Synonymous in the English Language 37 (1794) (emphasis added).

Some have made the argument, bordering on the frivolous, that only those arms in existence in the 18th century are protected by the Second Amendment. We do not interpret constitutional rights that way. Just as the First Amendment protects modern forms of communications, and the Fourth Amendment applies to modern forms of search, the Second Amendment extends, prima facie, to all instruments that constitute bearable arms, even those that were not in existence at the time of the founding.

We turn to the phrases "keep arms" and "bear arms." Johnson defined "keep" as, most relevantly, "[t]o retain; not to lose," and "[t]o have in custody." Webster defined it as "[t]o hold; to retain in one's power or possession." No party has apprised us of an idiomatic meaning of "keep Arms." Thus, the most natural reading of "keep Arms" in the Second Amendment is to "have weapons."

The phrase "keep arms" was not prevalent in the written documents of the founding period that we have found, but there are a few examples, all of which favor viewing the right to "keep Arms" as an individual right unconnected with militia service. William Blackstone, for example, wrote that Catholics convicted of not attending service in the Church of England suffered certain penalties, one of which was that they were not permitted to "keep arms in their houses." 4 Commentaries on the Laws of England 55 (1769) (hereinafter Blackstone); see also 1 W. & M., c. 15, §4 (1689) ("[N]o Papist . . . shall or may have or keep in his House . . . any Arms . . ."). Petitioners point to militia laws of the founding period that required militia members to "keep" arms in connection with militia service, and they conclude from this that the phrase "keep Arms" has a militia-related connotation. This is rather like saying that, since there are many statutes that authorize aggrieved employees to "file complaints" with federal agencies, the phrase "file complaints" has an employment-related connotation. "Keep arms" was simply a common way of referring to possessing arms, for militiamen *and everyone else.*[4]

4. See, e.g., 3 A Compleat Collection of State-Tryals 185 (1719) ("Hath not every Subject power to keep Arms, as well as Servants in his House for defence of his Person?"); T. Wood, A New Institute of the Imperial or Civil Law 282 (1730) ("Those are guilty of *publick* Force, who keep Arms in their Houses, and make use of them otherwise than upon Journeys or Hunting, or for Sale . . ."); A Collection of All the Acts of Assembly, Now in Force, in the Colony of Virginia 596

At the time of the founding, as now, to "bear" meant to "carry." See Johnson; Webster; T. Sheridan, A Complete Dictionary of the English Language (1796); 2 Oxford English Dictionary 20 (2d ed. 1989). When used with "arms," however, the term has a meaning that refers to carrying for a particular purpose—confrontation. In Muscarello v. United States (1998), in the course of analyzing the meaning of "carries a firearm" in a federal criminal statute, JUSTICE GINSBURG wrote that "[s]urely a most familiar meaning is, as the Constitution's Second Amendment . . . indicate[s]: 'wear, bear, or carry . . . upon the person or in the clothing or in a pocket, for the purpose . . . of being armed and ready for offensive or defensive action in a case of conflict with another person.'" (dissenting opinion) (quoting Black's Law Dictionary (6th ed. 1998)). We think that JUSTICE GINSBURG accurately captured the natural meaning of "bear arms." Although the phrase implies that the carrying of the weapon is for the purpose of "offensive or defensive action," it in no way connotes participation in a structured military organization.

From our review of founding-era sources, we conclude that this natural meaning was also the meaning that "bear arms" had in the 18th century. In numerous instances, "bear arms" was unambiguously used to refer to the carrying of weapons outside of an organized militia. The most prominent examples are those most relevant to the Second Amendment: Nine state constitutional provisions written in the 18th century or the first two decades of the 19th, which enshrined a right of citizens to "bear arms in defense of themselves and the state" or "bear arms in defense of himself and the state."[5] It is clear from those

---

(1733) ("Free Negros, Mulattos, or Indians, and Owners of Slaves, seated at Frontier Plantations, may obtain Licence from a Justice of Peace, for keeping Arms, &c."); J. Ayliffe, A New Pandect of *Roman* Civil Law 195 (1734) ("Yet a Person might keep Arms in his House, or on his Estate, on the Account of Hunting, Navigation, Travelling, and on the Score of Selling them in the way of Trade or Commerce, or such Arms as accrued to him by way of Inheritance"); J. Trusler, A Concise View of the Common Law and Statute Law of England 270 (1781) ("if [papists] keep arms in their houses, such arms may be seized by a justice of the peace"); Some Considerations on the Game Laws 54 (1796) ("Who has been deprived by [the law] of keeping arms for his own defence? What law forbids the veriest pauper, if he can raise a sum sufficient for the purchase of it, from mounting his Gun on his Chimney Piece . . . ?"); 3 B. Wilson, The Works of the Honourable James Wilson 84 (1804) (with reference to state constitutional right: "This is one of our many renewals of the Saxon regulations. 'They were bound,' says Mr. Selden, 'to keep arms for the preservation of the kingdom, and of their own person'"); W. Duer, Outlines of the Constitutional Jurisprudence of the United States 31–32 (1833) (with reference to colonists' English rights: "The right of every individual to keep arms for his defence, suitable to his condition and degree; which was the public allowance, under due restrictions of the natural right of resistance and self-preservation"); 3 R. Burn, Justice of the Peace and the Parish Officer 88 (1815) ("It is, however, laid down by Serjeant Hawkins, . . . that if a lessee, after the end of the term, keep arms in his house to oppose the entry of the lessor, . . ."); State v. Dempsey, 31 N. C. 384, 385 (1849) (citing 1840 state law making it a misdemeanor for a member of certain racial groups "to carry about his person or keep in his house any shot gun or other arms").

5. See Pa. Declaration of Rights ("That the people have a right to bear arms for the defence of themselves and the state . . ."); Vt. Declaration of Rights ("That the people have a right to bear arms for the defence of themselves and the State . . ."); Ky. Const. (1792) ("That the right of the citizens to bear arms in defence of themselves and the State shall not be questioned"); Ohio Const. (1802)

formulations that "bear arms" did not refer only to carrying a weapon in an organized military unit. Justice James Wilson interpreted the Pennsylvania Constitution's arms-bearing right, for example, as a recognition of the natural right of defense "of one's person or house"—what he called the law of "self preservation." 2 Collected Works of James Wilson (citing Pa. Const., (1790)). . . . These provisions demonstrate—again, in the most analogous linguistic context—that "bear arms" was not limited to the carrying of arms in a militia.

The phrase "bear Arms" also had at the time of the founding an idiomatic meaning that was significantly different from its natural meaning: "to serve as a soldier, do military service, fight" or "to wage war." But it *unequivocally* bore that idiomatic meaning only when followed by the preposition "against," which was in turn followed by the target of the hostilities. See 2 Oxford 21. (That is how, for example, our Declaration of Independence ¶28, used the phrase: "He has constrained our fellow Citizens taken Captive on the high Seas to bear Arms against their Country. . . ."). Every example given by petitioners' *amici* for the idiomatic meaning of "bear arms" from the founding period either includes the preposition "against" or is not clearly idiomatic. . . .

In any event, the meaning of "bear arms" that petitioners and JUSTICE STEVENS propose is *not even* the (sometimes) idiomatic meaning. Rather, they manufacture a hybrid definition, whereby "bear arms" connotes the actual carrying of arms (and therefore is not really an idiom) but only in the service of an organized militia. No dictionary has ever adopted that definition, and we have been apprised of no source that indicates that it carried that meaning at the time of the founding. But it is easy to see why petitioners and the dissent are driven to the hybrid definition. Giving "bear Arms" its idiomatic meaning would cause the protected right to consist of the right to be a soldier or to wage war—an absurdity that no commentator has ever endorsed. Worse still, the phrase "keep and bear Arms" would be incoherent. The word "Arms" would have two different meanings at once: "weapons" (as the object of "keep") and (as the object of "bear") one-half of an idiom. It would be rather like saying "He filled and kicked the bucket" to mean "He filled the bucket and died." Grotesque.

Petitioners justify their limitation of "bear arms" to the military context by pointing out the unremarkable fact that it was often used in that context—the same mistake they made with respect to "keep arms." It is especially unremarkable that the phrase was often used in a military context in the federal legal sources (such as records of congressional debate) that have been the focus of

---

("That the people have a right to bear arms for the defence of themselves and the State . . ."); Ind. Const. (1816) ("That the people have a right to bear arms for the defense of themselves and the State . . ."); Miss. Const. (1817) ("Every citizen has a right to bear arms, in defence of himself and the State"); Conn. Const. (1818) ("Every citizen has a right to bear arms in defence of himself and the state"); Ala. Const. (1819) ("Every citizen has a right to bear arms in defence of himself and the State"); Mo. Const. (1820) ("[T]hat their right to bear arms in defence of themselves and of the State cannot be questioned"). See generally Volokh, State Constitutional Rights to Keep and Bear Arms, 11 Tex. Rev. L. & Politics 191 (2006).

petitioners' inquiry. Those sources would have had little occasion to use it *except* in discussions about the standing army and the militia. And the phrases used primarily in those military discussions include not only "bear arms" but also "carry arms," "possess arms," and "have arms"—though no one thinks that those other phrases also had special military meanings. See Barnett, Was the Right to Keep and Bear Arms Conditioned on Service in an Organized Militia?, 83 Tex. L. Rev. 237, 261 (2004). . . . Other legal sources frequently used "bear arms" in nonmilitary contexts.[6] Cunningham's legal dictionary, cited above, gave as an example of its usage a sentence unrelated to military affairs ("Servants and labourers shall use bows and arrows on *Sundays*, &c. and not bear other arms"). . . .

JUSTICE STEVENS points to a study by *amici* supposedly showing that the phrase "bear arms" was most frequently used in the military context. Of course, as we have said, the fact that the phrase was commonly used in a particular context does not show that it is limited to that context, and, in any event, we have given many sources where the phrase was used in nonmilitary contexts. Moreover, the study's collection appears to include (who knows how many times) the idiomatic phrase "bear arms against," which is irrelevant. The *amici* also dismiss examples such as "*bear arms . . . for the purpose of killing game*" because those uses are "expressly qualified." . . . That analysis is faulty. A purposive qualifying phrase that contradicts the word or phrase it modifies is unknown this side of the looking glass (except, apparently, in some courses on Linguistics). If "bear arms" means, as we think, simply the carrying of arms, a modifier can limit the purpose of the carriage ("for the purpose of self-defense" or "to make war against the King"). But if "bear arms" means, as the petitioners and the dissent think, the carrying of arms only for military purposes, one simply cannot add "for the purpose of killing game." The right "to carry arms in the militia for the purpose of killing game" is worthy of the mad hatter. Thus, these purposive

6. See J. Brydall, Privilegia Magnatud apud Anglos (1704) (Privilege XXXIII) ("In the 21st Year of King Edward the Third, a Proclamation Issued, that no Person should bear any Arms within London, and the Suburbs"); J. Bond, A Compleat Guide to Justices of the Peace (1707) ("Sheriffs, and all other Officers in executing their Offices, and all other persons pursuing Hu[e] and Cry may lawfully bear arms"); 1 An Abridgment of the Public Statutes in Force and Use Relative to Scotland (1755) (entry for "Arms" : "And if any person above described shall have in his custody, use, or bear arms, being thereof convicted before one justice of peace, or other judge competent, summarily, he shall for the first offense forfeit all such arms"); Statute Law of Scotland Abridged (2d ed. 1769) ("Acts for disarming the highlands" but "exempting those who have particular licenses to bear arms"); E. de Vattel, The Law of Nations, or, Principles of the Law of Nature (1792) ("Since custom has allowed persons of rank and gentlemen of the army to bear arms in time of peace, strict care should be taken that none but these should be allowed to wear swords"); E. Roche, Proceedings of a Court-Martial, Held at the Council-Chamber, in the City of Cork (1798) (charge VI: "With having held traitorous conferences, and with having conspired, with the like intent, for the purpose of attacking and despoiling of the arms of several of the King's subjects, qualified by law to bear arms"); C. Humphreys, A Compendium of the Common Law in force in Kentucky (1822) ("[I]n this country the constitution guaranties to all persons the right to bear arms; then it can only be a crime to exercise this right in such a manner, as to terrify people unnecessarily").

qualifying phrases positively establish that "to bear arms" is not limited to military use.[7]

JUSTICE STEVENS places great weight on James Madison's inclusion of a conscientious-objector clause in his original draft of the Second Amendment: "but no person religiously scrupulous of bearing arms, shall be compelled to render military service in person." He argues that this clause establishes that the drafters of the Second Amendment intended "bear Arms" to refer only to military service. It is always perilous to derive the meaning of an adopted provision from another provision deleted in the drafting process. In any case, what JUSTICE STEVENS would conclude from the deleted provision does not follow. It was not meant to exempt from military service those who objected to going to war but had no scruples about personal gunfights. Quakers opposed the use of arms not just for militia service, but for any violent purpose whatsoever—so much so that Quaker frontiersmen were forbidden to use arms to defend their families, even though "[i]n such circumstances the temptation to seize a hunting rifle or knife in self-defense . . . must sometimes have been almost overwhelming." P. Brock, Pacifism in the United States 359 (1968). The Pennsylvania Militia Act of 1757 exempted from service those "*scrupling the use of arms*"—a phrase that no one contends had an idiomatic meaning. Thus, the most natural interpretation of Madison's deleted text is that those opposed to carrying weapons for potential violent confrontation would not be "compelled to render military service," in which such carrying would be required.

Finally, JUSTICE STEVENS suggests that "keep and bear Arms" was some sort of term of art, presumably akin to "hue and cry" or "cease and desist." (This suggestion usefully evades the problem that there is no evidence whatsoever to support a military reading of "keep arms.") JUSTICE STEVENS believes that the unitary meaning of "keep and bear Arms" is established by the Second Amendment's calling it a "right" (singular) rather than "rights" (plural). There is nothing to this. State constitutions of the founding period routinely grouped multiple (related) guarantees under a singular "right," and the First Amendment protects the "right [singular] of the people peaceably to assemble, and to petition the Government for a redress of grievances." And even if "keep and bear Arms" were a unitary phrase, we find no evidence that it bore a military meaning.[8]

7. JUSTICE STEVENS contends that since we assert that adding "against" to "bear arms" gives it a military meaning we must concede that adding a purposive qualifying phrase to "bear arms" can alter its meaning. But the difference is that we do not maintain that "against" *alters* the meaning of "bear arms" but merely that it *clarifies* which of various meanings (one of which is military) is intended. JUSTICE STEVENS, however, argues that "[t]he term 'bear arms' is a familiar idiom; when used unadorned by any additional words, its meaning is 'to serve as a soldier, do military service, fight.'" He therefore must establish that adding a contradictory purposive phrase can *alter* a word's meaning.

8. Faced with this clear historical usage, JUSTICE STEVENS resorts to the bizarre argument that because the word "to" is not included before "bear" (whereas it is included before "petition" in the First Amendment), the unitary meaning of "to keep and bear" is established. We have never heard of the proposition that omitting repetition of the "to" causes two verbs with different meanings to become one. A promise "to support and to defend the Constitution of the United States" is not a whit different from a promise "to support and defend the Constitution of the United States."

Although the phrase was not at all common (which would be unusual for a term of art), we have found instances of its use with a clearly nonmilitary connotation. In a 1780 debate in the House of Lords, for example, Lord Richmond described an order to disarm private citizens (not militia members) as "a violation of the constitutional right of Protestant subjects to keep and bear arms for their own defense." In response, another member of Parliament referred to "the right of bearing arms for personal defence," making clear that no special military meaning for "keep and bear arms" was intended in the discussion.

c. Meaning of the Operative Clause. Putting all of these textual elements together, we find that they guarantee the individual right to possess and carry weapons in case of confrontation. This meaning is strongly confirmed by the historical background of the Second Amendment. We look to this because it has always been widely understood that the Second Amendment, like the First and Fourth Amendments, codified a *pre-existing* right. The very text of the Second Amendment implicitly recognizes the pre-existence of the right and declares only that it "shall not be infringed." As we said in United States v. Cruikshank (1876), "[t]his is not a right granted by the Constitution. Neither is it in any manner dependent upon that instrument for its existence. The Second amendment declares that it shall not be infringed. . . ."

Between the Restoration and the Glorious Revolution, the Stuart Kings Charles II and James II succeeded in using select militias loyal to them to suppress political dissidents, in part by disarming their opponents. See J. Malcolm, To Keep and Bear Arms (1994). Under the auspices of the 1671 Game Act, for example, the Catholic James II had ordered general disarmaments of regions home to his Protestant enemies. These experiences caused Englishmen to be extremely wary of concentrated military forces run by the state and to be jealous of their arms. They accordingly obtained an assurance from William and Mary, in the Declaration of Right (which was codified as the English Bill of Rights), that Protestants would never be disarmed: "That the subjects which are Protestants may have arms for their defense suitable to their conditions and as allowed by law." (1689). This right has long been understood to be the predecessor to our Second Amendment. It was clearly an individual right, having nothing whatever to do with service in a militia. To be sure, it was an individual right not available to the whole population, given that it was restricted to Protestants, and like all written English rights it was held only against the Crown, not Parliament. But it was secured to them as individuals, according to "libertarian political principles," not as members of a fighting force.

By the time of the founding, the right to have arms had become fundamental for English subjects. Blackstone . . . cited the arms provision of the Bill of Rights as one of the fundamental rights of Englishmen. See 1 Blackstone 136, 139-140 (1765). His description of it cannot possibly be thought to tie it to militia or military service. It was, he said, "the natural right of resistance and self-preservation," and "the right of having and using arms for self-preservation and defence." Other contemporary authorities concurred. Thus, the right secured in 1689 as a result of the Stuarts' abuses was by the time of the founding understood to be an individual right protecting against both public and private violence.

And, of course, what the Stuarts had tried to do to their political enemies, George III had tried to do to the colonists. In the tumultuous decades of the 1760's and 1770's, the Crown began to disarm the inhabitants of the most rebellious areas. That provoked polemical reactions by Americans invoking their rights as Englishmen to keep arms. A New York article of April 1769 said that "[i]t is a natural right which the people have reserved to themselves, confirmed by the Bill of Rights, to keep arms for their own defence." They understood the right to enable individuals to defend themselves. As the most important early American edition of Blackstone's Commentaries (by the law professor and former Antifederalist St. George Tucker) made clear in the notes to the description of the arms right, Americans understood the "right of self-preservation" as permitting a citizen to "repe[l] force by force" when "the intervention of society in his behalf, may be too late to prevent an injury." Blackstone's Commentaries (1803) (hereinafter Tucker's Blackstone).

There seems to us no doubt, on the basis of both text and history, that the Second Amendment conferred an individual right to keep and bear arms. Of course the right was not unlimited, just as the First Amendment's right of free speech was not, see, e.g., United States v. Williams (2008). Thus, we do not read the Second Amendment to protect the right of citizens to carry arms for any sort of confrontation, just as we do not read the First Amendment to protect the right of citizens to speak for any purpose. Before turning to limitations upon the individual right, however, we must determine whether the prefatory clause of the Second Amendment comports with our interpretation of the operative clause.

2. Prefatory Clause

The prefatory clause reads: "A well regulated Militia, being necessary to the security of a free State. . . ."

a. "Well-Regulated Militia." In United States v. Miller (1939), we explained that "the Militia comprised all males physically capable of acting in concert for the common defense." That definition comports with founding-era sources. See, e.g., Webster ("The militia of a country are the able bodied men organized into companies, regiments and brigades . . . and required by law to attend military exercises on certain days only, but at other times left to pursue their usual occupations"); The Federalist No. 46 (J. Madison) ("near half a million of citizens with arms in their hands"); Letter to Destutt de Tracy (Jan. 26, 1811), in The Portable Thomas Jefferson ("[T]he militia of the State, that is to say, of every man in it able to bear arms").

Petitioners take a seemingly narrower view of the militia, stating that "[m]ilitias are the state- and congressionally-regulated military forces described in the Militia Clauses (art. I, §8)." Although we agree with petitioners' interpretive assumption that "militia" means the same thing in Article I and the

Second Amendment, we believe that petitioners identify the wrong thing, namely, the organized militia. Unlike armies and navies, which Congress is given the power to create ("to raise . . . Armies"; "to provide . . . a Navy," Art. I, §8), the militia is assumed by Article I already to be *in existence*. Congress is given the power to "provide for calling forth the militia," §8; and the power not to create, but to "organiz[e]" it — and not to organize "a" militia, which is what one would expect if the militia were to be a federal creation, but to organize "the" militia, connoting a body already in existence. This is fully consistent with the ordinary definition of the militia as all able-bodied men. From that pool, Congress has plenary power to organize the units that will make up an effective fighting force. That is what Congress did in the first militia Act, which specified that "each and every free able-bodied white male citizen of the respective states, resident therein, who is or shall be of the age of eighteen years, and under the age of forty-five years (except as is herein after excepted) shall severally and respectively be enrolled in the militia." Act of May 8, 1792. To be sure, Congress need not conscript every able-bodied man into the militia, because nothing in Article I suggests that in exercising its power to organize, discipline, and arm the militia, Congress must focus upon the entire body. Although the militia consists of all able-bodied men, the federally organized militia may consist of a subset of them.

Finally, the adjective "well-regulated" implies nothing more than the imposition of proper discipline and training. See Johnson ("Regulate": "To adjust by rule or method"); cf. Va. Declaration of Rights (1776) (referring to "a well-regulated militia, composed of the body of the people, trained to arms").

b. "Security of a Free State." The phrase "security of a free state" meant "security of a free polity," not security of each of the several States. . . . Joseph Story wrote in his treatise on the Constitution that "the word 'state' is used in various senses [and in] its most enlarged sense, it means the people composing a particular nation or community." 1 Story §208; see also 3 *id.*, §1890 (in reference to the Second Amendment's prefatory clause: "The militia is the natural defence of a free country"). It is true that the term "State" elsewhere in the Constitution refers to individual States, but the phrase "security of a free state" and close variations seem to have been terms of art in 18th-century political discourse, meaning a "'free country'" or free polity. See Volokh, "Necessary to the Security of a Free State," 83 Notre Dame L. Rev. 1, 5 (2007). Moreover, the other instances of "state" in the Constitution are typically accompanied by modifiers making clear that the reference is to the several States — "each state," "several states," "any state," "that state," "particular states," "one state," "no state." And the presence of the term "foreign state" in Article I and Article III shows that the word "state" did not have a single meaning in the Constitution.

There are many reasons why the militia was thought to be "necessary to the security of a free state." First, of course, it is useful in repelling invasions and suppressing insurrections. Second, it renders large standing armies unnecessary — an argument that Alexander Hamilton made in favor of federal control over the militia. Third, when the able-bodied men of a nation are trained in arms and organized, they are better able to resist tyranny.

3. Relationship between Prefatory Clause and Operative Clause

We reach the question, then: Does the preface fit with an operative clause that creates an individual right to keep and bear arms? It fits perfectly, once one knows the history that the founding generation knew and that we have described above. That history showed that the way tyrants had eliminated a militia consisting of all the able-bodied men was not by banning the militia but simply by taking away the people's arms, enabling a select militia or standing army to suppress political opponents. This is what had occurred in England that prompted codification of the right to have arms in the English Bill of Rights.

The debate with respect to the right to keep and bear arms, as with other guarantees in the Bill of Rights, was not over whether it was desirable (all agreed that it was) but over whether it needed to be codified in the Constitution. During the 1788 ratification debates, the fear that the federal government would disarm the people in order to impose rule through a standing army or select militia was pervasive in Antifederalist rhetoric. John Smilie, for example, worried not only that Congress's "command of the militia" could be used to create a "select militia," or to have "no militia at all," but also, as a separate concern, that "[w]hen a select militia is formed; the people in general may be disarmed." Federalists responded that because Congress was given no power to abridge the ancient right of individuals to keep and bear arms, such a force could never oppress the people. It was understood across the political spectrum that the right helped to secure the ideal of a citizen militia, which might be necessary to oppose an oppressive military force if the constitutional order broke down.

It is therefore entirely sensible that the Second Amendment's prefatory clause announces the purpose for which the right was codified: to prevent elimination of the militia. The prefatory clause does not suggest that preserving the militia was the only reason Americans valued the ancient right; most undoubtedly thought it even more important for self-defense and hunting. But the threat that the new Federal Government would destroy the citizens' militia by taking away their arms was the reason that right—unlike some other English rights—was codified in a written Constitution. . . .

[P]etitioners' interpretation does not even achieve the narrower purpose that prompted codification of the right. If, as they believe, the Second Amendment right is no more than the right to keep and use weapons as a member of an organized militia—if, that is, the *organized* militia is the sole institutional beneficiary of the Second Amendment's guarantee—it does not assure the existence of a "citizens' militia" as a safeguard against tyranny. For Congress retains plenary authority to organize the militia, which must include the authority to say who will belong to the organized force. That is why the first Militia Act's requirement that only whites enroll caused States to amend their militia laws to exclude free blacks. Thus, if petitioners are correct, the Second Amendment protects citizens' right to use a gun in an organization from which Congress has plenary authority to exclude them. It guarantees a select militia of the sort the Stuart kings found useful, but not the people's militia that was the concern of the founding generation. . . .

[Discussion of contemporaneous state constitutions omitted.]

C

JUSTICE STEVENS relies on the drafting history of the Second Amendment—the various proposals in the state conventions and the debates in Congress. It is dubious to rely on such history to interpret a text that was widely understood to codify a pre-existing right, rather than to fashion a new one. But even assuming that this legislative history is relevant, JUSTICE STEVENS flatly misreads the historical record.

It is true, as JUSTICE STEVENS says, that there was concern that the Federal Government would abolish the institution of the state militia. That concern found expression, however, *not* in the various Second Amendment precursors proposed in the State conventions, but in separate structural provisions that would have given the States concurrent and seemingly nonpreemptible authority to organize, discipline, and arm the militia when the Federal Government failed to do so. The Second Amendment precursors, by contrast, referred to the individual English right already codified in two (and probably four) State constitutions. The Federalist-dominated first Congress chose to reject virtually all major structural revisions favored by the Antifederalists, including the proposed militia amendments. Rather, it adopted primarily the popular and uncontroversial (though, in the Federalists' view, unnecessary) individual-rights amendments. The Second Amendment right, protecting only individuals' liberty to keep and carry arms, did nothing to assuage Antifederalists' concerns about federal control of the militia.

JUSTICE STEVENS thinks it significant that the Virginia, New York, and North Carolina Second Amendment proposals were "embedded . . . within a group of principles that are distinctly military in meaning," such as statements about the danger of standing armies. But so was the highly influential minority proposal in Pennsylvania, yet that proposal, with its reference to hunting, plainly referred to an individual right. Other than that erroneous point, JUSTICE STEVENS has brought forward absolutely no evidence that those proposals conferred only a right to carry arms in a militia. By contrast, New Hampshire's proposal, the Pennsylvania minority's proposal, and Samuel Adams' proposal in Massachusetts unequivocally referred to individual rights, as did two state constitutional provisions at the time. JUSTICE STEVENS' view thus relies on the proposition, unsupported by any evidence, that different people of the founding period had vastly different conceptions of the right to keep and bear arms. That simply does not comport with our longstanding view that the Bill of Rights codified venerable, widely understood liberties.

D

We now address how the Second Amendment was interpreted from immediately after its ratification through the end of the 19th century. Before proceeding, however, we take issue with JUSTICE STEVENS' equating of these sources with post enactment legislative history, a comparison that betrays a fundamental misunderstanding of a court's interpretive task. "Legislative history," of course, refers to the pre-enactment statements of those who drafted or voted for a law; it is considered persuasive by some, not because they reflect the general understanding of the disputed terms, but because the legislators who heard or read those statements presumably voted with that understanding. "Postenactment legislative history," a deprecatory contradiction in terms, refers to statements of those who drafted or voted for the law that are made after its enactment and hence could have had no effect on the congressional vote. It most certainly does not refer to the examination of a variety of legal and other sources to determine *the public understanding* of a legal text in the period after its enactment or ratification. That sort of inquiry is a critical tool of constitutional interpretation. As we will show, virtually all interpreters of the Second Amendment in the century after its enactment interpreted the amendment as we do.

1. Post-ratification Commentary

Three important founding-era legal scholars interpreted the Second Amendment in published writings. All three understood it to protect an individual right unconnected with militia service.

St. George Tucker's version of Blackstone's Commentaries, as we explained above, conceived of the Blackstonian arms right as necessary for self-defense. He equated that right, absent the religious and class-based restrictions, with the Second Amendment. In Note D, entitled, "View of the Constitution of the United States," Tucker elaborated on the Second Amendment: "This may be considered as the true palladium of liberty. . . . The right to self-defence is the first law of nature: in most governments it has been the study of rulers to confine the right within the narrowest limits possible. Wherever standing armies are kept up, and the right of the people to keep and bear arms is, under any colour or pretext whatsoever, prohibited, liberty, if not already annihilated, is on the brink of destruction." (ellipsis in original). He believed that the English game laws had abridged the right by prohibiting "keeping a gun or other engine for the destruction of game." He later grouped the right with some of the individual rights included in the First Amendment and said that if "a law be passed by congress, prohibiting" any of those rights, it would "be the province of the judiciary to pronounce whether any such act were constitutional, or not; and if not, to acquit the accused. . . ." It is unlikely that Tucker was referring to a person's being "accused" of violating a law making it a crime to bear arms in a state militia.[9]

[Discussion of William Rawle and Joseph Story omitted.]

9. JUSTICE STEVENS quotes some of Tucker's unpublished notes, which he claims show that Tucker had ambiguous views about the Second Amendment. But it is clear from the notes that Tucker located the power of States to arm their militias in the Tenth Amendment, and that he cited the Second Amendment for the proposition that such armament could not run afoul of any power of the federal government (since the amendment prohibits Congress from ordering disarmament). Nothing in the passage implies that the Second Amendment pertains only to the carrying of arms in the organized militia.

Antislavery advocates routinely invoked the right to bear arms for self-defense. Joel Tiffany, for example, citing Blackstone's description of the right, wrote that "the right to keep and bear arms, also implies the right to use them if necessary in self defence; without this right to use the guaranty would have hardly been worth the paper it consumed." A Treatise on the Unconstitutionality of American Slavery (1849); see also L. Spooner, The Unconstitutionality of Slavery 116 (1845) (right enables "personal defence"). In his famous Senate speech about the 1856 "Bleeding Kansas" conflict, Charles Sumner proclaimed:

> The rifle has ever been the companion of the pioneer and, under God, his tutelary protector against the red man and the beast of the forest. Never was this efficient weapon more needed in just self-defence, than now in Kansas, and at least one article in our National Constitution must be blotted out, before the complete right to it can in any way be impeached. And yet such is the madness of the hour, that, in defiance of the solemn guarantee, embodied in the Amendments to the Constitution, that 'the right of the people to keep and bear arms shall not be infringed,' the people of Kansas have been arraigned for keeping and bearing them, and the Senator from South Carolina has had the face to say openly, on this floor, that they should be disarmed — of course, that the fanatics of Slavery, his allies and constituents, may meet no impediment.

We have found only one early 19th-century commentator who clearly conditioned the right to keep and bear arms upon service in the militia — and he recognized that the prevailing view was to the contrary. "The provision of the constitution, declaring the right of the people to keep and bear arms, &c. was probably intended to apply to the right of the people to bear arms for such [militia-related] purposes only, and not to prevent congress or the legislatures of the different states from enacting laws to prevent the citizens from always going armed. A different construction however has been given to it." B. Oliver, The Rights of an American Citizen 177 (1832). . . .

III

Like most rights, the right secured by the Second Amendment is not unlimited. From Blackstone through the 19th-century cases, commentators and courts routinely explained that the right was not a right to keep and carry any weapon whatsoever in any manner whatsoever and for whatever purpose. For example, the majority of the 19th-century courts to consider the question held that prohibitions on carrying concealed weapons were lawful under the Second Amendment or state analogues. Although we do not undertake an exhaustive historical analysis today of the full scope of the Second Amendment, nothing in our opinion should be taken to cast doubt on longstanding prohibitions on the possession of firearms by felons and the mentally ill, or laws forbidding the carrying of firearms in sensitive places such as schools and government buildings, or laws imposing conditions and qualifications on the commercial sale of arms.[10]

10. We identify these presumptively lawful regulatory measures only as examples; our list does not purport to be exhaustive.

We also recognize another important limitation on the right to keep and carry arms. *Miller* said, as we have explained, that the sorts of weapons protected were those "in common use at the time." We think that limitation is fairly supported by the historical tradition of prohibiting the carrying of "dangerous and unusual weapons." See 4 Blackstone 148-149 (1769); 3 B. Wilson, Works of the Honourable James Wilson 79 (1804). . . .

It may be objected that if weapons that are most useful in military service — M-16 rifles and the like — may be banned, then the Second Amendment right is completely detached from the prefatory clause. But as we have said, the conception of the militia at the time of the Second Amendment's ratification was the body of all citizens capable of military service, who would bring the sorts of lawful weapons that they possessed at home to militia duty. It may well be true today that a militia, to be as effective as militias in the 18th century, would require sophisticated arms that are highly unusual in society at large. Indeed, it may be true that no amount of small arms could be useful against modern-day bombers and tanks. But the fact that modern developments have limited the degree of fit between the prefatory clause and the protected right cannot change our interpretation of the right.

IV

We turn finally to the law at issue here. As we have said, the law totally bans handgun possession in the home. It also requires that any lawful firearm in the home be disassembled or bound by a trigger lock at all times, rendering it inoperable.

As the quotations earlier in this opinion demonstrate, the inherent right of self-defense has been central to the Second Amendment right. The handgun ban amounts to a prohibition of an entire class of "arms" that is overwhelmingly chosen by American society for that lawful purpose. The prohibition extends, moreover, to the home, where the need for defense of self, family, and property is most acute. Under any of the standards of scrutiny that we have applied to enumerated constitutional rights,[11] banning from the home "the most preferred firearm in the nation to 'keep' and use for protection of one's home and family," would fail constitutional muster.

11. Justice Breyer correctly notes that this law, like almost all laws, would pass rational-basis scrutiny. But rational-basis scrutiny is a mode of analysis we have used when evaluating laws under constitutional commands that are themselves prohibitions on irrational laws. In those cases, "rational basis" is not just the standard of scrutiny, but the very substance of the constitutional guarantee. Obviously, the same test could not be used to evaluate the extent to which a legislature may regulate a specific, enumerated right, be it the freedom of speech, the guarantee against double jeopardy, the right to counsel, or the right to keep and bear arms. See United States v. Carolene Products Co. n. 4 (1938) ("There may be narrower scope for operation of the presumption of constitutionality [*i.e.*, narrower than that provided by rational-basis review] when legislation appears on its face to be within a specific prohibition of the Constitution, such as those of the first ten amendments . . ."). If all that was required to overcome the right to keep and bear arms was a rational basis, the Second Amendment would be redundant with the separate constitutional prohibitions on irrational laws, and would have no effect.

Few laws in the history of our Nation have come close to the severe restriction of the District's handgun ban. . . . It is no answer to say, as petitioners do, that it is permissible to ban the possession of handguns so long as the possession of other firearms (*i.e.*, long guns) is allowed. It is enough to note, as we have observed, that the American people have considered the handgun to be the quintessential self-defense weapon. There are many reasons that a citizen may prefer a handgun for home defense: It is easier to store in a location that is readily accessible in an emergency; it cannot easily be redirected or wrestled away by an attacker; it is easier to use for those without the upper-body strength to lift and aim a long gun; it can be pointed at a burglar with one hand while the other hand dials the police. Whatever the reason, handguns are the most popular weapon chosen by Americans for self-defense in the home, and a complete prohibition of their use is invalid.

We must also address the District's requirement (as applied to respondent's handgun) that firearms in the home be rendered and kept inoperable at all times. This makes it impossible for citizens to use them for the core lawful purpose of self-defense and is hence unconstitutional. . . .

JUSTICE BREYER has devoted most of his separate dissent to the handgun ban. . . . He criticizes us for declining to establish a level of scrutiny for evaluating Second Amendment restrictions. He proposes, explicitly at least, none of the traditionally expressed levels (strict scrutiny, intermediate scrutiny, rational basis), but rather a judge-empowering "interest-balancing inquiry" that "asks whether the statute burdens a protected interest in a way or to an extent that is out of proportion to the statute's salutary effects upon other important governmental interests." After an exhaustive discussion of the arguments for and against gun control, JUSTICE BREYER arrives at his interest-balanced answer: because handgun violence is a problem, because the law is limited to an urban area, and because there were somewhat similar restrictions in the founding period (a false proposition that we have already discussed [omitted from this excerpt]), the interest-balancing inquiry results in the constitutionality of the handgun ban. QED.

We know of no other enumerated constitutional right whose core protection has been subjected to a freestanding "interest-balancing" approach. The very enumeration of the right takes out of the hands of government—even the Third Branch of Government—the power to decide on a case-by-case basis whether the right is *really worth* insisting upon. A constitutional guarantee subject to future judges' assessments of its usefulness is no constitutional guarantee at all. Constitutional rights are enshrined with the scope they were understood to have when the people adopted them, whether or not future legislatures or (yes) even future judges think that scope too broad. We would not apply an "interest-balancing" approach to the prohibition of a peaceful neo-Nazi march through Skokie. See National Socialist Party of America v. Skokie (1977) (*per curiam*). The First Amendment contains the freedom-of-speech guarantee that the people ratified, which included exceptions for obscenity, libel, and disclosure of state secrets, but not for the expression of extremely unpopular and wrong-headed views. The Second Amendment is no different. Like the First, it is the very *product* of an interest-balancing by the people — which JUSTICE BREYER would now conduct for them anew. And whatever else it leaves to future evaluation, it surely elevates above all other interests the right of law-abiding, responsible citizens to use arms in defense of hearth and home. . . .

In sum, we hold that the District's ban on handgun possession in the home violates the Second Amendment, as does its prohibition against rendering any lawful firearm in the home operable for the purpose of immediate self-defense. Assuming that Heller is not disqualified from the exercise of Second Amendment rights, the District must permit him to register his handgun and must issue him a license to carry it in the home.

* * *

We are aware of the problem of handgun violence in this country, and we take seriously the concerns raised by the many *amici* who believe that prohibition of handgun ownership is a solution. The Constitution leaves the District of Columbia a variety of tools for combating that problem, including some measures regulating handguns. But the enshrinement of constitutional rights necessarily takes certain policy choices off the table. These include the absolute prohibition of handguns held and used for self-defense in the home. Undoubtedly some think that the Second Amendment is outmoded in a society where our standing army is the pride of our Nation, where well-trained police forces provide personal security, and where gun violence is a serious problem. That is perhaps debatable, but what is not debatable is that it is not the role of this Court to pronounce the Second Amendment extinct.

We affirm the judgment of the Court of Appeals.

It is so ordered.

JUSTICE STEVENS, with whom JUSTICE SOUTER, JUSTICE GINSBURG, and JUSTICE BREYER join, dissenting.

The question presented by this case is not whether the Second Amendment protects a "collective right" or an "individual right." Surely it protects a right that can be enforced by individuals. But a conclusion that the Second Amendment protects an individual right does not tell us anything about the scope of that right.

Guns are used to hunt, for self-defense, to commit crimes, for sporting activities, and to perform military duties. The Second Amendment plainly does not protect the right to use a gun to rob a bank; it is equally clear that it does encompass the right to use weapons for certain military purposes. Whether it also protects the right to possess and use guns for nonmilitary purposes like hunting and personal self-defense is the question presented by this case. . . .

I

The text of the Second Amendment is brief. It provides: "A well regulated Militia, being necessary to the security of a free State, the right of the people to keep and bear Arms, shall not be infringed."

Three portions of that text merit special focus: the introductory language defining the Amendment's purpose, the class of persons encompassed within its reach, and the unitary nature of the right that it protects.

"A well regulated Militia, being necessary to the security of a free State"

The preamble to the Second Amendment makes three important points. It identifies the preservation of the militia as the Amendment's purpose; it explains that the militia is necessary to the security of a free State; and it recognizes that the militia must be "well regulated." . . . In all three respects it is comparable to provisions in several State Declarations of Rights that were adopted roughly contemporaneously with the Declaration of Independence.[12] Those state provisions highlight the importance members of the founding generation attached to the maintenance of state militias; they also underscore the profound fear shared by many in that era of the dangers posed by standing armies. While the need for state militias has not been a matter of significant public interest for almost two centuries, that fact should not obscure the contemporary concerns that animated the Framers.

The parallels between the Second Amendment and these state declarations, and the Second Amendment's omission of any statement of purpose related to the right to use firearms for hunting or personal self-defense, is especially striking in light of the fact that the Declarations of Rights of Pennsylvania and Vermont *did* expressly protect such civilian uses at the time. Article XIII of Pennsylvania's 1776 Declaration of Rights announced that "the people have a right to bear arms for the defence *of themselves* and the state," (emphasis added); §43 of the Declaration assured that "the inhabitants of this state shall have the liberty to fowl and hunt in seasonable times on the lands they hold, and on all other lands therein not inclosed." And Article XV of the 1777 Vermont Declaration of Rights guaranteed "[t]hat the people have a right to bear arms for the defence *of themselves* and the State." (emphasis added). The contrast

12. The Virginia Declaration of Rights (1776), provided: "That a well-regulated militia, composed of the body of the people, trained to arms, is the proper, natural, and safe defence of a free State; that Standing Armies, in time of peace, should be avoided, as dangerous to liberty; and that, in all cases, the military should be under strict subordination to, and governed by, the civil power." Maryland's Declaration of Rights (1776), provided: "That a well-regulated militia is the proper and natural defence of a free government"; "That standing armies are dangerous to liberty, and ought not to be raised or kept up, without consent of the Legislature"; "That in all cases, and at all times, the military ought to be under strict subordination to and control of the civil power." Delaware's Declaration of Rights (1776), provided: "That a well regulated militia is the proper, natural, and safe defence of a free government"; "That standing armies are dangerous to liberty, and ought not to be raised or kept up without the consent of the Legislature"; "That in all cases and at all times the military ought to be under strict subordination to and governed by the civil power." Finally, New Hampshire's Bill of Rights (1783), read: "A well regulated militia is the proper, natural, and sure defence of a state"; "Standing armies are dangerous to liberty, and ought not to be raised or kept up without consent of the legislature"; "In all cases, and at all times, the military ought to be under strict subordination to, and governed by the civil power." It elsewhere provided: "No person who is conscientiously scrupulous about the lawfulness of bearing arms, shall be compelled thereto, provided he will pay an equivalent."

between those two declarations and the Second Amendment reinforces the clear statement of purpose announced in the Amendment's preamble. It confirms that the Framers' single-minded focus in crafting the constitutional guarantee "to keep and bear arms" was on military uses of firearms, which they viewed in the context of service in state militias.

The preamble thus both sets forth the object of the Amendment and informs the meaning of the remainder of its text. Such text should not be treated as mere surplusage, for "[i]t cannot be presumed that any clause in the constitution is intended to be without effect." Marbury v. Madison (1803).

The Court today tries to denigrate the importance of this clause of the Amendment by beginning its analysis with the Amendment's operative provision and returning to the preamble merely "to ensure that our reading of the operative clause is consistent with the announced purpose." That is not how this Court ordinarily reads such texts, and it is not how the preamble would have been viewed at the time the Amendment was adopted. While the Court makes the novel suggestion that it need only find some "logical connection" between the preamble and the operative provision, it does acknowledge that a prefatory clause may resolve an ambiguity in the text. Without identifying any language in the text that even mentions civilian uses of firearms, the Court proceeds to "find" its preferred reading in what is at best an ambiguous text, and then concludes that its reading is not foreclosed by the preamble. Perhaps the Court's approach to the text is acceptable advocacy, but it is surely an unusual approach for judges to follow.

"The right of the people"

The centerpiece of the Court's textual argument is its insistence that the words "the people" as used in the Second Amendment must have the same meaning, and protect the same class of individuals, as when they are used in the First and Fourth Amendments. According to the Court, in all three provisions — as well as the Constitution's preamble, section 2 of Article I, and the Tenth Amendment — "the term unambiguously refers to all members of the political community, not an unspecified subset." But the Court *itself* reads the Second Amendment to protect a "subset" significantly narrower than the class of persons protected by the First and Fourth Amendments; when it finally drills down on the substantive meaning of the Second Amendment, the Court limits the protected class to "law-abiding, responsible citizens." But the class of persons protected by the First and Fourth Amendments is not so limited; for even felons (and presumably irresponsible citizens as well) may invoke the protections of those constitutional provisions. The Court offers no way to harmonize its conflicting pronouncements.

The Court also overlooks the significance of the way the Framers used the phrase "the people" in these constitutional provisions. In the First Amendment, no words define the class of individuals entitled to speak, to publish, or to worship; in that Amendment it is only the right peaceably to assemble, and to petition the Government for a redress of grievances, that is described as a right of "the people." These rights contemplate collective action. While the right peaceably to assemble protects the individual rights of those persons participating in the assembly, its concern is with action engaged in by members of a group, rather than any single individual. Likewise, although the act of petitioning the Government is a right that can be exercised by individuals, it is primarily collective in nature. For if they are to be effective, petitions must involve groups of individuals acting in concert.

Similarly, the words "the people" in the Second Amendment refer back to the object announced in the Amendment's preamble. They remind us that it is the collective action of individuals having a duty to serve in the militia that the text directly protects and, perhaps more importantly, that the ultimate purpose of the Amendment was to protect the States' share of the divided sovereignty created by the Constitution.

As used in the Fourth Amendment, "the people" describes the class of persons protected from unreasonable searches and seizures by Government officials. It is true that the Fourth Amendment describes a right that need not be exercised in any collective sense. But that observation does not settle the meaning of the phrase "the people" when used in the Second Amendment. For, as we have seen, the phrase means something quite different in the Petition and Assembly Clauses of the First Amendment. Although the abstract definition of the phrase "the people" could carry the same meaning in the Second Amendment as in the Fourth Amendment, the preamble of the Second Amendment suggests that the uses of the phrase in the First and Second Amendments are the same in referring to a collective activity. By way of contrast, the Fourth Amendment describes a right *against* governmental interference rather than an affirmative right to engage in protected conduct, and so refers to a right to protect a purely individual interest. As used in the Second Amendment, the words "the people" do not enlarge the right to keep and bear arms to encompass use or ownership of weapons outside the context of service in a well-regulated militia.

"To keep and bear Arms"

Although the Court's discussion of these words treats them as two "phrases"—as if they read "to keep" and "to bear"—they describe a unitary right: to possess arms if needed for military purposes and to use them in conjunction with military activities.

As a threshold matter, it is worth pausing to note an oddity in the Court's interpretation of "to keep and bear arms." Unlike the Court of Appeals, the Court does not read that phrase to create a right to possess arms for "lawful, private purposes." Instead, the Court limits the Amendment's protection to the right "to possess and carry weapons in case of confrontation." No party or *amicus* urged this interpretation; the Court appears to have fashioned it out of whole cloth. But although this novel limitation lacks support in the text of the Amendment, the Amendment's text *does* justify a different limitation: the "right to keep and bear arms" protects only a right to possess and use firearms in connection with service in a state-organized militia.

The term "bear arms" is a familiar idiom; when used unadorned by any additional words, its meaning is "to serve as a soldier, do military service, fight." 1 Oxford English Dictionary 634 (2d ed. 1989). It is derived from the Latin *arma ferre*, which, translated literally, means "to bear [*ferre*] war equipment [*arma*]." Brief for Professors of Linguistics and English as *Amici Curiae*. One 18th-century dictionary defined "arms" as "weapons of offence, or armour of defence," 1 S. Johnson, A Dictionary of the English Language (1755), and another contemporaneous source explained that "[b]y *arms*, we understand those instruments of offence generally made use of in war; such as firearms, swords, & c. By *weapons*, we more particularly mean instruments of other kinds (exclusive of fire-arms), made use of as offensive, on special occasions." 1 J. Trusler, The Distinction Between Words Esteemed Synonymous in the English Language (1794).[13] Had the Framers wished to expand the meaning of the phrase "bear arms" to encompass civilian possession and use, they could have done so by the addition of phrases such as "for the defense of themselves," as was done in the Pennsylvania and Vermont Declarations of Rights. The *unmodified* use of "bear arms," by contrast, refers most naturally to a military purpose, as evidenced by its use in literally dozens of contemporary texts.[14] The absence of any reference to civilian uses of weapons tailors the text of the Amendment to the purpose identified in its preamble. But when discussing these words, the Court simply ignores the preamble.

The Court argues that a "qualifying phrase that contradicts the word or phrase it modifies is unknown this side of the looking glass." But this fundamentally fails to grasp the point. The stand-alone phrase "bear arms" most naturally conveys a military meaning *unless* the addition of a qualifying phrase signals that a different meaning is intended. When, as in this case, there is no such qualifier, the most natural meaning is the military one; and, in the absence of any qualifier, it is all the more appropriate to look to the preamble to confirm the

13. The Court's repeated citation to the dissenting opinion in Muscarello v. United States (1998), as illuminating the meaning of "bear arms," borders on the risible. At issue in *Muscarello* was the proper construction of the word "carries" in 18 U.S.C. §924(c); the dissent in that case made passing reference to the Second Amendment only in the course of observing that both the Constitution and Black's Law Dictionary suggested that something more active than placement of a gun in a glove compartment might be meant by the phrase "carries a firearm."

14. *Amici* professors of Linguistics and English reviewed uses of the term "bear arms" in a compilation of books, pamphlets, and other sources disseminated in the period between the Declaration of Independence and the adoption of the Second Amendment [and] . . . determined that of 115 texts that employed the term, all but five usages were in a clearly military context, and in four of the remaining five instances, further qualifying language conveyed a different meaning.

The Court allows that the phrase "bear Arms" did have as an idiomatic meaning, "to serve as a soldier, do military service, fight," but asserts that it "*unequivocally* bore that idiomatic meaning only when followed by the preposition 'against,' which was in turn followed by the target of the hostilities." But contemporary sources make clear that the phrase "bear arms" was often used to convey a military meaning without those additional words. See, e.g., To The Printer, Providence Gazette, (May 27, 1775) ("By the common estimate of three millions of people in America, allowing one in five to bear arms, there will be found 600,000 fighting men") . . . [5 additional examples omitted].

natural meaning of the text. The Court's objection is particularly puzzling in light of its own contention that the addition of the modifier "against" changes the meaning of "bear arms."

The Amendment's use of the term "keep" in no way contradicts the military meaning conveyed by the phrase "bear arms" and the Amendment's preamble. To the contrary, a number of state militia laws in effect at the time of the Second Amendment's drafting used the term "keep" to describe the requirement that militia members store their arms at their homes, ready to be used for service when necessary.[15] The Virginia military law, for example, ordered that "every one of the said officers, non-commissioned officers, and privates, shall constantly *keep* the aforesaid arms, accoutrements, and ammunition, ready to be produced whenever called for by his commanding officer." Act for Regulating and Disciplining the Militia, 1785 (emphasis added). "[K]eep and bear arms" thus perfectly describes the responsibilities of a framing-era militia member. . . . Different language surely would have been used to protect nonmilitary use and possession of weapons from regulation if such an intent had played any role in the drafting of the Amendment.

* * *

When each word in the text is given full effect, the Amendment is most naturally read to secure to the people a right to use and possess arms in conjunction with service in a well-regulated militia. So far as appears, no more than that was contemplated by its drafters or is encompassed within its terms. Even if the meaning of the text were genuinely susceptible to more than one interpretation, the burden would remain on those advocating a departure from the purpose identified in the preamble and from settled law to come forward with persuasive new arguments or evidence. The textual analysis offered by respondent and embraced by the Court falls far short of sustaining that heavy burden.[16] And the Court's emphatic reliance on the claim "that the Second Amendment . . . codified a *pre-existing* right," is of course beside the point because the right to keep and bear arms for service in a state militia was also a pre-existing right.

Indeed, not a word in the constitutional text even arguably supports the Court's overwrought and novel description of the Second Amendment as

15. The Court notes that the First Amendment protects two separate rights with the phrase "the 'right [singular] of the people peaceably to assemble, and to petition the Government for a redress of grievances.'" But this only proves the point: In contrast to the language quoted by the Court, the Second Amendment does not protect a "right to keep *and to* bear arms," but rather a "right to keep and bear arms." . . .

16. The Court's atomistic, word-by-word approach to construing the Amendment calls to mind the parable of the six blind men and the elephant, famously set in verse by John Godfrey Saxe. In the parable, each blind man approaches a single elephant; touching a different part of the elephant's body in isolation, each concludes that he has learned its true nature. One touches the animal's leg, and concludes that the elephant is like a tree; another touches the trunk and decides that the elephant is like a snake; and so on. Each of them, of course, has fundamentally failed to grasp the nature of the creature.

"elevat[ing] above all other interests" "the right of law-abiding, responsible citizens to use arms in defense of hearth and home."

II

The proper allocation of military power in the new Nation was an issue of central concern for the Framers. The compromises they ultimately reached, reflected in Article I's Militia Clauses and the Second Amendment, represent quintessential examples of the Framers' "splitting the atom of sovereignty." [U.S. Term Limits, Inc. v. Thornton (1995) (KENNEDY, J., concurring)].

Two themes relevant to our current interpretive task ran through the debates on the original Constitution. "On the one hand, there was a widespread fear that a national standing Army posed an intolerable threat to individual liberty and to the sovereignty of the separate States." Perpich v. Department of Defense (1990).[17] . . . On the other hand, the Framers recognized the dangers inherent in relying on inadequately trained militia members "as the primary means of providing for the common defense," *Perpich*. . . . [18] In order to respond to those twin concerns, a compromise was reached: Congress would be authorized to raise and support a national Army and Navy, and also to organize, arm, discipline, and provide for the calling forth of "the Militia." U. S. Const., Art. I, §8. The President, at the same time, was empowered as the "Commander in Chief of the Army and Navy of the United States, and of the Militia of the several States, when called into the actual Service of the United States." Art. II, §2. But, with respect to the militia, a significant reservation was made to the States: Although Congress would have the power to call forth, organize, arm, and discipline the militia, as well as to govern "such Part of them as may be employed in the Service of the United States," the States respectively would retain the right to appoint the officers and to train the militia in accordance with the discipline prescribed by Congress. Art. I, §8.

But the original Constitution's retention of the militia and its creation of divided authority over that body did not prove sufficient to allay fears about the dangers posed by a standing army. For it was perceived by some that Article I contained a significant gap: While it empowered Congress to organize, arm, and discipline the militia, it did not prevent Congress from providing for the militia's

17. Indeed, this was one of the grievances voiced by the colonists: Paragraph 13 of the Declaration of Independence charged of King George, "He has kept among us, in times of peace, Standing Armies without the Consent of our legislatures."

18. George Washington, writing to Congress on September 24, 1776, warned that for Congress "[t]o place any dependance upon Militia, is, assuredly, resting upon a broken staff." . . . And Alexander Hamilton argued this view in many debates. In 1787, he wrote:

> Here I expect we shall be told that the militia of the country is its natural bulwark, and would be at all times equal to the national defense. This doctrine, in substance, had like to have lost us our independence. . . . War, like most other things, is a science to be acquired and perfected by diligence, by perseverance, by time, and by practice.

The Federalist No. 25.

*dis*armament. As George Mason argued during the debates in Virginia on the ratification of the original Constitution:

> The militia may be here destroyed by that method which has been practiced in other parts of the world before; that is, by rendering them useless — by disarming them. Under various pretences, Congress may neglect to provide for arming and disciplining the militia; and the state governments cannot do it, for Congress has the exclusive right to arm them.

This sentiment was echoed at a number of state ratification conventions; indeed, it was one of the primary objections to the original Constitution voiced by its opponents. The Anti-Federalists were ultimately unsuccessful in persuading state ratification conventions to condition their approval of the Constitution upon the eventual inclusion of any particular amendment. But a number of States did propose to the first Federal Congress amendments reflecting a desire to ensure that the institution of the militia would remain protected under the new Government. The proposed amendments sent by the States of Virginia, North Carolina, and New York focused on the importance of preserving the state militias and reiterated the dangers posed by standing armies. New Hampshire sent a proposal that differed significantly from the others; while also invoking the dangers of a standing army, it suggested that the Constitution should more broadly protect the use and possession of weapons, without tying such a guarantee expressly to the maintenance of the militia. The States of Maryland, Pennsylvania, and Massachusetts sent no relevant proposed amendments to Congress, but in each of those States a minority of the delegates advocated related amendments. While the Maryland minority proposals were exclusively concerned with standing armies and conscientious objectors, the unsuccessful proposals in both Massachusetts and Pennsylvania would have protected a more broadly worded right, less clearly tied to service in a state militia. Faced with all of these options, it is telling that James Madison chose to craft the Second Amendment as he did.

The relevant proposals sent by the Virginia Ratifying Convention read as follows:

> 17th, That the people have a right to keep and bear arms; that a well regulated Militia composed of the body of the people trained to arms is the proper, natural and safe defence of a free State. That standing armies are dangerous to liberty, and therefore ought to be avoided, as far as the circumstances and protection of the Community will admit; and that in all cases the military should be under strict subordination to and be governed by the civil power.
>
> 19th. That any person religiously scrupulous of bearing arms ought to be exempted, upon payment of an equivalent to employ another to bear arms in his stead.

North Carolina adopted Virginia's proposals and sent them to Congress as its own, although it did not actually ratify the original Constitution until Congress had sent the proposed Bill of Rights to the States for ratification.

New York produced a proposal with nearly identical language. It read:

> That the people have a right to keep and bear Arms; that a well regulated Militia, including the body of the People capable of bearing Arms, is the proper, natural, and safe defence of a free State. . . . That standing Armies, in time of Peace, are dangerous to Liberty, and ought not to be kept up, except in Cases of necessity; and that at all times, the Military should be kept under strict Subordination to the civil Power.

Notably, each of these proposals used the phrase "keep and bear arms," which was eventually adopted by Madison. And each proposal embedded the phrase within a group of principles that are distinctly military in meaning.

By contrast, New Hampshire's proposal, although it followed another proposed amendment that echoed the familiar concern about standing armies, described the protection involved in more clearly personal terms. Its proposal read:

> *Twelfth*, Congress shall never disarm any Citizen unless such as are or have been in Actual Rebellion.

The proposals considered in the other three States, although ultimately rejected by their respective ratification conventions, are also relevant to our historical inquiry. First, the Maryland proposal, endorsed by a minority of the delegates and later circulated in pamphlet form, read:

> 4. That no standing army shall be kept up in time of peace, unless with the consent of two thirds of the members present of each branch of Congress. . . .
>
> 10. That no person conscientiously scrupulous of bearing arms in any case, shall be compelled personally to serve as a soldier.

The rejected Pennsylvania proposal, which was later incorporated into a critique of the Constitution titled "The Address and Reasons of Dissent of the Pennsylvania Minority of the Convention of the State of Pennsylvania to Their Constituents (1787)," signed by a minority of the State's delegates (those who had voted against ratification of the Constitution), read:

> 7. That the people have a right to bear arms for the defense of themselves and their own State, or the United States, or for the purpose of killing game; and no law shall be passed for disarming the people or any of them unless for crimes committed, or real danger of public injury from individuals; and as standing armies in the time of peace are dangerous to liberty, they ought not to be kept up; and that the military shall be kept under strict subordination to, and be governed by the civil powers.

Finally, after the delegates at the Massachusetts Ratification Convention had compiled a list of proposed amendments and alterations, a motion was made to add to the list the following language: "[T]hat the said Constitution never be construed to authorize Congress to . . . prevent the people of the United States, who are peaceable citizens, from keeping their own arms." This motion, however, failed to achieve the necessary support, and the proposal was excluded from the list of amendments the State sent to Congress.

Madison, charged with the task of assembling the proposals for amendments sent by the ratifying States, was the principal draftsman of the Second Amendment. He had before him, or at the very least would have been aware of, all of these proposed formulations. In addition, Madison had been a member, some years earlier, of the committee tasked with drafting the Virginia Declaration of Rights. That committee considered a proposal by Thomas Jefferson that would have included within the Virginia Declaration the following language: "No freeman shall ever be debarred the use of arms [within his own lands or tenements]." But the committee rejected that language, adopting instead the provision drafted by George Mason.[19]

With all of these sources upon which to draw, it is strikingly significant that Madison's first draft omitted any mention of nonmilitary use or possession of weapons. Rather, his original draft repeated the essence of the two proposed amendments sent by Virginia, combining the substance of the two provisions succinctly into one, which read: "The right of the people to keep and bear arms shall not be infringed; a well armed, and well regulated militia being the best security of a free country; but no person religiously scrupulous of bearing arms, shall be compelled to render military service in person."

Madison's decision to model the Second Amendment on the distinctly military Virginia proposal is therefore revealing, since it is clear that he considered and rejected formulations that would have unambiguously protected civilian uses of firearms. When Madison prepared his first draft, and when that draft was debated and modified, it is reasonable to assume that all participants in the drafting process were fully aware of the other formulations that would have protected civilian use and possession of weapons and that their choice to craft the Amendment as they did represented a rejection of those alternative formulations.

Madison's initial inclusion of an exemption for conscientious objectors sheds revelatory light on the purpose of the Amendment. It confirms an intent to describe a duty as well as a right, and it unequivocally identifies the military character of both. The objections voiced to the conscientious-objector clause only confirm the central meaning of the text. Although records of the debate in the Senate, which is where the conscientious-objector clause was removed, do not survive, the arguments raised in the House illuminate the perceived problems with the clause: Specifically, there was concern that Congress "can declare who are those religiously scrupulous, and prevent them from bearing arms."[20] The ultimate removal of the clause, therefore, only serves to confirm the purpose of

19. The adopted language, Virginia Declaration of Rights ¶13 (1776), read as follows: "That a well-regulated Militia, composed of the body of the people, trained to arms, is the proper, natural, and safe defence of a free State; that Standing Armies, in time of peace, should be avoided as dangerous to liberty; and that, in all cases, the military should be under strict subordination to, and governed by, the civil power."

20. This was the objection voiced by Elbridge Gerry, who went on to remark, in the next breath: "What, sir, is the use of a militia? It is to prevent the establishment of a standing army, the bane of liberty. . . . Whenever government mean to invade the rights and liberties of the people, they always attempt to destroy the militia, in order to raise an army upon their ruins."

the Amendment—to protect against congressional disarmament, by whatever means, of the States' militias.

The Court also contends that because "Quakers opposed the use of arms not just for militia service, but for any violent purpose whatsoever," the inclusion of a conscientious-objector clause in the original draft of the Amendment does not support the conclusion that the phrase "bear arms" was military in meaning. But that claim cannot be squared with the record. In the proposals cited [above], both Virginia and North Carolina included the following language: "That any person religiously scrupulous of bearing arms ought to be exempted, upon payment of an equivalent *to employ another to bear arms in his stead*" (emphasis added). There is no plausible argument that the use of "bear arms" in those provisions was not unequivocally and exclusively military: The State simply does not compel its citizens to carry arms for the purpose of private "confrontation," or for self-defense.

The history of the adoption of the Amendment thus describes an overriding concern about the potential threat to state sovereignty that a federal standing army would pose, and a desire to protect the States' militias as the means by which to guard against that danger. But state militias could not effectively check the prospect of a federal standing army so long as Congress retained the power to disarm them, and so a guarantee against such disarmament was needed. . . . The evidence plainly refutes the claim that the Amendment was motivated by the Framers' fears that Congress might act to regulate any civilian uses of weapons. And even if the historical record were genuinely ambiguous, the burden would remain on the parties advocating a change in the law to introduce facts or arguments "newly ascertained"; the Court is unable to identify any such facts or arguments. . . .

V

The Court concludes its opinion by declaring that it is not the proper role of this Court to change the meaning of rights "enshrine[d]" in the Constitution. But the right the Court announces was not "enshrined" in the Second Amendment by the Framers; it is the product of today's law-changing decision. The majority's exegesis has utterly failed to establish that as a matter of text or history, "the right of law-abiding, responsible citizens to use arms in defense of hearth and home" is "elevate[d] above all other interests" by the Second Amendment.

Until today, it has been understood that legislatures may regulate the civilian use and misuse of firearms so long as they do not interfere with the preservation of a well-regulated militia. The Court's announcement of a new constitutional right to own and use firearms for private purposes upsets that settled understanding, but leaves for future cases the formidable task of defining the scope of permissible regulations. Today judicial craftsmen have confidently asserted that a policy choice that denies a "law-abiding, responsible citize[n]" the right to keep and use weapons in the home for self-defense is "off the table." Given the presumption that most citizens are law abiding, and the reality that the need to defend oneself may suddenly arise in a host of locations outside the home, I fear that the District's policy choice may well be just the first of an unknown number of dominoes to be knocked off the table.

I do not know whether today's decision will increase the labor of federal judges to the "breaking point" envisioned by Justice Cardozo, but it will surely give rise to a far more active judicial role in making vitally important national policy decisions than was envisioned at any time in the 18th, 19th, or 20th centuries.

The Court properly disclaims any interest in evaluating the wisdom of the specific policy choice challenged in this case, but it fails to pay heed to a far more important policy choice — the choice made by the Framers themselves. The Court would have us believe that over 200 years ago, the Framers made a choice to limit the tools available to elected officials wishing to regulate civilian uses of weapons, and to authorize this Court to use the common-law process of case-by-case judicial lawmaking to define the contours of acceptable gun control policy. Absent compelling evidence that is nowhere to be found in the Court's opinion, I could not possibly conclude that the Framers made such a choice.

For these reasons, I respectfully dissent.

JUSTICE BREYER, with whom JUSTICE STEVENS, JUSTICE SOUTER, and JUSTICE GINSBURG join, dissenting.

We must decide whether a District of Columbia law that prohibits the possession of handguns in the home violates the Second Amendment. The majority, relying upon its view that the Second Amendment seeks to protect a right of personal self-defense, holds that this law violates that Amendment. In my view, it does not.

The majority's conclusion is wrong for two independent reasons. The first reason is that set forth by JUSTICE STEVENS — namely, that the Second Amendment protects militia-related, not self-defense-related, interests. . . . The second independent reason is that the protection the Amendment provides is not absolute. The Amendment permits government to regulate the interests that it serves. Thus, irrespective of what those interests are — whether they do or do not include an independent interest in self-defense — the majority's view cannot be correct unless it can show that the District's regulation is unreasonable or inappropriate in Second Amendment terms. This the majority cannot do. . . . In this opinion . . . I shall show that the District's law is consistent with the Second Amendment even if that Amendment is interpreted as protecting a wholly separate interest in individual self-defense. That is so because the District's regulation, which focuses upon the presence of handguns in high-crime urban areas, represents a permissible legislative response to a serious, indeed life-threatening, problem.

Thus I here assume that one objective (but, as the majority concedes, not the *primary* objective) of those who wrote the Second Amendment was to help assure citizens that they would have arms available for purposes of self-defense. Even so, a legislature could reasonably conclude that the law will advance goals of great public importance, namely, saving lives, preventing injury, and reducing crime. The law is tailored to the urban crime problem in that it is local in scope and thus affects only a geographic area both limited in size and entirely urban; the law concerns handguns, which are specially linked to urban gun deaths and injuries, and which are the overwhelmingly favorite weapon of armed criminals; and at the same time, the law imposes a burden upon gun owners that seems proportionately no greater than restrictions in existence at the time the Second Amendment was adopted. In these circumstances, the District's law falls within the zone that the Second Amendment leaves open to regulation by legislatures. . . .

How is a court to determine whether a particular firearm regulation (here, the District's restriction on handguns) is consistent with the Second Amendment? What kind of constitutional standard should the court use? How high a protective hurdle does the Amendment erect?

The question matters. The majority is wrong when it says that the District's law is unconstitutional "[u]nder any of the standards of scrutiny that we have applied to enumerated constitutional rights." How could that be? It certainly would not be unconstitutional under, for example, a "rational basis" standard, which requires a court to uphold regulation so long as it bears a "rational relationship" to a "legitimate governmental purpose." The law at issue here, which in part seeks to prevent gun-related accidents, at least bears a "rational relationship" to that "legitimate" life-saving objective. . . .

Respondent proposes that the Court adopt a "strict scrutiny" test, which would require reviewing with care each gun law to determine whether it is "narrowly tailored to achieve a compelling governmental interest." But the majority implicitly, and appropriately, rejects that suggestion by broadly approving a set of laws—prohibitions on concealed weapons, forfeiture by criminals of the Second Amendment right, prohibitions on firearms in certain locales, and governmental regulation of commercial firearm sales—whose constitutionality under a strict scrutiny standard would be far from clear.

Indeed, adoption of a true strict-scrutiny standard for evaluating gun regulations would be impossible. That is because almost every gun-control regulation will seek to advance (as the one here does) a "primary concern of every government—a concern for the safety and indeed the lives of its citizens." United States v. Salerno (1987). The Court has deemed that interest, as well as "the Government's general interest in preventing crime," to be "compelling," and the Court has in a wide variety of constitutional contexts found such public-safety concerns sufficiently forceful to justify restrictions on individual liberties, see, e.g., Brandenburg v. Ohio (1969) (*per curiam*) (First Amendment free speech rights); Sherbert v. Verner (1963) (First Amendment religious rights). . . . Thus, any attempt in theory to apply strict scrutiny to gun regulations will in practice turn into an interest-balancing inquiry, with the interests protected by the Second Amendment on one side and the governmental public-safety concerns on the other, the only question being whether the regulation at issue impermissibly burdens the former in the course of advancing the latter.

I would simply adopt such an interest-balancing inquiry explicitly. The fact that important interests lie on both sides of the constitutional equation suggests that review of gun-control regulation is not a context in which a court should effectively presume either constitutionality (as in rational-basis review) or unconstitutionality (as in strict scrutiny). Rather, "where a law significantly implicates competing constitutionally protected interests in complex ways," the Court generally asks whether the statute burdens a protected interest in a way or to an extent that is out of proportion to the statute's salutary effects upon other important governmental interests. Any answer would take account both of the statute's effects upon the competing interests and the existence of any clearly superior less restrictive alternative. Contrary to the majority's unsupported suggestion that this sort of "proportionality" approach is unprecedented, the Court has applied it in various constitutional contexts, including election-law cases, speech cases, and due process cases.

In applying this kind of standard the Court normally defers to a legislature's empirical judgment in matters where a legislature is likely to have greater expertise and greater institutional factfinding capacity. Nonetheless, a court, not a legislature, must make the ultimate constitutional conclusion, exercising its "independent judicial judgment" in light of the whole record to determine whether a law exceeds constitutional boundaries.

The above-described approach seems preferable to a more rigid approach here for a further reason. Experience as much as logic has led the Court to decide that in one area of constitutional law or another the interests are likely to prove stronger on one side of a typical constitutional case than on the other. See, e.g., United States v. Virginia (1996) (applying heightened scrutiny to gender-based classifications, based upon experience with prior cases); Williamson v. Lee Optical of Okla., Inc. (1955) (applying rational-basis scrutiny to economic legislation, based upon experience with prior cases). Here, we have little prior experience. Courts that *do* have experience in these matters have uniformly taken an approach that treats empirically-based legislative judgment with a degree of deference. See Winkler, Scrutinizing the Second Amendment, 105 Mich. L. Rev. 683, 687, 716-718 (2007) (describing hundreds of gun-law decisions issued in the last half-century by Supreme Courts in 42 States, which courts with "surprisingly little variation," have adopted a standard more deferential than strict scrutiny). While these state cases obviously are not controlling, they are instructive. And they thus provide some comfort regarding the practical wisdom of following the approach that I believe our constitutional precedent would in any event suggest. . . .

In weighing needs and burdens, we must take account of the possibility that there are reasonable, but less restrictive alternatives. Are there *other* potential measures that might similarly promote the same goals while imposing lesser restrictions? Here I see none.

The reason there is no clearly superior, less restrictive alternative to the District's handgun ban is that the ban's very objective is to reduce significantly the number of handguns in the District, say, for example, by allowing a law enforcement officer immediately to assume that *any* handgun he sees is an *illegal* handgun. And there is no plausible way to achieve that objective other than to ban the guns. . . . [A]ny measure less restrictive in respect to the use of handguns for self-defense will, to that same extent, prove less effective in preventing the use of handguns for illicit purposes. If a resident has a handgun in the home that he can use for self-defense, then he has a handgun in the home that he can use to commit suicide or engage in acts of domestic violence. If it is indeed the case, as the District believes, that the number of guns contributes to the number of gun-related crimes, accidents, and deaths, then, although there may be *less restrictive*, less effective substitutes for an outright ban, there is no less restrictive *equivalent* of an outright ban.

Licensing restrictions would not similarly reduce the handgun population, and the District may reasonably fear that even if guns are initially restricted to law-abiding citizens, they might be stolen and thereby placed in the hands of criminals. Permitting certain types of handguns, but not others, would affect the commercial market for handguns, but not their availability. And requiring safety devices such as trigger locks, or imposing safe-storage requirements would interfere with any self-defense interest while simultaneously leaving operable weapons in the hands of owners (or others capable of acquiring the weapon and disabling the safety device) who might use them for domestic violence or other crimes. . . .

The upshot is that the District's objectives are compelling; its predictive judgments as to its law's tendency to achieve those objectives are adequately supported; the law does impose a burden upon any self-defense interest that the Amendment seeks to secure; and there is no clear less restrictive alternative. I turn now to the final portion of the "permissible regulation" question: Does the District's law *disproportionately* burden Amendment-protected interests? . . . [T]he District law is tailored to the life-threatening problems it attempts to address. The law concerns one class of weapons, handguns, leaving residents free to possess shotguns and rifles, along with ammunition. The area that falls within its scope is totally urban. That urban area suffers from a serious handgun-fatality problem. The District's law directly aims at that compelling problem. And there is no less restrictive way to achieve the problem-related benefits that it seeks. . . .

The majority derides my approach as "judge-empowering." I take this criticism seriously, but I do not think it accurate. As I have previously explained, this is an approach that the Court has taken in other areas of constitutional law. Application of such an approach, of course, requires judgment, but the very nature of the approach — requiring careful identification of the relevant interests and evaluating the law's effect upon them — limits the judge's choices; and the method's necessary transparency lays bare the judge's reasoning for all to see and to criticize.

The majority's methodology is, in my view, substantially less transparent than mine. At a minimum, I find it difficult to understand the reasoning that seems to underlie certain conclusions that it reaches. . . . [It is not] at all clear to me how the majority decides *which* loaded "arms" a homeowner may keep. The majority says that that Amendment protects those weapons "typically possessed by law-abiding citizens for lawful purposes." This definition conveniently excludes machineguns, but permits handguns, which the majority describes as "the most popular weapon chosen by Americans for self-defense in the home." But what sense does this approach make? According to the majority's reasoning, if Congress and the States lift restrictions on the possession and use of machineguns, and people buy machineguns to protect their homes, the Court will have to reverse course and find that the Second Amendment *does*, in fact, protect the individual self-defense-related right to possess a machinegun. On the majority's reasoning, if tomorrow someone invents a particularly useful, highly dangerous self-defense weapon, Congress and the States had better ban it immediately, for once it becomes popular Congress will no longer possess the constitutional authority to do so. In essence, the majority determines what regulations are permissible by looking to see what existing regulations permit. There is no basis for believing that the Framers intended such circular reasoning. . . .

At the same time the majority ignores a more important question: Given the purposes for which the Framers enacted the Second Amendment, how should it be applied to modern-day circumstances that they could not have anticipated? Assume, for argument's sake, that the Framers did intend the Amendment to offer a degree of self-defense protection. Does that mean that the Framers also intended to guarantee a right to possess a loaded gun near swimming pools, parks, and playgrounds? That they would not have cared about the children who might pick up a loaded gun on their parents' bedside table? That they (who certainly showed concern for the risk of fire) would have lacked concern for the risk of accidental deaths or suicides that readily accessible loaded handguns in urban areas might bring? Unless we believe that they intended future generations to ignore such matters, answering questions such as the questions in this case requires judgment—judicial judgment exercised within a framework for constitutional analysis that guides that judgment and which makes its exercise transparent. One cannot answer those questions by combining inconclusive historical research with judicial *ipse dixit*.

The argument about method, however, is by far the less important argument surrounding today's decision. Far more important are the unfortunate consequences that today's decision is likely to spawn. Not least of these, as I have said, is the fact that the decision threatens to throw into doubt the constitutionality of gun laws throughout the United States. I can find no sound legal basis for launching the courts on so formidable and potentially dangerous a mission. In my view, there simply is no untouchable constitutional right guaranteed by the Second Amendment to keep loaded handguns in the house in crime-ridden urban areas.

For these reasons, I conclude that the District's measure is a proportionate, not a disproportionate, response to the compelling concerns that led the District to adopt it. And, for these reasons as well as the independently sufficient reasons set forth by JUSTICE STEVENS, I would find the District's measure consistent with the Second Amendment's demands.

With respect, I dissent.

SECTION B: DOES THE INDIVIDUAL RIGHT TO KEEP AND BEAR ARMS APPLY TO STAATES?

ASSIGNMENT S-14

McDonald v. City of Chicago provides a useful culmination of all the themes developed in Part III concerning constitutional rights: the nature and scope of the rights included in the Bill of Rights, their application to the states, and how the text should be interpreted. The opinions discuss the doctrine of "fundamental rights" under the Due Process Clauses and highlight the difference between this doctrine and an assessment of the original meaning of the text. In addition, Justice Thomas provides an exhaustive account of the original meaning of the Privileges or Immunities Clause of the Fourteenth Amendment.

STUDY GUIDE*: When reading the following opinions, pay attention to how history is being used to identify a right as "fundamental" and whether this is the same thing as identifying the original meaning of the text. How do the two sides define the right at issue? Is the outcome of this case consistent with the original meaning of the Fourteenth Amendment? Is Justice Alito employing an original meaning methodology? If not, why does he so extensively discuss historical evidence? How does his approach differ from that of Justice Thomas? What reasons does Justice Alito give for declining to apply the Privileges or Immunities Clause? When Justice Alito writes, "[w]e take no position with respect to this academic debate," to what "academic debate" is he referring? Do you agree that this debate can be avoided? Why does Justice Thomas not accept the Due Process Clause theory of the plurality? Note how he explains the relevance of certain evidence for assessing original public meaning. How does Justice Stevens propose that "substantive due process" cases be decided? Is that method in any tension with his discussion of the meaning of the Second Amendment? Is there any irony in the fact that his seemingly more capacious analysis of "liberty" in the Due Process Clause leads him to* deny *the claim of liberty being asserted here, whereas a more historical approach leads to the protection of a liberty? Notice his shift from "liberty" to "liberty interest," which doctrinally receives the most minimal judicial scrutiny. If you support the recognition of an individual right, how do you respond to Justice Breyer's description of the empirical issues raised by gun regulations? Is there any tension between his invocation of state experimentation and his dissenting opinions in the Commerce Clause cases of* Lopez *and* Morrison *(Chapter 9)? Does this debate reveal anything about the merits of identifying whether a right is "deeply rooted in the nation's history and tradition," as compared with identifying the original meaning of the text?*

McDONALD v. CITY OF CHICAGO

561 U.S. _____ (2010)

JUSTICE ALITO announced the judgment of the Court and delivered the opinion of the Court with respect to Parts I, II–A, II–B, II–D, III–A, and III–B, in which THE CHIEF JUSTICE, JUSTICE SCALIA, JUSTICE KENNEDY, and JUSTICE THOMAS join, and an opinion with respect to Parts II–C, IV, and V, in which THE CHIEF JUSTICE, JUSTICE SCALIA, and JUSTICE KENNEDY join.

Two years ago, in District of Columbia v. Heller (2008), we held that the Second Amendment protects the right to keep and bear arms for the purpose of self-defense, and we struck down a District of Columbia law that banned the possession of handguns in the home. The city of Chicago (City) and the village of Oak Park, a Chicago suburb, have laws that are similar to the District of Columbia's, but Chicago and Oak Park argue that their laws are constitutional because the Second Amendment has no application to the States. We have previously held that most of the provisions of the Bill of Rights apply with full force to both the Federal Government and the States. Applying the standard that is well established in our case law, we hold that the Second Amendment right is fully applicable to the States.

I

[Chicago petitioners] are Chicago residents who would like to keep handguns in their homes for self defense but are prohibited from doing so by Chicago's firearms laws. A City ordinance provides that "[n]o person shall . . . possess . . . any firearm unless such person is the holder of a valid registration certificate for such firearm." The Code then prohibits registration of most handguns, thus effectively banning handgun possession by almost all private citizens who reside in the City. . . . Chicago enacted its handgun ban to protect its residents "from the loss of property and injury or death from firearms." The Chicago petitioners and their *amici*, however, argue that the handgun ban has left them vulnerable to criminals. Chicago Police Department statistics, we are told, reveal that the City's handgun murder rate has actually increased since the ban was enacted and that Chicago residents now face one of the highest murder rates in the country and rates of other violent crimes that exceed the average in comparable cities. . . .

II

A

Petitioners argue that the Chicago and Oak Park laws violate the right to keep and bear arms for two reasons. Petitioners' primary submission is that this right is among the "privileges or immunities of citizens of the United States" and that the narrow interpretation of the Privileges or Immunities Clause adopted in the

Slaughter-House Cases (1873) should now be rejected. As a secondary argument, petitioners contend that the Fourteenth Amendment's Due Process Clause "incorporates" the Second Amendment right.

Chicago and Oak Park (municipal respondents) maintain that a right set out in the Bill of Rights applies to the States only if that right is an indispensable attribute of *any* "'civilized'" legal system. If it is possible to imagine a civilized country that does not recognize the right, the municipal respondents tell us, then that right is not protected by due process. And since there are civilized countries that ban or strictly regulate the private possession of handguns, the municipal respondents maintain that due process does not preclude such measures. In light of the parties' far-reaching arguments, we begin by recounting this Court's analysis over the years of the relationship between the provisions of the Bill of Rights and the States.

B

The Bill of Rights, including the Second Amendment, originally applied only to the Federal Government. In Barron v. Mayor of Baltimore (1833), the Court, in an opinion by Chief Justice Marshall, explained that this question was "of great importance" but "not of much difficulty." In less than four pages, the Court firmly rejected the proposition that the first eight Amendments operate as limitations on the States, holding that they apply only to the Federal Government.

The constitutional Amendments adopted in the aftermath of the Civil War fundamentally altered our country's federal system. The provision at issue in this case, §1 of the Fourteenth Amendment, provides, among other things, that a State may not abridge "the privileges or immunities of citizens of the United States" or deprive "any person of life, liberty, or property, without due process of law."

Four years after the adoption of the Fourteenth Amendment, this Court was asked to interpret the Amendment's reference to "the privileges or immunities of citizens of the United States." The Slaughter-House Cases involved challenges to a Louisiana law permitting the creation of a state-sanctioned monopoly on the butchering of animals within the city of New Orleans. Justice Samuel Miller's opinion for the Court concluded that the Privileges or Immunities Clause protects only those rights "which owe their existence to the Federal government, its National character, its Constitution, or its laws." The Court held that other fundamental rights — rights that predated the creation of the Federal Government and that "the State governments were created to establish and secure" — were not protected by the Clause.

In drawing a sharp distinction between the rights of federal and state citizenship, the Court relied on two principal arguments. First, the Court emphasized that the Fourteenth Amendment's Privileges or Immunities Clause spoke of "the privileges or immunities of *citizens of the United States*," and the Court contrasted this phrasing with the wording in the first sentence of the Fourteenth

Amendment and in the Privileges and Immunities Clause of Article IV, both of which refer to *state* citizenship.[21] (Emphasis added.) Second, the Court stated that a contrary reading would "radically chang[e] the whole theory of the relations of the State and Federal governments to each other and of both these governments to the people," and the Court refused to conclude that such a change had been made "in the absence of language which expresses such a purpose too clearly to admit of doubt." Finding the phrase "privileges or immunities of citizens of the United States" lacking by this high standard, the Court reasoned that the phrase must mean something more limited.

Under the Court's narrow reading, the Privileges or Immunities Clause protects such things as the right

> "to come to the seat of government to assert any claim [a citizen] may have upon that government, to transact any business he may have with it, to seek its protection, to share its offices, to engage in administering its functions . . . [and to] become a citizen of any State of the Union by a *bonâ fide* residence therein, with the same rights as other citizens of that State."

Finding no constitutional protection against state intrusion of the kind envisioned by the Louisiana statute, the Court upheld the statute. Four Justices dissented. Justice Field, joined by Chief Justice Chase and Justices Swayne and Bradley, criticized the majority for reducing the Fourteenth Amendment's Privileges or Immunities Clause to "a vain and idle enactment, which accomplished nothing, and most unnecessarily excited Congress and the people on its passage." Justice Field opined that the Privileges or Immunities Clause protects rights that are "in their nature . . . fundamental," including the right of every man to pursue his profession without the imposition of unequal or discriminatory restrictions. Justice Bradley's dissent observed that "we are not bound to resort to implication . . . to find an authoritative declaration of some of the most important privileges and immunities of citizens of the United States. It is in the Constitution itself." Justice Bradley would have construed the Privileges or Immunities Clause to include those rights enumerated in the Constitution as well as some unenumerated rights. Justice Swayne described the majority's narrow reading of the Privileges or Immunities Clause as "turn[ing] . . . what was meant for bread into a stone." (dissenting opinion).

Today, many legal scholars dispute the correctness of the narrow *Slaughter-House* interpretation. See, e.g., Saenz v. Roe (THOMAS, J., dissenting) (scholars of the Fourteenth Amendment agree "that the Clause does not mean what the

21. The first sentence of the Fourteenth Amendment makes "[a]ll persons born or naturalized in the United States and subject to the jurisdiction thereof . . . citizens of the United States *and of the State wherein they reside*." (Emphasis added.) The Privileges and Immunities Clause of Article IV provides that "[t]he Citizens of each State shall be entitled to all Privileges and Immunities of *Citizens in the several States*." (Emphasis added.)

Court said it meant in 1873"); Amar, Substance and Method in the Year 2000, 28 Pepperdine L. Rev. 601, 631, n. 178 (2001) ("Virtually no serious modern scholar — left, right, and center — thinks that this [interpretation] is a plausible reading of the Amendment"); Brief for Constitutional Law Professors (claiming an "overwhelming consensus among leading constitutional scholars" that the opinion is "egregiously wrong"); C. Black, A New Birth of Freedom 74–75 (1997).

Three years after the decision in the Slaughter-House Cases, the Court decided [United States v. Cruikshank (1876)], the first of the three 19th-century cases on which the Seventh Circuit relied. In that case, the Court reviewed convictions stemming from the infamous Colfax Massacre in Louisiana on Easter Sunday 1873. Dozens of blacks, many unarmed, were slaughtered by a rival band of armed white men.[22] Cruikshank himself allegedly marched unarmed African-American prisoners through the streets and then had them summarily executed. Ninety-seven men were indicted for participating in the massacre, but only nine went to trial. Six of the nine were acquitted of all charges; the remaining three were acquitted of murder but convicted under the Enforcement Act of 1870 for banding and conspiring together to deprive their victims of various constitutional rights, including the right to bear arms.

The Court reversed all of the convictions, including those relating to the deprivation of the victims' right to bear arms. The Court wrote that the right of bearing arms for a lawful purpose "is not a right granted by the Constitution" and is not "in any manner dependent upon that instrument for its existence." "The second amendment," the Court continued, "declares that it shall not be infringed; but this . . . means no more than that it shall not be infringed by Congress." "Our later decisions in Presser v. Illinois (1886) and Miller v. Texas (1894) reaffirmed that the Second Amendment applies only to the Federal Government." *Heller*.

C[23]

[T]he Seventh Circuit concluded that *Cruikshank*, *Presser*, and *Miller* doomed petitioners' claims at the Court of Appeals level. Petitioners argue, however, that we should overrule those decisions and hold that the right to keep and bear arms is one of the "privileges or immunities of citizens of the United States." In petitioners' view, the Privileges or Immunities Clause protects all of the rights set out in the Bill of Rights, as well as some others, but petitioners are unable to identify the Clause's full scope. Nor is there any consensus on that question among the scholars who agree that the Slaughter-House Cases' interpretation is flawed.

22. See C. Lane, The Day Freedom Died 265-266 (2008).
23. [Justice Thomas did not join this section — ED.]

We see no need to reconsider that interpretation here. For many decades, the question of the rights protected by the Fourteenth Amendment against state infringement has been analyzed under the Due Process Clause of that Amendment and not under the Privileges or Immunities Clause. We therefore decline to disturb the *Slaughter-House* holding.

At the same time, however, this Court's decisions in *Cruikshank*, *Presser*, and *Miller* do not preclude us from considering whether the Due Process Clause of the Fourteenth Amendment makes the Second Amendment right binding on the States. None of those cases "engage[d] in the sort of Fourteenth Amendment inquiry required by our later cases." See *Heller*. As explained more fully below, *Cruikshank*, *Presser*, and *Miller* all preceded the era in which the Court began the process of "selective incorporation" under the Due Process Clause, and we have never previously addressed the question whether the right to keep and bear arms applies to the States under that theory.

Indeed, *Cruikshank* has not prevented us from holding that other rights that were at issue in that case are binding on the States through the Due Process Clause. In *Cruikshank*, the Court held that the general "right of the people peaceably to assemble for lawful purposes," which is protected by the First Amendment, applied only against the Federal Government and not against the States. Nonetheless, over 60 years later the Court held that the right of peaceful assembly was a "fundamental righ[t] . . . safeguarded by the due process clause of the Fourteenth Amendment." De Jonge v. Oregon (1937). We follow the same path here and thus consider whether the right to keep and bear arms applies to the States under the Due Process Clause.

D

1

In the late 19th century, the Court began to consider whether the Due Process Clause prohibits the States from infringing rights set out in the Bill of Rights. See Hurtado v. California (1884) (due process does not require grand jury indictment); Chicago, B. & Q. R. Co. v. Chicago (1897) (due process prohibits States from taking of private property for public use without just compensation). Five features of the approach taken during the ensuing era should be noted.

First, the Court viewed the due process question as entirely separate from the question whether a right was a privilege or immunity of national citizenship. See Twining v. New Jersey (1908).

Second, the Court explained that the only rights protected against state infringement by the Due Process Clause were those rights "of such a nature that they are included in the conception of due process of law." *Ibid.* See also, *e.g.*, Adamson v. California (1947); Betts v. Brady (1942), Palko v. Connecticut (1937). . . . While it was "possible that some of the personal rights safeguarded by the first eight Amendments against National action [might] also be safeguarded against state action," the Court stated, this was "not because those rights are enumerated in the first eight Amendments." *Twining*.

The Court used different formulations in describing the boundaries of due process. For example, in *Twining*, the Court referred to "immutable principles of justice which inhere in the very idea of free government which no member of the Union may disregard." In Snyder v. Massachusetts (1934), the Court spoke of rights that are "so rooted in the traditions and conscience of our people as to be ranked as fundamental." And in *Palko*, the Court famously said that due process protects those rights that are "the very essence of a scheme of ordered liberty" and essential to "a fair and enlightened system of justice."

Third, in some cases decided during this era the Court "can be seen as having asked, when inquiring into whether some particular procedural safeguard was required of a State, if a civilized system could be imagined that would not accord the particular protection." Duncan v. Louisiana (1968). Thus, in holding that due process prohibits a State from taking private property without just compensation, the Court described the right as "a principle of natural equity, recognized by all temperate and civilized governments, from a deep and universal sense of its justice." *Chicago, B. & Q. R. Co.* Similarly, the Court found that due process did not provide a right against compelled incrimination in part because this right "has no place in the jurisprudence of civilized and free countries outside the domain of the common law." *Twining.*

Fourth, the Court during this era was not hesitant to hold that a right set out in the Bill of Rights failed to meet the test for inclusion within the protection of the Due Process Clause. The Court found that some such rights qualified. See, *e.g.*, [cases applying the rights of freedom of speech and press, assistance of counsel in capital cases, freedom of assembly, and free exercise of religion]. But others did not. See, *e.g.*, [cases refusing to apply the right to a grand jury indictment requirement or the privilege against self-incrimination].

Finally, even when a right set out in the Bill of Rights was held to fall within the conception of due process, the protection or remedies afforded against state infringement sometimes differed from the protection or remedies provided against abridgment by the Federal Government. To give one example, in *Betts* the Court held that, although the Sixth Amendment required the appointment of counsel in all federal criminal cases in which the defendant was unable to retain an attorney, the Due Process Clause required appointment of counsel in state criminal proceedings only where "want of counsel in [the] particular case . . . result[ed] in a conviction lacking in . . . fundamental fairness." Similarly, in Wolf v. Colorado (1949), the Court held that the "core of the Fourth Amendment" was implicit in the concept of ordered liberty and thus "enforceable against the States through the Due Process Clause" but that the exclusionary rule, which applied in federal cases, did not apply to the States.

2

An alternative theory regarding the relationship between the Bill of Rights and §1 of the Fourteenth Amendment was championed by Justice Black. This theory held that §1 of the Fourteenth Amendment totally incorporated all of the provisions of the Bill of Rights. As Justice Black noted, the chief congressional proponents of the Fourteenth Amendment espoused the view that the Amendment made the Bill of Rights applicable to the States and, in so doing, overruled this Court's decision in *Barron*.[24] *Adamson*, (dissenting opinion).[25] Nonetheless, the Court never has embraced Justice Black's "total incorporation" theory.

While Justice Black's theory was never adopted, the Court eventually moved in that direction by initiating what has been called a process of "selective incorporation," *i.e.*, the Court began to hold that the Due Process Clause fully incorporates particular rights contained in the first eight Amendments. The decisions during this time abandoned three of the previously noted characteristics of the earlier period.[26] The Court made it clear that the governing standard

24. Senator Jacob Howard, who spoke on behalf of the Joint Committee on Reconstruction and sponsored the Amendment in the Senate, stated that the Amendment protected all of "the personal rights guarantied and secured by the first eight amendments of the Constitution." Cong. Globe (1866). Representative John Bingham, the principal author of the text of §1, said that the Amendment would "arm the Congress . . . with the power to enforce the bill of rights as it stands in the Constitution today." After ratification of the Amendment, Bingham maintained the view that the rights guaranteed by §1 of the Fourteenth Amendment "are chiefly defined in the first eight amendments to the Constitution of the United States." Cong. Globe (1871). Finally, Representative Thaddeus Stevens, the political leader of the House and acting chairman of the Joint Committee on Reconstruction, stated during the debates on the Amendment that "the Constitution limits only the action of Congress, and is not a limitation on the States. This amendment supplies that defect, and allows Congress to correct the unjust legislation of the States." Cong. Globe; see also M. Curtis, No State Shall Abridge: The Fourteenth Amendment and the Bill of Rights (1986) (counting at least 30 statements during the debates in Congress interpreting §1 to incorporate the Bill of Rights); Brief for Constitutional Law Professors (collecting authorities and stating that "[n]ot a single senator or representative disputed [the incorporationist] understanding" of the Fourteenth Amendment).

25. The municipal respondents and some of their *amici* dispute the significance of these statements. They contend that the phrase "privileges or immunities" is not naturally read to mean the rights set out in the first eight Amendments, see Brief for Historians, and that "there is 'support in the legislative history for no fewer than four interpretations of the . . . Privileges or Immunities Clause.'" Brief for Municipal Respondents (quoting Currie, The Reconstruction Congress, 75 U. Chi. L. Rev. 383, 406 (2008); brackets omitted). They question whether there is sound evidence of "'any strong public awareness of nationalizing the entire Bill of Rights.'" Brief for Municipal Respondents (quoting Wildenthal, Nationalizing the Bill of Rights: Revisiting the Original Understanding of the Fourteenth Amendment in 1866–67, 68 Ohio St. L. J. 1509, 1600 (2007)). Scholars have also disputed the total incorporation theory. See, e.g., Fairman, Does the Fourteenth Amendment Incorporate the Bill of Rights? 2 Stan. L. Rev. 5 (1949); Berger, Incorporation of the Bill of Rights in the Fourteenth Amendment: A Nine-Lived Cat, 42 Ohio St.L. J. 435 (1981).

Proponents of the view that §1 of the Fourteenth Amendment makes all of the provisions of the Bill of Rights applicable to the States respond that the terms privileges, immunities, and rights were used interchangeably at the time, see, e.g., Curtis, and that the position taken by the leading congressional proponents of the Amendment was widely publicized and understood, see, e.g., Wildenthal; Hardy, Original Popular Understanding of the Fourteenth Amendment as Reflected in the Print Media of 1866-1868, 30 Whittier L. Rev. 695 (2009). A number of scholars have found support for the total incorporation of the Bill of Rights. See Curtis at 57-130; Aynes, On Misreading John Bingham and the Fourteenth Amendment, 103 Yale L. J. 57, 61 (1993); see also Amar, [The] Bill of Rights 181-230. We take no position with respect to this academic debate.

26. By contrast, the Court has never retreated from the proposition that the Privileges or Immunities Clause and the Due Process Clause present different questions. And in recent cases addressing unenumerated rights, we have required that a right also be "implicit in the concept of ordered liberty." See, e.g., Washington v. Glucksberg (1997).

is not whether *any* "civilized system [can] be imagined that would not accord the particular protection." *Duncan*. Instead, the Court inquired whether a particular Bill of Rights guarantee is fundamental to *our* scheme of ordered liberty and system of justice.

The Court also shed any reluctance to hold that rights guaranteed by the Bill of Rights met the requirements for protection under the Due Process Clause. The Court eventually incorporated almost all of the provisions of the Bill of Rights. Only a handful of the Bill of Rights protections remain unincorporated.[27]

Finally, the Court abandoned "the notion that the Fourteenth Amendment applies to the States only a watered-down, subjective version of the individual guarantees of the Bill of Rights," stating that it would be "incongruous" to apply different standards "depending on whether the claim was asserted in a state or federal court." [Malloy v. Hogan (1964)]. Instead, the Court decisively held that incorporated Bill of Rights protections "are all to be enforced against the States under the Fourteenth Amendment according to the same standards that protect those personal rights against federal encroachment." *Id.*[28] Employing this approach, the Court overruled earlier decisions in which it had held that particular Bill of Rights guarantees or remedies did not apply to the States.

III

With this framework in mind, we now turn directly to the question whether the Second Amendment right to keep and bear arms is incorporated in the concept of due process. In answering that question, as just explained, we must decide whether the right to keep and bear arms is fundamental to our scheme of ordered liberty, *Duncan*, or as we have said in a related context, whether this right is "deeply rooted in this Nation's history and tradition," Washington v. Glucksberg (1997).

A

Our decision in *Heller* points unmistakably to the answer. Self-defense is a basic right, recognized by many legal systems from ancient times to the present

27. In addition to the right to keep and bear arms (and the Sixth Amendment right to a unanimous jury verdict), the only rights not fully incorporated are (1) the Third Amendment's protection against quartering of soldiers; (2) the Fifth Amendment's grand jury indictment requirement; (3) the Seventh Amendment right to a jury trial in civil cases; and (4) the Eighth Amendment's prohibition on excessive fines. We never have decided whether the Third Amendment or the Eighth Amendment's prohibition of excessive fines applies to the States through the Due Process Clause. Our governing decisions regarding the Grand Jury Clause of the Fifth Amendment and the Seventh Amendment's civil jury requirement long predate the era of selective incorporation.

28. There is one exception to this general rule. The Court has held that although the Sixth Amendment right to trial by jury requires a unanimous jury verdict in federal criminal trials, it does not require a unanimous jury verdict in state criminal trials. See Apodaca v. Oregon (1972). But that ruling was the result of an unusual division among the Justices, not an endorsement of the two-track approach to incorporation. . . .

day,[29] and in *Heller*, we held that individual self-defense is "*the central component*" of the Second Amendment right. Explaining that "the need for defense of self, family, and property is most acute" in the home, we found that this right applies to handguns because they are "the most preferred firearm in the nation to 'keep' and use for protection of one's home and family." Thus, we concluded, citizens must be permitted "to use [handguns] for the core lawful purpose of self-defense."

Heller makes it clear that this right is "deeply rooted in this Nation's history and tradition." *Glucksberg*. *Heller* explored the right's origins, noting that the 1689 English Bill of Rights explicitly protected a right to keep arms for self-defense, and that by 1765, Blackstone was able to assert that the right to keep and bear arms was "one of the fundamental rights of Englishmen."

Blackstone's assessment was shared by the American colonists. As we noted in *Heller*, King George III's attempt to disarm the colonists in the 1760's and 1770's "provoked polemical reactions by Americans invoking their rights as Englishmen to keep arms."

The right to keep and bear arms was considered no less fundamental by those who drafted and ratified the Bill of Rights. "During the 1788 ratification debates, the fear that the federal government would disarm the people in order to impose rule through a standing army or select militia was pervasive in Antifederalist rhetoric." *Heller*. Federalists responded, not by arguing that the right was insufficiently important to warrant protection but by contending that the right was adequately protected by the Constitution's assignment of only limited powers to the Federal Government. Thus, Antifederalists and Federalists alike agreed that the right to bear arms was fundamental to the newly formed system of government. But those who were fearful that the new Federal Government would infringe traditional rights such as the right to keep and bear arms insisted on the adoption of the Bill of Rights as a condition for ratification of the Constitution. This is surely powerful evidence that the right was regarded as fundamental in the sense relevant here.

This understanding persisted in the years immediately following the ratification of the Bill of Rights. In addition to the four States that had adopted Second Amendment analogues before ratification, nine more States adopted state constitutional provisions protecting an individual right to keep and bear arms between 1789 and 1820. *Heller*. . . .

B

1

By the 1850's, the perceived threat that had prompted the inclusion of the Second Amendment in the Bill of Rights — the fear that the National Govern-

29. Citing Jewish, Greek, and Roman law, Blackstone wrote that if a person killed an attacker, "the slayer is in no kind of fault whatsoever, not even in the minutest degree; and is therefore to be totally acquitted and discharged, with commendation rather than blame." W. Blackstone, Commentaries on the Laws of England.

ment would disarm the universal militia—had largely faded as a popular concern, but the right to keep and bear arms was highly valued for purposes of self-defense. Abolitionist authors wrote in support of the right. See L. Spooner, The Unconstitutionality of Slavery (1860); J. Tiffany, A Treatise on the Unconstitutionality of American Slavery (1849). And when attempts were made to disarm "Free-Soilers" in "Bloody Kansas," Senator Charles Sumner, who later played a leading role in the adoption of the Fourteenth Amendment, proclaimed that "[n]ever was [the rifle] more needed in just self-defense than now in Kansas." The Crime Against Kansas: The Apologies for the Crime: The True Remedy, Speech of Hon. Charles Sumner in the Senate of the United States (1856). Indeed, the 1856 Republican Party Platform protested that in Kansas the constitutional rights of the people had been "fraudulently and violently taken from them" and the "right of the people to keep and bear arms" had been "infringed." National Party Platforms 1840–1972, p. 27 (5th ed. 1973).[30]

After the Civil War, many of the over 180,000 African Americans who served in the Union Army returned to the States of the old Confederacy, where systematic efforts were made to disarm them and other blacks. The laws of some States formally prohibited African Americans from possessing firearms. For example, a Mississippi law provided that "no freedman, free negro or mulatto, not in the military service of the United States government, and not licensed so to do by the board of police of his or her county, shall keep or carry fire-arms of any kind, or any ammunition, dirk or bowie knife."[31]

Throughout the South, armed parties, often consisting of ex-Confederate soldiers serving in the state militias, forcibly took firearms from newly freed slaves. In the first session of the 39th Congress, Senator Wilson told his colleagues: "In Mississippi rebel State forces, men who were in the rebel armies, are traversing the State, visiting the freedmen, disarming them, perpetrating murders and outrages upon them; and the same things are done in other sections of the country." The Report of the Joint Committee on Reconstruction—which was widely reprinted in the press and distributed by Members of the 39th Congress to their constituents shortly after Congress approved the Fourteenth Amendment—contained numerous examples of such abuses. In one town, the "marshal [took] all arms from returned colored soldiers, and [was] very prompt in shooting the blacks whenever an opportunity occur[red]." As Senator Wilson put it during the debate on a failed proposal to disband Southern militias: "There

30. Abolitionists and Republicans were not alone in believing that the right to keep and bear arms was a fundamental right. The 1864 Democratic Party Platform complained that the confiscation of firearms by Union troops occupying parts of the South constituted "the interference with and denial of the right of the people to bear arms in their defense."

31. In South Carolina, prominent black citizens held a convention to address the State's black code. They drafted a memorial to Congress, in which they included a plea for protection of their constitutional right to keep and bear arms: "We ask that, inasmuch as the Constitution of the United States explicitly declares that the right to keep and bear arms shall not be infringed . . . that the late efforts of the Legislature of this State to pass an act to deprive us [of] arms be forbidden, as a plain violation of the Constitution." Senator Charles Sumner relayed the memorial to the Senate and described the memorial as a request that black citizens "have the constitutional protection in keeping arms."

is one unbroken chain of testimony from all people that are loyal to this country, that the greatest outrages are perpetrated by armed men who go up and down the country searching houses, disarming people, committing outrages of every kind and description."[32]

Union Army commanders took steps to secure the right of all citizens to keep and bear arms,[33] but the 39th Congress concluded that legislative action was necessary. Its efforts to safeguard the right to keep and bear arms demonstrate that the right was still recognized to be fundamental.

The most explicit evidence of Congress' aim appears in §14 of the Freedmen's Bureau Act of 1866, which provided that "the right . . . to have full and equal benefit of all laws and proceedings concerning personal liberty, personal security, and the acquisition, enjoyment, and disposition of estate, real and personal, *including the constitutional right to bear arms*, shall be secured to and enjoyed by all the citizens . . . without respect to race or color, or previous condition of slavery." (emphasis added).[34] Section 14 thus explicitly guaranteed that "all the citizens," black and white, would have "the constitutional right to bear arms."

The Civil Rights Act of 1866, which was considered at the same time as the Freedmen's Bureau Act, similarly sought to protect the right of all citizens to keep and bear arms.[35] Section 1 of the Civil Rights Act guaranteed the "full and

32. Disarmament by bands of former Confederate soldiers eventually gave way to attacks by the Ku Klux Klan. In debates over the later enacted Enforcement Act of 1870, Senator John Pool observed that the Klan would "order the colored men to give up their arms; saying that everybody would be Kukluxed in whose house fire-arms were found."

33. For example, the occupying Union commander in South Carolina issued an order stating that "[t]he constitutional rights of all loyal and well disposed inhabitants to bear arms, will not be infringed." Union officials in Georgia issued a similar order, declaring that "[a]ll men, without the distinction of color, have the right to keep arms to defend their homes, families or themselves." In addition, when made aware of attempts by armed parties to disarm blacks, the head of the Freedmen's Bureau in Alabama "made public [his] determination to maintain the right of the negro to keep and to bear arms, and [his] disposition to send an armed force into any neighborhood in which that right should be systematically interfered with." Joint Committee on Reconstruction (1866).

34. The Freedmen's Bureau bill was amended to include an express reference to the right to keep and bear arms, even though at least some Members believed that the unamended version alone would have protected the right.

35. There can be no doubt that the principal proponents of the Civil Rights Act of 1866 meant to end the disarmament of African Americans in the South. In introducing the bill, Senator Trumbull described its purpose as securing to blacks the "privileges which are essential to freemen." He then pointed to the previously described Mississippi law that "prohibit[ed] any negro or mulatto from having fire-arms" and explained that the bill would "destroy" such laws. Similarly, Representative Sidney Clarke cited disarmament of freedmen in Alabama and Mississippi as a reason to support the Civil Rights Act and to continue to deny Alabama and Mississippi representation in Congress: "I regret, sir, that justice compels me to say, to the disgrace of the Federal Government, that the 'reconstructed' State authorities of Mississippi were allowed to rob and disarm our veteran soldiers and arm the rebels fresh from the field of treasonable strife. Sir, the disarmed loyalists of Alabama, Mississippi, and Louisiana are powerless to-day, and oppressed by the pardoned and encouraged rebels of those States. They appeal to the American Congress for protection. In response to this appeal I shall vote for every just measure of protection, for I do not intend to be among the treacherous violators of the solemn pledge of the nation."

equal benefit of all laws and proceedings for the security of person and property, as is enjoyed by white citizens." This language was virtually identical to language in §14 of the Freedmen's Bureau Act ("the right . . . to have full and equal benefit of all laws and proceedings concerning personal liberty, personal security, and the acquisition, enjoyment, and disposition of estate, real and personal"). And as noted, the latter provision went on to explain that one of the "laws and proceedings concerning personal liberty, personal security, and the acquisition, enjoyment, and disposition of estate, real and personal" was "the constitutional right to bear arms." Representative Bingham believed that the Civil Rights Act protected the same rights as enumerated in the Freedmen's Bureau bill, which of course explicitly mentioned the right to keep and bear arms. The unavoidable conclusion is that the Civil Rights Act, like the Freedmen's Bureau Act, aimed to protect "the constitutional right to bear arms" and not simply to prohibit discrimination.

Congress, however, ultimately deemed these legislative remedies insufficient. Southern resistance, Presidential vetoes, and this Court's pre-Civil-War precedent persuaded Congress that a constitutional amendment was necessary to provide full protection for the rights of blacks. Today, it is generally accepted that the Fourteenth Amendment was understood to provide a constitutional basis for protecting the rights set out in the Civil Rights Act of 1866.

In debating the Fourteenth Amendment, the 39th Congress referred to the right to keep and bear arms as a fundamental right deserving of protection. Senator Samuel Pomeroy described three "indispensable" "safeguards of liberty under our form of Government." One of these, he said, was the right to keep and bear arms:

> "Every man . . . should have the right to bear arms for the defense of himself and family and his homestead. And if the cabin door of the freedman is broken open and the intruder enters for purposes as vile as were known to slavery, then should a well-loaded musket be in the hand of the occupant to send the polluted wretch to another world, where his wretchedness will forever remain complete."

Even those who thought the Fourteenth Amendment unnecessary believed that blacks, as citizens, "have equal right to protection, and to keep and bear arms for self defense." (Sen. James Nye).[36]

Evidence from the period immediately following the ratification of the Fourteenth Amendment only confirms that the right to keep and bear arms was considered fundamental. In an 1868 speech addressing the disarmament of freedmen, Representative Stevens emphasized the necessity of the right: "Disarm a community and you rob them of the means of defending life. Take away their weapons of defense and you take away the inalienable right of defending

36. Other Members of the 39th Congress stressed the importance of the right to keep and bear arms in discussing other measures. In speaking generally on reconstruction, Representative Roswell Hart listed the "right of the people to keep and bear arms" as among those rights necessary to a "republican form of government." . . .

liberty." "The fourteenth amendment, now so happily adopted, settles the whole question." And in debating the Civil Rights Act of 1871, Congress routinely referred to the right to keep and bear arms and decried the continued disarmament of blacks in the South. Finally, legal commentators from the period emphasized the fundamental nature of the right. See, e.g., T. Farrar, Manual of the Constitution of the United States of America §118 (1867); J. Pomeroy, An Introduction to the Constitutional Law of the United States §239 (3d ed. 1875).

The right to keep and bear arms was also widely protected by state constitutions at the time when the Fourteenth Amendment was ratified. In 1868, 22 of the 37 States in the Union had state constitutional provisions explicitly protecting the right to keep and bear arms. Quite a few of these state constitutional guarantees, moreover, explicitly protected the right to keep and bear arms as an individual right to self-defense. What is more, state constitutions adopted during the Reconstruction era by former Confederate States included a right to keep and bear arms. A clear majority of the States in 1868, therefore, recognized the right to keep and bear arms as being among the foundational rights necessary to our system of Government.

In sum, it is clear that the Framers and ratifiers of the Fourteenth Amendment counted the right to keep and bear arms among those fundamental rights necessary to our system of ordered liberty.

2

Despite all this evidence, municipal respondents contend that Congress, in the years immediately following the Civil War, merely sought to outlaw "discriminatory measures taken against freedmen, which it addressed by adopting a non-discrimination principle" and that even an outright ban on the possession of firearms was regarded as acceptable, "so long as it was not done in a discriminatory manner." Brief for Municipal Respondents. They argue that Members of Congress overwhelmingly viewed §1 of the Fourteenth Amendment "as an antidiscrimination rule," and they cite statements to the effect that the section would outlaw discriminatory measures. This argument is implausible.

First, while §1 of the Fourteenth Amendment contains "an antidiscrimination rule," namely, the Equal Protection Clause, municipal respondents can hardly mean that §1 does no more than prohibit discrimination. If that were so, then the First Amendment, as applied to the States, would not prohibit nondiscriminatory abridgments of the rights to freedom of speech or freedom of religion; the Fourth Amendment, as applied to the States, would not prohibit all unreasonable searches and seizures but only discriminatory searches and seizures — and so on. We assume that this is not municipal respondents' view, so what they must mean is that the Second Amendment should be singled out for special — and specially unfavorable — treatment. We reject that suggestion.

Second, municipal respondents' argument ignores the clear terms of the Freedmen's Bureau Act of 1866, which acknowledged the existence of the right to bear arms. If that law had used language such as "the equal benefit of laws concerning the bearing of arms," it would be possible to interpret it as simply a prohibition of racial discrimination. But §14 speaks of and protects "the constitutional right to bear arms," an unmistakable reference to the right protected by the Second Amendment. And it protects the "full and equal benefit" of this right in the States. It would have been nonsensical for Congress to guarantee the full and equal benefit of a constitutional right that does not exist.

Third, if the 39th Congress had outlawed only those laws that discriminate on the basis of race or previous condition of servitude, African Americans in the South would likely have remained vulnerable to attack by many of their worst abusers: the state militia and state peace officers. In the years immediately following the Civil War, a law banning the possession of guns by all private citizens would have been nondiscriminatory only in the formal sense. Any such law — like the Chicago and Oak Park ordinances challenged here — presumably would have permitted the possession of guns by those acting under the authority of the State and would thus have left firearms in the hands of the militia and local peace officers. And as the Report of the Joint Committee on Reconstruction revealed, those groups were widely involved in harassing blacks in the South.

Fourth, municipal respondents' purely antidiscrimination theory of the Fourteenth Amendment disregards the plight of whites in the South who opposed the Black Codes. If the 39th Congress and the ratifying public had simply prohibited racial discrimination with respect to the bearing of arms, opponents of the Black Codes would have been left without the means of self-defense — as had abolitionists in Kansas in the 1850's.

Fifth, the 39th Congress' response to proposals to disband and disarm the Southern militias is instructive. Despite recognizing and deploring the abuses of these militias, the 39th Congress balked at a proposal to disarm them. Disarmament, it was argued, would violate the members' right to bear arms, and it was ultimately decided to disband the militias but not to disarm their members. It cannot be doubted that the right to bear arms was regarded as a substantive guarantee, not a prohibition that could be ignored so long as the States legislated in an evenhanded manner.

IV[37]

. . . Municipal respondents maintain that the Second Amendment differs from all of the other provisions of the Bill of Rights because it concerns the right to possess a deadly implement and thus has implications for public safety. And they note that there is intense disagreement on the question whether the private possession of guns in the home increases or decreases gun deaths and injuries.

The right to keep and bear arms, however, is not the only constitutional right that has controversial public safety implications. All of the constitutional provisions that impose restrictions on law enforcement and on the prosecution of crimes fall into the same category. See, e.g., Hudson v. Michigan (2006) ("The exclusionary rule generates 'substantial social costs,' which sometimes include

37. [Justice Thomas did not join this part — Ed.]

setting the guilty free and the dangerous at large"); Barker v. Wingo (1972) (reflecting on the serious consequences of dismissal for a speedy trial violation, which means "a defendant who may be guilty of a serious crime will go free"). . . . Municipal respondents cite no case in which we have refrained from holding that a provision of the Bill of Rights is binding on the States on the ground that the right at issue has disputed public safety implications.

We likewise reject municipal respondents' argument that we should depart from our established incorporation methodology on the ground that making the Second Amendment binding on the States and their subdivisions is inconsistent with principles of federalism and will stifle experimentation. . . . There is nothing new in the argument that, in order to respect federalism and allow useful state experimentation, a federal constitutional right should not be fully binding on the States. This argument was made repeatedly and eloquently by Members of this Court who rejected the concept of incorporation and urged retention of the two-track approach to incorporation. Throughout the era of "selective incorporation," Justice Harlan in particular, invoking the values of federalism and state experimentation, fought a determined rearguard action to preserve the two-track approach.

Time and again, however, those pleas failed. Unless we turn back the clock or adopt a special incorporation test applicable only to the Second Amendment, municipal respondents' argument must be rejected. Under our precedents, if a Bill of Rights guarantee is fundamental from an American perspective, then, unless *stare decisis* counsels otherwise, that guarantee is fully binding on the States and thus limits (but by no means eliminates) their ability to devise solutions to social problems that suit local needs and values. As noted by the 38 States that have appeared in this case as *amici* supporting petitioners, "[s]tate and local experimentation with reasonable firearms regulations will continue under the Second Amendment." Brief for State of Texas et al. . . .

We made it clear in *Heller* that our holding did not cast doubt on such longstanding regulatory measures as "prohibitions on the possession of firearms by felons and the mentally ill," "laws forbidding the carrying of firearms in sensitive places such as schools and government buildings, or laws imposing conditions and qualifications on the commercial sale of arms." We repeat those assurances here. Despite municipal respondents' doomsday proclamations, incorporation does not imperil every law regulating firearms. . . .

V[38]

A

. . . Justice Breyer's dissent makes several points to which we briefly respond. To begin, while there is certainly room for disagreement about *Heller*'s analysis of the history of the right to keep and bear arms, nothing written since

38. [Justice Thomas did not join this part — Ed.]

Heller persuades us to reopen the question there decided. Few other questions of original meaning have been as thoroughly explored.

JUSTICE BREYER'S conclusion that the Fourteenth Amendment does not incorporate the right to keep and bear arms appears to rest primarily on four factors: First, "there is no popular consensus" that the right is fundamental; second, the right does not protect minorities or persons neglected by those holding political power; third, incorporation of the Second Amendment right would "amount to a significant incursion on a traditional and important area of state concern, altering the constitutional relationship between the States and the Federal Government" and preventing local variations; and fourth, determining the scope of the Second Amendment right in cases involving state and local laws will force judges to answer difficult empirical questions regarding matters that are outside their area of expertise. Even if we believed that these factors were relevant to the incorporation inquiry, none of these factors undermines the case for incorporation of the right to keep and bear arms for self-defense.

First, we have never held that a provision of the Bill of Rights applies to the States only if there is a "popular consensus" that the right is fundamental, and we see no basis for such a rule. But in this case, as it turns out, there is evidence of such a consensus. An *amicus* brief submitted by 58 Members of the Senate and 251 Members of the House of Representatives urges us to hold that the right to keep and bear arms is fundamental. See Brief for Senator Kay Bailey Hutchison et al.. Another brief submitted by 38 States takes the same position. Brief for State of Texas et al.

Second, petitioners and many others who live in high-crime areas dispute the proposition that the Second Amendment right does not protect minorities and those lacking political clout. The plight of Chicagoans living in high-crime areas was recently highlighted when two Illinois legislators representing Chicago districts called on the Governor to deploy the Illinois National Guard to patrol the City's streets. The legislators noted that the number of Chicago homicide victims during the current year equaled the number of American soldiers killed during that same period in Afghanistan and Iraq and that 80% of the Chicago victims were black. *Amici* supporting incorporation of the right to keep and bear arms contend that the right is especially important for women and members of other groups that may be especially vulnerable to violent crime. If, as petitioners believe, their safety and the safety of other law-abiding members of the community would be enhanced by the possession of handguns in the home for self-defense, then the Second Amendment right protects the rights of minorities and other residents of high-crime areas whose needs are not being met by elected public officials.

Third, JUSTICE BREYER is correct that incorporation of the Second Amendment right will to some extent limit the legislative freedom of the States, but this is always true when a Bill of Rights provision is incorporated. Incorporation always restricts experimentation and local variations, but that has not stopped the Court from incorporating virtually every other provision of the Bill of Rights. "[T]he enshrinement of constitutional rights necessarily takes certain policy choices off the table." *Heller*. This conclusion is no more remarkable with respect to the Second Amendment than it is with respect to all the other limitations on state power found in the Constitution.

Finally, JUSTICE BREYER is incorrect that incorporation will require judges to assess the costs and benefits of firearms restrictions and thus to make difficult empirical judgments in an area in which they lack expertise. As we have noted, while his opinion in *Heller* recommended an interest-balancing test, the Court specifically rejected that suggestion. "The very enumeration of the right takes out of the hands of government—even the Third Branch of Government—the power to decide on a case-by-case basis whether the right is really worth insisting upon."

* * *

In *Heller*, we held that the Second Amendment protects the right to possess a handgun in the home for the purpose of self-defense. Unless considerations of *stare decisis* counsel otherwise, a provision of the Bill of Rights that protects a right that is fundamental from an American perspective applies equally to the Federal Government and the States. We therefore hold that the Due Process Clause of the Fourteenth Amendment incorporates the Second Amendment right recognized in *Heller*.

The judgment of the Court of Appeals is reversed, and the case is remanded for further proceedings.

It is so ordered.

JUSTICE SCALIA, concurring.

I join the Court's opinion. Despite my misgivings about Substantive Due Process as an original matter, I have acquiesced in the Court's incorporation of certain guarantees in the Bill of Rights "because it is both long established and narrowly limited." Albright v. Oliver (1994) (SCALIA, J., concurring). This case does not require me to reconsider that view, since straightforward application of settled doctrine suffices to decide it. . . .

[T]he question to be decided is not whether the historically focused method is a *perfect means* of restraining aristocratic judicial Constitution writing; but whether it is the *best means available* in an imperfect world. Or indeed, even more narrowly than that: whether it is demonstrably much better than what JUSTICE STEVENS proposes. I think it beyond all serious dispute that it is much less subjective, and intrudes much less upon the democratic process. It is less subjective because it depends upon a body of evidence susceptible of reasoned analysis rather than a variety of vague ethico-political First Principles whose combined conclusion can be found to point in any direction the judges favor. In the most controversial matters brought before this Court—for example, the constitutionality of prohibiting abortion, assisted suicide, or homosexual sodomy, or the constitutionality of the death penalty—*any* historical methodology, under *any* plausible standard of proof, would lead to the same conclusion. Moreover, the methodological differences that divide historians, and the varying interpretive assumptions they bring to their work are nothing compared to the differences among the American people (though perhaps not among graduates of prestigious law schools) with regard to the moral judgments JUSTICE STEVENS would have courts pronounce. And whether or not special expertise is needed to answer historical questions, judges most certainly have no "comparative . . . advantage" in resolving moral disputes. What is more, his approach would not eliminate, but multiply, the hard questions courts must confront, since he would not *replace* history with moral philosophy, but would have courts consider *both*.

And the Court's approach intrudes less upon the democratic process because the rights it acknowledges are those established by a constitutional history formed by democratic decisions; and the rights it fails to acknowledge are left to be democratically adopted or rejected by the people, with the assurance that their decision is not subject to judicial revision. JUSTICE STEVENS' approach, on the other hand, deprives the people of that power, since whatever the Constitution and laws may say, the list of protected rights will be whatever courts wish it to be. After all, he notes, the people have been wrong before and courts may conclude they are wrong in the future. . . . It is JUSTICE STEVENS' approach, not the Court's, that puts democracy in peril.

JUSTICE THOMAS, concurring in part and concurring in the judgment.

I agree with the Court that the Fourteenth Amendment makes the right to keep and bear arms set forth in the Second Amendment "fully applicable to the States." I write separately because I believe there is a more straightforward path to this conclusion, one that is more faithful to the Fourteenth Amendment's text and history.

Applying what is now a well-settled test, the plurality opinion concludes that the right to keep and bear arms applies to the States through the Fourteenth Amendment's Due Process Clause because it is "fundamental" to the American "scheme of ordered liberty," and "'deeply rooted in this Nation's history and tradition[.]'" I agree with that description of the right. But I cannot agree that it is enforceable against the States through a clause that speaks only to "process." Instead, the right to keep and bear arms is a privilege of American citizenship that applies to the States through the Fourteenth Amendment's Privileges or Immunities Clause.

I

. . . The provision at issue here, §1 of the Fourteenth Amendment, significantly altered our system of government. The first sentence of that section provides that "[a]ll persons born or naturalized in the United States and subject to the jurisdiction thereof, are citizens of the United States and of the State wherein they reside." This unambiguously overruled this Court's contrary holding in Dred Scott v. Sandford (1857) that the Constitution did not recognize black Americans as citizens of the United States or their own State. The meaning of §1's next sentence has divided this Court for many years. That sentence begins with the command that "[n]o State shall make or enforce any law which shall abridge the privileges or immunities of citizens of the United States." On its face, this appears to grant the persons just made United States citizens a certain collection of rights — *i.e.*, privileges or immunities — attributable to that status.

This Court's precedents accept that point, but define the relevant collection of rights quite narrowly. In the Slaughter-House Cases (1873), decided just five years after the Fourteenth Amendment's adoption, the Court interpreted this text, now known as the Privileges or Immunities Clause, for the first time. In a closely divided decision, the Court drew a sharp distinction between the privileges and immunities of state citizenship and those of federal citizenship, and held that the Privileges or Immunities Clause protected only the latter category of rights from state abridgment. The Court defined that category to include only those rights "which owe their existence to the Federal government, its National character, its Constitution, or its laws." This arguably left open the possibility that certain individual rights enumerated in the Constitution could be considered privileges or immunities of federal citizenship. See *ibid.* (listing "[t]he right to peaceably assemble" and "the privilege of the writ of habeas corpus" as rights potentially protected by the Privileges or Immunities Clause). But the Court soon rejected that proposition, interpreting the Privileges or Immunities Clause even more narrowly in its later cases.

Chief among those cases is United States v. Cruikshank (1876). There, the Court held that members of a white militia who had brutally murdered as many as 165 black Louisianians congregating outside a courthouse had not deprived the victims of their privileges as American citizens to peaceably assemble or to keep and bear arms. According to the Court, the right to peaceably assemble codified in the First Amendment was not a privilege of United States citizenship because "[t]he right . . . existed long *before* the adoption of the Constitution." (emphasis added). Similarly, the Court held that the right to keep and bear arms was not a privilege of United States citizenship because it was not "in any manner dependent upon that instrument for its existence." In other words, the reason the Framers codified the right to bear arms in the Second Amendment — its nature as an inalienable right that pre-existed the Constitution's adoption — was the very reason citizens could not enforce it against States through the Fourteenth.

That circular reasoning effectively has been the Court's last word on the Privileges or Immunities Clause. . . . As a consequence of this Court's marginalization of the Clause, litigants seeking federal protection of fundamental rights turned to the remainder of §1 in search of an alternative fount of such rights. They found one in a most curious place — that section's command that every State guarantee "due process" to any person before depriving him of "life, liberty, or property." At first, litigants argued that this Due Process Clause "incorporated" certain procedural rights codified in the Bill of Rights against the States. The Court generally rejected those claims, however, on the theory that the rights in question were not sufficiently "fundamental" to warrant such treatment.

That changed with time. The Court came to conclude that certain Bill of Rights guarantees *were* sufficiently fundamental to fall within §1's guarantee of "due process." . . . While this Court has at times concluded that a right gains "fundamental" status only if it is essential to the American "scheme of ordered liberty" or "'deeply rooted in this Nation's history and tradition,'" the Court has just as often held that a right warrants Due Process Clause protection if it satisfies a far less measurable range of criteria, see Lawrence v. Texas (2003) (concluding that the Due Process Clause protects "liberty of the person both in its spatial and in its more transcendent dimensions"). Using the latter approach, the Court has determined that the Due Process Clause applies rights against the States that are not mentioned in the Constitution at all, even without seriously arguing that the Clause was originally understood to protect such rights. See, e.g., Lochner v. New York (1905); Roe v. Wade (1973); *Lawrence*.

All of this is a legal fiction. The notion that a constitutional provision that guarantees only "process" before a person is deprived of life, liberty, or property could define the substance of those rights strains credulity for even the most casual user of words. Moreover, this fiction is a particularly dangerous one. The one theme that links the Court's substantive due process precedents together is their lack of a guiding principle to distinguish "fundamental" rights that warrant protection from nonfundamental rights that do not. Today's decision illustrates the point. Replaying a debate that has endured from the inception of the Court's substantive due process jurisprudence, the dissents laud the "flexibility" in this Court's substantive due process doctrine, while the plurality makes yet another effort to impose principled restraints on its exercise. But neither side argues that the meaning they attribute to the Due Process Clause was consistent with public understanding at the time of its ratification.

To be sure, the plurality's effort to cabin the exercise of judicial discretion under the Due Process Clause by focusing its inquiry on those rights deeply rooted in American history and tradition invites less opportunity for abuse than the alternatives. But any serious argument over the scope of the Due Process Clause must acknowledge that neither its text nor its history suggests that it protects the many substantive rights this Court's cases now claim it does.

I cannot accept a theory of constitutional interpretation that rests on such tenuous footing. This Court's substantive due process framework fails to account for both the text of the Fourteenth Amendment and the history that led to its adoption, filling that gap with a jurisprudence devoid of a guiding principle. I believe the original meaning of the Fourteenth Amendment offers a superior alternative, and that a return to that meaning would allow this Court to enforce the rights the Fourteenth Amendment is designed to protect with greater clarity and predictability than the substantive due process framework has so far managed.

I acknowledge the volume of precedents that have been built upon the substantive due process framework, and I further acknowledge the importance of *stare decisis* to the stability of our Nation's legal system. But *stare decisis* is only an "adjunct" of our duty as judges to decide by our best lights what the Constitution means. It is not "an inexorable command." *Lawrence*. Moreover, as judges, we interpret the Constitution one case or controversy at a time. The question presented in this case is not whether our entire Fourteenth Amendment jurisprudence must be preserved or revised, but only whether, and to what extent, a particular clause in the Constitution protects the particular right at issue here. With the inquiry appropriately narrowed, I believe this case presents an opportunity to reexamine, and begin the process of restoring, the meaning of the Fourteenth Amendment agreed upon by those who ratified it.

II

"It cannot be presumed that any clause in the constitution is intended to be without effect." Marbury v. Madison (1803) (Marshall, C.J.). Because the Court's Privileges or Immunities Clause precedents have presumed just that, I set them aside for the moment and begin with the text. The Privileges or Immunities Clause of the Fourteenth Amendment declares that "[n]o State . . . shall abridge the privileges or immunities of citizens of the United States." In interpreting this language, it is important to recall that constitutional provisions are "'written to be understood by the voters.'" *Heller*. Thus, the objective of this inquiry is to discern what "ordinary citizens" at the time of ratification would have understood the Privileges or Immunities Clause to mean.

A

1

At the time of Reconstruction, the terms "privileges" and "immunities" had an established meaning as synonyms for "rights." The two words, standing alone or paired together, were used interchangeably with the words "rights," "liberties," and "freedoms," and had been since the time of Blackstone. See 1 W. Blackstone, Commentaries *129 (describing the "rights and liberties" of Englishmen as "private immunities" and "civil privileges"). A number of antebellum judicial decisions used the terms in this manner. See, e.g., Magill v. Brown, (CC ED Pa. 1833) (Baldwin, J.) ("The words 'privileges and immunities' relate to the rights of persons, place or property; a privilege is a peculiar right, a private law, conceded to particular persons or places"). In addition, dictionary definitions confirm that the public shared this understanding. See, e.g., N. Webster, An American Dictionary of the English Language (rev. 1865) (defining "privilege" as "a right or immunity not enjoyed by others or by all" and listing among its synonyms the words "immunity," "franchise," "right," and "liberty"); *id.* (defining "immunity" as "[f]reedom from an obligation" or "particular privilege"); *id.* (defining "right" as "[p]rivilege or immunity granted by authority").

The fact that a particular interest was designated as a "privilege" or "immunity," rather than a "right," "liberty," or "freedom," revealed little about its substance. Blackstone, for example, used the terms "privileges" and "immunities" to describe both the inalienable rights of individuals and the positive-law rights of corporations. See Commentaries, (describing "private immunities" as a "residuum of natural liberty," and "civil privileges" as those "which society has engaged to provide, in lieu of the natural liberties so given up by individuals" (footnote omitted)); *id.* (stating that a corporate charter enables a corporation to "establish rules and orders" that serve as "the privileges and immunities . . . of the corporation"). Writers in this country at the time of Reconstruction followed a similar practice. The nature of a privilege or immunity thus varied depending on the person, group, or entity to whom those rights were assigned. See Lash, The Origins of the Privileges or Immunities Clause, Part I: "Privileges and Immunities" as an Antebellum Term of Art, 98 Geo. L. J. 1241, 1256-1257 (2010) (surveying antebellum usages of these terms).

2

The group of rights-bearers to whom the Privileges or Immunities Clause applies is, of course, "citizens." By the time of Reconstruction, it had long been established that both the States and the Federal Government existed to preserve their citizens' inalienable rights, and that these rights were considered "privileges" or "immunities" of citizenship. This tradition begins with our country's English roots. Parliament declared the basic liberties of English citizens in a series of documents ranging from the Magna Carta to the Petition of Right and the English Bill of Rights. These fundamental rights, according to the English tradition, belonged to all people but became legally enforceable only when recognized in legal texts, including acts of Parliament and the decisions of common-law judges. These rights included many that later would be set forth in our Federal Bill of Rights, such as the right to petition for redress of grievances, the right to a jury trial, and the right of "Protestants" to "have arms for their defence." English Bill of Rights (1689).

As English subjects, the colonists considered themselves to be vested with the same fundamental rights as other Englishmen. They consistently claimed the rights of English citizenship in their founding documents, repeatedly referring to these rights as "privileges" and "immunities." For example, a Maryland law provided that

> "[A]ll the Inhabitants of this Province being Christians (Slaves excepted) Shall have and enjoy all such *rights liberties immunities priviledges and free customs* within this Province as any naturall born subject of England hath or ought to have or enjoy in the Realm of England. . . ." Md. Act for the Liberties of the People (1639) (emphasis added).

As tensions between England and the Colonies increased, the colonists adopted protest resolutions reasserting their claim to the inalienable rights of Englishmen. Again, they used the terms "privileges" and "immunities" to describe these rights. As the Massachusetts Resolves declared:

> "*Resolved*, That there are certain essential Rights of the *British* Constitution of Government, which are founded in the Law of God and Nature, and are the common Rights of Mankind—Therefore.. . . .
>
> "*Resolved*, That no Man can justly take the Property of another without his Consent: And that upon this original Principle the Right of Representation . . . is evidently founded. . . . *Resolved*, That this *inherent* Right, together with all other, essential *Rights, Liberties, Privileges and Immunities* of the People of *Great Britain*,

have been fully confirmed to them by *Magna Charta*." The Massachusetts Resolves (Oct. 29, 1765) (some emphasis added).

In keeping with this practice, the First Continental Congress declared in 1774 that the King had wrongfully denied the colonists "the rights, liberties, and immunities of free and natural-born subjects . . . within the realm of England." In an address delivered to the inhabitants of Quebec that same year, the Congress described those rights as including the "great" "right[s]" of "trial by jury," "Habeas Corpus," and "freedom of the press."

After declaring their independence, the newly formed States replaced their colonial charters with constitutions and state bills of rights, almost all of which guaranteed the same fundamental rights that the former colonists previously had claimed by virtue of their English heritage. See, *e.g.*, Pa. Declaration of Rights (1776) (declaring that "all men are born equally free and independent, and have certain natural, inherent and inalienable rights," including the "right to worship Almighty God according to the dictates of their own consciences" and the "right to bear arms for the defence of themselves and the state").

Several years later, the Founders amended the Constitution to expressly protect many of the same fundamental rights against interference by the Federal Government. Consistent with their English heritage, the founding generation generally did not consider many of the rights identified in these amendments as new entitlements, but as inalienable rights of all men, given legal effect by their codification in the Constitution's text. See, e.g., 1 Annals of Cong. (1834) (statement of Rep. Madison) (proposing Bill of Rights in the first Congress); The Federalist No. 84 (A. Hamilton); see also *Heller*, "[I]t has always been widely understood that the Second Amendment, like the First and Fourth Amendments, codified a *pre-existing* right"). The Court's subsequent decision in *Barron*, however, made plain that the codification of these rights in the Bill made them legally enforceable only against the Federal Government, not the States.

3

Even though the Bill of Rights did not apply to the States, other provisions of the Constitution did limit state interference with individual rights. Article IV, §2, cl. 1 provides that "[t]he Citizens of each State shall be entitled to all Privileges and Immunities of Citizens in the several States." The text of this provision resembles the Privileges or Immunities Clause, and it can be assumed that the public's understanding of the latter was informed by its understanding of the former. Article IV, §2 was derived from a similar clause in the Articles of Confederation, and reflects the dual citizenship the Constitution provided to all Americans after replacing that "league" of separate sovereign States. By virtue of a person's citizenship in a particular State, he was guaranteed whatever rights and liberties that State's constitution and laws made available. Article IV, §2 vested citizens of each State with an additional right: the assurance that they would be afforded the "privileges and immunities" of citizenship in any of the several States in the Union to which they might travel.

What were the "Privileges and Immunities of Citizens in the several States"? That question was answered perhaps most famously by Justice Bushrod Washington sitting as Circuit Justice in Corfield v. Coryell (CC ED Pa. 1825). In that case, a Pennsylvania citizen claimed that a New Jersey law prohibiting nonresidents from harvesting oysters from the State's waters violated Article IV, §2 because it deprived him, as an out-of-state citizen, of a right New Jersey availed to its own citizens. Justice Washington rejected that argument, refusing to "accede to the proposition" that Article IV, §2 entitled "citizens of the several states . . . to participate in *all* the rights which belong exclusively to the citizens of any other particular state." (emphasis added). In his view, Article IV, §2 did not guarantee equal access to all public benefits a State might choose to make available to its citizens. Instead, it applied only to those rights "which are, in their nature, *fundamental*; which belong, of right, to the citizens of all free governments." (emphasis added). Other courts generally agreed with this principle.

When describing those "fundamental" rights, Justice Washington thought it "would perhaps be more tedious than difficult to enumerate" them all, but suggested that they could "be all comprehended under" a broad list of "general heads," such as "[p]rotection by the government," "the enjoyment of life and liberty, with the right to acquire and possess property of every kind," "the benefit of the writ of habeas corpus," and the right of access to "the courts of the state," among others.

Notably, Justice Washington did not indicate whether Article IV, §2 *required* States to recognize these fundamental rights in their own citizens and thus in sojourning citizens alike, or whether the Clause simply prohibited the States from discriminating against sojourning citizens with respect to whatever fundamental rights state law happened to recognize. On this question, the weight of legal authorities at the time of Reconstruction indicated that Article IV, §2 prohibited States from discriminating against sojourning citizens when recognizing fundamental rights, but did not require States to recognize those rights and did not prescribe their content. . . . This Court adopted the same conclusion in a unanimous opinion just one year after the Fourteenth Amendment was ratified. See Paul v. Virginia (1869).

* * *

The text examined so far demonstrates three points about the meaning of the Privileges or Immunities Clause in §1. First, "privileges" and "immunities" were synonyms for "rights." Second, both the States and the Federal Government had long recognized the inalienable rights of their citizens. Third, Article IV, §2 of the Constitution protected traveling citizens against state discrimination with respect to the fundamental rights of state citizenship.

Two questions still remain, both provoked by the textual similarity between §1's Privileges or Immunities Clause and Article IV, §2. The first involves the nature of the rights at stake: Are the privileges or immunities of "citizens of the United States" recognized by §1 the same as the privileges and immunities of "citizens in the several States" to which Article IV, §2 refers? The second involves the restriction imposed on the States: Does §1, like Article IV, §2, prohibit only discrimination with respect to certain rights *if* the State chooses to recognize them, or does it require States to recognize those rights? I address each question in turn.

B

I start with the nature of the rights that §1's Privileges or Immunities Clause protects. Section 1 overruled *Dred Scott*'s holding that blacks were not citizens of either the United States or their own State and, thus, did not enjoy "the privileges and immunities of citizens" embodied in the Constitution. The Court in *Dred Scott* did not distinguish between privileges and immunities of citizens of the United States and citizens in the several States, instead referring to the rights of citizens generally. It did, however, give examples of what the rights of citizens were—the constitutionally enumerated rights of "the full liberty of speech" and the right "to keep and carry arms."

Section 1 protects the rights of citizens "of the United States" specifically. The evidence overwhelmingly demonstrates that the privileges and immunities of such citizens included individual rights enumerated in the Constitution, including the right to keep and bear arms.

1

Nineteenth-century treaties through which the United States acquired territory from other sovereigns routinely promised inhabitants of the newly acquired territories that they would enjoy all of the "rights," "privileges," and "immunities" of United States citizens. Commentators of the time explained that the rights and immunities of "citizens of the United States" recognized in these treaties "undoubtedly mean[t] those privileges that are common to all citizens of this republic." Marcus, An Examination of the Expediency and Constitutionality of Prohibiting Slavery in the State of Missouri 17 (1819). It is therefore altogether unsurprising that several of these treaties identify liberties enumerated in the Constitution as privileges and immunities common to all United States citizens.

For example, the Louisiana Cession Act of 1803, which codified a treaty between the United States and France culminating in the Louisiana Purchase, provided that

> "The inhabitants of the ceded territory shall be incorporated in the Union of the United States, and admitted as soon as possible, according to the principles of the Federal constitution, to the enjoyments of *all the rights, advantages and immunities of citizens of the United States*; and in the mean time they shall be maintained and protected in *the free enjoyment of their liberty, property and the religion which they profess*." Treaty Between the United States of America and the French Republic, Art. III, Apr. 30, 1803 (emphasis added).

The Louisiana Cession Act reveals even more about the privileges and immunities of United States citizenship because it provoked an extensive public debate on the meaning of that term. In 1820, when the Missouri Territory (which the United States acquired through the Cession Act) sought to enter the Union as a new State, a debate ensued over whether to prohibit slavery within Missouri as a condition of its admission. Some congressmen argued that prohibiting slavery in Missouri would deprive its inhabitants of the "privileges and immunities" they had been promised by the Cession Act. But those who opposed slavery in Missouri argued that the right to hold slaves was merely a matter of state property law, not one of the privileges and immunities of United States citizenship guaranteed by the Act.

Daniel Webster was among the leading proponents of the antislavery position. In his "Memorial to Congress," Webster argued that "[t]he rights, advantages and immunities here spoken of [in the Cession Act] must . . . be such as are recognized or communicated by the Constitution of the United States," not the "rights, advantages and immunities, derived exclusively from the *State* governments. . . ." D. Webster, A Memorial to the Congress of the United States on the Subject of Restraining the Increase of Slavery in New States to be Admitted into the Union (Dec. 15, 1819) (emphasis added). "The obvious meaning" of the Act, in Webster's view, was that "*the rights derived under the federal Constitution* shall be enjoyed by the inhabitants of [the territory]." (emphasis added). In other words, Webster articulated a distinction between the rights of United States citizenship and the rights of state citizenship, and argued that the former included those rights "recognized or communicated by the Constitution." Since the right to hold slaves was not mentioned in the Constitution, it was not a right of federal citizenship.

Webster and his allies ultimately lost the debate over slavery in Missouri and the territory was admitted as a slave State as part of the now-famous Missouri Compromise. But their arguments continued to inform public understanding of the privileges and immunities of United States citizenship. . . .

2

Evidence from the political branches in the years leading to the Fourteenth Amendment's adoption demonstrates broad public understanding that the privileges and immunities of United States citizenship included rights set forth in the Constitution, just as Webster and his allies had argued. In 1868, President Andrew Johnson issued a proclamation granting amnesty to former Confederates, guaranteeing "to all and to every person who directly or indirectly participated in the late insurrection or rebellion, a full pardon and amnesty for the offence of treason . . . with restoration of *all rights, privileges, and immunities under the Constitution* and the laws which have been made in pursuance thereof."

Records from the 39th Congress further support this understanding.

a

After the Civil War, Congress established the Joint Committee on Reconstruction to investigate circumstances in the Southern States and to determine whether, and on what conditions, those States should be readmitted to the Union. See . . . M. Curtis, No State Shall Abridge: The Fourteenth Amendment and the Bill of Rights (1986). That Committee would ultimately recommend the adoption of the Fourteenth Amendment, justifying its recommendation by submitting a report to Congress that extensively catalogued the abuses of civil rights in the former slave States and argued that "adequate security for future peace and safety . . . can only be found in such changes of the organic law as shall determine the civil rights and privileges of all citizens in all parts of the republic."

As the Court notes, the Committee's Report "was widely reprinted in the press and distributed by members of the 39th Congress to their constituents." In addition, newspaper coverage suggests that the wider public was aware of the Committee's work even before the Report was issued. For example, the Fort Wayne Daily Democrat (which appears to have been unsupportive of the Committee's work) paraphrased a motion instructing the Committee to

> "enquire into [the] expediency of amending the Constitution of the United States so as to declare with greater certainty the power of Congress to enforce and determine by appropriate legislation all the guarantees contained in *that instrument*." The Nigger Congress!, Fort Wayne Daily Democrat, Feb. 1, 1866 (emphasis added).

b

Statements made by Members of Congress leading up to, and during, the debates on the Fourteenth Amendment point in the same direction. . . . Before considering that record here, it is important to clarify its relevance. When interpreting constitutional text, the goal is to discern the most likely public understanding of a particular provision at the time it was adopted. Statements by legislators can assist in this process to the extent they demonstrate the manner in which the public used or understood a particular word or phrase. They can further assist to the extent there is evidence that these statements were disseminated to the public. In other words, this evidence is useful not because it demonstrates what the draftsmen of the text may have been thinking, but only insofar as it illuminates what the public understood the words chosen by the draftsmen to mean.

(1)

Three speeches stand out as particularly significant. Representative John Bingham, the principal draftsman of §1, delivered a speech on the floor of the House in February 1866 introducing his first draft of the provision. Bingham began by discussing *Barron* and its holding that the Bill of Rights did not apply to the States. He then argued that a constitutional amendment was necessary to provide "an express grant of power in Congress to enforce by penal enactment these great canons of the supreme law, securing to all the citizens in every State all the privileges and immunities of citizens, and to all the people all the sacred rights of person." Bingham emphasized that §1 was designed "to arm the Congress of the United States, by the consent of the people of the United States, with the power to enforce the bill of rights as it stands in the Constitution today. It 'hath that extent — no more.'"

Bingham's speech was printed in pamphlet form and broadly distributed in 1866 under the title, "One Country, One Constitution, and One People," and the subtitle, "In Support of the Proposed Amendment to Enforce the Bill of Rights." Newspapers also reported his proposal, with the New York Times providing particularly extensive coverage, including a full reproduction of Bingham's first draft of §1 and his remarks that a constitutional amendment to "enforc[e]" the "immortal bill of rights" was "absolutely essential to American nationality." N.Y. Times, Feb. 27, 1866.

Bingham's first draft of §1 was different from the version ultimately adopted. Of particular importance, the first draft granted Congress the "power to make all laws . . . necessary and proper to secure" the "citizens of each State all privileges and immunities of citizens in the several States," rather than restricting state power to "abridge" the privileges or immunities of citizens of the United States.[39]

That draft was met with objections, which the *Times* covered extensively. A front-page article hailed the "Clear and Forcible Speech" by Representative Robert Hale against the draft, explaining — and endorsing — Hale's view that Bingham's proposal would "confer upon Congress all the rights and power of legislation now reserved to the States" and would "in effect utterly obliterate State rights and State authority over their own internal affairs."

Critically, Hale did *not* object to the draft insofar as it purported to protect constitutional liberties against state interference. Indeed, Hale stated that he believed (incorrectly in light of *Barron*) that individual rights enumerated in the Constitution were already enforceable against the States. See 39th Cong. Globe ("I have, somehow or other, gone along with the impression that there is that sort of protection thrown over us in some way, whether with or without the sanction of a judicial decision that we are so protected"). Hale's misperception was not uncommon among members of the Reconstruction generation. But that is secondary to the point that the *Times*' coverage of this debate over §1's meaning suggests public awareness of its main contours — *i.e.*, that §1 would, at a minimum, enforce constitutionally enumerated rights of United States citizens against the States.

Bingham's draft was tabled for several months. In the interim, he delivered a second well-publicized speech, again arguing that a constitutional amendment was required to give Congress the power to enforce the Bill of Rights against the States. That speech was printed in pamphlet form, and the New York Times covered the speech on its front page.

By the time the debates on the Fourteenth Amendment resumed, Bingham had amended his draft of §1 to include the text of the Privileges or Immunities

39. The full text of Bingham's first draft of §1 provided as follows: "The Congress shall have power to make all laws which shall be necessary and proper to secure to the citizens of each State all privileges and immunities of citizens in the several States, and to all persons in the several States equal protection in the rights of life, liberty, and property."

Clause that was ultimately adopted. Senator Jacob Howard introduced the new draft on the floor of the Senate in the third speech relevant here. Howard explained that the Constitution recognized "a mass of privileges, immunities, and rights, some of them secured by the second section of the fourth article of the Constitution, . . . some by the first eight amendments of the Constitution," and that "there is no power given in the Constitution to enforce and to carry out any of these guarantees" against the States. Howard then stated that "the great object" of §1 was to "restrain the power of the States and compel them at all times to respect these great fundamental guarantees." Section 1, he indicated, imposed "a general prohibition upon all the States, as such, from abridging the privileges and immunities of the citizens of the United States."

In describing these rights, Howard explained that they included "the privileges and immunities spoken of" in Article IV, §2. Although he did not catalogue the precise "nature" or "extent" of those rights, he thought "Corfield v. Coryell" provided a useful description. Howard then submitted that

> "[t]o these privileges and immunities, whatever they may be— . . . should be *added the personal rights guarantied and secured by the first eight amendments of the Constitution;* such as the freedom of speech and of the press; the right of the people peaceably to assemble and petition the Government for a redress of grievances, [and] . . . *the right to keep and to bear arms.*" (emphasis added).

News of Howard's speech was carried in major newspapers across the country, including the New York Herald, which was the best selling paper in the Nation at that time. The New York Times carried the speech as well, reprinting a lengthy excerpt of Howard's remarks, including the statements quoted above. The following day's *Times* editorialized on Howard's speech, predicting that "[t]o this, the first section of the amendment, the Union party throughout the country will yield a ready acquiescence, and the South could offer no justifiable resistance," suggesting that Bingham's narrower second draft had not been met with the same objections that Hale had raised against the first.

As a whole, these well-circulated speeches indicate that §1 was understood to enforce constitutionally declared rights against the States, and they provide no suggestion that any language in the section other than the Privileges or Immunities Clause would accomplish that task.

(2)

When read against this backdrop, the civil rights legislation adopted by the 39th Congress in 1866 further supports this view. Between passing the Thirteenth Amendment—which outlawed slavery alone—and the Fourteenth Amendment, Congress passed two significant pieces of legislation. The first was the Civil Rights Act of 1866, which provided that "all persons born in the United States" were "citizens of the United States" and that "such citizens, of every race and color, . . . shall have the same right" to, among other things, "full and equal benefit of all laws and proceedings for the security of person and property, as is enjoyed by white citizens."

Both proponents and opponents of this Act described it as providing the "privileges" of citizenship to freedmen, and defined those privileges to include constitutional rights, such as the right to keep and bear arms. See 39th Cong. Globe (remarks of Sen. Trumbull) (stating that the "the late slaveholding States" had enacted laws "depriving persons of African descent of privileges which are essential to freemen," including "prohibit[ing] any negro or mulatto from having fire-arms" and stating that "[t]he purpose of the bill under consideration is to destroy all these discriminations"); *id.* (remarks of Rep. Raymond) (opposing the Act, but recognizing that to "[m]ake a colored man a citizen of the United States" would guarantee to him, *inter alia*, "a defined *status* . . . a right to defend himself and his wife and children; a right to bear arms").

Three months later, Congress passed the Freedmen's Bureau Act, which also entitled all citizens to the "full and equal benefit of all laws and proceedings concerning personal liberty" and "personal security." The Act stated expressly that the rights of personal liberty and security protected by the Act "includ[ed] the constitutional right to bear arms."

(3)

There is much else in the legislative record. Many statements by Members of Congress corroborate the view that the Privileges or Immunities Clause enforced constitutionally enumerated rights against the States. I am not aware of any statement that directly refutes that proposition. That said, the record of the debates — like most legislative history — is less than crystal clear. In particular, much ambiguity derives from the fact that at least several Members described §1 as protecting the privileges and immunities of citizens "in the several States," harkening back to Article IV, §2. These statements can be read to support the view that the Privileges or Immunities Clause protects some or all the fundamental rights of "citizens" described in *Corfield*. They can also be read to support the view that the Privileges or Immunities Clause, like Article IV, §2, prohibits only state discrimination with respect to those rights it covers, but does not deprive States of the power to deny those rights to all citizens equally. I examine the rest of the historical record with this understanding. But for purposes of discerning what the public most likely thought the Privileges or Immunities Clause to mean, it is significant that the most widely publicized statements by the legislators who voted on §1 — Bingham, Howard, and even Hale — point unambiguously toward the conclusion that the Privileges or Immunities Clause enforces at least those fundamental rights enumerated in the Constitution against the States, including the Second Amendment right to keep and bear arms.

3

Interpretations of the Fourteenth Amendment in the period immediately following its ratification help to establish the public understanding of the text at the time of its adoption. Some of these interpretations come from Members of Congress. During an 1871 debate on a bill to enforce the Fourteenth Amendment, Representative Henry Dawes listed the Constitution's first eight

Amendments, including "the right to keep and bear arms," before explaining that after the Civil War, the country "gave the most grand of all these rights, privileges, and immunities, by one single amendment to the Constitution, to four millions of American citizens" who formerly were slaves. "It is all these," Dawes explained, "which are comprehended in the words 'American citizen.'" Even opponents of Fourteenth Amendment enforcement legislation acknowledged that the Privileges or Immunities Clause protected constitutionally enumerated individual rights.

Legislation passed in furtherance of the Fourteenth Amendment demonstrates even more clearly this understanding. For example, Congress enacted the Civil Rights Act of 1871, which was titled in pertinent part "An Act to enforce the Provisions of the Fourteenth Amendment to the Constitution of the United States," and which is codified in the still-existing 42 U. S. C. §1983. That statute prohibits state officials from depriving citizens of "any rights, privileges, or immunities *secured by the Constitution*." (emphasis added). Although the Judiciary ignored this provision for decades after its enactment, this Court has come to interpret the statute, unremarkably in light of its text, as protecting constitutionally enumerated rights. Monroe v. Pape (1961).

A Federal Court of Appeals decision written by a future Justice of this Court adopted the same understanding of the Privileges or Immunities Clause. See, e.g., United States v. Hall (CC SD Ala. 1871) (Woods, J.) ("We think, therefore, that the . . . rights enumerated in the first eight articles of amendment to the constitution of the United States, are the privileges and immunities of citizens of the United States"). In addition, two of the era's major constitutional treatises reflected the understanding that §1 would protect constitutionally enumerated rights from state abridgment.[40] A third such treatise unambiguously indicates that the Privileges or Immunities Clause accomplished this task. G. Paschal, The Constitution of the United States 290 (1868) (explaining that the rights listed in §1 had "already been guarantied" by Article IV and the Bill of Rights, but that "[t]he new feature declared" by §1 was that these rights, "which had been construed to apply only to the national government, are thus imposed upon the States").

Another example of public understanding comes from United States Attorney Daniel Corbin's statement in an 1871 Ku Klux Klan prosecution. Corbin cited *Barron* and declared:

> "[T]he fourteenth amendment changes all that theory, and lays the same restriction upon the States that before lay upon the Congress of the United States—that, as Congress heretofore could not interfere with the right of the citizen to keep and bear arms, now, after the adoption of the fourteenth amendment, the State cannot in-

40. See J. Pomeroy, An Introduction to the Constitutional Law of the United States (E. Bennett ed. 1886) (describing §1, which the country was then still considering, as a "needed" "remedy" for *Barron ex rel. Tiernan v. Mayor of Baltimore* (1833), which held that the Bill of Rights was not enforceable against the States); T. Farrar, Manual of the Constitution of the United States of America (1867); *id.*, (3d ed. 1872)(describing the Fourteenth Amendment as having "swept away" the "decisions of many courts" that "the popular rights guaranteed by the Constitution are secured only against [the federal] government").

terfere with the right of the citizen to keep and bear arms. The right to keep and bear arms is included in the fourteenth amendment, under 'privileges and immunities.'"

* * *

This evidence plainly shows that the ratifying public understood the Privileges or Immunities Clause to protect constitutionally enumerated rights, including the right to keep and bear arms. As the Court demonstrates, there can be no doubt that §1 was understood to enforce the Second Amendment against the States. In my view, this is because the right to keep and bear arms was understood to be a privilege of American citizenship guaranteed by the Privileges or Immunities Clause.

C

. . . Chicago and Oak Park, . . . contend that the Second Amendment, as applied to the States through the Fourteenth, authorizes a State to impose an outright ban on handgun possession such as the ones at issue here so long as a State applies it to all citizens equally. The Court explains why this antidiscrimination-only reading of §1 as a whole is "implausible." I agree, but because I think it is the Privileges or Immunities Clause that applies this right to the States, I must explain why this Clause in particular protects against more than just state discrimination, and in fact establishes a minimum baseline of rights for all American citizens. . . .

I begin, again, with the text. The Privileges or Immunities Clause opens with the command that "*No State shall*" abridge the privileges or immunities of citizens of the United States. Amdt. 14, §1 (emphasis added). The very same phrase opens Article I, §10 of the Constitution, which prohibits the States from "pass[ing] any Bill of Attainder" or "ex post facto Law," among other things. Article I, §10 is one of the few constitutional provisions that limits state authority. In *Barron*, when Chief Justice Marshall interpreted the Bill of Rights as lacking "plain and intelligible language" restricting state power to infringe upon individual liberties, he pointed to Article I, §10 as an example of text that would have accomplished that task. Indeed, Chief Justice Marshall would later describe Article I, §10 as "a bill of rights for the people of each state." Fletcher v. Peck (1810). Thus, the fact that the Privileges or Immunities Clause uses the command "[n]o State shall"—which Article IV, §2 does not—strongly suggests that the former imposes a greater restriction on state power than the latter.

This interpretation is strengthened when one considers that the Privileges or Immunities Clause uses the verb "abridge," rather than "discriminate," to describe the limit it imposes on state authority. The Webster's dictionary in use at the time of Reconstruction defines the word "abridge" to mean "[t]o deprive; to cut off; . . . as, to *abridge* one of his rights." The Clause is thus best understood to impose a limitation on state power to infringe upon pre-existing substantive rights. It raises no indication that the Framers of the Clause used the word "abridge" to prohibit only discrimination.

This most natural textual reading is underscored by a well-publicized revision to the Fourteenth Amendment that the Reconstruction Congress rejected. After several Southern States refused to ratify the Amendment, President Johnson met with their Governors to draft a compromise. Their proposal eliminated Congress' power to enforce the Amendment (granted in §5), and replaced the Privileges or Immunities Clause in §1 with the following:

> "All persons born or naturalized in the United States, and subject to the jurisdiction thereof, are citizens of the United States, and of the States in which they reside, and the Citizens of each State shall be entitled to all *the privileges and immunities of citizens in the several States.*"

Significantly, this proposal removed the "[n]o State shall" directive and the verb "abridge" from §1, and also changed the class of rights to be protected from those belonging to "citizens of the United States" to those of the "citizens in the several States." This phrasing is materially indistinguishable from Article IV, §2, which generally was understood as an antidiscrimination provision alone. The proposal thus strongly indicates that at least the President of the United States and several southern Governors thought that the Privileges or Immunities Clause, which they unsuccessfully tried to revise, prohibited more than just state-sponsored discrimination. . . . [41]

III

My conclusion is contrary to this Court's precedents, which hold that the Second Amendment right to keep and bear arms is not a privilege of United States citizenship. I must, therefore, consider whether *stare decisis* requires retention of those precedents. As mentioned at the outset, my inquiry is limited to the right at issue here. Thus, I do not endeavor to decide in this case whether, or to what extent, the Privileges or Immunities Clause applies any other rights enumerated in the Constitution against the States.[42] Nor do I suggest that the *stare decisis* considerations surrounding the application of the right to keep and bear arms against the States would be the same as those surrounding another

41. I conclude that the right to keep and bear arms applies to the States through the Privileges or Immunities Clause, which recognizes the rights of United States "citizens." The plurality concludes that the right applies to the States through the Due Process Clause, which covers all "person[s]." Because this case does not involve a claim brought by a noncitizen, I express no view on the difference, if any, between my conclusion and the plurality's with respect to the extent to which the States may regulate firearm possession by noncitizens.

42. I note, however, that I see no reason to assume that the constitutionally enumerated rights protected by the Privileges or Immunities Clause should consist of all the rights recognized in the Bill of Rights and no others. Constitutional provisions outside the Bill of Rights protect individual rights, see, e.g., Art. I, §9, cl. 2 (granting the "Privilege of the Writ of Habeas Corpus"), and there is no obvious evidence that the Framers of the Privileges or Immunities Clause meant to exclude them. In addition, certain Bill of Rights provisions prevent federal interference in state affairs and are not readily construed as protecting rights that belong to individuals. The Ninth and Tenth Amendments are obvious examples, as is the First Amendment's Establishment Clause, which "does not purport to protect individual rights." Elk Grove Unified School Dist. v. Newdow (2004) (THOMAS, J., concurring in judgment).

right protected by the Privileges or Immunities Clause. I consider *stare decisis* only as it applies to the question presented here.

A

This inquiry begins with the *Slaughter-House Cases* [in which] the Court defined the rights of state citizenship as "embrac[ing] nearly every civil right for the establishment and protection of which organized government is instituted"—that is, all those rights listed in *Corfield*. That left very few rights of federal citizenship for the Privileges or Immunities Clause to protect. The Court suggested a handful of possibilities, such as the "right of free access to [federal] seaports," protection of the Federal Government while traveling "on the high seas," and even two rights listed in the Constitution ([such as] "[t]he right to peaceably assemble" and "the privilege of the writ of *habeas corpus*"). But its decision to interpret the rights of state and federal citizenship as mutually exclusive led the Court in future cases to conclude that constitutionally enumerated rights were excluded from the Privileges or Immunities Clause's scope. See *Cruikshank*.

I reject that understanding. There was no reason to interpret the Privileges or Immunities Clause as putting the Court to the extreme choice of interpreting the "privileges and immunities" of federal citizenship to mean either all those rights listed in *Corfield*, or almost no rights at all. . . . For one thing, *Corfield* listed the "elective franchise" as one of the privileges and immunities of "citizens of the several states," yet Congress and the States still found it necessary to adopt the Fifteenth Amendment—which protects "[t]he right of citizens of the United States to vote"—two years after the Fourteenth Amendment's passage. If the Privileges or Immunities Clause were understood to protect every conceivable civil right from state abridgment, the Fifteenth Amendment would have been redundant.

The better view, in light of the States and Federal Government's shared history of recognizing certain inalienable rights in their citizens, is that the privileges and immunities of state and federal citizenship overlap. This is not to say that the privileges and immunities of state and federal citizenship are the same. At the time of the Fourteenth Amendment's ratification, States performed many more functions than the Federal Government, and it is unlikely that, simply by referring to "privileges or immunities," the Framers of §1 meant to transfer every right mentioned in *Corfield* to congressional oversight. As discussed, "privileges" and "immunities" were understood only as synonyms for "rights." It was their attachment to a particular group that gave them content, and the text and history recounted here indicate that the rights of United States citizens were not perfectly identical to the rights of citizens "in the several States." Justice Swayne, one of the dissenters in *Slaughter-House*, made the point clear:

> "The citizen of a State has the *same* fundamental rights as a citizen of the United States, *and also certain others*, local in their character, arising from his relation to the State, and in addition, those which belong to the citizen of the United States, he being in that relation also. There may thus be a double citizenship, each having some rights peculiar to itself. It is only over those which belong to the citizen of the

United States that the category here in question throws the shield of its protection." (emphasis added).

Because the privileges and immunities of American citizenship include rights enumerated in the Constitution, they overlap to at least some extent with the privileges and immunities traditionally recognized in citizens in the several States.

A separate question is whether the privileges and immunities of American citizenship include any rights besides those enumerated in the Constitution. The four dissenting Justices in *Slaughter-House* would have held that the Privileges or Immunities Clause protected the unenumerated right that the butchers in that case asserted. Because this case does not involve an unenumerated right, it is not necessary to resolve the question whether the Clause protects such rights, or whether the Court's judgment in *Slaughter-House* was correct.

Still, it is argued that the mere possibility that the Privileges or Immunities Clause may enforce unenumerated rights against the States creates "'special hazards'" that should prevent this Court from returning to the original meaning of the Clause.[43] (STEVENS, J., dissenting). Ironically, the same objection applies to the Court's substantive due process jurisprudence, which illustrates the risks of granting judges broad discretion to recognize individual constitutional rights in the absence of textual or historical guideposts. But I see no reason to assume that such hazards apply to the Privileges or Immunities Clause. The mere fact that the Clause does not expressly list the rights it protects does not render it incapable of principled judicial application. The Constitution contains many provisions that require an examination of more than just constitutional text to determine whether a particular act is within Congress' power or is otherwise prohibited. See, e.g., Art. I, §8, cl. 18 (Necessary and Proper Clause); Amdt. 8 (Cruel and Unusual Punishments Clause). When the inquiry focuses on what the ratifying era understood the Privileges or Immunities Clause to mean, interpreting it should be no more "hazardous" than interpreting these other constitutional provisions by using the same approach. To be sure, interpreting the Privileges or Immunities Clause may produce hard questions. But they will have the advantage of being questions the Constitution asks us to answer. I believe those questions are more worthy of this Court's attention — and far more likely to yield discernable answers — than the substantive due process questions the Court has for years created on its own, with neither textual nor historical support.

Finding these impediments to returning to the original meaning overstated, I reject *Slaughter-House* insofar as it precludes any overlap between the privileges and immunities of state and federal citizenship. I next proceed to the *stare decisis* considerations surrounding the precedent that expressly controls the question presented here.

43. To the extent JUSTICE STEVENS is concerned that reliance on the Privileges or Immunities Clause may invite judges to "write their personal views of appropriate public policy into the Constitution," his celebration of the alternative — the "flexibility," "transcend[ence]," and "dynamism" of substantive due process — speaks for itself.

B

Three years after *Slaughter-House*, the Court in *Cruikshank* squarely held that the right to keep and bear arms was not a privilege of American citizenship, thereby overturning the convictions of militia members responsible for the brutal Colfax Massacre. *Cruikshank* is not a precedent entitled to any respect. The flaws in its interpretation of the Privileges or Immunities Clause are made evident by the preceding evidence of its original meaning, and I would reject the holding on that basis alone. But, the consequences of *Cruikshank* warrant mention as well.

Cruikshank's holding that blacks could look only to state governments for protection of their right to keep and bear arms enabled private forces, often with the assistance of local governments, to subjugate the newly freed slaves and their descendants through a wave of private violence designed to drive blacks from the voting booth and force them into peonage, an effective return to slavery. Without federal enforcement of the inalienable right to keep and bear arms, these militias and mobs were tragically successful in waging a campaign of terror against the very people the Fourteenth Amendment had just made citizens.

Take, for example, the Hamburg Massacre of 1876. There, a white citizen militia sought out and murdered a troop of black militiamen for no other reason than that they had dared to conduct a celebratory Fourth of July parade through their mostly black town. The white militia commander, "Pitchfork" Ben Tillman, later described this massacre with pride: "[T]he leading white men of Edgefield" had decided "to seize the first opportunity that the negroes might offer them to provoke a riot and teach the negroes a lesson by having the whites demonstrate their superiority by killing as many of them as was justifiable." None of the perpetrators of the Hamburg murders was ever brought to justice.[44]

Organized terrorism like that perpetuated by Tillman and his cohorts proliferated in the absence of federal enforcement of constitutional rights. Militias such as the Ku Klux Klan, the Knights of the White Camellia, the White Brotherhood, the Pale Faces, and the '76 Association spread terror among blacks and white Republicans by breaking up Republican meetings, threatening political leaders, and whipping black militiamen. These groups raped, murdered, lynched, and robbed as a means of intimidating, and instilling pervasive fear in, those whom they despised.

Although Congress enacted legislation to suppress these activities,[45] Klan tactics remained a constant presence in the lives of Southern blacks for decades. Between 1882 and 1968, there were at least 3,446 reported lynchings of blacks in the South. They were tortured and killed for a wide array of alleged crimes,

44. Tillman went on to a long career as South Carolina's Governor and, later, United States Senator. Tillman's contributions to campaign finance law have been discussed in our recent cases on that subject. See Citizens United v. Federal Election Comm'n, (2010) (Stevens, J., dissenting) (discussing at length the Tillman Act of 1907). His contributions to the culture of terrorism that grew in the wake of *Cruikshank* had an even more dramatic and tragic effect.

45. In an effort to enforce the Fourteenth Amendment and halt this violence, Congress enacted a series of civil rights statutes, including the Force Acts and the Ku Klux Klan Act.

without even the slightest hint of due process. Emmit Till, for example, was killed in 1955 for allegedly whistling at a white woman. The fates of other targets of mob violence were equally depraved. See, e.g., Lynched Negro and Wife Were First Mutilated, Vicksburg (Miss.) Evening Post, Feb. 8, 1904; Negro Shot Dead for Kissing His White Girlfriend, Chi. Defender, Feb. 31, 1915 (reporting incident in Florida); La. Negro Is Burned Alive Screaming "I Didn't Do It," Cleveland Gazette, Dec. 13, 1914 (reporting incident in Louisiana).

The use of firearms for self-defense was often the only way black citizens could protect themselves from mob violence. As Eli Cooper, one target of such violence, is said to have explained, "[t]he Negro has been run over for fifty years, but it must stop now, and pistols and shotguns are the only weapons to stop a mob." Church Burnings Follow Negro Agitator's Lynching, Chicago Defender, Sept. 6,1919. Sometimes, as in Cooper's case, self-defense did not succeed. He was dragged from his home by a mob and killed as his wife looked on. But at other times, the use of firearms allowed targets of mob violence to survive. One man recalled the night during his childhood when his father stood armed at a jail until morning to ward off lynchers. The experience left him with a sense, "not 'of powerlessness, but of the "possibilities of salvation"'" that came from standing up to intimidation.

In my view, the record makes plain that the Framers of the Privileges or Immunities Clause and the ratifying-era public understood — just as the Framers of the Second Amendment did — that the right to keep and bear arms was essential to the preservation of liberty. The record makes equally plain that they deemed this right necessary to include in the minimum baseline of federal rights that the Privileges or Immunities Clause established in the wake of the War over slavery. There is nothing about *Cruikshank*'s contrary holding that warrants its retention.

* * *

I agree with the Court that the Second Amendment is fully applicable to the States. I do so because the right to keep and bear arms is guaranteed by the Fourteenth Amendment as a privilege of American citizenship.

JUSTICE STEVENS, dissenting.

In District of Columbia v. Heller, the Court answered the question whether a federal enclave's "prohibition on the possession of usable handguns in the home violates the Second Amendment to the Constitution." The question we should be answering in this case is whether the Constitution "guarantees individuals a fundamental right," enforceable against the States, "to possess a functional, personal firearm, including a handgun, within the home." [Complaint.] That is a different — and more difficult — inquiry than asking if the Fourteenth Amendment "incorporates" the Second Amendment. The so-called incorporation question was squarely and, in my view, correctly resolved in the late 19th century.[46] . . .

46. See United States v. Cruikshank (1876); Presser v. Illinois (1886); Miller v. Texas (1894). This is not to say that I agree with all other aspects of these decisions.

I agree with the plurality's refusal to accept petitioners' primary submission. Their briefs marshal an impressive amount of historical evidence for their argument that the Court interpreted the Privileges or Immunities Clause too narrowly in the Slaughter-House Cases (1873). But the original meaning of the Clause is not as clear as they suggest — and not nearly as clear as it would need to be to dislodge 137 years of precedent. The burden is severe for those who seek radical change in such an established body of constitutional doctrine. Moreover, the suggestion that invigorating the Privileges or Immunities Clause will reduce judicial discretion, strikes me as implausible, if not exactly backwards. "For the very reason that it has so long remained a clean slate, a revitalized Privileges or Immunities Clause holds special hazards for judges who are mindful that their proper task is not to write their personal views of appropriate public policy into the Constitution." [47]

I further agree with the plurality that there are weighty arguments supporting petitioners' second submission, insofar as it concerns the possession of firearms for lawful self-defense in the home. But these arguments are less compelling than the plurality suggests; they are much less compelling when applied outside the home; and their validity does not depend on the Court's holding in *Heller*. For that holding sheds no light on the meaning of the Due Process Clause of the Fourteenth Amendment. Our decisions construing that Clause to render various procedural guarantees in the Bill of Rights enforceable against the States likewise tell us little about the meaning of the word "liberty" in the Clause or about the scope of its protection of nonprocedural rights.

This is a substantive due process case.

I

Section 1 of the Fourteenth Amendment decrees that no State shall "deprive any person of life, liberty, or property, without due process of law." The Court has filled thousands of pages expounding that spare text. As I read the vast corpus of substantive due process opinions, they confirm several important principles that ought to guide our resolution of this case. The principal opinion's lengthy summary of our "incorporation" doctrine, and its implicit (and untenable) effort to wall off that doctrine from the rest of our substantive due process jurisprudence, invite a fresh survey of this old terrain.

Substantive Content

The first, and most basic, principle established by our cases is that the rights protected by the Due Process Clause are not merely procedural in nature. . . . [T]he

47. Wilkinson, The Fourteenth Amendment Privileges or Immunities Clause, 12 Harv. J. L. & Pub. Pol'y 43, 52 (1989). Judge Wilkinson's point is broader than the privileges or immunities debate. As he observes, "there may be more structure imposed by provisions subject to generations of elaboration and refinement than by a provision in it pristine state. The fortuities of uneven constitutional development must be respected, not cast aside in the illusion of reordering the landscape anew."

historical evidence suggests that, at least by the time of the Civil War if not much earlier, the phrase "due process of law" had acquired substantive content as a term of art within the legal community.[48] This understanding is consonant with the venerable "notion that governmental authority has implied limits which preserve private autonomy," a notion which predates the founding and which finds reinforcement in the Constitution's Ninth Amendment, see Griswold v. Connecticut (1965) (Goldberg, J., concurring). The Due Process Clause cannot claim to be the source of our basic freedoms — no legal document ever could — but it stands as one of their foundational guarantors in our law. . . .

Liberty

The second principle woven through our cases is that substantive due process is fundamentally a matter of personal liberty. For it is the liberty clause of the Fourteenth Amendment that grounds our most important holdings in this field. It is the liberty clause that enacts the Constitution's "promise" that a measure of dignity and self-rule will be afforded to all persons. Planned Parenthood of Southeastern Pa. v. Casey (1992). It is the liberty clause that reflects and renews "the origins of the American heritage of freedom [and] the abiding interest in individual liberty that makes certain state intrusions on the citizen's right to decide how he will live his own life intolerable." Fitzgerald v. Porter Memorial Hospital (CA7 1975) (STEVENS, J.). Our substantive due process cases have episodically invoked values such as privacy and equality as well, values that in certain contexts may intersect with or complement a subject's liberty interests in profound ways. But as I have observed on numerous occasions, "most of the significant [20th-century] cases raising Bill of Rights issues have, in the final analysis, actually interpreted the word 'liberty' in the Fourteenth Amendment."[49]

It follows that the term "incorporation," like the term "unenumerated rights," is something of a misnomer. Whether an asserted substantive due process interest is explicitly named in one of the first eight Amendments to the Constitution or is not mentioned, the underlying inquiry is the same: We must ask whether the interest is "comprised within the term liberty." [Whitney v.

48. See, e.g., Ely, The Oxymoron Reconsidered: Myth and Reality in the Origins of Substantive Due Process, 16 Const. Commentary 315, 326-327 (1999) (concluding that founding-era "American statesmen accustomed to viewing due process through the lens of [Sir Edward] Coke and [William] Blackstone could [not] have failed to understand due process as encompassing substantive as well as procedural terms"); Gedicks, An Originalist Defense of Substantive Due Process: Magna Carta, Higher-Law Constitutionalism, and the Fifth Amendment, 58 Emory L. J. 585, 594 (2009) (arguing "that one widely shared understanding of the Due Process Clause of the Fifth Amendment in the late eighteenth century encompassed judicial recognition and enforcement of unenumerated substantive rights"); Maltz, Fourteenth Amendment Concepts in the Antebellum Era, 32 Am. J. Legal Hist. 305, 317-318 (1988) (explaining that in the antebellum era a "substantial number of states," as well as antislavery advocates, "imbued their [constitutions']respective due process clauses with a substantive content"). . . .

49. Stevens, The Bill of Rights: A Century of Progress, 59 U. Chi. L. Rev. 13, 20 (1992). . . .

California (1927)] (Brandeis, J., concurring). As the second Justice Harlan has shown, ever since the Court began considering the applicability of the Bill of Rights to the States, "the Court's usual approach has been to ground the prohibitions against state action squarely on due process, without intermediate reliance on any of the first eight Amendments." Malloy v. Hogan (1964) (dissenting opinion).

In his own classic opinion in *Griswold* (concurring in judgment), Justice Harlan memorably distilled these precedents' lesson: "While the relevant inquiry may be aided by resort to one or more of the provisions of the Bill of Rights, it is not dependent on them or any of their radiations. The Due Process Clause of the Fourteenth Amendment stands . . . on its own bottom." Inclusion in the Bill of Rights is neither necessary nor sufficient for an interest to be judicially enforceable under the Fourteenth Amendment. This Court's "'selective incorporation'" doctrine is not simply "related" to substantive due process; it is a subset thereof. . . .

II

So far, I have explained that substantive due process analysis generally requires us to consider the term "liberty" in the Fourteenth Amendment, and that this inquiry may be informed by but does not depend upon the content of the Bill of Rights. How should a court go about the analysis, then? . . . Several of our most important recent decisions confirm the proposition that substantive due process analysis—from which, once again, "incorporation" analysis derives—must not be wholly backward looking. See, e.g., Lawrence v. Texas (2003) ("[H]istory and tradition are the starting point but not in all cases the ending point of the substantive due process inquiry". . . .[50] To the extent the Court's opinion could be read to imply that the historical pedigree of a right is the exclusive or dispositive determinant of its status under the Due Process Clause, the opinion is seriously mistaken.

A rigid historical test is inappropriate in this case, most basically, because our substantive due process doctrine has never evaluated substantive rights in purely, or even predominantly, historical terms. . . . The right to free speech, for instance, has been safeguarded from state infringement not because the States have always honored it, but because it is "essential to free government" and "to the maintenance of democratic institutions"—that is, because the right to free speech is implicit in the concept of ordered liberty. Thornhill v. Alabama (1940). While the verbal formula has varied, the Court has largely been consistent in its liberty-based approach to substantive interests outside of the adjudicatory system. As the question before us indisputably concerns such an interest, the answer

50. I acknowledge that some have read the Court's opinion in *Glucksberg* as an attempt to move substantive due process analysis, for all purposes, toward an exclusively historical methodology—and thereby to debilitate the doctrine. If that were ever *Glucksberg*'s aspiration, *Lawrence* plainly renounced it. As between *Glucksberg* and *Lawrence*, I have little doubt which will prove the more enduring precedent.

cannot be found in a granular inspection of state constitutions or congressional debates.

More fundamentally, a rigid historical methodology is unfaithful to the Constitution's command. For if it were really the case that the Fourteenth Amendment's guarantee of liberty embraces only those rights "so rooted in our history, tradition, and practice as to require special protection," *Glucksberg*, then the guarantee would serve little function, save to ratify those rights that state actors have *already* been according the most extensive protection. That approach is unfaithful to the expansive principle Americans laid down when they ratified the Fourteenth Amendment and to the level of generality they chose when they crafted its language; it promises an objectivity it cannot deliver and masks the value judgments that pervade any analysis of what customs, defined in what manner, are sufficiently "'rooted'"; it countenances the most revolting injustices in the name of continuity, for we must never forget that not only slavery but also the subjugation of women and other rank forms of discrimination are part of our history; and it effaces this Court's distinctive role in saying what the law is, leaving the development and safekeeping of liberty to majoritarian political processes. It is judicial abdication in the guise of judicial modesty.

No, the liberty safeguarded by the Fourteenth Amendment is not merely preservative in nature but rather is a "dynamic concept." Stevens, The Bill of Rights. Its dynamism provides a central means through which the Framers enabled the Constitution to "endure for ages to come," McCulloch v. Maryland (1819), a central example of how they "wisely spoke in general language and left to succeeding generations the task of applying that language to the unceasingly changing environment in which they would live," Rehnquist, The Notion of a Living Constitution, 54 Tex. L. Rev. 693, 694 (1976). "The task of giving concrete meaning to the term 'liberty,'" I have elsewhere explained at some length, "was a part of the work assigned to future generations." Stevens, The Third Branch of Liberty, 41 U. Miami L. Rev. 277, 291 (1986).[51] The judge who would outsource the interpretation of "liberty" to historical sentiment has turned his back on a task the Constitution assigned to him and drained the document of its intended vitality. . . .

IV

The question in this case, then, is not whether the Second Amendment right to keep and bear arms (whatever that right's precise contours) applies to the States because the Amendment has been incorporated into the Fourteenth Amendment.

51. Justice Kennedy has made the point movingly: "Had those who drew and ratified the Due Process Clauses of the Fifth Amendment or the Fourteenth Amendment known the components of liberty in its manifold possibilities, they might have been more specific. They did not presume to have this insight. They knew times can blind us to certain truths and later generations can see that laws once thought necessary and proper in fact serve only to oppress. As the Constitution endures, persons in every generation can invoke its principles in their own search for greater freedom." *Lawrence*.

It has not been. The question, rather, is whether the particular right asserted by petitioners applies to the States because of the Fourteenth Amendment itself, standing on its own bottom. And to answer that question, we need to determine, first, the nature of the right that has been asserted and, second, whether that right is an aspect of Fourteenth Amendment "liberty." Even accepting the Court's holding in *Heller*, it remains entirely possible that the right to keep and bear arms identified in that opinion is not judicially enforceable against the States, or that only part of the right is so enforceable. . . .

Understood as a plea to keep their preferred type of firearm in the home, petitioners' argument has real force. The decision to keep a loaded handgun in the house is often motivated by the desire to protect life, liberty, and property. It is comparable, in some ways, to decisions about the education and upbringing of one's children. For it is the kind of decision that may have profound consequences for every member of the family, and for the world beyond. In considering whether to keep a handgun, heads of households must ask themselves whether the desired safety benefits outweigh the risks of deliberate or accidental misuse that may result in death or serious injury, not only to residents of the home but to others as well. Millions of Americans have answered this question in the affirmative, not infrequently because they believe they have an inalienable right to do so — because they consider it an aspect of "the supreme human dignity of being master of one's fate rather than a ward of the State," Indiana v. Edwards (2008) (Scalia, J., dissenting). Many such decisions have been based, in part, on family traditions and deeply held beliefs that are an aspect of individual autonomy the government may not control.

Bolstering petitioners' claim, our law has long recognized that the home provides a kind of special sanctuary in modern life. Consequently, we have long accorded special deference to the privacy of the home, whether a humble cottage or a magnificent manse. This veneration of the domestic harkens back to the common law. William Blackstone recognized a "right of habitation," and opined that "every man's house is looked upon by the law to be his castle of defence and asylum." *Heller* carried forward this legacy, observing that "the need for defense of self, family, and property is most acute" in one's abode, and celebrating "the right of law-abiding, responsible citizens to use arms in defense of hearth and home."

While the individual's interest in firearm possession is thus heightened in the home, the State's corresponding interest in regulation is somewhat weaker. The State generally has a lesser basis for regulating private as compared to public acts, and firearms kept inside the home generally pose a lesser threat to public welfare as compared to firearms taken outside. The historical case for regulation is likewise stronger outside the home, as many States have for many years imposed stricter, and less controversial, restrictions on the carriage of arms than on their domestic possession.

It is significant, as well, that a rule limiting the federal constitutional right to keep and bear arms to the home would be less intrusive on state prerogatives and easier to administer. Having unleashed in *Heller* a tsunami of legal uncertainty, and thus litigation, and now on the cusp of imposing a national rule on the States in this area for the first time in United States history, the Court could at least moderate the confusion, upheaval, and burden on the States by adopting a rule that is clearly and tightly bounded in scope. . . .

V

While I agree with the Court that our substantive due process cases offer a principled basis for holding that petitioners have a constitutional right to possess a usable fiream [*sic*] in the home, I am ultimately persuaded that a better reading of our case law supports the city of Chicago. I would not foreclose the possibility that a particular plaintiff—say, an elderly widow who lives in a dangerous neighborhood and does not have the strength to operate a long gun—may have a cognizable liberty interest in possessing a handgun. But I cannot accept petitioners' broader submission. A number of factors, taken together, lead me to this conclusion.

First, firearms have a fundamentally ambivalent relationship to liberty. Just as they can help homeowners defend their families and property from intruders, they can help thugs and insurrectionists murder innocent victims. The threat that firearms will be misused is far from hypothetical, for gun crime has devastated many of our communities. . . .

Hence, in evaluating an asserted right to be free from particular gun-control regulations, liberty is on both sides of the equation. Guns may be useful for self-defense, as well as for hunting and sport, but they also have a unique potential to facilitate death and destruction and thereby to destabilize ordered liberty. *Your* interest in keeping and bearing a certain firearm may diminish *my* interest in being and feeling safe from armed violence. And while granting you the right to own a handgun might make you safer on any given day—assuming the handgun's marginal contribution to self-defense outweighs its marginal contribution to the risk of accident, suicide, and criminal mischief—it may make you and the community you live in less safe overall, owing to the increased number of handguns in circulation. It is at least reasonable for a democratically elected legislature to take such concerns into account in considering what sorts of regulations would best serve the public welfare. . . .

Second, the right to possess a firearm of one's choosing is different in kind from the liberty interests we have recognized under the Due Process Clause. Despite the plethora of substantive due process cases that have been decided in the post-*Lochner* century, I have found none that holds, states, or even suggests that the term "liberty" encompasses either the common-law right of self-defense or a right to keep and bear arms. I do not doubt for a moment that many Americans feel deeply passionate about firearms, and see them as critical to their way of life as well as to their security. Nevertheless, it does not appear to be the case that the ability to own a handgun, or any particular type of firearm, is critical to leading a life of autonomy, dignity, or political equality: The marketplace offers many tools for self-defense, even if they are imperfect substitutes, and neither petitioners nor their *amici* make such a contention.

Petitioners' claim is not the kind of substantive interest, accordingly, on which a uniform, judicially enforced national standard is presumptively appropriate.

Indeed, in some respects the substantive right at issue may be better viewed as a property right. Petitioners wish to *acquire* certain types of firearms, or to *keep* certain firearms they have previously acquired. Interests in the possession of chattels have traditionally been viewed as property interests subject to definition and regulation by the States. Under that tradition, Chicago's ordinance is unexceptional.[52]

The liberty interest asserted by petitioners is also dissimilar from those we have recognized in its capacity to undermine the security of others. To be sure, some of the Bill of Rights' procedural guarantees may place "restrictions on law enforcement" that have "controversial public safety implications." (plurality opinion). But those implications are generally quite attenuated. A defendant's invocation of his right to remain silent, to confront a witness, or to exclude certain evidence cannot directly cause any threat. The defendant's liberty interest is constrained by (and is itself a constraint on) the adjudicatory process. The link between handgun ownership and public safety is much tighter. The handgun is itself a tool for crime; the handgun's bullets *are* the violence.

Similarly, it is undeniable that some may take profound offense at a remark made by the soapbox speaker, the practices of another religion, or a gay couple's choice to have intimate relations. But that offense is moral, psychological, or theological in nature; the actions taken by the rights-bearers do not actually threaten the physical safety of any other person. Firearms may be used to kill another person. If a legislature's response to dangerous weapons ends up impinging upon the liberty of any individuals in pursuit of the greater good, it invariably does so on the basis of more than the majority's "'own moral code,'" *Lawrence*. . . .

Third, the experience of other advanced democracies, including those that share our British heritage, undercuts the notion that an expansive right to keep and bear arms is intrinsic to ordered liberty. Many of these countries place restrictions on the possession, use, and carriage of firearms far more onerous than the restrictions found in this Nation. See Municipal Respondents' Brief (discussing laws of England, Canada, Australia, Japan, Denmark, Finland, Luxembourg, and New Zealand). That the United States is an international outlier in the permissiveness of its approach to guns does not suggest that our laws are bad laws. It does suggest that this Court may not need to assume responsibility for making our laws still more permissive.

Admittedly, these other countries differ from ours in many relevant respects, including their problems with violent crime and the traditional role that firearms have played in their societies. But they are not so different from the United

52. It has not escaped my attention that the Due Process Clause refers to "property" as well as "liberty." . . . I am open to property claims under the Fourteenth Amendment. This case just involves a weak one. And ever since the Court "incorporated" the more specific property protections of the Takings Clause in 1897, see *Chicago, B. & Q. R. Co.*, substantive due process doctrine has focused on liberty.

States that we ought to dismiss their experience entirely. The fact that our oldest allies have almost uniformly found it appropriate to regulate firearms extensively tends to weaken petitioners' submission that the right to possess a gun of one's choosing is fundamental to a life of liberty. While the "American perspective" must always be our focus, it is silly—indeed, arrogant—to think we have nothing to learn about liberty from the billions of people beyond our borders.

Fourth, the Second Amendment differs in kind from the Amendments that surround it, with the consequence that its inclusion in the Bill of Rights is not merely unhelpful but positively harmful to petitioners' claim. Generally, the inclusion of a liberty interest in the Bill of Rights points toward the conclusion that it is of fundamental significance and ought to be enforceable against the States. But the Second Amendment plays a peculiar role within the Bill, as announced by its peculiar opening clause. Even accepting the *Heller* Court's view that the Amendment protects an individual right to keep and bear arms disconnected from militia service, it remains undeniable that "the purpose for which the right was codified" was "to prevent elimination of the militia." *Heller*. It was the States, not private persons, on whose immediate behalf the Second Amendment was adopted. Notwithstanding the *Heller* Court's efforts to write the Second Amendment's preamble out of the Constitution, the Amendment still serves the structural function of protecting the States from encroachment by an overreaching Federal Government.

The Second Amendment, in other words, "is a federalism provision" . . . directed at preserving the autonomy of the sovereign States, and its logic therefore "resists" incorporation by a federal court *against* the States. No one suggests that the Tenth Amendment, which provides that powers not given to the Federal Government remain with "the States," applies to the States; such a reading would border on incoherent, given that the Tenth Amendment exists (in significant part) to safeguard the vitality of state governance. The Second Amendment is no different. . . .

Fifth, although it may be true that Americans' interest in firearm possession and state-law recognition of that interest are "deeply rooted" in some important senses, it is equally true that the States have a long and unbroken history of regulating firearms. The idea that States may place substantial restrictions on the right to keep and bear arms short of complete disarmament is, in fact, far more entrenched than the notion that the Federal Constitution protects any such right. . . . From the early days of the Republic, through the Reconstruction era, to the present day, States and municipalities have placed extensive licensing requirements on firearm acquisition, restricted the public carriage of weapons, and banned altogether the possession of especially dangerous weapons, including handguns. After the 1860's just as before, the state courts almost uniformly upheld these measures. . . .

Finally, even apart from the States' long history of firearms regulation and its location at the core of their police powers, this is a quintessential area in which federalism ought to be allowed to flourish without this Court's meddling.

Whether or not we *can* assert a plausible constitutional basis for intervening, there are powerful reasons why we *should not* do so.

Across the Nation, States and localities vary significantly in the patterns and problems of gun violence they face, as well as in the traditions and cultures of lawful gun use they claim. The city of Chicago, for example, faces a pressing challenge in combating criminal street gangs. Most rural areas do not. The city of Chicago has a high population density, which increases the potential for a gunman to inflict mass terror and casualties. Most rural areas do not. The city of Chicago offers little in the way of hunting opportunities. Residents of rural communities are, one presumes, much more likely to stock the dinner table with game they have personally felled.

Given that relevant background conditions diverge so much across jurisdictions, the Court ought to pay particular heed to state and local legislatures' "right to experiment." [New State Ice Co. v. Liebmann (1932)] (BRANDEIS, J., dissenting). So long as the regulatory measures they have chosen are not "arbitrary, capricious, or unreasonable," we should be allowing them to "try novel social and economic" policies. It "is more in keeping . . . with our status as a court in a federal system," under these circumstances, "to avoid imposing a single solution . . . from the top down." Smith v. Robbins (2000).

It is all the more unwise for this Court to limit experimentation in an area "where the best solution is far from clear." United States v. Lopez (1995) (KENNEDY, J., concurring). Few issues of public policy are subject to such intensive and rapidly developing empirical controversy as gun control. Chicago's handgun ban, in itself, has divided researchers. Of course, on some matters the Constitution requires that we ignore such pragmatic considerations. But the Constitution's text, history, and structure are not so clear on the matter before us — as evidenced by the groundbreaking nature of today's fractured decision — and this Court lacks both the technical capacity and the localized expertise to assess "the wisdom, need, and propriety" of most gun control measures. *Griswold.*[53] . . .

VII

The fact that the right to keep and bear arms appears in the Constitution should not obscure the novelty of the Court's decision to enforce that right against the States. By its terms, the Second Amendment does not apply to the States; read properly, it does not even apply to individuals outside of the militia context. The Second Amendment was adopted to protect the *States* from federal encroachment. And the Fourteenth Amendment has never been understood by the Court

53. . . . I agree with the plurality that for a right to be eligible for substantive due process recognition, there need not be "a 'popular consensus' that the right is fundamental." In our remarkably diverse, pluralistic society, there will almost never be such uniformity of opinion. But to the extent that popular consensus is relevant, I do not agree with the Court that the *amicus* brief filed in this case by numerous state attorneys general constitutes evidence thereof. It is puzzling that so many state lawmakers have asked us to limit their *option* to regulate a dangerous item.

to have "incorporated" the entire Bill of Rights. There was nothing foreordained about today's outcome.

Although the Court's decision in this case might be seen as a mere adjunct to its decision in *Heller*, the consequences could prove far more destructive — quite literally — to our Nation's communities and to our constitutional structure. Thankfully, the Second Amendment right identified in *Heller* and its newly minted Fourteenth Amendment analogue are limited, at least for now, to the home. But neither the "assurances" provided by the plurality, nor the many historical sources cited in its opinion should obscure the reality that today's ruling marks a dramatic change in our law — or that the Justices who have joined it have brought to bear an awesome amount of discretion in resolving the legal question presented by this case. . . .

Accordingly, I respectfully dissent.

JUSTICE BREYER, with whom JUSTICE GINSBURG and JUSTICE SOTOMAYOR join, dissenting.

In my view, JUSTICE STEVENS has demonstrated that the Fourteenth Amendment's guarantee of "substantive due process" does not include a general right to keep and bear firearms for purposes of private self-defense. . . . The Court, however, does not expressly rest its opinion upon "substantive due process" concerns. Rather, it directs its attention to this Court's "incorporation" precedents and asks whether the Second Amendment right to private self-defense is "fundamental" so that it applies to the States through the Fourteenth Amendment.

I shall therefore separately consider the question of "incorporation." I can find nothing in the Second Amendment's text, history, or underlying rationale that could warrant characterizing it as "fundamental" insofar as it seeks to protect the keeping and bearing of arms for private self-defense purposes. Nor can I find any justification for interpreting the Constitution as transferring ultimate regulatory authority over the private uses of firearms from democratically elected legislatures to courts or from the States to the Federal Government. I therefore conclude that the Fourteenth Amendment does not "incorporate" the Second Amendment's right "to keep and bear Arms." And I consequently dissent. . . .

[II]

In my own view, the Court should not look to history alone but to other factors as well — above all, in cases where the history is so unclear that the experts themselves strongly disagree. . . . I would include among those factors the nature of the right; any contemporary disagreement about whether the right is fundamental; the extent to which incorporation will further other, perhaps more basic, constitutional aims; and the extent to which incorporation will advance or hinder the Constitution's structural aims, including its division of powers among different governmental institutions (and the people as well). Is incorporation needed, for example, to further the Constitution's effort to ensure that the government treats each individual with equal respect? Will it help maintain the democratic form of government that the Constitution foresees? In a word, will incorporation prove consistent, or inconsistent, with the Constitution's efforts to create governmental institutions well suited to the carrying out of its constitutional promises?

Finally, I would take account of the Framers' basic reason for believing the Court ought to have the power of judicial review. Alexander Hamilton feared granting that power to Congress alone, for he feared that Congress, acting as judges, would not overturn as unconstitutional a popular statute that it had recently enacted, as legislators. The Federalist No. 78 (A. Hamilton) ("This independence of the judges is equally requisite to guard the constitution and the rights of individuals from the effects of those ill humours, which" can, at times, lead to "serious oppressions of the minor part in the community"). Judges, he thought, may find it easier to resist popular pressure to suppress the basic rights of an unpopular minority. See United States v. Carolene Products Co., n. 4 (1938). That being so, it makes sense to ask whether that particular comparative judicial advantage is relevant to the case at hand. See, e.g., J. Ely, Democracy and Distrust (1980). . . .

How do these considerations apply here? For one thing, I would apply them only to the private self-defense right directly at issue. After all, the Amendment's militia related purpose is primarily to protect *States* from *federal* regulation, not to protect individuals from militia-related regulation. *Heller*. . . . [But] there is no popular consensus that the private self-defense right described in *Heller* is fundamental. The plurality suggests that two *amici* briefs filed in the case show such a consensus, but, of course, numerous *amici* briefs have been filed opposing incorporation as well. Moreover, every State regulates firearms extensively, and public opinion is sharply divided on the appropriate level of regulation. Much of this disagreement rests upon empirical considerations. One side believes the right essential to protect the lives of those attacked in the home; the other side believes it essential to regulate the right in order to protect the lives of others attacked with guns. It seems unlikely that definitive evidence will develop one way or the other. And the appropriate level of firearm regulation has thus long been, and continues to be, a hotly contested matter of political debate.

Moreover, there is no reason here to believe that incorporation of the private self-defense right will further any other or broader constitutional objective. We are aware of no argument that gun-control regulations target or are passed with the purpose of targeting "discrete and insular minorities." *Carolene Products Co.*, n. 4. Nor will incorporation help to assure equal respect for individuals. Unlike the First Amendment's rights of free speech, free press, assembly, and petition, the private self-defense right does not comprise a necessary part of the democratic process that the Constitution seeks to establish. Unlike the First Amendment's religious protections, the Fourth Amendment's protection against unreasonable searches and seizures, the Fifth and Sixth Amendments' insistence upon fair criminal procedure, and the Eighth Amendment's protection against cruel and unusual punishments, the private self-defense right does not significantly seek to protect individuals who might otherwise suffer unfair or inhumane treatment at the hands of a majority. Unlike the protections offered by many of these same Amendments, it does not involve matters as to which judges possess a comparative expertise, by virtue of their close familiarity with the justice system and its operation. And, unlike the Fifth Amendment's insistence on just compensation, it does not involve a matter where a majority might unfairly seize for itself property belonging to a minority.

Finally, incorporation of the right *will* work a significant disruption in the constitutional allocation of decision-making authority, thereby interfering with the Constitution's ability to further its objectives.

First, on any reasonable accounting, the incorporation of the right recognized in *Heller* would amount to a significant incursion on a traditional and important area of state concern, altering the constitutional relationship between the States and the Federal Government. Private gun regulation is the quintessential exercise of a State's "police power"—*i.e.*, the power to "protec[t] . . . the lives, limbs, health, comfort, and quiet of all persons, and the protection of all property within the State," by enacting "all kinds of restraints and burdens" on both "persons and property." *Slaughter-House Cases*. The Court has long recognized that the Constitution grants the States special authority to enact laws pursuant to this power. A decade ago, we wrote that there is "no better example of the police power" than "the suppression of violent crime." United States v. Morrison (2000). And examples in which the Court has deferred to state legislative judgments in respect to the exercise of the police power are legion. See, *e.g.*, Gonzales v. Oregon (2006) (assisted suicide); Washington v. Glucksberg (1997) (same). . . .

Second, determining the constitutionality of a particular state gun law requires finding answers to complex empirically based questions of a kind that legislatures are better able than courts to make. And it may require this kind of analysis in virtually every case.

Government regulation of the right to bear arms normally embodies a judgment that the regulation will help save lives. The determination whether a gun regulation is constitutional would thus almost always require the weighing of the constitutional right to bear arms against the "primary concern of every government—a concern for the safety and indeed the lives of its citizens." United States v. Salerno (1987). With respect to other incorporated rights, this sort of inquiry is *sometimes* present. See, e.g., Brandenburg v. Ohio (1969) (free speech); Sherbert v. Verner (1963) (religion); Brigham City v. Stuart (2006) (Fourth Amendment); New York v. Quarles (1984) (Fifth Amendment). . . . But here, this inquiry—calling for the fine tuning of protective rules—is likely to be part of a daily judicial diet.

Given the competing interests, courts will have to try to answer empirical questions of a particularly difficult kind. Suppose, for example, that after a gun regulation's adoption the murder rate went up. Without the gun regulation would the murder rate have risen even faster? How is this conclusion affected by the local recession which has left numerous people unemployed? What about budget cuts that led to a downsizing of the police force? How effective was that police force to begin with? And did the regulation simply take guns from those who use them for lawful purposes without affecting their possession by criminals?

Consider too that countless gun regulations of many shapes and sizes are in place in every State and in many local communities. Does the right to possess weapons for self-defense extend outside the home? To the car? To work? What sort of guns are necessary for self-defense? Handguns? Rifles? Semiautomatic weapons? When is a gun semi-automatic? Where are different kinds of weapons likely needed? Does time-of-day matter? Does the presence of a child in the house matter? Does the presence of a convicted felon in the house matter? Do police need special rules permitting patdowns designed to find guns? When do registration requirements become severe to the point that they amount to an unconstitutional ban? Who can possess guns and of what kind? Aliens? Prior drug offenders? Prior alcohol abusers? How would the right interact with a state or local government's ability to take special measures during, say, national security emergencies? . . .

The difficulty of finding answers to these questions is exceeded only by the importance of doing so. Firearms cause well over 60,000 deaths and injuries in the United States each year. Those who live in urban areas, police officers, women, and children, all may be particularly at risk. And gun regulation may save their lives. Some experts have calculated, for example, that Chicago's handgun ban has saved several hundred lives, perhaps close to 1,000, since it was enacted in 1983. Other experts argue that stringent gun regulations "can help protect police officers operating on the front lines against gun violence," have reduced homicide rates in Washington, D.C., and Baltimore, and have helped to lower New York's crime and homicide rates.

At the same time, the opponents of regulation cast doubt on these studies. And who is right? Finding out may require interpreting studies that are only indirectly related to a particular regulatory statute, say one banning handguns in the home. Suppose studies find more accidents and suicides where there is a handgun in the home than where there is a long gun in the home or no gun at all? To what extent do such studies justify a ban? What if opponents of the ban put forth counter studies?

In answering such questions judges cannot simply refer to judicial homilies, such as Blackstone's 18th-century perception that a man's home is his castle. Nor can the plurality so simply reject, by mere assertion, the fact that "incorporation will require judges to assess the costs and benefits of firearms restrictions." How can the Court assess the strength of the government's regulatory interests without addressing issues of empirical fact? How can the Court determine if a regulation is appropriately tailored without considering its impact? And how can the Court determine if there are less restrictive alternatives without considering what will happen if those alternatives are implemented?

Perhaps the Court could lessen the difficulty of the mission it has created for itself by adopting a jurisprudential approach similar to the many state courts that administer a state constitutional right to bear arms. But the Court has not yet done so. Rather, the Court has haphazardly created a few simple rules, such as that it will not touch "prohibitions on the possession of firearms by felons and the mentally ill," "laws forbidding the carrying of firearms in sensitive places such as schools and government buildings," or "laws imposing conditions and qualifications on the commercial sale of arms." But why these rules and not others? Does the Court know that these regulations are justified by some special gun-related risk of death? In fact, the Court does not know. It has simply invented rules that sound sensible without being able to explain why or how Chicago's handgun ban is different.

The fact is that judges do not know the answers to the kinds of empirically based questions that will often determine the need for particular forms of gun regulation. Nor do they have readily available "tools" for finding and evaluating the technical material submitted by others. Judges cannot easily make empirically based predictions; they have no way to gather and evaluate the data required to see if such predictions are accurate; and the nature of litigation and concerns about *stare decisis* further make it difficult for judges to change course if predictions prove inaccurate. Nor can judges rely upon local community views and values when reaching judgments in circumstances where prediction is difficult because the basic facts are unclear or unknown.

At the same time, there is no institutional need to send judges off on this "mission-almost-impossible." Legislators . . . are far better suited than judges to uncover facts and to understand their relevance. And legislators, unlike Article III judges, can be held democratically responsible for their empirically based and value laden conclusions. We have thus repeatedly affirmed our preference for "legislative not judicial solutions" to this kind of problem, just as we have repeatedly affirmed the Constitution's preference for democratic solutions legislated by those whom the people elect.

In New State Ice Co. v. Liebmann (1932), Justice Brandeis stated in dissent:

> "Some people assert that our present plight is due, in part, to the limitations set by courts upon experimentation in the fields of social and economic science; and to the discouragement to which proposals for betterment there have been subjected otherwise. There must be power in the States and the Nation to remould, through experimentation, our economic practices and institutions to meet changing social and economic needs. I cannot believe that the framers of the Fourteenth Amendment, or the States which ratified it, intended to deprive us of the power to correct [the social problems we face]."

There are 50 state legislatures. The fact that this Court may already have refused to take this wise advice with respect to Congress in *Heller* is no reason to make matters worse here.

Third, the ability of States to reflect local preferences and conditions—both key virtues of federalism—here has particular importance. The incidence of gun ownership varies substantially as between crowded cities and uncongested rural communities, as well as among the different geographic regions of the country. Thus, approximately 60% of adults who live in the relatively sparsely populated Western States of Alaska, Montana, and Wyoming report that their household keeps a gun, while fewer than 15% of adults in the densely populated Eastern States of Rhode Island, New Jersey, and Massachusetts say the same.

The nature of gun violence also varies as between rural communities and cities. Urban centers face significantly greater levels of firearm crime and homicide, while rural communities have proportionately greater problems with nonhomicide gun deaths, such as suicides and accidents. And idiosyncratic local factors can lead to two cities finding themselves in dramatically different circumstances: For example, in 2008, the murder rate was 40 times higher in New Orleans than it was in Lincoln, Nebraska.

It is thus unsurprising that States and local communities have historically differed about the need for gun regulation as well as about its proper level. Nor is it surprising that "primarily, and historically," the law has treated the exercise of police powers, including gun control, as "matter[s] of local concern." [Medtronic, Inc. v. Lohr (1996)].

Fourth, although incorporation of any right removes decisions from the democratic process, the incorporation of this particular right does so without strong offsetting justification — as the example of Oak Park's handgun ban helps to show. Oak Park decided to ban handguns in 1983, after a local attorney was shot to death with a handgun that his assailant had smuggled into a courtroom in a blanket. A citizens committee spent months gathering information about handguns. It secured 6,000 signatures from community residents in support of a ban. And the village board enacted a ban into law.

Subsequently, at the urging of ban opponents the Board held a community referendum on the matter. The citizens committee argued strongly in favor of the ban. It pointed out that most guns owned in Oak Park were handguns and that handguns were misused more often than citizens used them in self-defense. The ban opponents argued just as strongly to the contrary. The public decided to keep the ban by a vote of 8,031 to 6,368. And since that time, Oak Park now tells us, crime has decreased and the community has seen no accidental handgun deaths.

Given the empirical and local value-laden nature of the questions that lie at the heart of the issue, why, in a Nation whose Constitution foresees democratic decisionmaking, is it so *fundamental* a matter as to require taking that power from the people? What is it here that the people did not know? What is it that a judge knows better?

* * *

In sum, the police power, the superiority of legislative decisionmaking, the need for local decisionmaking, the comparative desirability of democratic decisionmaking, the lack of a manageable judicial standard, and the life-threatening harm that may flow from striking down regulations all argue against incorporation. Where the incorporation of other rights has been at issue, *some* of these problems have arisen. But in this instance *all* these problems are present, *all* at the same time, and *all* are likely to be present in most, perhaps nearly all, of the cases in which the constitutionality of a gun regulation is at issue. At the same time, the important factors that favor incorporation in other instances — *e.g.*, the protection of broader constitutional objectives — are not present here.

The upshot is that all factors militate against incorporation—with the possible exception of historical factors.

III

I must, then, return to history. . . . I can find much in the historical record that shows that some Americans in some places at certain times thought it important to keep and bear arms for private self-defense. For instance, the reader will see that many States have constitutional provisions protecting gun possession. But, as far as I can tell, those provisions typically do no more than guarantee that a gun regulation will be a *reasonable* police power regulation. It is thus altogether unclear whether such provisions would prohibit cities such as Chicago from enacting laws, such as the law before us, banning handguns. The majority, however, would incorporate a right that is likely *inconsistent* with Chicago's law; and the majority would almost certainly *strike down* that law.

Thus, the specific question before us is not whether there are references to the right to bear arms for self defense throughout this Nation's history—of course there are—or even whether the Court should incorporate a simple constitutional requirement that firearms regulations not unreasonably burden the right to keep and bear arms, but rather whether there is a consensus that *so substantial* a private self-defense right as the one described in *Heller* applies to the States. . . . In my view, that record is insufficient to say that the right to bear arms for private self-defense, as explicated by *Heller*, is fundamental in the sense relevant to the incorporation inquiry. . . . States and localities have consistently enacted firearms regulations, including regulations similar to those at issue here, throughout our Nation's history. Courts have repeatedly upheld such regulations. And it is, at the very least, possible, and perhaps likely, that incorporation will impose on every, or nearly every, State a different right to bear arms than they currently recognize—a right that threatens to destabilize settled state legal principles.

I thus cannot find a historical consensus with respect to whether the right described by *Heller* is "fundamental" as our incorporation cases use that term. Nor can I find sufficient historical support for the majority's conclusion that that right is "deeply rooted in this Nation's history and tradition." Instead, I find no more than ambiguity and uncertainty that perhaps even expert historians would find difficult to penetrate. And a historical record that is so ambiguous cannot itself provide an adequate basis for incorporating a private right of self-defense and applying it against the States. . . .

[Discussion of the regulation of firearms in the Eighteeth, Nineteenth, Twentieth, and Twenty-First Century omitted.]

* * *

In sum, the Framers did not write the Second Amendment in order to protect a private right of armed self-defense. There has been, and is, no consensus that the right is, or was, "fundamental." No broader constitutional interest or principle supports legal treatment of that right as fundamental. To the contrary, broader constitutional concerns of an institutional nature argue strongly against that treatment. Moreover, nothing in 18th-, 19th-, 20th-, or 21st-century history shows a consensus that the right to private armed self-defense, as described in *Heller*, is "deeply rooted in this Nation's history or tradition" or is otherwise "fundamental." Indeed, incorporating the right recognized in *Heller* may change the law in many of the 50 States. Read in the majority's favor, the historical evidence is at most ambiguous. And, in the absence of any other support for its conclusion, ambiguous history cannot show that the Fourteenth Amendment incorporates a private right of self-defense against the States.

With respect, I dissent.

SECTION C: How Should Regulations of Firearms Be Scrutinized?

ASSIGNMENT S-15

Study Guide: Having now found that the right to keep and bear arms applies both to the federal and state governments, the next question facing the courts will be how to evaluate the constitutionality of gun regulations falling short of a complete ban. The next excerpt from a student note proposes adapting the First Amendment doctrine governing" time, place and manner" regulations of speech to the Second Amendment context. Is there any difference between the freedom of speech and the right to possess and carry weapons that affects the scrutiny of laws regulating these two types of conduct? Is the note making the same point as Justice Breyer? Or could this analysis be considered a response to Justice Breyer?

GARY E. BARNETT, THE REASONABLE REGULATION OF THE RIGHT TO KEEP AND BEAR ARMS, 6 GEORGETOWN J. L. & PUB. POL'Y 607 (2008): Determining the extent to which a citizen has a right to keep and bear arms involves a two-step inquiry. The first step addresses whether the Second Amendment protects an individual right to keep and bear arms or a collective right of states to maintain a militia. This is the question dealt with in *Heller*. . . . After determining that the Second Amendment protects an individual right, the second step in determining the extent of Second Amendment protections is to ascertain whether a particular law is a proper exercise of the police power and is therefore a reasonable regulation, or whether it exceeds the police power and is an infringement of the individual right.

The answer to this question is not directly addressed by the Constitution. There is no clause specifically addressing how to identify a reasonable regulation of any liberty, much less a reasonable regulation of the right to keep and bear arms. Given that the government can reasonably regulate, the question is whether regulation goes too far, unduly infringing the rights of individuals.

The difficulty is that the term "infringe" is vague. A vague term is one that becomes important in borderline cases. . . . A determination of the proper location to draw the line when a term is vague usually requires employing a constructive method. . . . The issue is where—between the total prohibition on the possession of arms and no regulation at all—the boundaries of reasonable regulation should be drawn. The constructive theory that I advance is that of Common Law Construction. The theory is based on the idea that indeterminate constitutional meanings should be decided with reference to tradition and precedent.[54] The tradition and precedent I believe to be the most analogous and informative on the issue of reasonable regulation of a firearm is the First Amendment and its time, place, and manner jurisprudence. . . .

The Supreme Court reviews a content-neutral restriction on First Amendment protected rights under a heightened scrutiny standard. . . . While this standard is not the presumptively unconstitutional level of review that exists for content-based restrictions, if applied properly, the established time, place, and manner for content-neutral restrictions doctrine provides a standard with considerable bite. Two components of the Court's standard provide for meaningful scrutiny of restrictions on speech. These are the requirements that; (1) a restriction on speech be narrowly tailored to serve a significant government interest; and (2) there remain ample alternative channels of communication. . . .

The right to keep and bear arms, like rights protected by the First Amendment, is subject to regulation under the police power. If a regulation under the police power does not unduly "infringe" upon an individual's rights, it is reasonable and should be found constitutional. Although scholars and legal theorists have come to use the term "reasonable regulation" to describe a permissible exercise of the police power, the term is extremely broad and unhelpful. To determine whether a regulation infringes upon an individual's right to keep and bear arms, a doctrine with greater specificity is required. . . .

Narrowly Tailored to Serve a Significant Government Interest

Once "Arms" has been defined and the restrictions on the Second Amendment have been determined to apply to the public forum, a court must determine whether a regulation is "reasonable." The Common Law method of construction teaches an important lesson about the reasonable regulation of the right to keep and bear arms. If the very same degree of scrutiny that is applied to restrictions on speech in a public forum were applied to restrictions on guns in a public forum, far more gun laws would be upheld as constitutional than laws restricting speech. This is because, with gun laws, the government can almost always provide a safety rationale for enacting a particular regulation. In other words,

54. Adrian Vermeule, *Common Law Constitutionalism and the Limits of Reason*, 107 Colum. L. Rev. 1482, 1482 (2007).

any gun restriction can be justified on the grounds of safety. This effectively eliminates the half of the test requiring a significant government interest. In contrast, in First Amendment law, absent a clear and present danger, speech rarely threatens health and safety in the same way. This inability of the government to have an ever-present safety rationale creates an inherent protection for speech within First Amendment law. In other words, because it is more difficult for the government to articulate a significant interest, it can enact fewer restrictions. This lack of protection in the Second Amendment law should be supplemented by requiring a law be the least intrusive means to achieving the government's stated end. . . .

Determining whether a regulation is narrowly tailored . . . is a difficult task. This is where the wisdom embedded within First Amendment law is quite useful. The Supreme Court, in [its First Amendment cases], has already promulgated a feasible approach: if a government restriction results in a substantially adverse effect on the non-target group from effectively asserting their Second Amendment rights, then that restriction would be unreasonable. For example, a trigger lock requirement on a handgun, intended to combat the social harm of accidental firearm use, would most likely have a deleterious effect on an individual's ability to protect herself effectively against an armed robber. The non-target group, those wanting to exercise their right of self defense, would, for all intents and purposes, be prohibited from effectively acting in self-defense, a constitutionally protected end. Such a requirement would not be narrowly tailored . . . and therefore would be unconstitutional.

Ample Alternative Means to Achieve the Protected Ends

The second requirement for a government restriction to not infringe an individual's right to keep and bear arms, and thus be reasonable, mirrors the third prong of the First Amendment analysis — that any restriction leave open ample alternative channels of communication. This requirement is designed to safeguard against the encroachment on the protected ends of the First Amendment. To ensure that this requirement is satisfied, a law must allow for the continued accomplishment of the constitutionally protected end. The same is true of the Second Amendment. Although it does not expressly protect any specific means, it does protect specific ends. Therefore, as in First Amendment law, a restriction must leave ample means of accomplishing the ends protected by the Second Amendment.

The most obvious effect of this standard is to guarantee that a complete prohibition of "Arms" would be unconstitutional. What exactly qualifies as ample alternatives is a fact-intensive inquiry that must be undertaken on a case-by-case basis. But as in the First Amendment analysis, the protected end must be identified, and the court must make a determination as to whether that end can still be accomplished through the use of the remaining means. First Amendment case law can be instructive on this issue. By looking to Supreme Court decisions that have made determination on what constitutes an ample alternative channel of communication, a principle can be found that can be transposed on to the Second

Amendment issue in question. This transposition will not be perfect; however, it will offer more enlightenment than a blind determination by the Court. . . .

Study Guide: In the next case, the Court of Appeals for the Ninth Circuit attempts to identify an appropriate approach to scrutinizing gun regulations falling short of the bans struck down in Heller *and* McDonald. *It ends up borrowing reasoning from abortion cases to evaluate a Chicago ban on gun ranges within the city limits. Why does it reject a "strict scrutiny" approach? How does it analogize to "time, place, and manner" regulations of speech? How does its approach differ from that proposed in the previous note?*

NORDYKE v. KING

United States Court of Appeals for the Ninth Circuit, 07–15763 (2011)

O'Scannlain, Circuit Judge:

We must decide whether the Second Amendment prohibits a local government from banning gun shows on its property.

I

Russell and Sallie Nordyke operate a business that promotes gun shows throughout California. A typical gun show involves the display and sale of thousands of firearms, generally ranging from pistols to rifles. Since 1991, the Nordykes have promoted numerous shows across the state, including one at the public fairgrounds in Alameda County. The Alameda gun shows routinely draw about 4,000 people. In the summer of 1999, the county passed an ordinance making it a misdemeanor to bring onto or to possess a firearm or ammunition on county property. . . .

II

Because the Supreme Court has yet to articulate a standard of review in Second Amendment cases, that task falls to the courts of appeals and the district courts. It has been suggested that only regulations which substantially burden the right to keep and to bear arms should receive heightened scrutiny. . . . Other courts would apply strict scrutiny to all gun-control regulations. . . .

B

We are satisfied that a substantial burden framework will prove to be far more judicially manageable than an approach that would reflexively apply strict scrutiny to all gun-control laws. As *McDonald* recognized, "assess[ing] the costs and benefits of firearms restrictions" requires "difficult empirical judgments in an area in which [judges] lack expertise." Indeed, whether a gun-control regulation serves the government's interest in safety is likely to be a difficult question to answer. See *Heller* (Breyer, J., dissenting) ("[E]mpirically based arguments cannot prove either that handgun possession diminishes crime or that handgun bans are ineffective."); [Eugene Volokh, *Implementing the Right to Keep and Bear Arms for Self-Defense*, 56 UCLA L. Rev. 1443, 1461 (2009)] (arguing that it "is likely to be especially hard" to "estimate the effectiveness of [a gun-control] law in preventing future crime and injury").

Applying strict scrutiny to every gun regulation would require courts to assess the effectiveness of a myriad of gun-control laws. Whenever a law is challenged under the Second Amendment, the government is likely to claim that the law serves its interest in reducing crime. Because the Supreme Court has already held that "the Government's general interest in preventing crime" is "compelling," United States v. Salerno (1987), the question, under strict scrutiny, would be whether the regulation is narrowly tailored to that interest. But courts cannot determine whether a gun-control regulation is narrowly tailored to the prevention of crime without deciding whether the regulation is likely to be effective (or, at least, whether less burdensome regulations would be as effective). Sorting gun-control regulations based on their likely effectiveness is a task better fit for the legislature. Cf. Richard H. Fallon, Jr., *Judicially Manageable Standards and Constitutional Meaning*, 119 Harv. L. Rev. 1274, 1291 (2006) ("A test may be deemed judicially unmanageable if it would require courts to make empirical findings or predictive judgments for which they lack competence.").

By contrast, the substantial burden test, though hardly mechanical, will not produce nearly as many difficult empirical questions as strict scrutiny. See *Volokh* (arguing that it is easier to determine whether a law substantially burdens the right to bear arms than to figure out whether a law "will reduce the danger of gun crime"). Indeed, courts make similar determinations in other constitutional contexts. See, e.g., Planned Parenthood of Se. Pa. v. Casey (1992) (holding that pre-viability abortion regulations are unconstitutional if they impose an "undue burden" on a women's right to terminate her pregnancy). Courts can use the doctrines generated in these related contexts for guidance in determining whether a gun-control regulation is impermissibly burdensome, as we suggest below.

C

In their supplemental briefs, the Nordykes and their amici argue that McDonald requires this Court to give strict scrutiny to the Ordinance. This is so, the briefs assert, because McDonald held that the right to keep and to bear arms is "fundamental." For support, the briefs point to a number of cases noting that laws burdening fundamental rights trigger strict scrutiny.

But, the Supreme Court does not apply strict scrutiny to every law that regulates the exercise of a fundamental right, despite language in some cases suggesting the contrary. Instead, in a variety of contexts, the Court applies mere rational basis scrutiny to laws that regulate, but do not significantly burden, fundamental rights. Cf. *Casey* ("Not every law which makes a right more difficult to exercise is, ipso facto, an infringement of that right.").

For instance, even though the Supreme Court has recognized a constitutional right to obtain an abortion,[55] it has approved a number of regulations that had the "effect of increasing the cost or decreasing the availability" of abortions. These regulations command mere rational basis review so long as they do not pose an "undue burden" on the right to abort a non-viable fetus. See Gonzales v. Carhart (2007). Similarly, "the government may impose reasonable restrictions on the time, place, or manner of protected speech," provided, inter alia, that the restrictions are not too cumbersome. See Ward v. Rock Against Racism (1989). . . .

Accordingly, we hold that only regulations which substantially burden the right to keep and to bear arms trigger heightened scrutiny under the Second Amendment.[56]

III

Having determined the standard of review, the question becomes whether the Nordykes' Proposed Second Amended Complaint sufficiently alleged that the Ordinance substantially burdens their right to keep and to bear arms. The Nordykes only challenge the ordinance as an effective prohibition of gun shows on county fairgrounds. That is, they complain that they cannot display and sell guns on county property; they do not allege that they wish to carry guns on county property for the purpose of defending themselves while on that property. Thus, the proper inquiry is whether a ban on gun shows at the county fairgrounds substantially burdens the right to keep and to bear arms; not whether a county can ban all people from carrying firearms on all of its property for any purpose.

A

Where, as here, government restricts the distribution of a constitutionally protected good or service, courts typically ask whether the restriction leaves open sufficient alternative avenues for obtaining the good or service. For instance, courts reviewing a restriction on the time, place, or manner of protected speech will ask whether the restriction "leave[s] open ample alternative channels for communication of the information." *Ward.* Thus, the Supreme Court upheld an ordinance that prohibited "picketing before or about the residence . . . of any individual" because protestors were not barred from residential neighborhoods generally, but rather could "enter such neighborhoods, alone or in groups, even

55. Admittedly, there is some dispute over whether the right to obtain an abortion still enjoys "fundamental" status. See Lawrence v. Texas (2003) (Scalia, J., dissenting) (arguing that *Roe*'s statement that abortion is a "fundamental right" has been undermined by subsequent cases holding that only rights that are "'deeply rooted in this Nation's history and tradition'" are "fundamental" (quoting Washington v. Glucksberg (1997))). Compare Roe v. Wade (1973) (deeming the right to an abortion "fundamental"), *with Casey* (not once describing abortion as a "fundamental right" or a "fundamental liberty interest"). We express no opinion on this issue.

56. We need not decide today precisely what type of heightened scrutiny applies to laws that substantially burden Second Amendment rights.

marching," go "door-to-door to proselytize their views," "distribute literature," and "contact residents by telephone." Frisby v. Schultz (1988).

Likewise, the Supreme Court recently held that a ban on one particular method of performing an abortion did not constitute an "undue burden" on the right to an abortion in part because "[a]lternatives [were] available to the prohibited procedure." *Carhart*; see also *id.* ("[T]he Act allows . . . a commonly used and generally accepted [abortion] method, so it does not construct a substantial obstacle to the abortion right.").

Following this lead, when deciding whether a restriction on gun sales substantially burdens Second Amendment rights, we should ask whether the restriction leaves law-abiding citizens with reasonable alternative means for obtaining firearms sufficient for self-defense purposes.

Similarly, a law does not substantially burden a constitutional right simply because it makes the right more expensive or more difficult to exercise. See *Carhart* ("'The fact that a law which serves a valid purpose, one not designed to strike at the right itself, has the incidental effect of making it more difficult or more expensive to procure an abortion cannot be enough to invalidate it.'" (quoting *Casey*)). Thus, regulations of gun sales do not substantially burden Second Amendment rights merely because they make it more difficult to obtain a gun. Cf. *Heller* ("[N]othing in our opinion should be taken to cast doubt on . . . laws imposing conditions and qualifications on the commercial sale of arms.").

Finally, a regulation is particularly unlikely to impose a substantial burden on a constitutional right where it simply declines to use government funds or property to facilitate the exercise of that right. For instance, the Supreme Court held that excluding even medically necessary abortions from Medicaid coverage did not constitute an "unduly burdensome interference with [a pregnant women's] freedom to decide whether to terminate her pregnancy." Harris v. McRae (1980). Regulations that simply refuse to provide government subsidies to gun dealers, therefore, do not constitute a substantial burden on the right to keep and to bear arms.

B

Applying the foregoing considerations, we must determine whether the Proposed Second Amended Complaint alleged sufficient facts to suggest plausibly that the Ordinance substantially burdens the Nordykes' right to keep and to bear arms. It does not assert that the Ordinance makes it materially more difficult to obtain firearms. Nor does it allege a shortage of places to purchase guns in or near Alameda County. In any event, the Ordinance does not prohibit gun shows, but merely declines to host them on government premises. The Proposed Second Amended Complaint, therefore, does not allege sufficient facts to state a Second Amendment claim capable of surviving a motion to dismiss. . . .

But the Nordykes submitted the Proposed Second Amended Complaint over six years ago. Since then, all of the Supreme Court's modern Second Amendment case law has been created. Accordingly, there may well be facts which the Nordykes did not consider relevant in 2004, and thus did not allege in the

Proposed Second Amended Complaint, but which, if now alleged, might plausibly suggest that the Ordinance substantially burdens the Nordykes' Second Amendment rights.

Therefore, to the extent that the district court's denial of leave to amend was with prejudice, it must be vacated and the Nordykes given the opportunity further to amend their complaint. If they do, the district court should consider, in light of *Heller*, *McDonald*, and this opinion, whether the Nordykes have alleged a viable Second Amendment claim.

***Study Guide:** In the next case, the Court of Appeals for the Seventh Circuit also attempts to identify an appropriate approach to scrutinizing gun regulations. It ends up borrowing reasoning from the First Amendment to evaluate a Chicago ban on gun ranges within the city limits. Does it go about this task in a different manner than does the Ninth Circuit? Why does it reject the substantial burden approach adopted by the Ninth Circuit?*

EZELL v. CITY OF CHICAGO

United States Court of Appeals for the Seventh Circuit, No. 10-3525 (2011)

Sykes, Circuit Judge. . . .

In the wake of *McDonald*, the Chicago City Council lifted the City's laws banning handgun possession and adopted the Responsible Gun Owners Ordinance in their place. The plaintiffs here challenge the City Council's treatment of firing ranges. The Ordinance mandates one hour of range training as a prerequisite to lawful gun ownership, yet at the same time prohibits all firing ranges in the city. . . .

1. *Heller*, *McDonald*, and a framework for Second Amendment litigation

It's true that Second Amendment litigation is new, and Chicago's ordinance is unlike any firearms law that has received appellate review since *Heller*. But that doesn't mean we are without a framework for how to proceed. The Supreme Court's approach to deciding *Heller* points in a general direction. Although the critical question in *Heller*—whether the Amendment secures an individual or collective right—was interpretive rather than doctrinal, the Court's decision method is instructive.

With little precedent to synthesize, *Heller* focused almost exclusively on the original public meaning of the Second Amendment, consulting the text and relevant historical materials to determine how the Amendment was understood at the time of ratification. This inquiry led the Court to conclude that the Second Amendment secures a pre-existing natural right to keep and bear arms; that the right is personal and not limited to militia service; and that the "central component of the right" is the right of armed self-defense, most notably in the home. *Heller*. On this understanding the Court invalidated the District of Columbia's ban on handgun possession, as well as its requirement that all firearms in the home be kept inoperable. The Court said these laws were unconstitutional "[u]nder any . . . standard[] of scrutiny" because "the inherent right of self defense has been central to the Second Amendment right" and the District's restrictions "extend[] . . . to the home, where the need for defense of self, family, and property is most acute." *Id.* That was enough to decide the case. The Court resolved the Second Amendment challenge in *Heller* without specifying any doctrinal "test" for resolving future claims.

For our purposes, however, we know that *Heller*'s reference to "any standard of scrutiny" means any *heightened* standard of scrutiny; the Court specifically excluded rational-basis review. *Id.* ("If all that was required to overcome the right to keep and bear arms was a rational basis, the Second Amendment would be redundant with the separate constitutional prohibitions on irrational laws, and would have no effect."). Beyond that, the Court was not explicit about how Second Amendment challenges should be adjudicated now that the historic debate about the Amendment's status as an individual-rights guarantee has been settled. Instead, the Court concluded that "whatever else [the Second Amendment] leaves to future evaluation, it surely elevates above all other interests the right of law-abiding, responsible citizens to use arms in defense of hearth and home." *Id.*

And in a much-noted passage, the Court carved out some exceptions:

> [N]othing in our opinion should be taken to cast doubt on longstanding prohibitions on the possession of firearms by felons and the mentally ill, or laws forbidding the carrying of firearms in sensitive places such as schools and government buildings, or laws imposing conditions and qualifications on the commercial sale of arms.

Id. The Court added that this list of "presumptively lawful regulatory measures" was illustrative, not exhaustive. *Id.*

These now-familiar passages from *Heller* hold several key insights about judicial review of laws alleged to infringe Second Amendment rights. First, the threshold inquiry in some Second Amendment cases will be a "scope" question: Is the restricted activity protected by the Second Amendment in the first place? The answer requires a textual and historical inquiry into original meaning. *Heller* ("Constitutional rights are enshrined with the scope they were understood to have when the people adopted them, whether or not future legislatures or (yes) even future judges think that scope too broad."); *McDonald* ("[T]he scope of the Second Amendment right" is determined by textual and historical inquiry, not interest-balancing.).

McDonald confirms that when state- or local-government action is challenged, the focus of the original-meaning inquiry is carried forward in time; the Second Amendment's scope as a limitation on the States depends on how the right was understood when the Fourteenth Amendment was ratified. Setting aside the ongoing debate about which part of the Fourteenth Amendment does the work of incorporation, and how, this wider historical lens is required if we are to follow the Court's lead in resolving questions about the scope of the Second Amendment by consulting its original public meaning as both a starting point and an important constraint on the analysis.[57]

The Supreme Court's free-speech jurisprudence contains a parallel for this kind of threshold "scope" inquiry. The Court has long recognized that certain "well-defined and narrowly limited classes of speech"—e.g., obscenity, defamation, fraud, incitement—are categorically "outside the reach" of the First Amendment. United States v. Stevens (2010); see also Brown v. Entm't Merchants Ass'n (June 27, 2011). When the Court has "identified categories of speech as fully outside the protection of the First Amendment, it has not been on the basis of a simple cost-benefit analysis." *Stevens.* Instead, some categories of speech are unprotected as a matter of history and legal tradition. *Id.* So too with the Second Amendment.

Heller suggests that some federal gun laws will survive Second Amendment challenge because they regulate activity falling outside the terms of the right as publicly understood when the Bill of Rights was ratified; *McDonald* confirms that if the claim concerns a state or local law, the "scope" question asks how the right was publicly understood when the Fourteenth Amendment was proposed and ratified. Accordingly, if the government can establish that a challenged firearms law regulates activity falling outside the scope of the Second Amendment right as it was understood at the relevant historical moment—1791 or 1868—then the analysis can stop there; the regulated activity is categorically unprotected, and the law is not subject to further Second Amendment review.

If the government cannot establish this—if the historical evidence is inconclusive or suggests that the regulated activity is *not* categorically unprotected—then there must be a second inquiry into the strength of the government's justification for restricting or regulating the exercise of Second Amendment rights. *Heller*'s reference to "any . . . standard[] of scrutiny" suggests as much. *McDonald* emphasized that the Second Amendment "limits[,] but by no means eliminates," governmental discretion to regulate activity falling within the scope of the right. Deciding whether the government has transgressed the limits

57. On this aspect of originalist interpretive method as applied to the Second Amendment, see generally Akhil Reed Amar, The Bill of Rights: Creation and Reconstruction 215-30, 257-67 (1998); Brannon P. Denning & Glenn H. Reynolds, *Five Takes on* McDonald v. Chicago, 26 J.L & POL. 273, 285-87 (2011); Josh Blackmun & Ilya Shapiro, *Keeping Pandora's Box Sealed: Privileges or Immunities*, The Constitution in 2020, *and Properly Extending the Right to Keep and Bear Arms to the States*, 8 Geo J.L. Pub. Pol'y 1, 51-57 (2010); Clayton E. Cramer, Nicholas J. Johnson & George A. Mocsary, *"This Right Is Not Allowed by Governments That Are Afraid of the People": The Public Meaning of the Second Amendment When the Fourteenth Amendment Was Ratified*, 17 GEO. MASON L. REV. 823, 824-25 (2010); Steven G. Calabresi & Sarah E. Agudo, *Individual Rights Under State Constitutions When the Fourteenth Amendment Was Ratified in 1868: What Rights Are Deeply Rooted in American History and Tradition?*, 87 Tex. L. Rev. 7, 11-17, 50-54 (2008); Randy E. Barnett, *Was the Right to Keep and Bear Arms Conditioned on Service in an Organized Militia?*, 83 Tex. L. Rev. 237, 266-70 (2004); David B. Kopel, *The Second Amendment in the Nineteenth Century*, 1998 BYU L. Rev. 1359; Stephen P. Halbrook, *Personal Security, Personal Liberty, and "The Constitutional Right to Bear Arms": Visions of the Framers of the Fourteenth Amendment*, 5 Seton Hall Const. L.J. 341 (1995).

imposed by the Second Amendment—that is, whether it has "infringed" the right to keep and bear arms—requires the court to evaluate the regulatory means the government has chosen and the public-benefits end it seeks to achieve. Borrowing from the Court's First Amendment doctrine, the rigor of this judicial review will depend on how close the law comes to the core of the Second Amendment right and the severity of the law's burden on the right. See generally Volokh, *Implementing the Right to Keep and Bear Arms for Self-Defense*, 56 UCLA L. REV. at 1454-72 (explaining the scope, burden, and danger-reduction justifications for firearm regulations post-*Heller*); Nelson Lund, *The Second Amendment,* Heller, *and Originalist Jurisprudence*, 56 UCLA L. REV.. 1343, 1372-75 (2009); Adam Winkler, Heller*'s Catch-22,* 56 UCLA L. REV.. 1551, 1571-73 (2009); Lawrence B. Solum, District of Columbia v. Heller *and Originalism,* 103 NW. U. L. REV. 923, 979-80 (2009); Glenn H. Reynolds & Brannon P. Denning, Heller*'s Future in the Lower Courts*, 102 NW. U. L. REV. 2035, 2042-44 (2008).

Both *Heller* and *McDonald* suggest that broadly prohibitory laws restricting the core Second Amendment right—like the handgun bans at issue in those cases, which prohibited handgun possession even in the home—are categorically unconstitutional. *Heller* ("We know of no other enumerated constitutional right whose core protection has been subjected to a freestanding 'interest-balancing' approach."). For all other cases, however, we are left to choose an appropriate standard of review from among the heightened standards of scrutiny the Court applies to governmental actions alleged to infringe enumerated constitutional rights; the answer to the Second Amendment "infringement" question depends on the government's ability to satisfy whatever standard of means-end scrutiny is held to apply. . . . [58]

2. Applying the framework to Chicago's firing range ban

The plaintiffs challenge only the City's ban on firing ranges, so our first question is whether range training is categorically unprotected by the Second Amendment. *Heller* and *McDonald* suggest to the contrary. The Court emphasized in both cases that the "central component" of the Second Amendment is

58. The Ninth Circuit recently adopted a somewhat different framework for Second Amendment claims. In Nordyke v. King, a divided panel announced a gatekeeping "substantial burden" test before the court will apply heightened scrutiny. (9th Cir. May 2, 2011) (O'Scannlain, J.). Under this approach only laws that substantially burden Second Amendment rights will get some form of heightened judicial review. The *Nordyke* majority specifically deferred judgment on "what type of heightened scrutiny applies to laws that substantially burden Second Amendment rights." Judge Gould, concurring in *Nordyke*, would apply heightened scrutiny "only [to] arms regulations falling within the core purposes of the Second Amendment, that is, regulations aimed at restricting defense of the home, resistance of tyrannous government, and protection of country." All other firearms laws, he said, should be reviewed for reasonableness, although by this he meant the sort of reasonableness review that applies in the First Amendment context, not the deferential rational basis review that applies to all laws.

the right to keep and bear arms for defense of self, family, and home. *Heller.* The right to possess firearms for protection implies a corresponding right to acquire and maintain proficiency in their use; the core right wouldn't mean much without the training and practice that make it effective. . . . Indeed, the City considers live firing-range training so critical to responsible firearm ownership that it mandates this training as a condition of lawful firearm possession. At the same time, however, the City insists in this litigation that range training is categorically outside the scope of the Second Amendment and may be completely prohibited.

There is an obvious contradiction here, but we will set it aside for the moment and consider the City's support for its categorical position. The City points to a number of founding-era, antebellum, and Reconstruction state and local laws that limited the discharge of firearms in urban environments. As we have noted, the most relevant historical period for questions about the scope of the Second Amendment as applied to the States is the period leading up to and surrounding the ratification of the Fourteenth Amendment. That point aside, most of the statutes cited by the City are not specific to controlled target practice and, in any event, contained significant carve outs and exemptions. . . . The City cites other eighteenth- and nineteenth-century statutes regulating the discharge of firearms in cities, but most of these allowed citizens to obtain a permit or license to engage in firearms practice from the governor or city council. . . . These "time, place, and manner" regulations do not support the City's position that target practice is categorically unprotected. . . . [These and other examples provided by the City fall] far short of establishing that target practice is wholly outside the Second Amendment as it was understood when incorporated as a limitation on the States.

We proceed, then, to the second inquiry, which asks whether the City's restriction on range training survives Second Amendment scrutiny. As we have explained, this requires us to select an appropriate standard of review. Although the Supreme Court did not do so in either *Heller* or *McDonald*, the Court *did* make it clear that the deferential rational-basis standard is out, and with it the presumption of constitutionality. *Heller* (citing United States v. Carolene Prods., [footnote 4] (1938)). This necessarily means that the City bears the burden of justifying its action under *some* heightened standard of judicial review. . . .

The City urges us to import the "undue burden" test from the Court's abortion cases, see, e.g., Planned Parenthood of Se. Pa. v. Casey (1992), but we decline the invitation. Both *Heller* and *McDonald* suggest that First Amendment analogues are more appropriate, and on the strength of that suggestion, we and other circuits have already begun to adapt First Amendment doctrine to the Second Amendment context

In free-speech cases, the applicable standard of judicial review depends on the nature and degree of the governmental burden on the First Amendment right and sometimes also on the specific iteration of the right. For example, "[c]ontent-based regulations are presumptively invalid," R.A.V. v. City of St. Paul (1992), and thus get strict scrutiny, which means that the law must be narrowly tailored to serve a compelling governmental interest; see also Ariz. Free Enter. Club's

Freedom Club PAC v. Bennett, (June 27, 2011). Likewise, "[l]aws that burden political speech are subject to strict scrutiny." Citizens United v. Fed. Election Comm'n (2010). On the other hand, "time, place, and manner" regulations on speech need only be "reasonable"and "justified without reference to the content of the regulated speech." Ward v. Rock Against Racism (1989). The Supreme Court also uses a tiered standard of review in its speech-forum doctrine; regulations in a traditional public or designated public forum get strict scrutiny, while regulations in a nonpublic forum "must not discriminate on the basis of viewpoint and 'must be reasonable in light of the forum's purpose.'" Choose Life Ill., Inc. v. White (7th Cir. 2008) (quoting Good News Club v. Milford Cent. Sch. (2001)).

In election-law cases, regulations affecting the expressive association rights of voters, candidates, and parties are subject to a fluctuating standard of review that varies with the severity of the burden on the right; laws imposing severe burdens get strict scrutiny, while more modest regulatory measures need only be reasonable, politically neutral, and justified by an important governmental interest. . . . Similarly, restrictions imposed on adult bookstores are reviewed under an intermediate standard of scrutiny that requires the municipality to present "evidence that the restrictions actually have public benefits great enough to justify any curtailment of speech." Annex Books, Inc. v. City of Indianapolis, (7th Cir. 2009) (citing Los Angeles v. Alameda Books, Inc. (2002), and Renton v. Playtime Theatres, Inc. (1986)). And in commercial-speech cases, the Court applies an intermediate standard of review that accounts for the "subordinate position" that commercial speech occupies "in the scale of First Amendment values." Bd. of Trs. of State Univ. of N.Y. v. Fox (1989). In this context intermediate scrutiny requires "a fit between the legislature's ends and the means chosen to accomplish those ends, . . . a fit that is not necessarily perfect, but reasonable; that represents not necessarily the single best disposition but one whose scope is in proportion to the interest served." *Id.* at 480 (internal quotation marks and citation omitted).

Labels aside, we can distill this First Amendment doctrine and extrapolate a few general principles to the Second Amendment context. First, a severe burden on the core Second Amendment right of armed self-defense will require an extremely strong public-interest justification and a close fit between the government's means and its end. Second, laws restricting activity lying closer to the margins of the Second Amendment right, laws that merely regulate rather than restrict, and modest burdens on the right may be more easily justified. How much more easily depends on the relative severity of the burden and its proximity to the core of the right.

In [United States v. Skoien (7th Cir. 2010) (en banc)] we required a "form of strong showing"—a/k/a "intermediate scrutiny"—in a Second Amendment challenge to a prosecution under 18 U.S.C. §922(g)(9), which prohibits the possession of firearms by persons convicted of a domestic-violence misdemeanor. We held that "logic and data" established a "substantial relation" between dispossessing domestic-violence misdemeanants and the important governmental goal of "preventing armed mayhem." Intermediate scrutiny was appropriate in *Skoien* because the claim was not made by a "law-abiding, responsible citizen" as in *Heller*; nor did the case involve the central self-defense component of the right.

Here, in contrast, the plaintiffs *are* the "law-abiding, responsible citizens" whose Second Amendment rights are entitled to full solicitude under *Heller*, and their claim comes much closer to implicating the core of the Second Amendment right. The City's firing-range ban is not merely regulatory; it *prohibits* the "law-abiding, responsible citizens" of Chicago from engaging in target practice in the controlled environment of a firing range. This is a serious encroachment on the right to maintain proficiency in firearm use, an important corollary to the meaningful exercise of the core right to possess firearms for self-defense.

That the City conditions gun possession on range training is an additional reason to closely scrutinize the range ban. All this suggests that a more rigorous showing than that applied in *Skoien* should be required, if not quite "strict scrutiny." To be appropriately respectful of the individual rights at issue in this case, the City bears the burden of establishing a strong public-interest justification for its ban on range training: The City must establish a close fit between the range ban and the actual public interests it serves, and also that the public's interests are strong enough to justify so substantial an encumbrance on individual Second Amendment rights. Stated differently, the City must demonstrate that civilian target practice at a firing range creates such genuine and serious risks to public safety that prohibiting range training throughout the city is justified.

At this stage of the proceedings, the City has not come close to satisfying this standard. In the district court, the City presented no data or expert opinion to support the range ban, so we have no way to evaluate the seriousness of its claimed public-safety concerns. Indeed, on this record those concerns are entirely speculative and, in any event, can be addressed through sensible zoning and other appropriately tailored regulations. . . .

Perhaps the City can muster sufficient evidence to justify banning firing ranges everywhere in the city, though that seems quite unlikely. As the record comes to us at this stage of the proceedings, the firing-range ban is wholly out of proportion to the public interests the City claims it serves. Accordingly, the plaintiffs' Second Amendment claim has a strong likelihood of success on the merits. . . .

For the foregoing reasons, we REVERSE the district court's order denying the plaintiffs' motion for a preliminary injunction and REMAND with instructions to enter a preliminary injunction consistent with this opinion.